Beginning Unix®

Beginning Unix®

Paul Love, Joe Merlino, Craig Zimmerman,
Jeremy C. Reed, and Paul Weinstein

Wiley Publishing, Inc.

Beginning Unix®

Published by
Wiley Publishing, Inc.
10475 Crosspoint Boulevard
Indianapolis, IN 46256
www.wiley.com

Published simultaneously in Canada

ISBN 13: 978-0-7645-7994-3

ISBN 10: 0-7645-7994-0

Manufactured in the United States of America

10 9 8 7 6 5 4 3 2 1

1MA/RR/QU/QV/IN

For general information on our other products and services or to obtain technical support, please contact our Customer Care Department within the U.S. at (800) 762-2974, outside the U.S. at (317) 572-3993 or fax (317) 572-4002.

Wiley also publishes its books in a variety of electronic formats. Some content that appears in print may not be available in electronic books.

Library of Congress Cataloging-in-Publication Data: Available from publisher

About the Authors

Paul Love (Cincinnati, OH), CISSP, CISA, CISM, Security+, has been in the IT field for 15 years. Paul holds a Masters of Science degree in Network Security and a Bachelor's in Information Systems. He has co-authored two Linux security books, contributed to multiple Linux/Unix books, and has been the technical editor for over 10 best selling Linux and Unix books. Paul also ran a successful Linux portal site during the dot com era and has been an avid Unix/Linux user and administrator both professionally and as a hobby for many years.

Joe Merlino (Boston, MA) is an experienced system administrator with Unix and Linux for more than a decade.

Craig Zimmerman (New York, NY) manages UNIX, Macintosh, and Windows systems for Spontaneous, a post-production company in New York City. He previously worked at Chiat/Day helping build the world's most famous virtual advertising agency, managing and networking Unix and Macintosh systems in multiple offices.

Jeremy C. Reed (Marysville, WA) is a programmer, a member of NetBSD, and has actively taught FreeBSD, NetBSD, and OpenBSD administration classes for the past three years.

Paul Weinstein (Chicago, IL) has worked on various Unix-based computing platforms, from the mainframe (Harris HCX-9) to the desktop (Powerbook G4) and has developed applications on just about all of the current major branches of Unix in the course of the past 10 years. Recently he has been focusing a lot of his attention on developing and integrating Web-based systems using tools such as Linux, Apache, MySQL, and Perl, and in doing so has brought his unique understanding to a wide range of computing environments ranging from public elementary schools to pioneering open source companies. Currently, Paul works as President and Chief Consultant for the computer consulting firm Kepler Solutions, Inc.

David Mercer (Cape Town, South Africa) is a long-time Unix user and PHP programmer who contributed to *Beginning PHP4* and *Beginning PHP5*. He has maintained a keen interest in all things open source ever since he managed to put together a working Beowulf cluster by nicking old computer parts from colleagues and assembling them under his desk.

Credits

Acquisitions Editor
Debra Williams

Development Editor
Maryann Steinhart

Production Editor
Felicia Robinson

Technical Editors
Robert Berg
John Kennedy
David Mercer
David Bruce

Copy Editor
Publication Services

Editorial Manager
Mary Beth Wakefield

Vice President & Executive Group Publisher
Richard Swadley

Vice President and Publisher
Joseph B. Wikert

Project Coordinator
Erin Smith

Graphics and Production Specialists
April Farling
Carrie A. Foster
Lauren Goddard
Denny Hager
Lynsey Osborn

Quality Control Technicians
Amanda Briggs
Brian H. Walls

Proofreading and Indexing
TECHBOOKS Production Services

Contents

Acknowledgments

I would like to thank my family and those who mentored me throughout my career.

I would like to thank the staff at Wiley, particularly Debra Williams Cauley, who helped get this book started and whose participation during the writing of this book was instrumental in its completion. I would also like to thank Maryann and the technical editors whose tough first reviews and great insight helped develop the book into a far greater work. All others at the Wrox team who helped make this book a better product through their input or editing are greatly appreciated.

Finally, I would like to thank all the developers of the Unix systems and their derivatives. Their tireless pursuit of excellence has given us one of the most elegant and stable operating systems available today.

—Paul Love

Introduction

The new millennium has seen many changes in many areas of computing, from new forms of storage with massive amounts of storage space, to systems that are far more powerful than the first computer users could have ever imagined. Designed and initially created more than 30 years ago, the Unix operating system has been part of the evolution of computers, so it's no accident that Unix is still one of the most popular operating systems for mission-critical tasks.

Unix is the basis for some of the most-used operating systems today, from Apple's Mac OS X to Linux to the more commonly known Unix versions, such as Sun's Solaris Unix and IBM's AIX. Today many of the versions of Unix are available free to users and corporations, allowing for a larger use base than many had imagined when Unix was first being developed. Unix is now seen as a user-friendly, very secure, and robust operating system rather than the cold, command line–only operating system once thought to be useful only to computer experts.

Beginning Unix covers all basic aspects of the Unix operating system. What is unique about this book is that it covers not only the standard Unix systems, such as Sun's Solaris and IBM's AIX, but also Unix derivatives, such as Apple's Mac OS X and the various Linuxes. Additionally, this book includes a unique conversion section explaining how to convert Mac OS X–specific or Windows operating systems commands that you may already know into their Unix equivalents, making the transition from other operating systems much easier.

This book also includes a CD-ROM with the KNOPPIX operating system. This fully functional version of Linux enables you to restart your computer into a Linux environment. KNOPPIX requires no technical experience, and it will not damage or modify your current operating system. Using KNOPPIX is an easy way for you to follow along with the book, learning Unix without the consequences of having to lose any data or operating systems on your computer.

Who Is This Book For?

This book is for anyone who is interested in understanding the concepts and operation of the Unix operating system, including any of the Unix derivatives available today (Apple OS X, Linux, or BSD, for example). It is designed for absolute beginners to the Unix operating system, including those who have only worked with the many graphical user interfaces available for the different Unix systems (Apple's Aqua interface, KDE, GNOME, and so forth). This book can also be useful for veteran Unix users, because no one knows everything about Unix, as a refresher on known concepts or as a tool to fill gaps in some knowledge areas.

No assumptions are made about the reader's skill level or prior use of computers. If you have used computers and other operating systems such as Mac OS X or Microsoft Windows, you will understand some of the concepts faster, but all readers will gain some insight from this book, regardless of their present expertise.

What Does This Book Cover?

This book covers all versions of Unix in their most basic form, as well as commands and concepts common to all versions of Unix and its derivatives, including:

- Apple's Mac OS X
- Red Hat Linux
- Mandrakelinux
- IBM's AIX
- Any version of Linux
- Any version of BSD (FreeBSD, OpenBSD, NetBSD)

Special emphasis is placed on Sun's Solaris, Mac OS X, and Linux because they are the most popular available. The different versions of Unix utilize the same principles and commands with small differences, so any version of Unix can be used with this book.

This book also covers basic programming, including shell scripting and Perl programming, which enable you to automate your system as much as possible—one of the strengths of the Unix operating system. The coverage of these programming concepts creates a firm foundation for more advanced programming covered by other books.

How This Book Is Structured

This book presents basic concepts of the Unix operating system first, progressing to more advanced topics and programming later in the book. If you are familiar with the concepts or commands covered in one chapter, you can simply skip to one that has information you need to learn.

Chapters 1 through 4 provide the fundamental information you need to understand Unix methodology, how Unix is designed, and the basics of logging in to and out of a Unix system.

- **Chapter 1: Unix Fundamentals**. The basics of Unix, including the history and terminology as well as some of the core concepts of Unix design and philosophy. This chapter helps you understand some of the culture behind the Unix operating system.
- **Chapter 2: First Steps**. This chapter describes the very first steps you must take to utilize the Unix operating system effectively, including what occurs during the Unix boot process, how to log in, and how the user environment (shell) is structured, as well as how to shut down a Unix system properly.
- **Chapter 3: Understanding Users and Groups**. Learning how users and groups work within the system is crucial to understanding how you can effectively use your system. This chapter covers all aspects of user accounts and groups, including how to add, modify, and delete user accounts and how to become another user with the `su` command.
- **Chapter 4: File System Concepts**. The Unix file system is one of the most critical components of the Unix system as a whole. The file system allows you to store and manipulate your files. This

chapter shows you what the Unix file system is and how to use it from a user and system administrator point of view. You will learn how to utilize the file system effectively, so that you can prevent some of the common problems associated with file system management.

Chapters 5–7 put you to work, from customizing your working environment to editing files on Unix. These chapters extend your repertoire of Unix commands.

- **Chapter 5: Customize Your Working Environment**. The shell is the primary environment that you use for day-to-day work in Unix. Unix offers a multitude of ways to customize your working environment to suit your needs and whims. This chapter goes over the many different configuration options available for users in many of the different Unix shells.
- **Chapter 6: Unix Commands In-Depth**. Unix has hundreds of different commands that do many tasks. This chapter provides a foundation for some of the most commonly used commands you will need to understand in order to use the system effectively for day-to-day work.
- **Chapter 7: Editing Files with Vi**. The vi editor is one of the oldest and most widely used text editors in Unix. It is commonly seen as a monolithic and difficult-to-use editor, but as you will learn, it is a very powerful and fast way to edit files. This chapter explores all aspects of using the vi editor to create and edit files effectively.

With a good foundation in place, you're ready to move on to more-advanced topics. Chapters 8–11 discuss how to use some powerful Unix tools, how to manage processes, and how to schedule programs to run at specific times. Chapter 12 takes on the important subject of security.

- **Chapter 8: Advanced Tools**. This chapter introduces the concept of regular expressions and covers some of the more advanced tools available to the Unix user.
- **Chapter 9: Advanced Unix Commands: Sed and AWK**. `sed` and `awk` are two very powerful tools that enable a user to manipulate files in an efficient manner. These commands are essential, and you will find yourself using them frequently. This chapter goes from the ground up in showing you how to use these commands.
- **Chapter 10: Job Control and Process Management**. This chapter covers the basics of Unix processes and how to control and manage these crucial components of the Unix operating system. As an extension of processes, job control is reviewed and explained.
- **Chapter 11: Running Programs at Specified Times**. Running programs at specified times without user or administrator intervention provides a user or administrator with the capability to run programs with minimal system impact when the fewest users are utilizing the system. This chapter covers how to run commands at different times and discusses the environmental variables that affect this process.
- **Chapter 12: Security**. Unix has had security features ingrained for many years, but as with any operating system, it can be made more secure from malicious entities on the outside or inside. This chapter goes over the basics of system security and then covers some of the fundamental steps you can take to make your system more secure.

Chapters 13–17 delve into shell scripting and other methods of "automating" common tasks in Unix systems. Although these tasks often fall within the purview of system administrators, other users, including home users, may benefit.

- **Chapter 13: Basic Shell Scripting**. Shell scripting is the gateway to more advanced programming languages for many users. This chapter delves into the basics of programming with the major Unix shells, making the transition from user to beginning programmer easier.
- **Chapter 14: Advanced Shell Scripting**. This chapter takes Chapter 13 one step further, moving you into more advanced programming topics and leaving you with the capability to program shell scripts for any task.
- **Chapter 15: System Logging**. The importance of logging to users, administrators, and programmers cannot be overstated. Logging is the outlet for the system to communicate with the user, on everything from problems to successful system actions.
- **Chapter 16: Unix Networking**. This chapter covers all aspects of communicating with other systems, including network administration and scripting on common network tasks.
- **Chapter 17: Perl Programming for Unix Automation**. Perl is one of the most common programming languages on Unix, as well as on other operating systems. Perl enables you to quickly write concise, useful programs. This chapter goes over the basics of programming in the Perl language and tells you how to automate common Unix tasks with Perl.

Chapters 18 and 19 cover two important topics: backing up your data and installing Unix programs.

- **Chapter 18: Backup Tools**. This chapter describes some of the tools available on your Unix system for backing up and restoring your system in the event of accidental deletion or major system failure or catastrophe.
- **Chapter 19: Installing Software from Source Code**. Although Unix includes many programs in a default installation, there are often many other programs you will want to install. This chapter shows you how to install software from source code and from precompiled binaries.

Chapters 20 and 21 provide maps to Unix operating systems for those who are more familiar with Microsoft Windows, Microsoft DOS, Mac OS 9, and Mac OS X. These chapters are great references for those who have used other operating systems and want to compare Unix to what they already know.

- **Chapter 20: Conversion: Unix for Mac OS Users**. Mac OS X is built on a Unix foundation, but there are some minor differences between standard Unix and Apple's Mac OS X. This chapter converts typical Mac OS (X, 9, and below) commands and concepts into their equivalent Unix commands or concepts. This chapter makes the migration into Unix much easier for users of any version of Apple's operating systems.
- **Chapter 21: Conversion: Unix for Windows Users**. Microsoft Windows is the predominant operating system available today. This chapter converts the most common Windows and MS-DOS commands into their equivalent Unix commands, making the migration from those operating systems to Unix much simpler.

The book concludes with two appendixes. Appendix A, "Answers," provides the solutions to the exercise(s) at the end of most chapters. These exercises will enable you to test your grasp of the concepts presented in the chapter. Appendix B, "Useful Unix Web Sites," provides links to some of the best Unix-related Web sites on the Internet.

What Do You Need to Use This Book?

There are no requirements to use this book, but to make the learning process easier, the KNOPPIX distribution of Linux is provided on the CD-ROM accompanying this book. This enables you to use a Unix-based operating system any time, with no commitment of hard-drive resources or system alterations. The KNOPPIX distribution runs completely from CD-ROM and can be run at any time. If you have a Mac OS X system, you are already using a Unix operating system. The CD-ROM version of KNOPPIX runs only on Intel- or AMD-based systems; it will not work on Apple's line of hardware.

Conventions

This book uses the conventions discussed in this section to make the importance of specific information stand out.

> **Important notes or concepts appear in this format.**

Interesting tidbits or tips are formatted in italics, like this.

```
Code or commands are in this monotype format.
```

The text also uses specific styles to denote their significance:

- Keyboard commands that use function keys are denoted like: Shift+Q
- Web URLs are noted like this: `persistence.properties`.

Any actual Tab characters in code are represented by a right arrow: →.

Source Code

The source code for all the code in this book is available online if you prefer to cut and paste rather than copy by hand from the book. It is available at `www.wrox.com`. At the Wrox Web site, you can find the book's source code by searching for the book title (*Beginning Unix*) or ISBN (0-7645-7994-0).

Errata

This book has been checked for technical and grammatical errors, but as is human nature, errors can occur. The errata page for this book is available at `www.wrox.com`, in the book details section. If you find an error in the book that is not listed, the authors would greatly appreciate it if you go to `www.wrox.com/contact/techsupport.shtml` and complete the form to submit the error. By submitting any errors you discover, you help us to make this book even better.

Unix Fundamentals

The Unix operating system was created more than 30 years ago by a group of researchers at AT&T's Bell Laboratories. During the three decades of constant development that have followed, Unix has found a home in many places, from the ubiquitous mainframe to home computers to the smallest of embedded devices. This chapter provides a brief overview of the history of Unix, discusses some of the differences among the many Unix systems in use today, and covers the fundamental concepts of the basic Unix operating system.

Brief History

In terms of computers, Unix has a long history. Unix was developed at AT&T's Bell Laboratories after Bell Labs withdrew from a long-term collaboration with General Electric (G.E.) and MIT to create an operating system called MULTICS (Multiplexed Operating and Computing System) for G.E.'s mainframe. In 1969, Bell Labs researchers created the first version of Unix (then called UNICS, or Uniplexed Operating and Computing System), which has evolved into the common Unix systems of today.

Unix was gradually ported to different machine architectures from the original PDP-7 minicomputer and was used by universities. The source code was made available at a small fee to encourage its further adoption. As Unix gained acceptance by universities, students who used it began graduating and moving into positions where they were responsible for purchasing systems and software. When those people began purchasing systems for their companies, they considered Unix because they were familiar with it, spreading adoption further. Since the first days of Unix, the operating system has grown significantly, so that it now forms the backbone of many major corporations' computer systems.

Unix no longer is an acronym for anything, but it is derived from the UNICS acronym. Unix developers and users use a lot of acronyms to identify things in the system and for commands.

Unix Versions

In the early days Unix was made available as source code rather than in the typical binary form. This made it easier for others to modify the code to meet their needs, and it resulted in forks in the code, meaning that there are now many disparate versions (also known as flavors).

Source code represents the internal workings of a program, specifying line by line how a program or application operates. Access to source code makes it easier to understand what is occurring in the program and allows for easier modification of the program. Most commercial programs are distributed in binary form, meaning they are ready to be run, but the internal lines of code are not readable by people.

There are primarily two base versions of Unix available: AT&T System V and Berkley Software Distribution (BSD). The vast majority of all Unix flavors are built on one of these two versions. The primary differences between the two are the utilities available and the implementations of the file structure. Most of the Unix flavors incorporate features from each base version; some include the System V version utilities in `/usr/bin` and the BSD version in `/usr/ucb/bin`, for example, so that you have the choice of using a utility with which you are comfortable. This arrangement is indicative of the Unix way of providing the flexibility to do things in different ways.

The various versions of Unix systems provide the user the power of choice: you can select the flavor that best matches your needs or system requirements. This ability to choose is considered by many as a strength, although some see it as a weakness in that these slightly differing versions and flavors create some incompatibilities (in the implementation, commands, communications, or methods, for example). There is no "true" version of Unix or one that is more official than others; there are just different implementations. Linux, for example, is a variant of Unix that was built from the ground up as a free Unix-like alternative to the expensive commercial Unix versions available when Linux was first created in 1991. Here are some of the more popular flavors of Unix available:

Sun Microsystem's Solaris Unix

IBM AIX

Hewlett Packard HP-UX

Red Hat Enterprise Linux

Fedora Core

SUSE Linux

Debian GNU/Linux

Mac OS X

KNOPPIX

Yellow Dog Linux (for Apple systems)

Santa Cruz Operations SCO OpenServer

SGI IRIX

FreeBSD

OpenBSD

NetBSD

OS/390 Unix

Plan 9

Each of these flavors implements its version of Unix in a slightly different way, but even though the implementation of a command may vary on some systems, the core command and its functionality follow the principles of one of the two major variations. Most versions of Unix utilize SVR4 (System V) and add the BSD components as an option to allow for maximum interoperability. This is especially true with commands; for example, there are two versions of the `ps` command (for showing processes) available on most systems. One version of `ps` might reside in `/usr/bin/ps` (the System V version) while the other might exist in `/usr/ucb/bin` (BSD version); the commands operate similarly, but provide output or accept optional components in a different manner.

Many vendors have attempted to standardize the Unix operating system. The most successful attempt, a product of the noncommercial Institute for Electrical and Electronics Engineers, is standard 1003 (IEEE 1003), also known as the POSIX (Portable Operating Systems Interface) standard. That standard is also registered with the International Organization for Standardization under ISO/IEC 9945-1, which you can find at `http://iso.org/iso/en/CombinedQueryResult.CombinedQueryResult?queryString=9945`. The POSIX standard merged with the Single Unix Specification (SUS) standard to become one integrated standard for all Unix flavors. It retained the name POSIX standard. Not all Unix versions follow the POSIX standard to the letter, but most do adhere to the major principles outlined in the standard.

Early Unix systems were mainly commercial commodities like most software for sale; to run the operating system, you generally had to pay for that right. In 1984 an engineer named Richard Stallman began work on the GNU Project, which was an effort to create an operating system that was like Unix and that could be distributed and used freely by anyone. He currently runs the Free Software Foundation (`http://gnu.org/fsf/fsf.html`), and many of the programs he and his supporters have created are used in both commercial and open-source versions of Unix.

GNU stands for GNU's Not Unix, which is a recursive acronym. The GNU Project wanted to create a Unix-like operating system, not a Unix derivative (which would imply that it was a source-code copy of Unix).

In 1991 Linus Torvalds, a Finnish graduate student, began work on a Unix-like system called Linux. Linux is actually the kernel (kernels are discussed later in this chapter), while the parts with which most people are familiar — the tools, shell, and file system — are the creations of others (usually the GNU organization). As the Linux project gained momentum, it grew into a major contender in the Unix market. Many people are first introduced to Unix through Linux, which makes available to desktop machines the functionality of a Unix machine that used to costs thousands of dollars. The strength of Linux lies in its progressive licensing, which allows for the software to be freely distributable with no royalty requirements. The only requirement for the end user is that any changes made to the software be made available to others in the community, thus permitting the software to mature at an incredibly fast rate. The license under which Linux is distributed is called the GNU Public License (GPL), available at `http://gnu.org/licenses/licenses.html`.

Another free variant of Unix that has gained popularity is the BSD family of software, which uses the very lenient BSD License (`http://opensource.org/licenses/bsd-license.php`). This license allows for free modification without the requirement of providing the software source code to others. After a landmark 1994 lawsuit settlement, BSD Unix became freely distributable and has evolved into the NetBSD, FreeBSD, and OpenBSD projects, and it also forms the underlying technology for Darwin (upon which Mac OS X is based).

These freely available Unix derivatives have given new life to the Unix operating system, which had been experiencing a decline as the Microsoft Windows juggernaut advanced. Additionally, Apple has become the highest-volume supplier of Unix systems. Now Unix is moving forward in the corporate environment as well as in the end-user desktop market.

Operating System Components

An operating system is the software interface between the user and the hardware of a system. Whether your operating system is Unix, DOS, Windows, or OS/2, everything you do as a user or programmer interacts with the hardware in some way. In the very early days of computers, text output or a series of lights indicated the results of a system request. Unix started as a command-line interface (CLI) system—there was no graphical user interface (GUI) to make the system easier to use or more aesthetically pleasing. Now Unix has some of the most customizable user interfaces available, in the forms of the Mac OS X Aqua and Linux's KDE and GNOME interfaces among others, making the Unix system truly ready for the average user's desktop.

Let's take a brief look at the components that make up the Unix operating system: the kernel, the shell, the file system, and the utilities (applications).

Unix Kernel

The kernel is the lowest layer of the Unix system. It provides the core capabilities of the system and allows processes (programs) to access the hardware in an orderly manner. Basically, the kernel controls processes, input/output devices, file system operations, and any other critical functions required by the operating system. It also manages memory. These are all called autonomous functions, in that they are run without instructions by a user process. It is the kernel that allows the system to run in multiuser (more than one user accessing the system at the same time), multitasking (more than one program running at a time) mode.

A kernel is built for the specific hardware on which it is operating, so a kernel built for a Sun Sparc machine can't be run on an Intel processor machine without modifications. Because the kernel deals with very low-level tasks, such as accessing the hard drive or managing multitasking, and is not user friendly, it is generally not accessed by the user.

One of the most important functions of the kernel is to facilitate the creation and management of processes. Processes are executed programs (called jobs or tasks in some operating systems) that have owners—human or systems—who initiate their calling or execution. The management of these can be very complicated because one process often calls another (referred to as *forking* in Unix). Frequently processes also need to communicate with one another, sending and receiving information that allows other actions to be performed. The kernel manages all of this outside of the user's awareness.

The kernel also manages memory, a key element of any system. It must provide all processes with adequate amounts of memory, and some processes require a lot of it. Sometimes a process requires more memory than is available (too many other processes running, for example). This is where virtual memory comes in. When there isn't enough physical memory, the system tries to accommodate the process by moving portions of it to the hard disk. When the portion of the process that was moved to hard disk is needed again, it is returned to physical memory. This procedure, called *paging*, allows the system to provide multitasking capabilities, even with limited physical memory.

Another aspect of virtual memory is called *swap*, whereby the kernel identifies the least-busy process or a process that does not require immediate execution. The kernel then moves the entire process out of RAM to the hard drive until it is needed again, at which point it can be run from the hard drive or from physical RAM. The difference between the two is that paging moves only part of the process to the hard drive, while swapping moves the entire process to hard drive space. The segment of the hard drive used for virtual memory is called the *swap space* in Unix, a term you will want to remember as you move through this book. Running out of swap space can cause significant problems, up to and including system failure, so always be sure you have sufficient swap space. Whenever swapping occurs, you pay a heavy price in significantly decreased performance, because disks are appreciably slower than physical RAM. You can avoid swapping by ensuring that you have an adequate amount of physical RAM for the system.

Shells

The shell is a command line interpreter that enables the user to interact with the operating system. A shell provides the next layer of functionality for the system; it is what you use directly to administer and run the system. The shell you use will greatly affect the way you work. The original Unix shells have been heavily modified into many different types of shells over the years, all with some unique feature that the creator(s) felt was lacking in other shells. There are three major shells available on most systems: the Bourne shell (also called sh), the C shell (csh), and the Korn shell (ksh). The shell is used almost exclusively via the command line, a text-based mechanism by which the user interacts with the system.

The Bourne shell (also simply called Shell) was the first shell for Unix. It is still the most widely available shell on Unix systems, providing a language with which to script programs and basic user functionality to call other programs. Shell is good for everyday use and is especially good for shell scripting because its scripts are very portable (they work in other Unix versions' Bourne shells). The only problem with the Bourne shell is that it has fewer features for user interaction than some of the more modern shells.

The C shell is another popular shell commonly available on Unix systems. This shell, from the University of California at Berkeley, was created to address some of the shortcomings of the Bourne shell and to resemble the C language (which is what Unix is built on). Job control features and the capability to alias commands (discussed in Chapter 5) make this shell much easier for user interaction. The C shell had some early quirks when dealing with scripting and is often regarded as less robust than the Bourne shell for creating shell scripts. The quirks were eventually fixed, but the C shell still has slight variations, resulting from different implementations based on which entity (commercial provider or other resource) is providing the shell.

The Korn shell was created by David Korn to address the Bourne shell's user-interaction issues and to deal with the shortcomings of the C shell's scripting quirks. The Korn shell adds some functionality that neither the Bourne or C shell has while incorporating the strong points of each shell. The only drawback to the Korn shell is that it requires a license, so its adoption is not as widespread as that of the other two.

These are by no means the only shells available. Here's a list of some of the many shells available for the different Unix systems:

- sh (also known as the Bourne shell)[
- PDKSH (Public Domain Korn shell)
- bash (Bourne Again Shell — a revamped version of Bourne shell)
- Z shell
- TCSH (TENEX C shell)

As with everything Unix, there are many different implementations, and you are free to choose the shell that best suits your needs based on the features provided. Chapter 5 examines several shells in detail.

The Other Components

The other Unix components are the file system and the utilities. The file system enables the user to view, organize, secure, and interact with, in a consistent manner, files and directories located on storage devices. The file system is discussed in depth in Chapter 4.

Utilities are the applications that enable you to work on the system (not to be confused with the shell). These utilities include the Web browser for navigating the Internet, word processing utilities, e-mail programs, and other commands that will be discussed throughout this book.

Try It Out Run Unix from a CD-ROM

The best way to learn Unix is to follow along with the book and try some of the exercises while you are reading. If you don't have a current install of a Unix operating system, and you do have an Intel/AMD-based system (a PC that is Windows compatible), you can use KNOPPIX, a bootable Linux distribution. KNOPPIX enables you to try Unix right from a CD, without installing or modifying any other operating system on your computer. It provides a full-featured Linux environment and is a great way to see what Linux and Unix is about.

1. Use the copy of Knoppix included on this book's CD or download the KNOPPIX ISO image from one of the mirrors listed at `http://knopper.net/knoppix-mirrors/index-en.html`. There are usually two versions of the software, one in German and one in English; choose the image with the extension `-EN.iso`.
2. If you downloaded a copy of Knoppix, use your favorite CD-burning software to burn a copy of the ISO onto a CD-R.
3. Insert the CD-ROM included with this book or the CD-R you created into your CD-ROM drive and boot (load) from it. By default, most systems let you boot from a CD-ROM simply by putting the disk in the drive. (If the CD-ROM doesn't start automatically, you may need to contact your computer manufacturer's manual for instructions.) You'll see the opening KNOPPIX screen, which should be similar to the one in Figure 1-1.

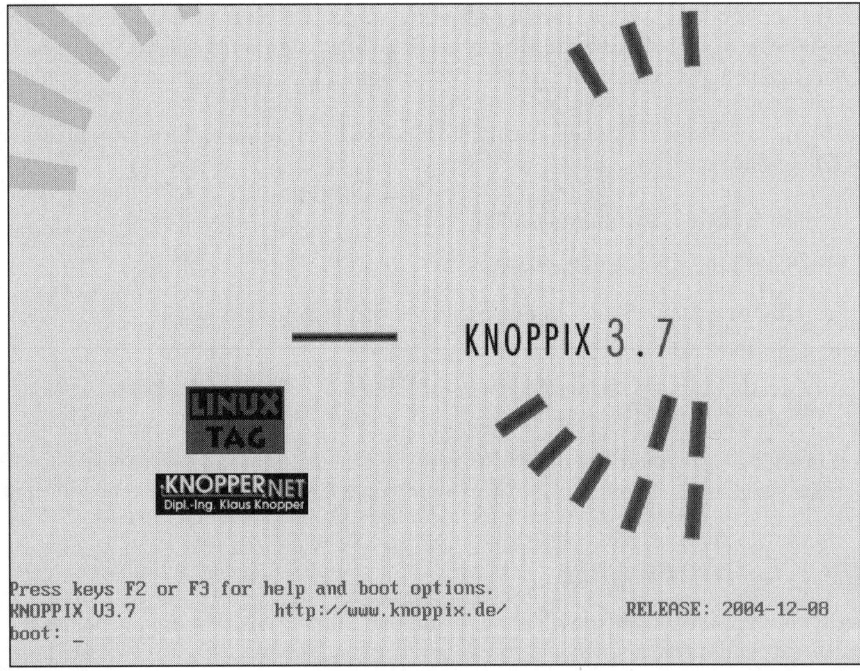

Figure 1-1

4. Press **Enter** (or **Return**) to continue the boot process. You'll see a screen similar to the one shown in Figure 1-2.

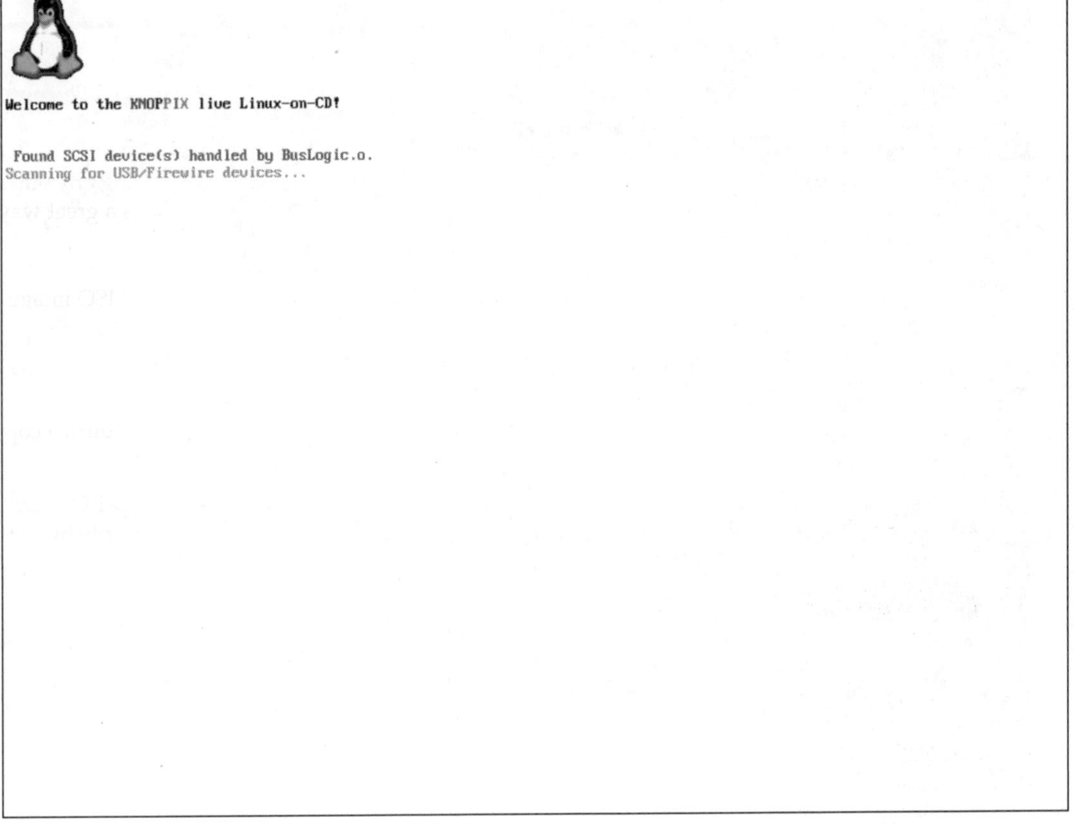

Welcome to the KNOPPIX live Linux-on-CD!
Found SCSI device(s) handled by BusLogic.o.
Scanning for USB/Firewire devices...

Figure 1-2

5. The boot sequence continues through a few more screens.

Because KNOPPIX is bootable and can be transported from system to system, you do not enter a password as you would with most Unix distributions.

Figure 1-3 shows the desktop loading.

6. When you are done, exit the system by rebooting (restarting) or shutting down your computer. You can do this by pressing **Ctrl+Alt+Del**. A dialog box provides you with options to Turn Off Computer or Restart Computer. If you select Restart Computer, take out the CD-ROM during the reboot to return to your regular operating system.

Figure 1-3

How It Works

The KNOPPIX distribution has been optimized to run within RAM from the CD-ROM. It does not need to modify the hard drive or install itself anywhere. It can be run without fear of damaging the current contents of your hard drive.

Summary

This chapter briefly discussed the history of Unix and introduced some of the versions of Unix. The Unix core components — the kernel, shells, file system, and utilities — were introduced.

In the past, Unix was considered a system geared to the most computer-savvy users and those who wanted a system for core functionality, with no regard to aesthetics or user friendliness. Unix has evolved to fit the needs of many different types of users, from the no-nonsense corporate environment to the novice computer user's desktop. There are rich desktop environments available for many flavors of Unix, for example, and every currently selling Macintosh computer is running a version of Unix right out of the box.

In Chapter 2, you begin using a Unix system from initial login to logout.

First Steps

This chapter introduces you to interacting with the Unix operating system. It examines the initial Unix boot process, shows you how to log in to the system and to properly shut down the system, and explains what the shell offers you. It also covers the `man` command, which is Unix's built-in system help facility. This chapter provides the foundation upon which other chapters will build.

System Startup

What occurs from the power-off position until your operating system is fully available is called the *boot process*. In the simplest terms, the boot process consists of the Read-Only Memory's (ROM, or NVRAM, or firmware) loading of the program for actually booting (starting) the system. This initial step (commonly called bootstrapping) identifies the devices on the system that can be booted or started from. You can boot or start from only one device at a time, but, because many different devices can be identified as bootable, one of those other identified devices can be used if one bootable device has a failure. These devices may load automatically, or you may be shown a list of devices from which you can choose. Figure 2-1 shows a list of bootable devices in a Solaris boot system on the Intel platform.

The boot device doesn't have to be a physical hard drive, because the system can boot from the network or from removable storage such as a CD-ROM or floppy diskette. A boot device simply holds the information about where to load the operating system. The bootstrap phase only identifies the hardware available for booting and whether it is usable.

Control is then transferred to the kernel. The operating system has not been loaded at this point, and the system is not usable for production processes. Some systems show the boot process by means of messages on the screen, and others hide the system messages from the users by using graphical figures to represent the boot process. Figure 2-2 shows the boot drive being identified during the Solaris boot process.

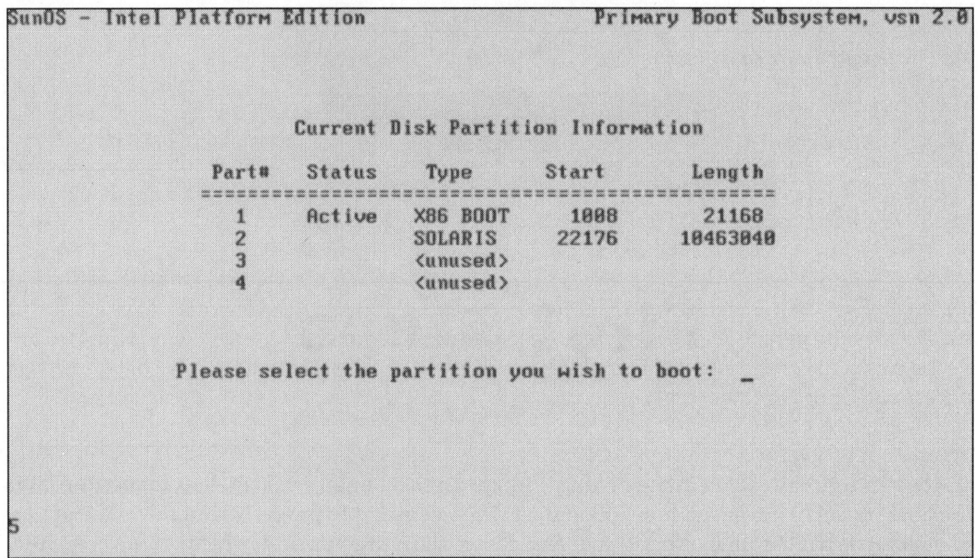

SunOS - Intel Platform Edition
Primary Boot Subsystem, vsn 2.0
Current Disk Partition Information
Part# Status Type Start Length
1 Active X86 BOOT 1008 21168
2 SOLARIS 22176 10463040
3 <unused>
4 <unused>
Please select the partition you wish to boot: _
5

Figure 2-1

```
SunOS Secondary Boot version 3.00

            Solaris Intel Platform Edition Booting System

Running Configuration Assistant...
Autobooting from bootpath: /pci@0,0/pci-ide@7,1/ide@0/cmdk@0,0:a

If the system hardware has changed, or to boot from a different
device, interrupt the autoboot process by pressing ESC.

Press ESCape to interrupt autoboot in 1 second.
```

Figure 2-2

After the initial bootstrapping, the boot program begins loading the Unix kernel, which typically resides in the root partition of the system. The kernel on most Unix systems is called unix; in Linux systems, it might be called vmunix or vmlinuz. Its location differs according to the Unix version, as these examples show:

- AIX: /unix
- Linux: /boot/vmlinuz
- Solaris: /kernel/unix

These are only a few of the different kernel locations, but in general you shouldn't have to modify the kernel in day-to-day or even development processes unless you are a system administrator or need to add/remove some functionality from the kernel for a specific need.

The kernel's initial tasks, which vary according to hardware and Unix version, are followed by the initialization phase, in which the system processes and scripts are started. The init process is the first job started and is the parent of all other processes. It must be running for the system to run. The init process calls the initialization scripts and completes administrative tasks relative to the system, such as starting sendmail, the X or window server (that provides the graphical user interface), and so on.

The init process looks into the initialization specification file, usually called /etc/inittab. This file identifies how init should interpret different run levels and what scripts and processes should be started in each run level. A *run level* is a grouping of processes (programs in the most basic sense) or daemons (processes that run all the time).

Figure 2-3 shows the initialization phase on a Mac OS X system.

Figure 2-3

Mac OS X and some of the newer versions of Unix are not as verbose as other Unix systems, because, as Unix has evolved, the makers of the different Unix systems have made ease of use their primary goal. Because the typical end user has no use for the information, a lot of the messages that appear on initialization screens of older versions of Unix generally aren't displayed by Mac OS X and user-friendly Linuxes.

> *You can use the escape sequence (Cmd+v) to view the boot messages on the Mac OS X.*

Figure 2-4 shows the end of the system initialization of a freshly installed Solaris 10 system.

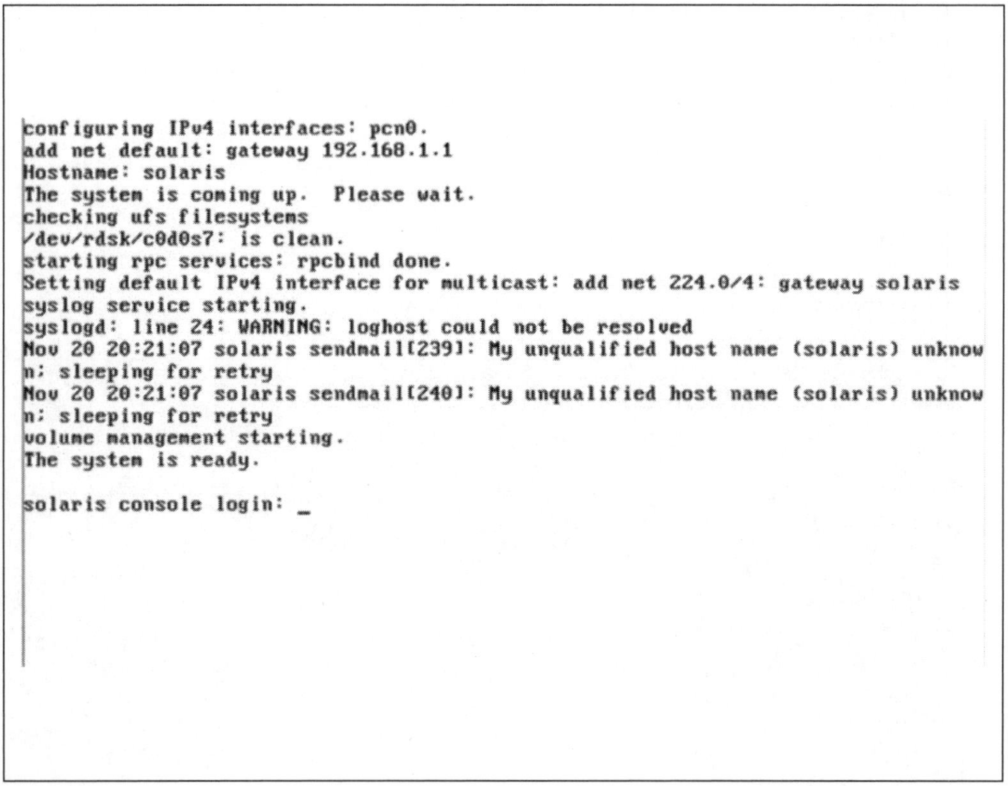

```
configuring IPv4 interfaces: pcn0.
add net default: gateway 192.168.1.1
Hostname: solaris
The system is coming up.  Please wait.
checking ufs filesystems
/dev/rdsk/c0d0s7: is clean.
starting rpc services: rpcbind done.
Setting default IPv4 interface for multicast: add net 224.0/4: gateway solaris
syslog service starting.
syslogd: line 24: WARNING: loghost could not be resolved
Nov 20 20:21:07 solaris sendmail[239]: My unqualified host name (solaris) unknow
n: sleeping for retry
Nov 20 20:21:07 solaris sendmail[240]: My unqualified host name (solaris) unknow
n: sleeping for retry
volume management starting.
The system is ready.

solaris console login: _
```

Figure 2-4

At first, this information may seem odd or even alarming, but there is generally an explanation of the message in the script or logs to track down a problem as your Unix knowledge progresses. For example, the 10th line shows an error in syslogd (the system logging daemon, which is discussed in Chapter 15): `syslogd: line 24: WARNING: loghost could not be resolved`. That may look like big trouble, but it is in fact a minor issue that can be resolved by adding a single entry in `/etc/hosts`. You'll learn more about these messages, how to identify them, and how to troubleshoot them in Chapter 15.

Figure 2-5 shows a Linux system booting (after the initialization phase), and again there are some messages that can be disconcerting, such as the one on line 3: `Your system appears to have shut down uncleanly.`

```
Initializing USB controller (usb-uhci):                              [  OK  ]
Mount USB filesystem                                                 [  OK  ]
Your system appears to have shut down uncleanly
Press Y within 2 seconds to force file system integrity check...y
Checking root filesystem
/dev/sda1: 114607/282240 files (0.5% non-contiguous), 507713/564275 blocks
                                                                     [  OK  ]
Remounting root filesystem in read-write mode:                       [  OK  ]
Activating swap partitions:                                          [  OK  ]
Starting up RAID devices:
Checking filesystems
/dev/sda6: recovering journal
/dev/sda6: 725/185856 files (0.7% non-contiguous), 15207/371495 blocks
                                                                     [  OK  ]
Mounting local filesystems:                                          [  OK  ]
Checking loopback filesystems                                        [  OK  ]
Mounting loopback filesystems:                                       [  OK  ]
Loading keymap: us                                                   [  OK  ]
Loading compose keys: compose.latin.inc                              [  OK  ]
The BackSpace key sends: ^?                                          [  OK  ]
Enabling swap space:                                                 [  OK  ]
Starting netprofile:                                                 [  OK  ]
INIT: Entering runlevel: 5
Entering non-interactive startup
Checking for new hardware_
```

Figure 2-5

These errors are usually fixed automatically or can be corrected using the `fsck` command, which is introduced in Chapter 4.

The boot-up screens contain a wealth of information, but you don't have to watch every message as it displays on your screen. You can use the command `dmesg` to gather boot-up messages that you can peruse at your leisure. To change the boot-up parameters, you must modify either the system Read-Only Memory (ROM) or the Unix operating system initialization scripts as discussed later in the book.

After the initialization phase has completed, the system is running and ready for users to log in. You will see a login prompt or graphical login screen on your system if you are logging in locally.

Logging In and Out of Unix

Logging in means that you are authenticating yourself to the Unix system as a valid user who needs to utilize resources. When you attempt to log in to a Unix system, you are typically asked to authenticate yourself by providing a username and password pair, although logins can include more advanced mechanisms such as biometrics (a retina eye scan, for example) or one-time-use tokens that change password combinations every few seconds. You can log in by using either a graphical user interface (GUI) or the command line.

Logging In via GUI

If you have a keyboard/mouse and monitor directly connected to the Unix system, you can log in much like users log in to their home systems. The initial login screen can take many forms, from the traditional command line that only presents text information to graphical logins complete with pictures. Let's look at a few examples. Figure 2-6 shows a command-line interface on a Mandrakelinux login screen via a command line interface.

```
Mandrake Linux release 10.0 (Official) for i586
Kernel 2.6.3-7mdksmp on an i686 / tty1
localhost login: beginningunix
Password:
Last login: Wed Nov 24 15:29:50 on :0
[beginningunix@localhost beginningunix]$ _
```

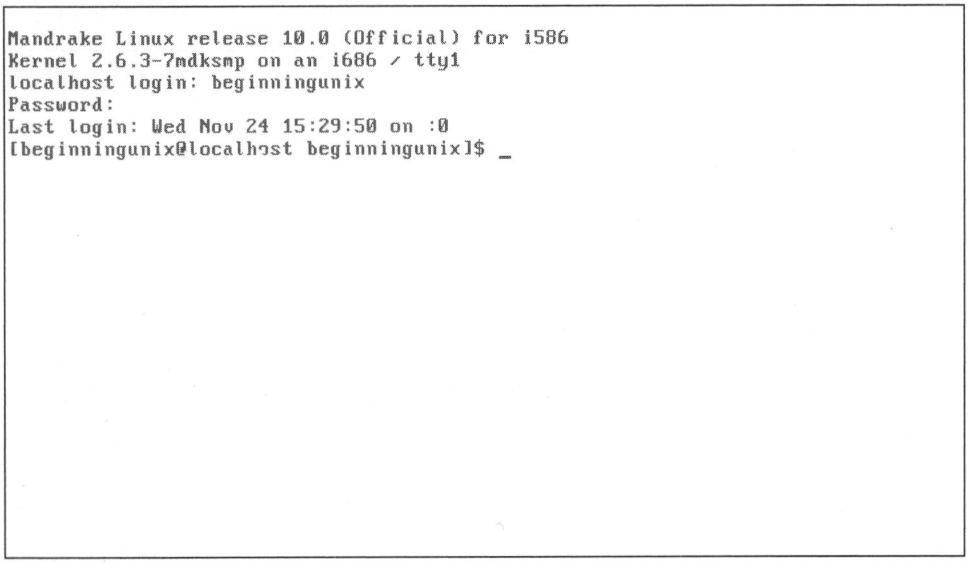

Figure 2-6

Figure 2-7 shows a graphical login for a Mandrakelinux system.

Figure 2-7

Figure 2-8 shows a Solaris 10 graphical login.

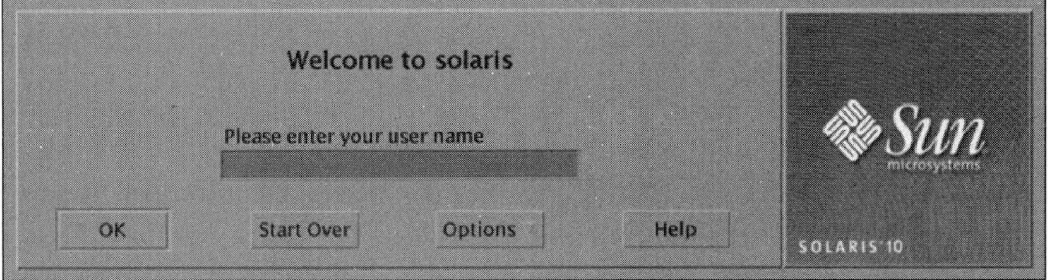

Figure 2-8

The username and password that you supply are against the internal system file or database containing a list of valid usernames and passwords. Figure 2-9 shows a Mac OS X login screen asking the user to select as whom he wants to log in.

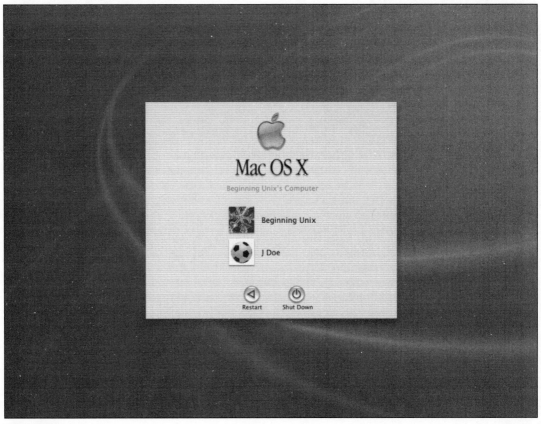

Figure 2-9

In this example, selecting Beginning Unix brings up the screen shown in Figure 2-10, where a valid password must be entered.

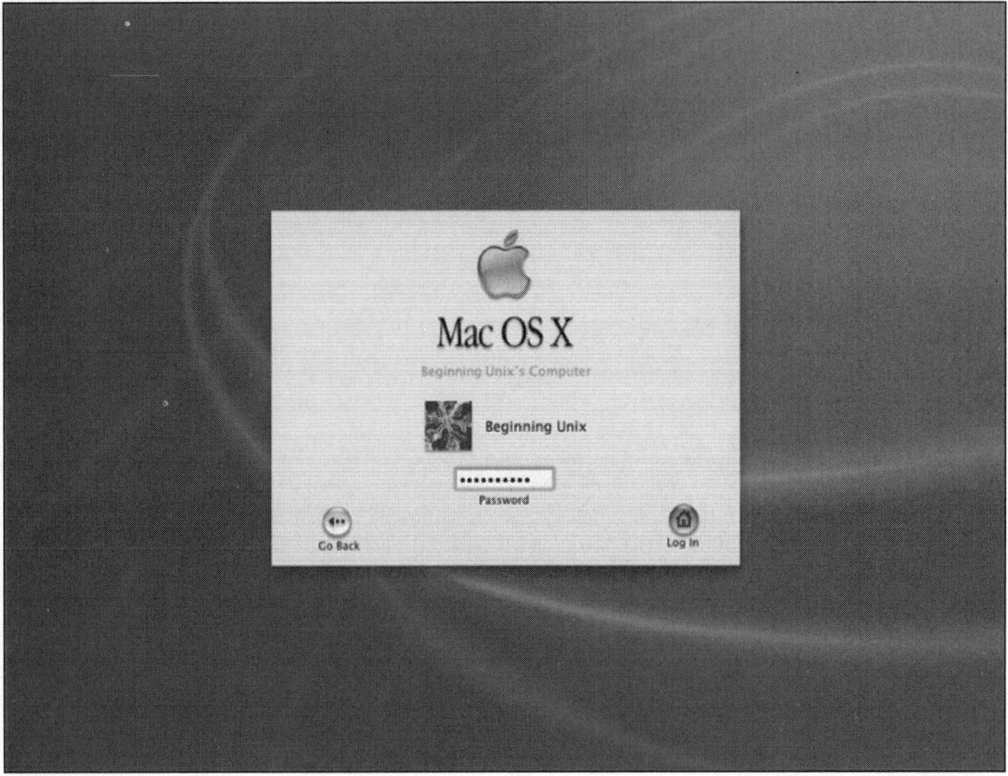

Figure 2-10

An incorrect password usually results in a text or graphic message letting the user know the password entered is invalid. Most Unix systems are set up to freeze an account or set a time delay if a user enters a password incorrectly more than three (or some other specified number of) times. This is for security reasons, so that someone cannot easily continue to enter different passwords in an attempt to log in to another person's account. A correct password starts the login process, which might look much like that shown in Figure 2-11.

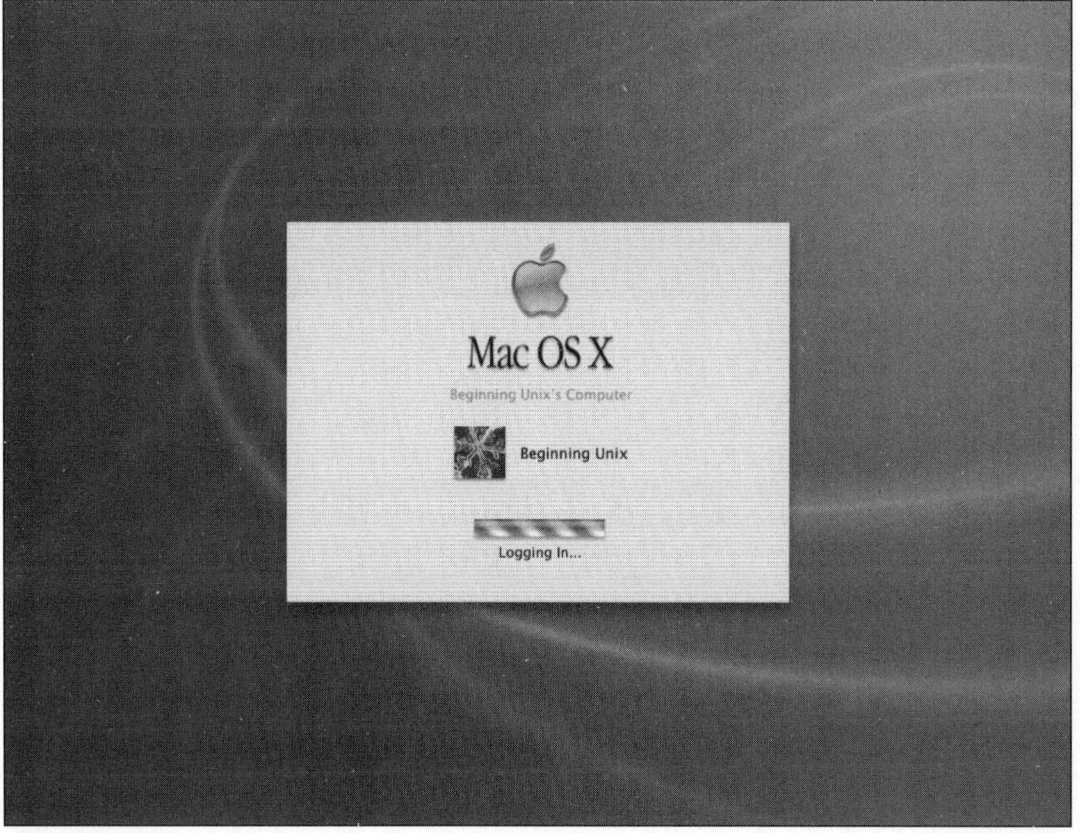

Figure 2-11

Logging In at the Command Line

There are instances where Unix systems aren't running graphical user interfaces and all work is done using the command line. In these cases, you typically see either a banner message indicating the type of machine you are logging in to or a message set up by the system administrator. Sometimes you won't see anything other than the login prompt. Figure 2-12 shows a sample login screen from a Linux system.

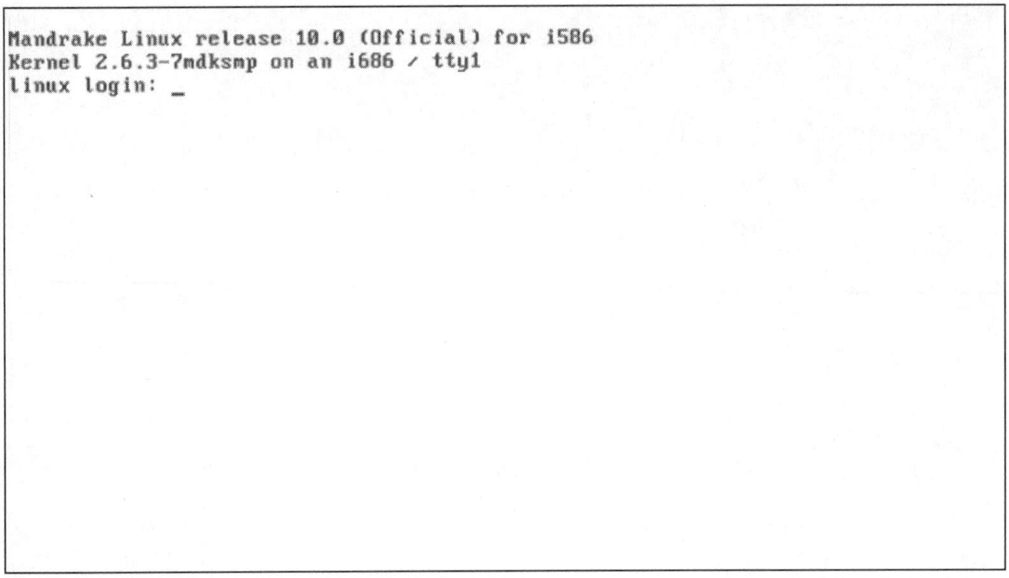

```
Mandrake Linux release 10.0 (Official) for i586
Kernel 2.6.3-7mdksmp on an i686 / tty1
linux login: _
```

Figure 2-12

The banner portion of this screen is this part:

```
Mandrake Linux release 10.0 (Official) for i586
Kernel 2.6.3-7ndksmp on an i686
```

The first line of the banner indicates that this is a Linux system, specifically the Mandrake 10 distribution. The second line indicates the kernel the system is running and also specifies the teletype number (screen). Banners differ from system to system, but you can generally figure out what information is being presented. Because of security concerns, this information may be absent on systems that are publicly accessible through the Internet (exact system specifications make it easier for hackers to attack the system).

The third line shows the hostname, which can be a name (linux, in Figure 2-12) or IP address (such as 192.168.1.1) and then the phrase `login:`. This is where you enter the username that you are logging in as. Notice that the command line login doesn't offer any hints about what username to use, so you have to know it ahead of time. Figure 2-13 shows a login failure, followed by the sequence of events for a successful logging in.

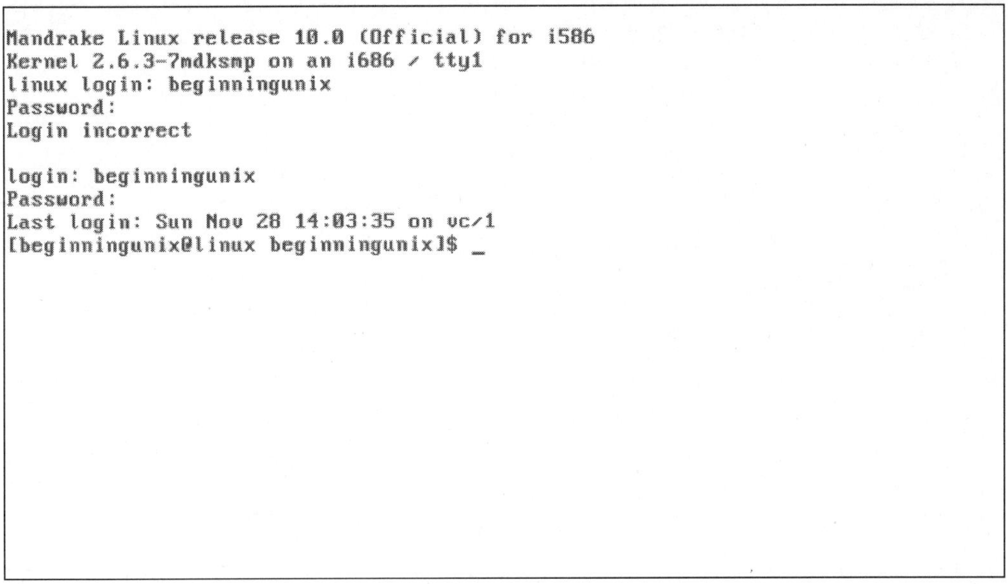

```
Mandrake Linux release 10.0 (Official) for i586
Kernel 2.6.3-7mdksmp on an i686 / tty1
linux login: beginningunix
Password:
Login incorrect

login: beginningunix
Password:
Last login: Sun Nov 28 14:03:35 on vc/1
[beginningunix@linux beginningunix]$ _
```

Figure 2-13

In this example, the user enters beginningunix as the username and presses **Enter** (or **Return**). The request for the password comes on the screen (line 4). The user enters a bad password for that account, and the system responds with the `Login incorrect` statement, followed by another chance to log in. This time the user enters the correct username and password. The system then displays the last time the user was logged in and provides access to a command line shell so that the user can begin working on the system.

The last time logged in is a security feature that enables you to see when the account was last used. If you notice that the last time logged in was a time when you weren't using the system, someone may have broken into your account. Contact the system administrator immediately.

If you use the command line to log in either remotely or locally and your username/password combination is rejected, the system does not tell you which part of the login is incorrect. You get the same message — `Login incorrect` — whether your username is invalid or your password is wrong. Figure 2-14 shows the username beginningunix entered with an erroneous password, followed by a bad username entered with beginningunix's password, and you can see that the system's response to both of these login attempts is the same: `Login incorrect`. This is another security mechanism to prevent malicious entities from attempting to guess usernames on the system; everyone must have a valid username/password combination to log in.

Do not forget your username and password, because there are usually no hints for either when you log in to Unix.

```
Mandrake Linux release 10.0 (Official) for i586
Kernel 2.6.3-7mdksmp on an i686 / tty1
linux login: beginningunix
Password:
Login incorrect

login: beginunix
Password:
Login incorrect

login: beginningunix
Password:
Last login: Sun Nov 28 14:21:19 on vc/1
[beginningunix@linux beginningunix]$ _
```

Figure 2-14

Remotely Logging In

Unix was built with networking in mind, allowing for remote operations via a command line or graphical user interface. When remotely logging in, you generally use a network protocol such as TCP/IP (discussed in Chapter 16).

A protocol is a standard method for transferring information between two different systems.

The following are some of the most common methods for logging in to a remote Unix system:

Command	Description
`ssh`	Logs in interactively to a shell to perform multiple functions such as running commands. This method uses encryption to scramble the session so that the username, password, and all communications with the remote system are encrypted* (not readable by others).
`telnet`	Logs in interactively to a shell to perform multiple functions such as running commands. Because this method is not encrypted,* the username, password, and all communications with the remote system are sent in plain text and possibly viewable by others on the network.
`sftp`	Logs in to transfer files between two different systems. This method is encrypted.* (`sftp` is discussed in Chapter 8.)
`ftp`	Logs in to transfer files between two different systems. This method is not encrypted.* (`ftp` is also discussed in Chapter 8.)

**Encrypted means that the text is not understandable by others and is in a sense scrambled. For example, if the phrase "this is my password" were encrypted, it might show up as "14N!&x&*0 | ~dB{2" to anyone else viewing the session over the network.*

These are by no means the only methods for remote logins. For example, the r commands — `rsh` (remote shell), `rcp` (remote copy), and `rlogin` (remote login) — were prevalent in the past, but because they offer little security, they're generally discouraged in today's environments. `rsh` and `rlogin` are similar in functionality to `telnet`, and `rcp` is similar to `ftp`.

To enable remote logins, the local and remote systems must have connectivity to each other and allow for access via the communications path (that is, no firewall or system restrictions).

Most Unix systems have support for the protocols/commands used to connect to external systems, but these services may not always be available to you for remote connections (the remote machine may not allow connections to the system, for example). In these cases, you must contact the system administrator of the Unix system in order to determine the method for connecting remotely.

Using ssh

`ssh` (Secure SHell) and `telnet` are two methods that enable you to log in to a remote system and run commands interactively; that is, you can use most if not all of the commands available to your account as if you were locally connected. To use these commands, you need the following information at a minimum:

command hostname

`command` indicates the protocol you want to use (preferably `ssh` if it's available, because the session would be encrypted) to connect, and *`hostname`* indicates the remote system to which you want to connect. *`hostname`* can be an actual name (such as darwin) or an IP address (such as 192.168.1.58). To connect to system darwin (IP address of 192.168.1.58) from a Linux system with `ssh`, you could type:

```
ssh darwin
```

or

```
ssh 192.168.1.58
```

An IP address is a numerical designation used by the computer to route information from one system to another. Because a long set of numbers is often difficult for humans to remember, you can use a common name to refer to a remote system if the system is set up properly. More on this is discussed in Chapter 16.

After typing either of these commands, you'd see the same type of prompt or information that you did when you logged in locally via the command line.

In Figure 2-15, for example, running the command `hostname` shows you the hostname of the system on which you're running the command. In this example, it's DARWIN, a Mac OS X system. Then the `ssh` command is typed: `ssh 192.168.1.65` (the IP address for the Linux system named linux).

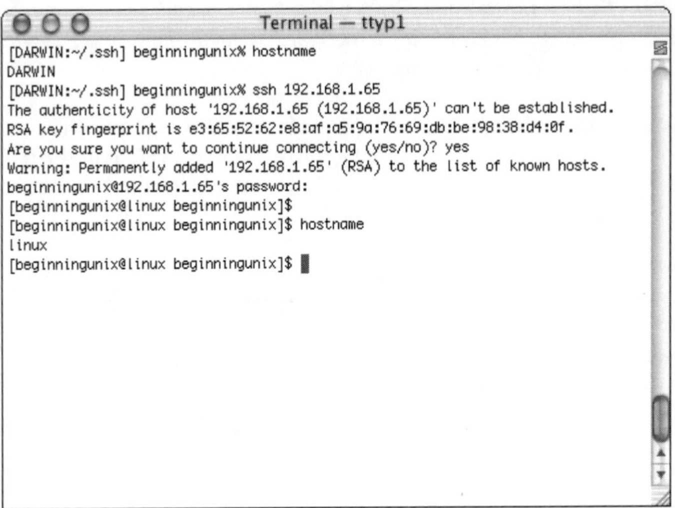

Terminal — ttyp1
[DARWIN:~/.ssh] beginningunix% hostname
DARWIN
[DARWIN:~/.ssh] beginningunix% ssh 192.168.1.65
The authenticity of host '192.168.1.65 (192.168.1.65)' can't be established.
RSA key fingerprint is e3:65:52:62:e8:af:a5:9a:76:69:db:be:98:38:d4:0f.
Are you sure you want to continue connecting (yes/no)? yes
Warning: Permanently added '192.168.1.65' (RSA) to the list of known hosts.
beginningunix@192.168.1.65's password:
[beginningunix@linux beginningunix]$
[beginningunix@linux beginningunix]$ hostname
linux
[beginningunix@linux beginningunix]$

Figure 2-15

If this is the first time you are using `ssh` to connect to the remote system, you are prompted to accept the remote system's keys, or identification, as shown on line 11 (this occurs only the first time you connect to the system). You can confirm the key with the remote system administrator. If someone changes the system or tries to pretend to be the server using `ssh` (and trying to steal your user credentials), you will be notified with a warning.

After entering the password for the user account, you are put into a shell on the remote system. The reason you are not asked your username is that the `ssh` command sends the username you are logged in with on the local system unless you specify a different username. Now execute `hostname`, and you see that you are truly remotely logged in to the machine named linux.

When you run `ssh` *`hostname`*, `ssh` assumes that you want to log in to the remote system with the same username that you're using on the local system. Your username on different systems may not always be the same because of differing naming conventions, so you may be jdoe on one system, johnd on another, and jd1234 on a third. If you need a different username to log on to a remote system, use the following syntax:

```
ssh username@hostname
```

If you are logged into system darwin as user johnd and want to remotely log in to system 192.168.1.65 (linux) as user jdoe, you type:

```
ssh jdoe@192.168.1.65
```

Remember that *`hostname`* can be an actual name (such as boardroom) or an IP address (such as 192.168.1.58).

Using telnet

`ssh` gives you encryption from local to remote server and vice versa, providing more security during the working session, but `ssh` may not always be available to you because of system restrictions or policy. If that's the case, you generally need to use `telnet`, which offers the same functionality, but with no encryption of data being transmitted between the local and remote systems. `telnet` is an older protocol that's in wide use even in today's security-conscious environment because it's available on many major platforms (including Microsoft Windows and DOS) by default. You use `telnet` much like `ssh` except that sometimes you are prompted for your username and password (`telnet` doesn't always assume you want to log in as the current user). To `telnet` from the darwin machine to the solaris machine (192.168.1.60), you'd type:

```
telnet solaris
```

or

```
telnet 192.168.1.60
```

as shown in Figure 2-16.

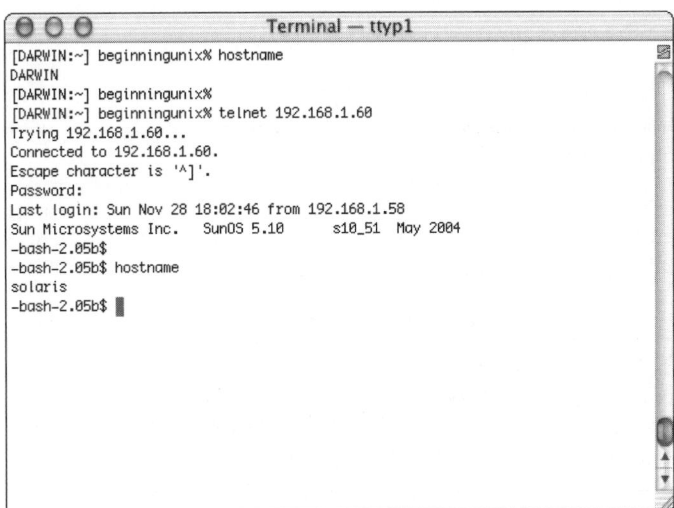

Figure 2-16

In Figure 2-16, `hostname` is run to determine the current system's hostname (DARWIN), and then the `telnet 192.168.1.60` command is issued. The system requests the user's password, and after it's provided, the last login and banner information is displayed. Running `hostname` again produces the expected results: solaris. The user can now run commands as if her screen and keyboard were directly connected to the solaris system.

The Shell

After you log in, you are taken to the shell predefined for you by your system administrator. (Shells were introduced in Chapter 1.) A command line interface or a graphical user interface (GUI) displays, giving you access to the shell. Figure 2-17 shows a typical command line interface.

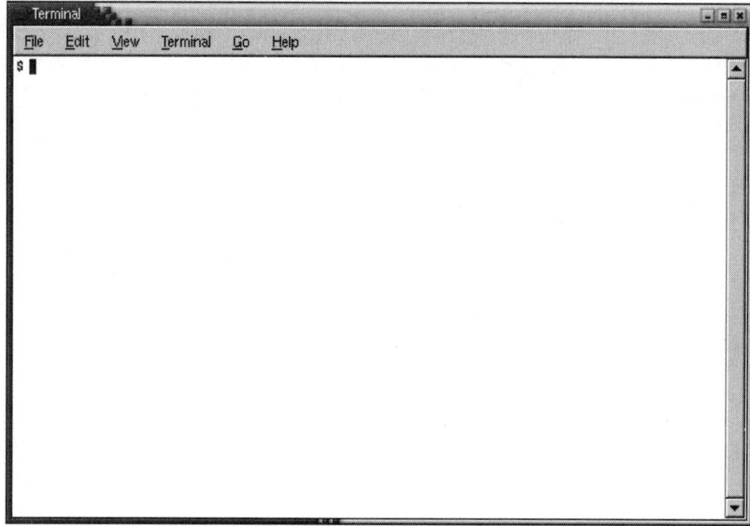

Figure 2-17

If you are using a GUI, locate the xterm or konsole application that gives you access to the shell. Then you're all set to enter the commands discussed throughout this book.

Logging Out

After you have completed the work you need to do on the system using your interactive login, you need to exit the system in a controlled and orderly manner to prevent processes or jobs from ending abruptly. The command `exit` ends your shell session (or you can use the command `logout` in the bash or c shell as described in Chapter 5). This closes the window that you are logged in to or ends your session completely. If you are using a GUI, there is typically a button or key sequence that logs you out of the session.

System Shutdown

Unix is a multiuser, multitasking system, so there are usually many processes or programs running at all times. Because the file system needs to be synchronized, just turning the power off creates issues with the file system and affects the stability of the system. There are always processes or tasks running on the system, even if no users are logged in, and an improper shutdown can cause numerous problems.

You typically need to be the superuser or root (the most privileged account on a Unix system) to shut down the system, but on some standalone or personally owned Unix boxes, an administrative user and sometimes regular users can do so. Some GUIs enable you to shut down your system by clicking a button.

The most consistent way to shut down a Unix system properly via the command line is to use one of the following commands:

Command	Function
`halt`	Brings the system down immediately.
`init 0`	Powers off the system using predefined scripts to synchronize and clean up the system prior to shutdown. (Not available on all Unix systems.)
`init 6`	Reboots the system by shutting it down completely and then bringing it completely back up. (Not available on all systems.)
`poweroff`	Shuts down the system by powering off.
`reboot`	Reboots the system.
`shutdown`	Shuts down the system.

The preferred method is to use `shutdown`, which is available on all Unix systems. It uses scripts provided by the system for a proper shutdown and has most of the functionality of the other commands. The `halt` command typically brings down the system immediately without going through the recommended shutdown sequence, causing file system synchronization issues (possible corruption of data or worse).

Another way to shut down and restart the system is to use the following command:

```
shutdown -r
```

To shut down the computer so that you can use the poweroff button to physically power the system down safely, you can use the following command:

```
shutdown -h
```

Using the `shutdown` command is the most proper way to bring the system down without corrupting data or creating system inconsistencies.

Getting Help with Man Pages

Unix commands have always had a multitude of arguments or options to allow different types of functionality with the same command. Because no one can possibly remember every Unix command and all its options, there has been online help available since Unix's earliest days. Unix's version of help files are called *man pages*. Man (manual) pages present online documentation in a standard format that is readable by any user and is set up in a consistent and logical manner. The command is used by simply typing the following syntax:

```
man command
```

You replace *command* with the name of the command you want more information about. For example, to see the man page for the command `man`, you would type:

```
man man
```

at which point you would see output similar to the following (from a Linux system):

```
man(1)                                                     man(1)

NAME

man - format and display the on-line manual pages
manpath - determine user's search path for man pages

SYNOPSIS
       man  [-acdfFhkKtwW]  [--path]  [-m system] [-p string] [-C config_file]
       [-M pathlist] [-P pager] [-S section_list] [section] name ...


DESCRIPTION
       man formats and displays the on-line manual pages.  If you specify sec-
       tion,  man  only looks in that section of the manual. name is normally
       the name of the manual page, which is typically the name of a  command,
       function,  or  file.   However, if name contains a slash (/) then man
       interprets it as a file specification, so that you can do  man  ./foo.5
       or even man /cd/foo/bar.1.gz.

       See below for a description of where man looks for the manual page
       files.


OPTIONS
       -C  config_file
             Specify the  configuration  file  to  use;   the   default   is
             /etc/man.config.  (See man.config(5).)
...
```

This has been cut for brevity. To see the whole man page, type ***man man*** *at the command line.*

```
...
SEE ALSO
       apropos(1), whatis(1), less(1), groff(1), man.conf(5).


BUGS
       The -t option only works if a troff-like program is installed.
       If you see blinking  \255  or  <AD>  instead  of  hyphens,  put  `LESS-
       CHARSET=latin1' in your environment.


TIPS
       If you add the line
```

```
  (global-set-key  [(f1)]  (lambda () (interactive) (manual-entry (cur-
rent-word))))
```

to your *.emacs* file, then hitting F1 will give you the man page for the library call at the current cursor position.

To get a plain text version of a man page, without backspaces and underscores, try

```
  # man foo | col -b > foo.mantxt
```

September 2, 1995 **man(1)**

Man pages are generally divided into sections, which generally vary by the man page author's preference. Here are some of the more common sections:

- `NAME` — Name of the command.
- `SYNOPSIS` — General usage parameters of the command.
- `DESCRIPTION` — Generally describes of the command and what it does.
- `OPTIONS` — Describes all the arguments or options to the command.
- `SEE ALSO` — Lists other commands that are directly related to the command in the man page or closely resembling its functionality.
- `BUGS` — Explains any known issues or bugs that exist with the command or its output.
- `EXAMPLES` (or `TIPS`) — Common usage examples that give the reader an idea of how the command can be used.
- `AUTHORS` — The author of the man page/command.

You won't always know the command you need to use, but if you know what a major point of a command is, you can search the man pages using the `-k` option, which looks for keywords in the man pages. If you need to change the permission settings of a file, for example, but can't remember the command to use, you can type:

```
man -k permission
```

You'll get a list of commands with the word *permission* in their keywords.

Try It Out Use the Man Pages

1. Using the man pages, search for a keyword of your choice to see what commands show up. If you can't think of one, use this:

   ```
   man -k shell
   ```

2. Read the man page for one of the commands from your search result list.

How It Works

The results of your search show every command that matches with your keyword, and you can then view their man pages to find the command you need.

The man pages are a vital resource and the first avenue of research when you need information about commands or files in a Unix system.

Summary

This chapter covered the basics of using a Unix system, from logging in to shutting down the system. You also learned how to use the online help system in the form of the man pages, which enable you to become a self-reliant user as your toolbox of Unix commands grow.

Understanding Users and Groups

A user account provides you with access to the Unix system, whether by a shell, an ftp account, or other means. To use the resources that the Unix system provides, you need a valid user account and resource permissions (permissions are discussed in Chapter 4). Think of your account as your passport, identifying who you are to the Unix system.

For further Mac OS X–specific information regarding users and groups, see Chapter 20.

This chapter discusses the basics of accounts and what accounts are on the various Unix systems, examines how to administer accounts, and explores the purposes of groups and how groups work. It also includes other pertinent information about users and groups in Unix.

Account Basics

There are three primary types of accounts on a Unix system: the root user (or superuser) account, system accounts, and user accounts. Almost all accounts fall into one of those categories.

Root Account

The root account's user has complete and unfettered control of the system, to the point that he can run commands to completely destroy the system. The root user (also called root) can do absolutely anything on the system, with no restrictions on files that can be accessed, removed, and modified.

The Unix methodology assumes that root users know what they want to do, so if they issue a command that will completely destroy the system, Unix allows it. If you are used to working with Microsoft Windows, its administrator account is most like Unix's root account, except that Windows generally tries to protect itself from you — if you try to format the disk that the operating system is on, Windows prevents you from doing so, but Unix accepts the command and starts formatting with no regard to self-destruction. This basic tenet is why people generally use root for only the most important tasks, and then use it only for the time required — and very cautiously.

System Accounts

System accounts are those needed for the operation of system-specific components. They include, for example, the mail account (for electronic mail functions) and the sshd account (for ssh functionality). System accounts are generally provided by the operating system during installation or by a software manufacturer (including in-house developers). They generally assist in the running of services or programs that the users require.

There are many different types of system accounts, and some of them may not exist on your Unix system. For instance, some of the system account names you may find in your `/etc/passwd` file (discussed later in this chapter) are adm, alias, apache, backup, bin, bind, daemon, ftp, guest, gdm, gopher, halt, identd, irc, kmem, listen, mail, mysql, named, noaccess, nobody, nobody4, ntp, root, rpc, rpcuser, and sys. These accounts are usually needed for some specific function on your system, and any modifications to them could adversely affect the system. Do not modify them unless you have done your research on their functionality and have tested the system with any changes.

User Accounts

User accounts provide interactive access to the system for users and groups of users. General users are typically assigned to these accounts and usually have limited access to critical system files and directories. Generally you want to use eight characters or fewer in an account name, but this is no longer a requirement for all Unix systems. For interoperability with other Unix systems and services, however, you will most likely want to restrict your account names to eight characters or fewer.

An account name is the same as a username.

Group Accounts

Group accounts add the capability to assemble other accounts into logical arrangements for simplification of privilege (permission) management. Unix permissions (which are discussed in depth in Chapter 4) are placed on files and directories and are granted in three subsets: the owner of the file, also known as the user; the group assigned to the file, also known simply as group; and anyone who has a valid login to the system but does not fall into either the owner or group subsets, also known as *others*. The existence of a group enables a resource or file owner to grant access to files to a class of people. For example, say that a company with about 100 employees uses a central Unix server for all activities from production to research to support objectives. Three of the employees compose the company's human resources (HR) staff; they often deal with sensitive information, including salaries, pay raises, and disciplinary actions. The HR staff has to store its information on the server everyone else uses, but its directory, `Human_Resources`, needs to be protected so that others cannot view the contents. To enable HR to set specific permissions on its files that allow access only to HR staff, the three staff members are put into a group called hr. The permissions on the `Human_Resources` directory can then be set to allow those members to view and modify files, while excluding all who fall into the other group (everyone else).

One of the strengths of groups is that an account can belong to many groups, based on access requirements. For instance, the two members of the internal audit team may need to access everyone's data, but their directory, called `Audit`, needs to be protected from everyone else's account. To do this, they can belong to all groups and still have a special audit group in which they are the only members. This situation is discussed later in the chapter.

Managing Users and Groups

User management is a cornerstone activity for the healthy upkeep of a system. For security purposes, management should be limited to a few users who need to administer accounts. There are three main user administration files:

- `/etc/passwd`—Identifies the authorized accounts for the system.
- `/etc/shadow`—Holds the encrypted password of the corresponding account. Most Unix systems have this file.
- `/etc/group`—Contains information on group accounts.

/etc/passwd

The first—and the most important—administration file is `/etc/passwd`. This file holds the majority of information about accounts on the Unix system. Almost anyone with an account on the system can view the file, but only root can modify it. Figure 3-1 shows a sample `/etc/passwd` file from a Linux machine.

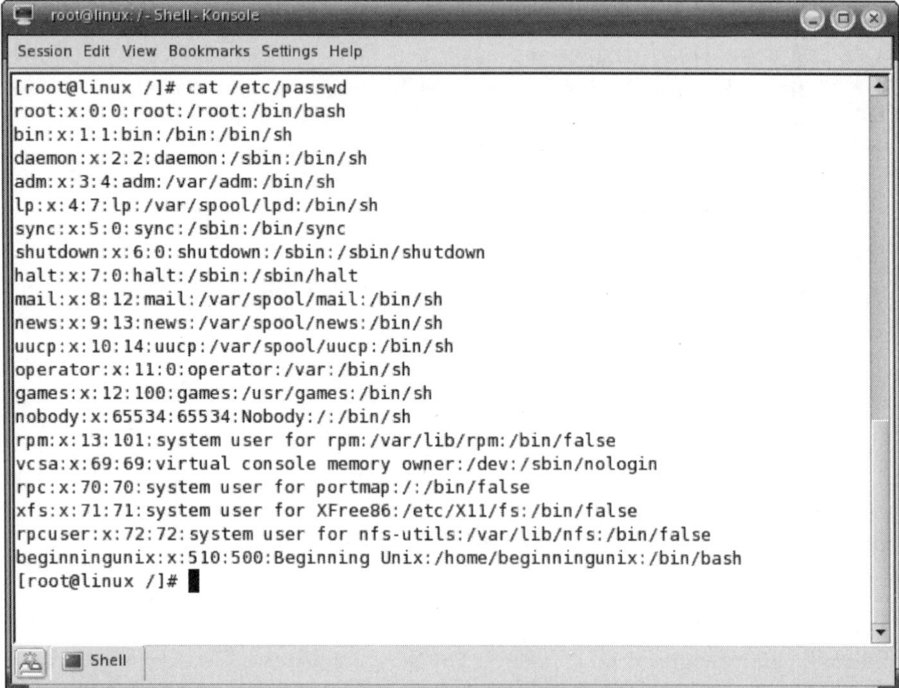

Figure 3-1

Figure 3-2 shows an `/etc/passwd` file from a Solaris 10 system. It's nearly identical to the file shown in Figure 3-1 because the format is the same among the various Unix systems.

```
Solaris
File Edit View Terminal Go Help
# cat /etc/passwd
root:x:0:1:Super-User:/:/sbin/sh
daemon:x:1:1::/:
bin:x:2:2::/usr/bin:
sys:x:3:3::/:
adm:x:4:4:Admin:/var/adm:
lp:x:71:8:Line Printer Admin:/usr/spool/lp:
uucp:x:5:5:uucp Admin:/usr/lib/uucp:
nuucp:x:9:9:uucp Admin:/var/spool/uucppublic:/usr/lib/uucp/uucico
smmsp:x:25:25:SendMail Message Submission Program:/:
listen:x:37:4:Network Admin:/usr/net/nls:
gdm:x:50:50:GDM Reserved UID:/:
webservd:x:80:80:WebServer Reserved UID:/:
nobody:x:60001:60001:NFS Anonymous Access User:/:
noaccess:x:60002:60002:No Access User:/:
nobody4:x:65534:65534:SunOS 4.x NFS Anonymous Access User:/:
beginningunix:x:510:100:Beginning Unix:/export/home/beginningunix:/usr/bin/bash
#
```

Figure 3-2

Take a look at any of the lines in the file (the example in Figure 3-3 uses the `beginningunix` line at the end of the file shown in Figure 3-1), and you can see that there are seven distinct parts — called fields — separated by colons. Although some fields can be left empty, each entry in the file must have all seven fields. Figure 3-3 indicates the location of each of the fields.

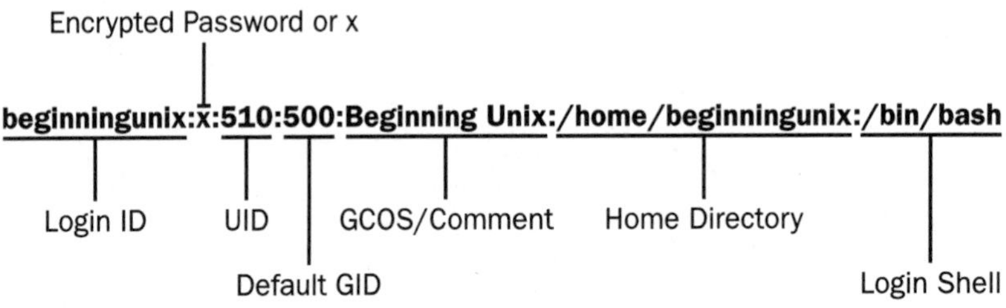

Figure 3-3

Here are descriptions of the file entry fields, with examples from the line shown in Figure 3-3:

1. Login ID (username) that a user enters to log in to the account. Usernames should be unique, so avoid duplicate names, which only introduce confusion and create serious permission problems. Usernames are generally assigned by the administrator. Because users must use their usernames to log in to the system, complexity versus ease of use must be weighed when selecting username schemas.

   beginningunix`:x:510:500:Beginning Unix:/home/beginningunix:/bin/bash`

2. Encrypted password or x. If shadow passwords are used, this field contains just an x. In the early days of Unix, the password field contained the user's encrypted password, but as

machines got more powerful, it became easier to crack or discover the passwords, and passwords were moved to a separate file called `/etc/shadow`. Permissions allow only specific accounts to view that file. Some versions of Unix still include the encrypted password in the `/etc/passwd` file, but this practice is generally frowned upon. An administrator usually assigns a user's initial password.

```
beginningunix:x:510:500:Beginning Unix:/home/beginningunix:/bin/bash
```

3. UID (user ID number) by which the system knows the account. This is how Unix represents the user (instead of using the username). A user often interacts with the system only through an account name, but the Unix system uses a number (UID) to represent the user. Every account is assigned a UID, generally in the range from 0 to 65535, with 0–99 reserved for system IDs (root — the superuser — is always 0). The 65535 limit is not valid on all systems (some allow for many more). The UID does not have to be unique, although having users share UIDs is a bad practice because logging and permissions become confusing when two users share a UID. (The functionality sought by having users share UIDs can be accomplished through groups.) An administrator typically assigns account names and UIDs.

```
beginningunix:x:510:500:Beginning Unix:/home/beginningunix:/bin/bash
```

The UID is what really identifies the user to the system. You can change your root account's name to admin but because the UID associated with the account is 0, the system identifies it as the superuser. You could also assign the 0 UID to another user, and that account would have superuser permissions (this assignment presents security issues and is highly discouraged).

4. Default GID (group ID) — the primary, or default, group to which the account belongs. This doesn't limit the total groups to which the account can belong; it only identifies the regular group the user belongs to upon login. This number doesn't need to be unique because many users can share the same group with no adverse effects on the system. Lower-number groups are generally used for system account groups.

```
beginningunix:x:510:500:Beginning Unix:/home/beginningunix:/bin/bash
```

5. The GCOS, or comment, field holds information about the accounts, such as the full name of the user, the telephone or office number, or any other human-readable information. This field can contain almost anything you want (except a colon, which would represent the end of the field). Most organizations use it to add some contact information for the account in case there is a problem. Anything in this file (and field) can be viewed by anyone on the system, so do not provide sensitive information such as credit card numbers or Social Security numbers. This field can be left blank with no adverse effect (you'll have two colons next to each other, the "blank field" in between).

```
beginningunix:x:510:500:Beginning Unix:/home/beginningunix:/bin/bash
```

Interestingly, the GCOS field derives its name from the General Electric Comprehensive Operating System (GECOS), or General Comprehensive Operating System. The field was originally used for holding GCOS identification for services that ran off GECOS systems (which was its own operating system). GCOS is not in much use these days, but the term survives today when referring to this field.

6. Location of the account's starting, or home, directory (used to store personal files). This can be any valid directory (usually but not always `/home`) on which the user has full permissions (read,

write, and execute). The directory is usually owned by the account with which it's aligned. Do not assign any account with `/tmp` as the home directory because this can create serious security vulnerabilities.

```
beginningunix:x:510:500:Beginning Unix:/home/beginningunix:/bin/bash
```

7. The user's login shell. It must be a valid shell (usually listed in the `/etc/shells` file), or else the user cannot log in interactively. All valid shells are usually identified in `/etc/shells`. (Shells are described in depth in Chapter 5.) If the shell identified in field seven doesn't exist (such as a misspelled entry), the user will not be able to log in interactively. Be very careful when manually editing this field.

```
beginningunix:x:510:500:Beginning Unix:/home/beginningunix:/bin/bash
```

/etc/shadow

The `/etc/shadow` file contains the encrypted password entries for local users as well as any password aging (which tells when passwords expire) or restrictions. Figure 3-4 shows a sample `/etc/shadow` file from a Linux system.

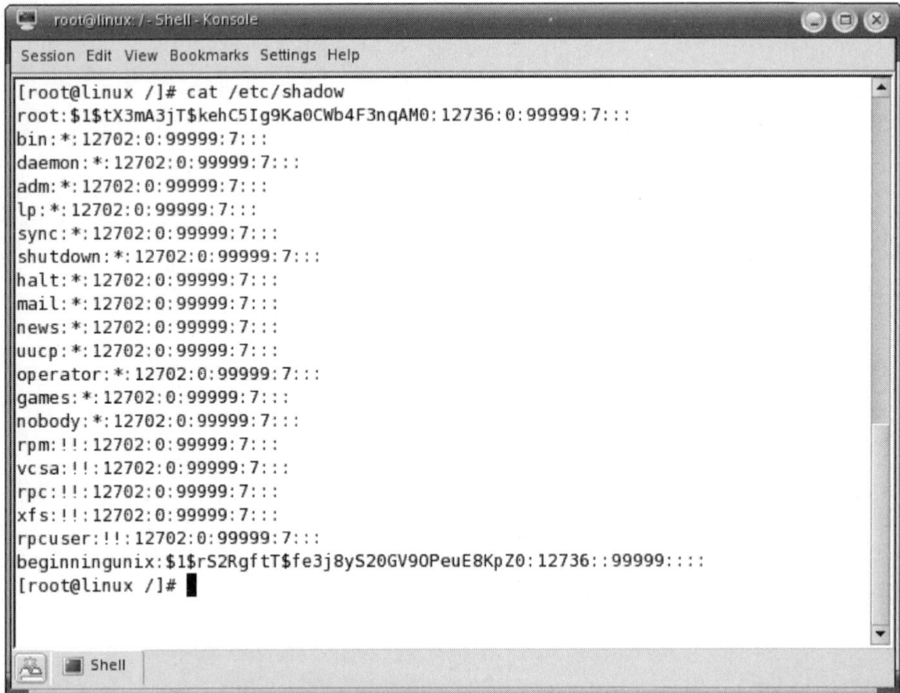

Figure 3-4

Figure 3-5 shows an `/etc/shadow` example from a Solaris 10 Unix system. The field content is slightly different from what is shown in Figure 3-4, but the nine fields are the same.

```
Solaris
File  Edit  View  Terminal  Go  Help
# cat /etc/shadow
root:t2Ckk31xvlPxQ:6445::::::
daemon:NP:6445::::::
bin:NP:6445::::::
sys:NP:6445::::::
adm:NP:6445::::::
lp:NP:6445::::::
uucp:NP:6445::::::
nuucp:NP:6445::::::
smmsp:NP:6445::::::
listen:*LK*:::::::
gdm:*LK*:::::::
webservd:*LK*:::::::
nobody:*LK*:6445::::::
noaccess:*LK*:6445::::::
nobody4:*LK*:6445::::::
beginningunix:t2Ckk31xvlPxQ:12735::::::
#
```

Figure 3-5

Figure 3-6 uses the last line in Figure 3-4 to indicate the colon-delimited fields.

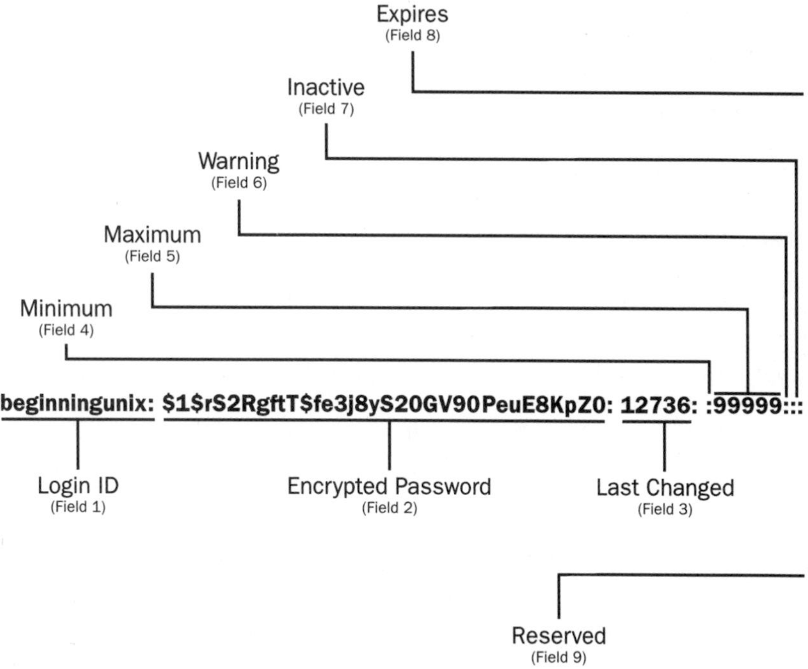

Figure 3-6

Here are descriptions of the file entry fields, with examples from the line in Figure 3-6:

1. The login ID (username, or account name). This information corresponds to the `/etc/passwd` entry for the account.

   beginningunix:`$1$cth3s70B$Sol7rv9u.UyKtEyZ0HP.V.:12736::9999::::`

2. The encrypted version of the password (which can be 13 or more characters depending on the Unix implementation). Because this file is readable only by root, the passwords are more protected than if they were in the openly readable in `/etc/passwd` file. If this field is blank, the user is not required to enter a password — a very dangerous situation, because only the account name need be discovered for the system to be compromised. There are ways to lock an account (prevent anyone from using it) with this field as well, depending on the version of Unix. On some systems, for example, NP in this field means that the user cannot actively log in to the account, but must log in with his own account and then use `sudo` (discussed later in this chapter). You can also put a `*` (`*LK*` for Solaris) to indicate that the account is locked.

   `beginningunix:`**1cth3s70B$Sol7rv9u.UyKtEyZ0HP.V.**`:12736::9999::::`

3. The number of days from January 1, 1970, until the password was changed. This is used in conjunction with the other fields to determine if the account and password are still valid and if the password requires updating.

   `beginningunix:$1$cth3s70B$Sol7rv9u.UyKtEyZ0HP.V.:`**12736**`::9999::::`

The January 1, 1970, date represents what is called the epoch. It's a date picked out by the creators of Unix as a good start time.

4. The minimum number of days before the user can change his password again. This allows the system administrator to protect the user from changing his password too soon after the previous change, reducing the chance an attacker can change the password if he finds it. This field is also used for administrative functions such as password propagation between systems.

   In this example, the field is blank:

   `beginningunix:$1$cth3s70B$Sol7rv9u.UyKtEyZ0HP.V.:12736::9999::::`

5. The maximum number of days the password is valid before requiring a change. The administrator uses this field to enforce password change policies and to reduce the likelihood that a malicious entity can use brute force (continually trying passwords) to crack the password, which can take a significant amount of time, depending on how good the password is.

   `beginningunix:$1$cth3s70B$Sol7rv9u.UyKtEyZ0HP.V.:12736::`**9999**`::::`

6. The number of days the user is warned before password expiration. It is a good practice to give each user warning that her password is going to expire, so that she has the opportunity to change it at a convenient time before its expiration. If the user fails to change her password in the given amount of time, she could be locked out of the system until the system administrator can intervene.

   In this example, the fields 6–9 are blank, as they are in most systems:

   `beginningunix:$1$cth3s70B$Sol7rv9u.UyKtEyZ0HP.V.:12736::9999::::`

7. Varies between the various Unix implementations but generally represents either the number of consecutive days of account inactivity that can elapse before the password is disabled, or the number of days after a password expires until that account is disabled.
8. The number of days from January 1, 1970, until the account expires. This is useful in creating limited-time accounts (such as for temporary employees with a fixed date of hire and contract end).
9. Reserved for future use.

/etc/group

The `/etc/group` file contains the group information for each account. Figure 3-7 shows a sample `/etc/group` file from a Linux system.

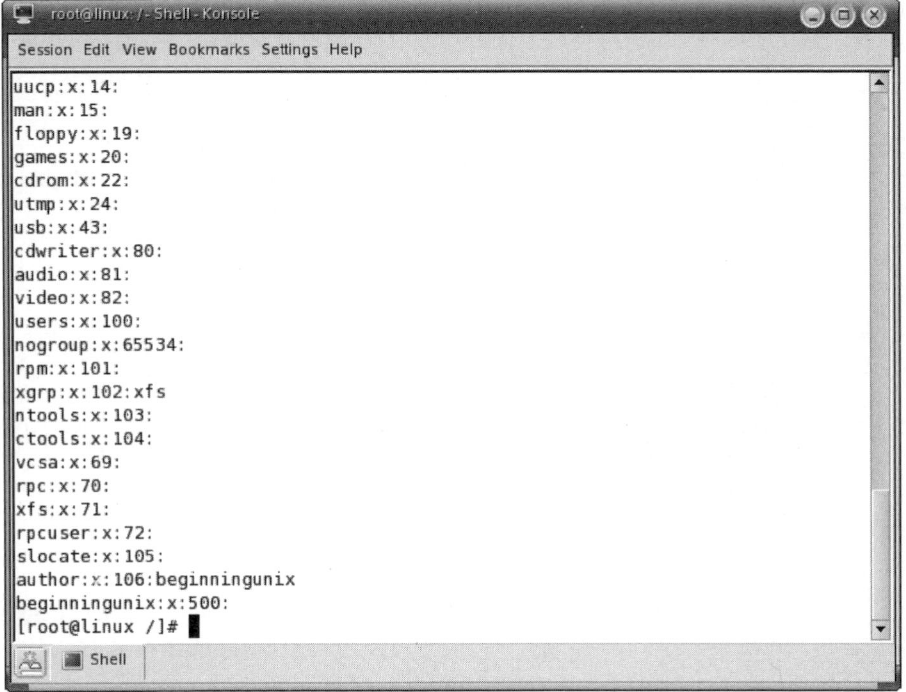

Figure 3-7

Figure 3-8 shows the same file on a Solaris 10 system.

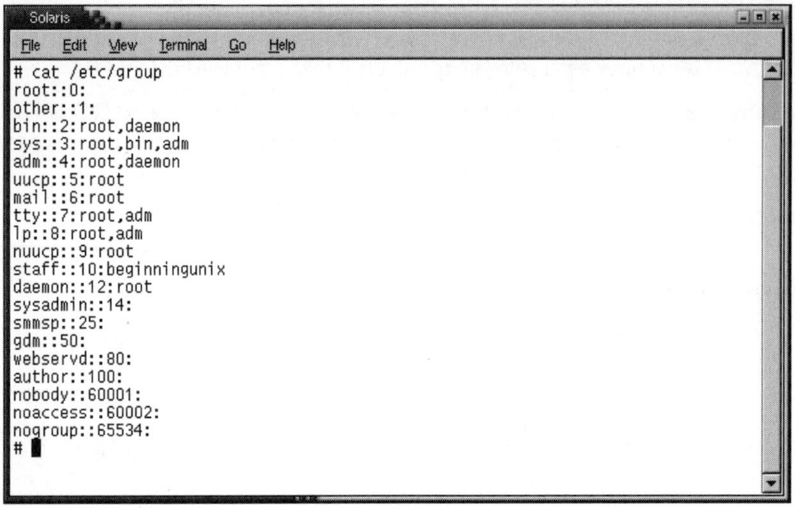

```
Solaris
File Edit View Terminal Go Help
# cat /etc/group
root::0:
other::1:
bin::2:root,daemon
sys::3:root,bin,adm
adm::4:root,daemon
uucp::5:root
mail::6:root
tty::7:root,adm
lp::8:root,adm
nuucp::9:root
staff::10:beginningunix
daemon::12:root
sysadmin::14:
smmsp::25:
gdm::50:
webservd::80:
author::100:
nobody::60001:
noaccess::60002:
nogroup::65534:
#
```

Figure 3-8

The files have the same format. Here are descriptions of the four colon-separated fields, using the next-to-last line in Figure 3-7 as an example:

1. The name of the group, which is how the group is identified to users. In this example, the group name is the same as the account name.

   beginningunix`:x:500:`

2. The password for using the group. This field is blank (no password) on most systems, but it can contain the encrypted password for the group or an x for a shadowed password. The `/etc/passwd` security issues also apply in this case, which is why some systems use a group shadow file. That file is generally located at `/etc/gshadow`; refer to your vendor documentation for more information on the file and its format.

   `beginningunix:x:500:`

3. The group ID (GID). This number identifies the group to the system. It is how Unix sees the group (similar to `/etc/passwd` UID).

   `beginningunix:x:`**500**`:`

4. Comma-separated list of accounts that belong to the group. The line preceding the example line in Figure 3-7 shows that the account beginningunix also belongs to the author group:

   `author:x:106:`**beginningunix**

   This information allows permissions to be set accordingly (discussed in Chapter 4). The field can be blank, as the example shows.

   `beginningunix:x:500:`

Mac OS X Differences

The preceding are primary user administration files on almost all Unix systems. Mac OS X is a notable exception to this. The `/etc/passwd`, `/etc/shadow`, and `/etc/group` files exist, but are used by the system only for single-user mode (discussed in Chapter 20). The primary repository for this information is the NetInfo database, which can be viewed and modified with the `niutil` command. Here's how to view a list of the current databases:

```
niutil -list . /
```

This command generates output similar to that shown in Figure 3-9.

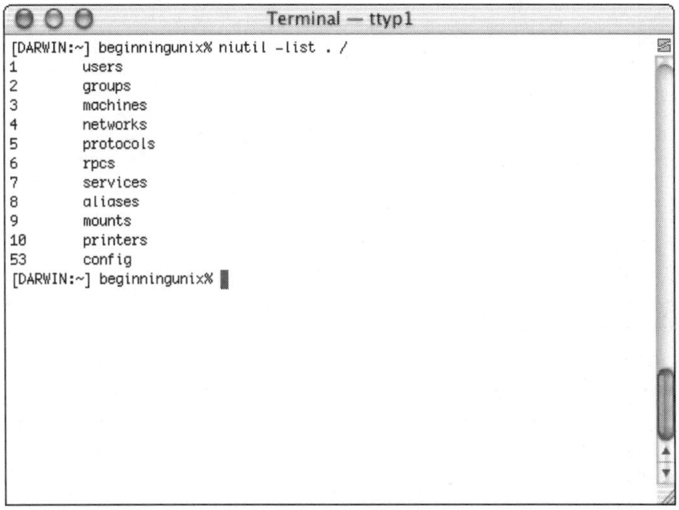

```
Terminal — ttyp1
[DARWIN:~] beginningunix% niutil -list . /
1       users
2       groups
3       machines
4       networks
5       protocols
6       rpcs
7       services
8       aliases
9       mounts
10      printers
53      config
[DARWIN:~] beginningunix%
```

Figure 3-9

To view one of the databases, such as a listing of current users, you can type the following:

```
niutil -read . /groups
```

The output of this command is shown in Figure 3-10.

For more information about NetInfo on Mac OS X, see Chapter 20.

The Mac OS X graphical user interface (GUI) makes it easy to manage user accounts because it was built with ease of use in mind from the start. This is an advantage over some of the other Unix systems.

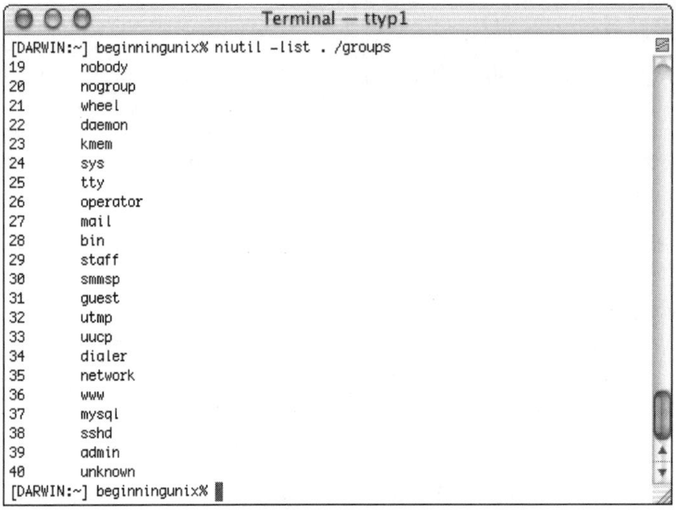

```
[DARWIN:~] beginningunix% niutil -list . /groups
19      nobody
20      nogroup
21      wheel
22      daemon
23      kmem
24      sys
25      tty
26      operator
27      mail
28      bin
29      staff
30      smmsp
31      guest
32      utmp
33      uucp
34      dialer
35      network
36      www
37      mysql
38      sshd
39      admin
40      unknown
[DARWIN:~] beginningunix%
```

Figure 3-10

Managing Accounts and Groups

Some Unix systems use different commands or command structures (options to the command), but using the command line to create, modify, and delete accounts and groups is fairly standardized among them. Following are commands available on the majority of Unix systems and their descriptions:

Command	Description
useradd	Adds accounts to the system.
usermod	Modifies account attributes.
userdel	Deletes accounts from the system.
groupadd	Adds groups to the system.
groupmod	Modifies group attributes.
groupdel	Removes groups from the system.

To add or delete an account manually (without using the preceding commands), you would have to:

- Modify /etc/passwd to add or remove the account line.
- Modify /etc/shadow to add or remove the account line.
- Modify /etc/group to add or remove the account references.
- Add or remove the account's home directory (if not shared, which by default it should not be).

You can avoid these steps by using the commands. You'll also reduce the risk of introducing a typo into one of the files, which could make your system unusable. To run these commands, you must be logged in as root (superuser).

Account Management

The `useradd` command enables you to add a user in a single command line. The following table describes some of the options to the `useradd` command.

Option	Description	File and Field Affected
`-c`	Comment for the GCOS or comment field (use quotes if you have a space in the comments).	`/etc/passwd`; Field 5
`-d`	Account's home directory.	`/etc/passwd`; Field 6
`-e`	Expiration date of the account in yyyy-mm-dd or mm/dd/yy format, depending on the Unix version. (The account is not valid after this date.)	`/etc/shadow`; Field 8
`-f`	Number of days the account can be inactive before being disabled or the number of days after the password has expired that the account will be disabled.	`/etc/shadow`; Field 7
`-g`	Initial group (default group).	`/etc/passwd`; Field 4
`-G`	Comma-separated list of supplementary or secondary groups to which the user belongs.	`/etc/group`; Field 4 of groups identified in the command line
`-m`	Creates the home directory if it doesn't exist.	Not applicable
`-s`	The user's shell for interactive logins.	`/etc/passwd`; Field 7
`-u`	Assigns user ID (unique unless `-o` option, which allows duplicate UIDs, is used). UIDs 0–99 are generally reserved for system accounts.	`/etc/passwd`; Field 3

The structure of the command is:

```
useradd -c comment -d home directory -e expiration date -f inactive days -g primary
(default) group -G secondary groups -m -s shell -u user id accountname
```

The last item is the account name. It is not optional. It's field 1 in the `/etc/passwd` file.

Here's an example that creates an account for a user named unixnewbie, whose real name is Jane Doe. Jane needs the account until July 4, 2006. Her primary group is users, and authors is her secondary group. She has requested the Bourne shell for her default shell. She isn't sure she will be using this system, so let's disable her account if she hasn't used it within 60 days. The `useradd` command to create this account is:

```
useradd -c "Jane Doe" -d /home/unixnewbie -e 040406 -f 60 -g users -G authors -m -s
/bin/ksh -u 1000 unixnewbie
```

After this command runs, a password to the account must be set using the `passwd` *`accountname`* command. To create the password for Jane Doe's account, root would type:

```
passwd unixnewbie
```

The new account owner should change the password immediately.

Try It Out Create an Account with **useradd**

A new temporary employee, Sarah Torvalds, has joined your company today (5/01/05). Sarah's manager has requested that you create an account for Sarah. She has joined the company to assist in some end-of-the-year human resources work, so she needs access to the default user group and to the hr group. Her contract with the company ends 120 days from her start day (the same day the account is created). Standard users are created with an inactive account timeout of 30 days, are assigned to the employees group by default, and are assigned the c shell. Usernames are created using the first initial and last name (no more than eight characters total for the account name, in this case for compatibility with other Unix systems). You need to create an account for Sarah using the `useradd` command because you do not have access to any graphical tools. First log in as root, then run the following commands:

```
# useradd -c "Sarah Torvalds" -d /home/storvald -e 05/01/05 -f 30 -g employees -G
hr -m -s /bin/csh -u 1005 storvald
# passwd storvald
Changing password for user storvald.
New UNIX password:
Retype UNIX password:
passwd: all authentication tokens updated successfully.
#
```

How It Works

The `useradd` command modifies the `/etc/passwd`, `/etc/shadow`, and `/etc/group` files and creates a home directory. Just think how much easier this is than having to manually edit all three files and create the home directory! `useradd` works quickly because the format for the files is standardized and can be easily used. You can also create scripts using this command to make the process even easier.

You can use the `-D` *option to assign default values to some of the* `useradd` *values, making the commands easier to run. Refer to the* `useradd` *man pages for more information.*

The `usermod` command enables you to make changes to an existing account from the command line (instead of modifying system files). It uses the same arguments as the `useradd` command, plus the `-l` argument, which allows you to change the account name. For instance, to change Sarah Torvalds' account name to saraht and provide her with a home directory, you'd issue the following command:

```
usermod -d /home/saraht -m -l saraht storvald
```

This command changes Sarah Torvalds' current account (storvald) and makes the new home directory `/home/saraht` (`-d /home/saraht -m`) and the new account name saraht (`-l saraht`). The `-m` creates the home directory that hadn't previously existed.

The `userdel` command is extremely easy to use and can therefore be dangerous if not used with caution. There is only one argument or option available for the command: `-r`, for removing the account's home directory and mail spool (mail file). Here's how to remove the saraht account:

```
userdel -r saraht
```

If you want to keep her home directory for backup purposes, omit the `-r` option. You can remove the home directory as needed at a later time.

The `useradd`, `usermod`, and `userdel` commands work similarly in most Unix systems (Solaris, Linux, BSD, and so on) but not in Mac OS X. If you want to modify accounts with the command line, you need to use `niutil` with the `-create`, `-createprop`, and `-appendprop` arguments. `niutil` is a Mac OS X–specific command; refer to your man pages for more information if you are using Mac OS X and need to add users at the command line.

Group Management

Managing groups is accomplished with the `groupadd`, `groupmod`, and `groupdel` commands on most Unix systems. `groupadd` has this syntax:

```
groupadd -g group_id group_name
```

To create a new group for the finance department called finance_2 and assign it a unique GID of 535, for example, you'd use:

```
groupadd -g 535 finance_2
```

This command makes the appropriate entry in the `/etc/group` file.

To modify a group, use the `groupmod` syntax:

```
groupmod -n new_modified_group_name old_group_name
```

To change the finance_2 group name to financial, type:

```
groupmod -n financial finance_2
```

You can also use the `-g` option with `groupmod` to change the GID of the group. Here's how you'd change the financial GID to 545:

```
groupmod -g 545 financial
```

To delete an existing group, all you need are the `groupdel` command and the group name. To delete the financial group, the command is:

```
groupdel financial
```

This removes only the group, not any files associated with that group. (The files are still accessible by their owners.)

User Management with Graphical User Interface Tools

There are many graphical user interface (GUI) tools available on the various Unix systems, and although space prohibits covering them in depth in this book, you should be aware of their existence. The use of GUI tools makes management much easier for new administrators, but a good understanding of the command line interface tools is necessary before you use them primarily. Let's take a look at a few of the GUI tools; refer to your own documentation for more information on the many tools available.

Mac OS X

Mac OS X has very straightforward user management tools. To access them, click the Apple icon in the upper-right corner of the screen and select System Preferences. Then choose Account in the section labeled System (bottom left). Figure 3-11 shows the screen that appears.

Figure 3-11

Two accounts — User and Beginning Unix (both of which are admin type accounts, meaning they can run system administrator commands on the system) — can be seen in Figure 3-11. From this screen, you can add, edit or modify, and delete an account. You can also set the account to log in automatically upon boot-up.

To edit an existing account, simply highlight the account and click the Edit User button. Figure 3-12 shows an example of the account screen that displays.

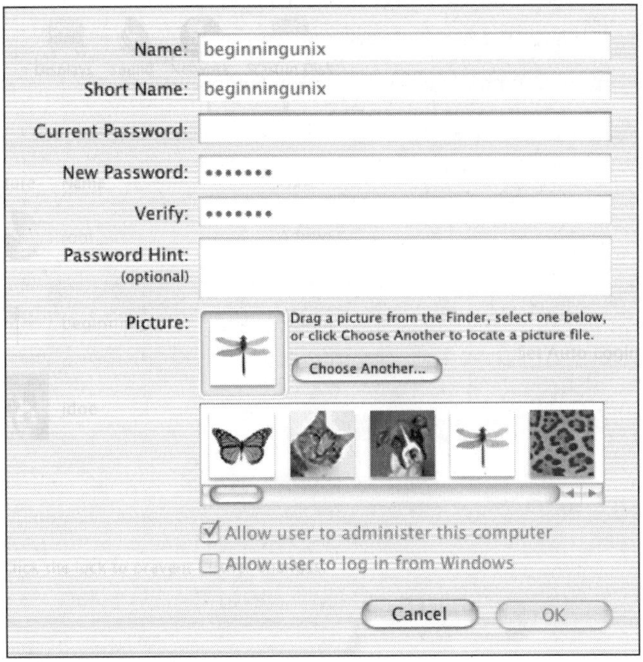

Figure 3-12

To set the auto login for an account or to delete an account, highlight the account and click the appropriate button. To create a new user, just click the New User button.

Linux

Linux offers many ways to manage accounts with a GUI. Every distribution has its own method of user administration. Here's a list of the commands that start the various graphical administration tools on the major distributions of Linux:

Distribution	Command
SUSE	`/sbin/yast2`
Red Hat (Fedora Core)	`/usr/bin/system-config-users`
Mandrakelinux	`/usr/sbin/userdrake`
All	webmin

The `webmin` command enables remote administration, typically with a graphic interface for users and other types of administrative tasks. It is available at `http://webmin.com` and works on most Unix systems, including Solaris's. Webmin is not installed by default on most versions of Unix.

The Linux tools vary in functionality, but generally provide all the capabilities of the command-line equivalents.

Solaris

Solaris provides a tool called `admintool`, which allows for granular management of accounts and groups. To access admintool, type the following at the command line:

```
admintool &
```

The ampersand (&) after the command puts the command process in the background so you can continue using the terminal window for other operations.

It has many features and can manage devices as well as users. To learn more about the capabilities of this tool, visit Sun Microsystems' Web site (`www.sun.com`) and search for admintool.

Becoming Another User

There are times when you will need to log into another account without logging out of the system. There are two commands that enable you to do this: `su` and `sudo`. The `su` (switch user) command is available on all versions of Unix. It enables you to remain logged in as yourself while accessing another account. You must know the password for the account you are trying to access using `su` unless you are the root user, in which case you don't need a password (on the local system). Here's the syntax for `su`:

```
su accountname
```

If you are logged in as jdoe, for example, and want to log in as jsmith, type:

```
su jsmith
```

When using `su`, you continue to use your own environment variables and profile (which you'll learn in Chapter 5). If you want to use the account's user environment, put a dash (-) between the `su` and the account name:

```
su - jsmith
```

You will be asked for the password of the account to which you are switching unless you are the root user, in which case you are immediately logged in to the account. If you type the `su` command with no account name (with or without the -), you are attempting to log in to the root account and will be asked for the root password. (Many people think `su` stands for superuser because running the `su` command by itself takes you to the root, or superuser, account). When you have completed the tasks requiring the account you've `su`'d to, type **exit**. You're returned to your original account (and environment, if applicable).

The `sudo` (superuser do) command enables the superuser, or root administrator, to delegate commands that can be run by others. It is not available on all Unix systems but can be downloaded from `http://courtesan.com/sudo/`. Here's the command's syntax:

```
sudo command to run
```

To list all the commands available for the user to run with `sudo`, type:

```
sudo -l
```

Before you can run any commands, the system generally requires you to enter your password so it can validate your credentials.

On Mac OS X, you cannot easily log in as the root user using the `su` command, but you can use the `sudo` command to achieve the same functionality by typing:

```
sudo /bin/sh
```

This command takes you to a root shell, which is equivalent to running `su` by itself with no arguments (this works with other versions of Unix as well).

User- and Group-Related Commands

A number of commands can give you important user and group information to help you manage your accounts and the systems. The `who` command, for example, identifies who is currently logged in to the system. To use it, just type **who** at the command line. Its output is similar to what is shown in Figure 3-13.

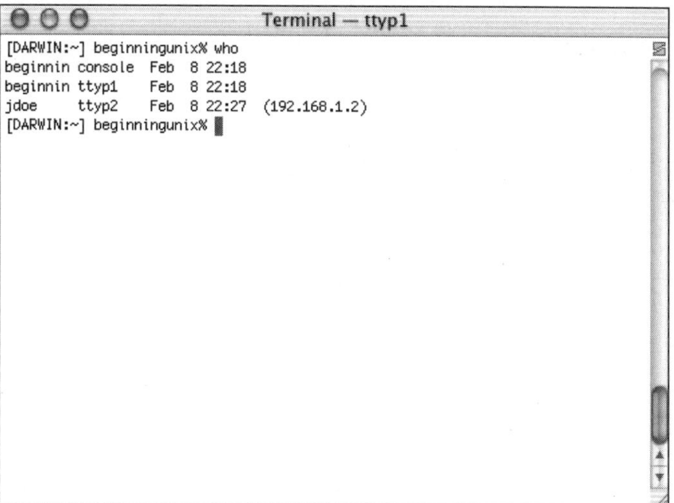

Figure 3-13

The output is in four columns: login name, terminal, login time, and remote hostname or X display. In Figure 3-13, three users are logged in: beginnin (beginningunix, but the name was truncated for space reasons on the output) twice and jdoe. The console is the terminal (screen display) as well as the ttyp1 and ttyp2, which are terminals (devices to identify what terminal the user is on). The next field identifies the date and time when each the user logged in, and you can see that jdoe came in from a remote connection (192.168.1.2).

Sometimes you will be logging in to different machines or will have switched users so much that you aren't sure what user you currently are. To do so, use the `whoami` or `who am i` command. These commands look almost the same, but the spaces make a big difference. `whoami` shows who you are currently logged in as, whereas `who am i` shows who you originally logged on to the system as. Figure 3-14 shows examples of the two commands.

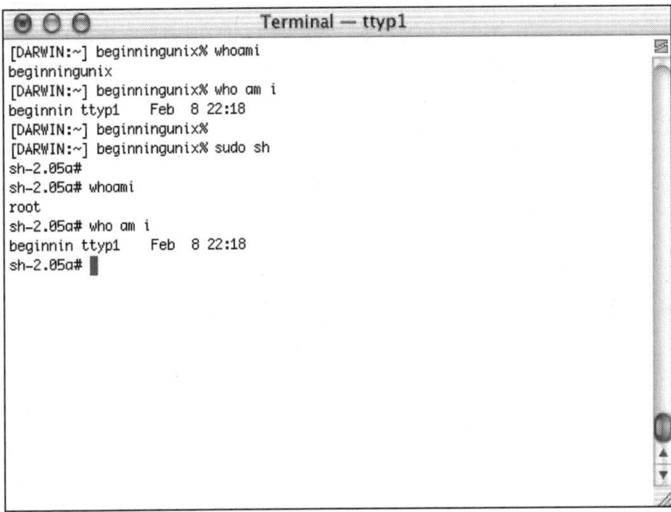

Figure 3-14

The first time the `whoami` command is run, it shows the user as beginningunix, which is the user who logged in to this system. Then the `who am i` command also shows that the user is beginning unix, along with the other information that appears with the `who` command. Following the `sudo sh` command in Figure 3-14, taking beginningunix to a root shell, `whoami` shows the user as root.

The `id` command shows information about the user logged in and about the user's groups. An example of `id` displaying the beginningunix account's information is shown in Figure 3-15, followed by an `id` after `sudo sh`, which shows the root user's information.

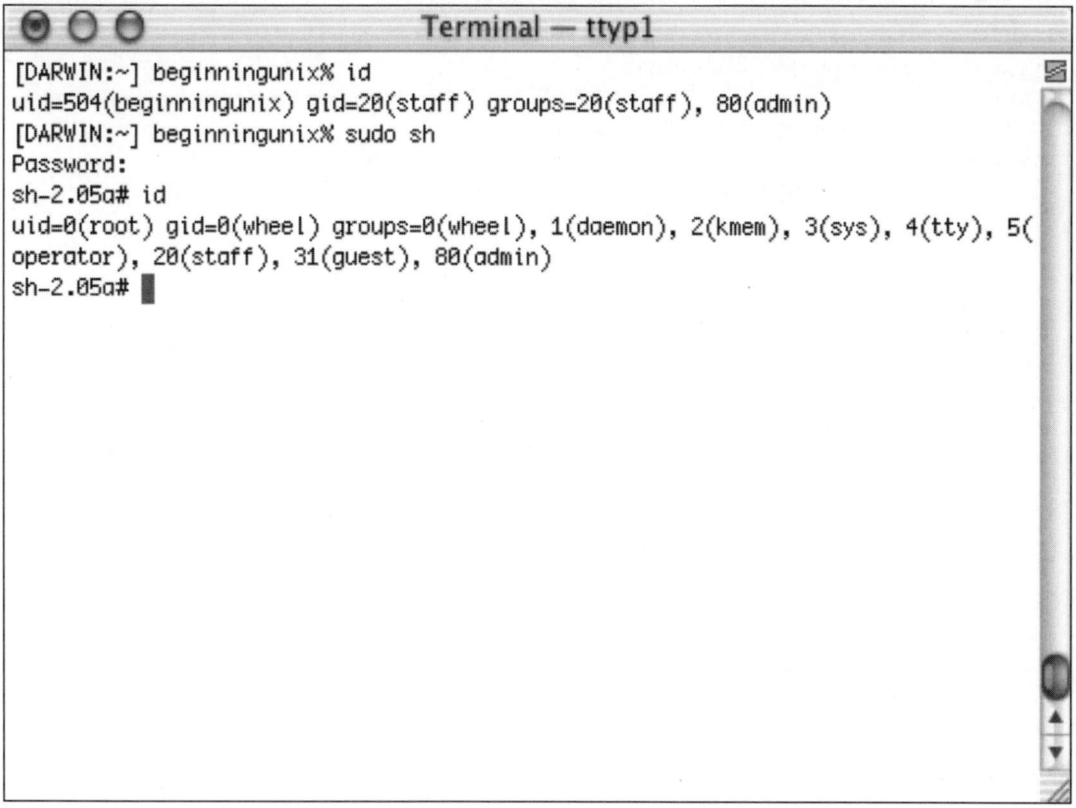

```
[DARWIN:~] beginningunix% id
uid=504(beginningunix) gid=20(staff) groups=20(staff), 80(admin)
[DARWIN:~] beginningunix% sudo sh
Password:
sh-2.05a# id
uid=0(root) gid=0(wheel) groups=0(wheel), 1(daemon), 2(kmem), 3(sys), 4(tty), 5(
operator), 20(staff), 31(guest), 80(admin)
sh-2.05a#
```

Figure 3-15

Everything after the `uid=` and before the `gid=` is the user ID information, and everything after the `gid=` pertains to primary and secondary (supplemental) groups to which the account belongs.

The `groups` command can identify the groups to which a user or your account belongs. Run by itself, it identifies the groups of the currently logged-in user. Supply an account name as an argument, and `groups` reports on that user's groups. Figure 3-16 shows examples of both.

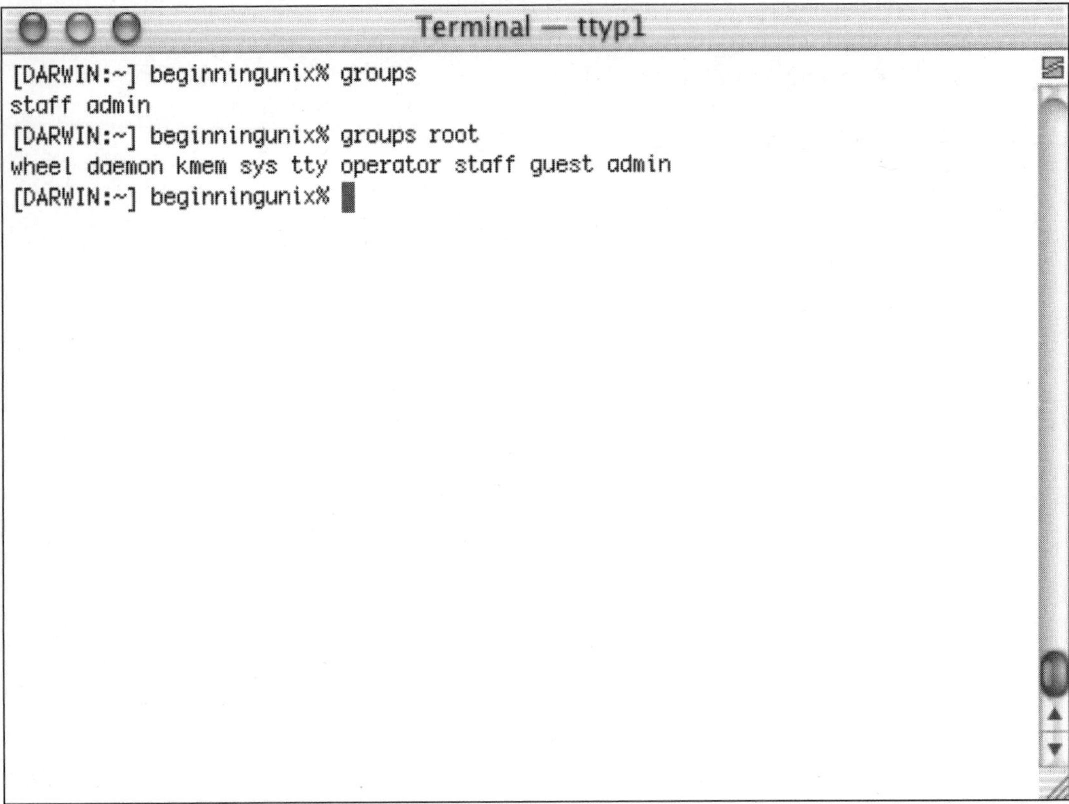

Terminal — ttyp1
[DARWIN:~] beginningunix% groups
staff admin
[DARWIN:~] beginningunix% groups root
wheel daemon kmem sys tty operator staff guest admin
[DARWIN:~] beginningunix%

Figure 3-16

All of these commands will help you manage your accounts and the systems.

Summary

In this chapter, you learned what accounts and groups are and how to manage them. You explored switching users and other important administrative commands that can help you build your Unix knowledge base as you progress into later chapters. Now that you understand accounts and groups, put your new knowledge to work on the following exercises.

Exercises

1. What are the three primary files that deal with user and group administration? What are they for?
2. Jane Doe is a new contractor who will be joining your company May 1, 2005, to work on an Information Technology project and also to assist in some end-of-fiscal-year Human Resources work. Jane's manager has requested that you create an account for Jane, who will need access to

the employees, info_tech_1, info_tech_2, and info_tech_5 groups. Her contract with the company ends 31 days from her start date. Create the account using `useradd`. Here's additional information you'll need: Standard users are created with an inactive account timeout of 10 days, and are assigned the Korn shell. A username (account name) is created using the person's first-initial-and-last-name combination (up to eight characters for the account name). In this company, all accounts have the employee name in the `/etc/passwd` file as well as a designation of E for full-time employees or C for contractors before the name, with one space between the designator and the employee name. The system uses the `/export/home` directory for home directories. Assign Jane's account the userid 1000 because the most recent account UID created was 999. You are already logged in as root.

File System Concepts

A file system is a component of Unix that enables the user to view, organize, secure, and interact with files and directories that are located on storage devices. There are different types of file systems within Unix: disk-oriented, network-oriented, and special, or virtual.

- Disk-oriented (or local) file system — Physically accessible file systems residing on a hard drive, CD-ROM, DVD ROM, USB drive, or other device. Examples include UFS (Unix File System), FAT (File Allocation Table, typically Windows and DOS systems), NTFS (New Technology File System, usually Windows NT, 2000, and XP systems), UDF (Universal Disk Format, typically DVD), HFS+ (Hierarchical File System, such as Mac OS X), ISO9660 (typically CD-ROM), and EXT2 (Extended Filesystem 2).
- Network-oriented (or network-based) file system — A file system accessed from a remote location. These are usually disk-oriented on the server side, and the clients access the data remotely over the network. Examples include Network File System (NFS), Samba (SMB/CIFS), AFP (Apple Filing Protocol), and WebDAV.
- Special, or virtual, file system — A file system that typically doesn't physically reside on disk, such as the TMPFS (temporary file system), PROCFS (Process File System), and LOOPBACKFS (the Loopback File System).

This chapter discusses disk-oriented file systems in depth and briefly covers the network-oriented and special file systems. Mac OS X users should keep in mind that, although their file system layout differs sharply from that of a traditional Unix system, all of the utilities mentioned in this chapter are available and useful on a Mac OS X system. Also, Unix is a case-sensitive operating system, but Mac OS X is a case-insensitive/case-preserving operating system. The significance of this difference will be discussed later in this chapter.

File System Basics

A file system is a logical collection of files on a partition or disk. A partition is a container for information and can span an entire hard drive if desired. An apple pie, for example, can be eaten whole or it can be cut into slices, which is similar to how a hard drive or other physical storage device can be manipulated. A slice of pie is akin to a partition on a drive, and the whole pie could represent a single partition that takes up a whole disk. There are more advanced meanings as well, but for this chapter, only a hard drive or the systematic division of a hard drive is considered to be a partition.

A partition usually contains only one file system, such as one file system housing the `/` file system or another containing the `/home` file system. One file system per partition allows for the logical maintenance and management of differing file systems. These partitions are invisible to users, who can move effortlessly among any number of file systems on their Unix systems without even knowing they've gone from one to another.

Everything in Unix is considered to be a file, including physical devices such as DVD-ROMs, USB devices, floppy drives, and so forth. This use of files allows Unix to be consistent in its treatment of resources and gives the user a consistent mechanism of interaction with the system. It's easy to understand, then, why file systems are an integral part of a Unix operating system.

Unix uses a hierarchical structure to organize files, providing a from-the-top approach to finding information by drilling down through successive layers in an organized fashion to locate what's needed. It's similar to the way that a filing cabinet works. The file cabinet itself is the holder of all information—in other words, it's the base of the filing system. To find hiring information about a certain employee, for example, you need to locate the correct file cabinet, the correct drawer in the cabinet, the correct folder in the drawer, and the correct page of information inside the folder.

In Unix, everything starts with the root directory, often designated only by `/`. (This directory is not to be confused with the user account named root, which was discussed in Chapter 3.) All other files and directories originate there. The root directory generally includes a set of commonplace directories (see the "Root's Basic Directories" section of this chapter), then subdirectories within those directories, and so on. To find specific information in Unix, you need to locate the correct directory, the correct subdirectories, and the correct file.

Directory Structure

Unix uses a hierarchical file system structure, much like an upside-down tree, with root (`/`) at the base of the file system and all other directories spreading from there. The vast majority of Unix systems use the directories shown in Figure 4-1 and described in the next table. (For information about the directory structure on Mac OS X, see Chapter 20.) Not every version of Unix will have all the directories listed, nor is this an all-inclusive list, because Unix vendors may incorporate their own directories.

> *Every vendor's Unix systems implement their own directory structures as needed by the vendor and its customers. No system has the exact same directory structure as another, but they generally have the directories described in this chapter and usually follow the conventions outlined as well.*

Essentially, you always start with the root directory to find any other directory or file. If the hiring information you wanted to find earlier is stored in your Unix computer, you might find the specific information (let's call the employee John Doe) in `/home/hr/A_J/John_Doe`, where `/` is the root directory, `home` is a subdirectory of root, `hr` is a subdirectory of `home`, `A_J` is a subdirectory of `hr`, and `John_Doe`, the file you want, is in the `A_J` directory.

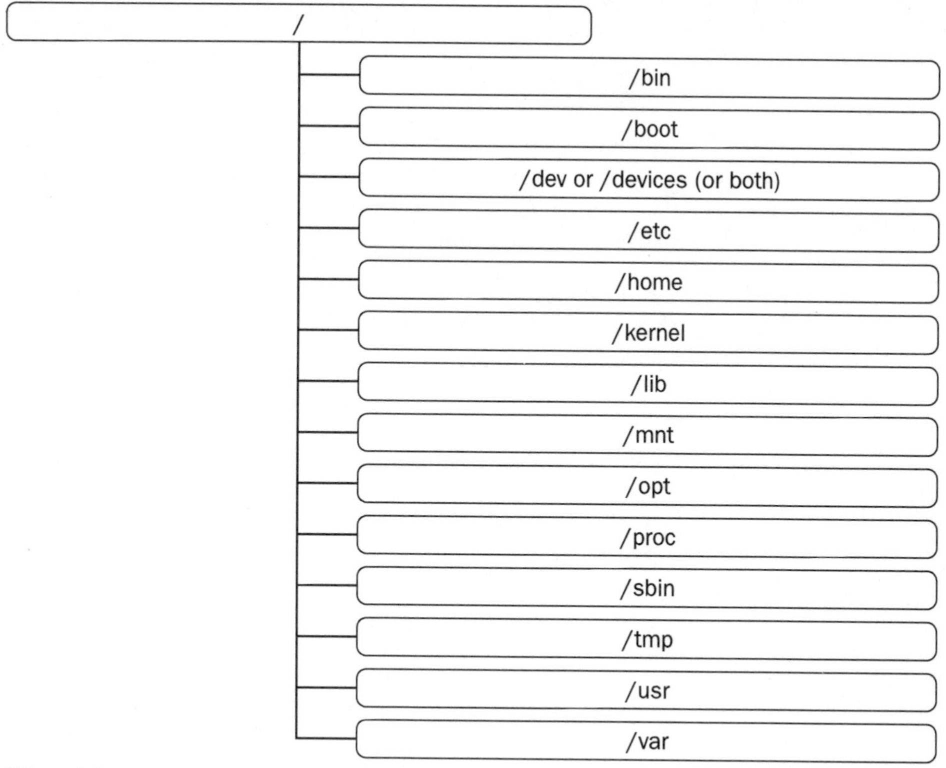

Figure 4-1

Root's Basic Directories

Remembering that root is the base of the file system, there are some core directories that generally exist on most Unix systems. The directories have specific purposes and generally hold the same types of information for easily locating files. Following are the directories that exist on the major versions of Unix:

Directory	Description
`/`	Root should contain only the directories needed at the top level of the file structure (or that come already installed in it). Unnecessary subdirectories under root can clutter your system, making administration more difficult and, depending on the system, filling up the space allocated for `/`.
`bin`	Usually contains binary (executable) files critical for system use, and often contains essential system programs, such as vi (for editing files), passwd (for changing passwords), and sh (the Bourne shell).
`boot`	Contains files for booting the system.

Table continued on following page

Directory	Description
dev devices	Either or both of these will exist. They contain device files, often including cdrom(CD-ROM drive), eth0 (Ethernet interface), and fd0 (floppy drive). (The devices are often named differently in the different Unix systems.)
etc	Contains system configuration files such as passwd (holds user account information and is not to be confused with /bin/passwd); hosts (contains information about host resolution); and shadow (contains encrypted passwords).
export	Often contains remote file systems (those external to the physical system), such as home directories exported from another system to save space and centralize home directories.
home	Contains the home directory for users and other accounts (specified in /etc/passwd, for example).
kernel	Contains kernel files.
lib	Contains shared library files and sometimes other kernel-related files.
mnt	Used to mount other temporary file systems, such as cdrom and floppy for the CD-ROM drive and floppy diskette drive, respectively.
proc	Contains all processes marked as a file by process number or other information that is dynamic to the system.
sbin	Contains binary (executable) files, usually for system administration. Examples include fdisk (for partitioning physical disks) and ifconfig (for configuring network interfaces).
tmp	Holds temporary files used between system boots (some Unix systems do not delete the contents of the tmp directory between boots).
usr	Used for miscellaneous purposes, or can be used by many users (such as for man pages). Can include administrative commands, shared files, library files, and others.
var	Typically contains variable-length files such as log and print files and any other type of file that may contain a variable amount of data. For instance, the log files (typically in /var/log) range in size from very small to very large, depending on the system configuration.

Your Unix system may contain more than, fewer than, or all of these directories, but it will generally contain five or six of them plus subdirectories that vary from implementation to implementation.

Paths and Case

There are two other important concepts you should know about before moving on: paths (absolute and relative) and case sensitivity.

Every file has an absolute path and a relative path. The absolute path refers to the exact location of the file in its file system, such as /etc/passwd. The relative path refers to the location of a file or directory in relation (relative) to your current location. If you are in the /etc directory, for example, the relative path to /etc/passwd is passwd because it's in the same directory you are. This is analogous to the location of your home. If you were giving your address to someone who lived in your neighborhood, you'd probably say that you lived two streets up at 1234 Anystreet. This would be your relative address— relative to your neighbor. If you were giving your address to someone in another country, you'd put it in more specific terms, such as 1234 Anystreet, Anytown, Montana, ZIP Code, USA, which would be your absolute address. Using a relative location is good if you're using it from a known location, but the absolute path is always a safer option because you are specifying the exact location.

Unix is a case-sensitive operating system. This means that the case (capitalization) of file and directory names matters. In DOS or Microsoft Windows systems, you can type a filename with no regard to the capitalization. In Unix, you must know the case of the file or directory name because you could have three different files named real_file, Real_file, and REAL_FILE. To make it easier for the user, though, Unix filenames are conventionally lowercase (this especially true for system-generated files). Mac OS X is a case-insensitive/case-preserving file system. This means that on Mac OS X there is no distinction between naming a file real_file, Real_file, or REAL_FILE but only one of those filenames can exist at a time. While Mac OS X does not distinguish between cases, it does retain the case as entered. Keep this in mind when exchanging files between Mac OS X computers and other Unix systems.

Navigating the File System

Now that you understand the basics of the file system, you can begin navigating to the files you need. The following are commands you'll use to navigate the system:

Command	Description
cat	Concatenate: displays a file.
cd	Change directory: moves you to the directory identified.
cp	Copy: copies one file/directory to specified location.
file	Identifies the file type (binary, text, etc).
find	Finds a file/directory.
head	Shows the beginning of a file.
less	Browses through a file from end or beginning.
ls	List: shows the contents of the directory specified.
mkdir	Make directory: creates the specified directory.
more	Browses through a file from beginning to end.
mv	Move: moves the location of or renames a file/directory.
pwd	Print working directory: shows the current directory the user is in.
rm	Remove: removes a file.

Table continued on following page

Command	Description
rmdir	Remove directory: removes a directory.
tail	Shows the end of a file.
touch	Creates a blank file or modifies an existing file's attributes.
whereis	Shows the location of a file.
which	Shows the location of a file if it is in your PATH.

Let's take a closer look at some of these commands.

pwd

The first command you need is `pwd`, which shows you your current location within the file system. Knowing where you are in the file system is critically important because you can cause serious damage to the system by running certain commands when you think you are in one directory but are actually in another. The `pwd` command has no arguments; just type **pwd** at the command line. The output is similar to that shown in Figure 4-2.

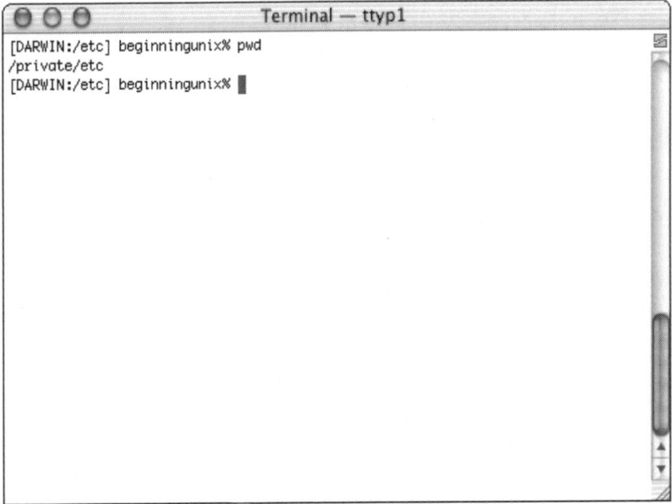

Figure 4-2

cd

The `cd` (change directory) command enables you to move around within the file system. Used without an argument, it returns you to your home directory. To move to another directory, that directory's name is required as the argument:

```
cd directory
```

If you type **cd /etc**, for example, you move to the `/etc` directory (you can use `pwd` to confirm your new location). `cd` takes you to the location you specify as long as you have permissions to enter that directory. To go to the `/var/adm` directory, you'd use this command:

```
cd /var/adm
```

The directory in which you typically start when you log in on your Unix system is called your *home* directory (you may be in a different directory if there is an administrative error or a problem with your identified home directory). You will usually control the contents (files and directories) in your home directory, which is defined in `/etc/passwd` and stores your files. You can use the ~ (tilde) to represent your home directory in many commands. For example, `cd ~` moves you to your home directory, and `ls ~` lists the contents of your home directory.

Remember that in Unix, everything is a file, including the current directory and the directory preceding (or above) the current directory. There are two files in every directory called `.` *(the current directory) and* `..` *(the next higher directory). If you are in* `/usr/openwin/share/etc/workspace/patterns`*, for example, and you want to move to* `/usr/openwin/share/etc/workspace`*, you can simply use* `cd ..` *instead of the longer* `cd /usr/openwin/share/etc/workspace`*. This convention has many scripting applications, as you'll learn in Chapters 13 and 14.*

which and whereis

The `which` and `whereis` commands assist in finding files for which you know the names but not the location. With the filename as the argument, `which` looks only through the files identified in your `PATH` (an environment variable that contains a list of directories where executable files might be located; `PATH` is discussed in Chapter 5).For example, if you are using the `ls` command and want to know where the actual `ls` command resides in the file system (most Unix systems contain both BSD and System V versions of `ls`), you can use the command `which ls`. It will show you the instances of the command `ls` in your `PATH`. The `whereis` command will locate the command in all its locations as defined by the system rather than the searching only the user's `PATH`. If the argument you supply after `which` or `whereis` doesn't exist on the file system, you receive a command not found type error message.

Figure 4-3 shows an example of the output of the `which` and `whereis` commands used with the `vi` command. (Vi, an editor, is discussed in Chapter 7.)

The `which` command shows only `/usr/bin/vi` because `/usr/bin` is before `/usr/ucb` in this user's `PATH` (as shown by the `echo $PATH` command in Figure 4-3). The output of the `whereis` command shows all locations of the command in a list of standard places defined by the system.

The `echo` *command repeats whatever arguments you provide. When used with a defined system variable, the command shows you what the variable represents.*

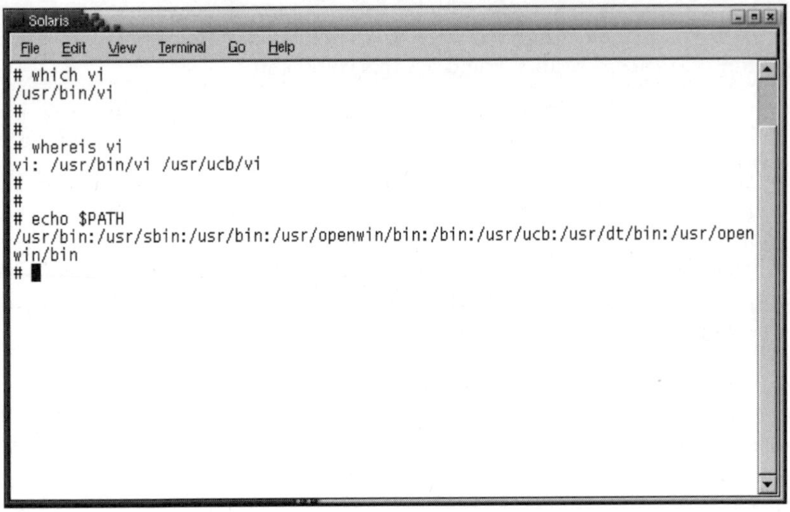

```
# which vi
/usr/bin/vi
#
#
# whereis vi
vi: /usr/bin/vi /usr/ucb/vi
#
#
# echo $PATH
/usr/bin:/usr/sbin:/usr/bin:/usr/openwin/bin:/bin:/usr/ucb:/usr/dt/bin:/usr/open
win/bin
#
```

Figure 4-3

find

You can also use the `find` command to locate files in Unix, although this command may consume a lot of resources (and make the system respond slowly). Here's the syntax:

`find` *pathname options*

If you want to find the `lostfile` file, for example, and you think it's somewhere in the `/usr/share` directory, you can use this command:

```
find /usr/share -name lostfile -print
```

There are many options to the `find` command, and you should refer to the man (manual) pages for more instructions on its many uses.

file

After you find a file, you will usually want to do something with it. The first step is to determine what type of file it is (such as binary or text), and that's where the `file` command comes in. The command has the following syntax:

`file` *filename*

The output shows that the file is binary, text, directory, device, or any of the other types of files in Unix. This is useful in determining whether a file can be viewed using the methods discussed next in this chapter. For instance, a binary or directory file won't show up very well using the `more` command because of the coding of the characters.

ls

The `ls` command enables you to list the contents of any directory that you have permissions to. The `ls` command by itself lists the contents of the current directory. To show the contents of any other directory, use `ls` *`path`*. For instance `ls /usr/bin` shows you the files and directories that reside in the `/usr/bin` directory. Using the `ls -l` command shows extended information about the directory contents. Figure 4-4 shows `ls` output, followed by `ls -l` output.

```
Solaris
File  Edit  View  Terminal  Go  Help
# ls
TT_DB      dev        home        mnt       platform    tmp
bin        devices    kernel      net       proc        usr
boot       etc        lib         nsmail    root        var
cdrom      export     lost+found  opt       sbin        vol
# ls -l
total 736
drwxr-xr-x   2 root     root         512 Oct 27 20:44 TT_DB
lrwxrwxrwx   1 root     root           9 Oct 27 20:32 bin -> ./usr/bin
drwxr-xr-x   1 root     root       16384 Dec 31  1969 boot
drwxr-xr-x   3 root     root         512 Nov 13 21:52 cdrom
drwxr-xr-x  17 root     sys         4096 Feb  8 19:54 dev
drwxr-xr-x   5 root     sys          512 Feb  8 19:53 devices
drwxr-xr-x  61 root     sys         4096 Feb  8 19:57 etc
drwxr-xr-x   3 root     sys          512 Oct 27 20:32 export
dr-xr-xr-x   1 root     root           1 Feb  8 19:54 home
drwxr-xr-x  14 root     sys          512 Oct 27 21:01 kernel
drwxr-xr-x   2 root     bin         4096 Oct 27 20:56 lib
drwx------  18 root     root        8192 Oct 27 20:32 lost+found
drwxr-xr-x   2 root     sys          512 Oct 27 20:32 mnt
dr-xr-xr-x   1 root     root           1 Feb  8 19:54 net
drwx------   2 root     other        512 Oct 27 21:18 nsmail
drwxr-xr-x   4 root     sys          512 Oct 27 20:59 opt
drwxr-xr-x   4 root     sys          512 Oct 27 20:36 platform
dr-xr-xr-x  63 root     root       59072 Feb  8 22:52 proc
-rw-r--r--   1 root     other     248320 Oct 27 21:36 root
drwxr-xr-x   2 root     sys         1024 Oct 27 20:52 sbin
drwxrwxrwt   8 root     sys          329 Feb  8 20:28 tmp
drwxr-xr-x  38 root     sys         1024 Oct 27 22:07 usr
drwxr-xr-x  34 root     sys          512 Oct 27 21:10 var
dr-xr-xr-x   6 root     root         512 Feb  8 19:54 vol
#
```

Figure 4-4

The following table describes what the extended information includes. The example output is from a line in the output shown in Figure 4-4:

```
drwxr-xr-x  61 root    sys     3584 Nov  3 19:20 etc
```

ls -l Output	Description
drwxr-xr-x	The type of file and the permissions associated with it (discussed in the "File and Directory Permissions" section later in this chapter)
61	The number of links to the file (discussed in the "File Types" section)
root	The owner of the file (discussed in Chapter 3)
sys	The group to which the file owner belongs (discussed in Chapter 3)

Table continued on following page

ls -l Output	Description
3584	Size of file (in characters)
Nov 3 19:20	The last time the file or directory was modified (changed)
etc	Name of file or directory

If the `ls` *command isn't available for some reason, you can use the* `echo` *command to display files. Simply use* `echo directory*` *to see the contents of a directory. For example, to view the contents of the / directory, use* `echo /*`*, which shows output similar to running the* `ls` *command with no options. To show hidden files (discussed in the following paragraph), use the* `echo /.*` *command. You must use the * metacharacter. (Metacharacters are discussed in Chapters 7 and 8.)*

Using the `-a` option with the `ls` command shows you all files or directories, including those that are hidden. A file or directory can be hidden by placing a `.` (period) in front of the filename. A standard `ls` command's output does not list hidden files. One legitimate reason to hide a file or directory is to reduce the amount of clutter shown when running `ls`. Figure 4-5 shows a directory's `ls` output, followed by its `ls -a` output so you can see the difference.

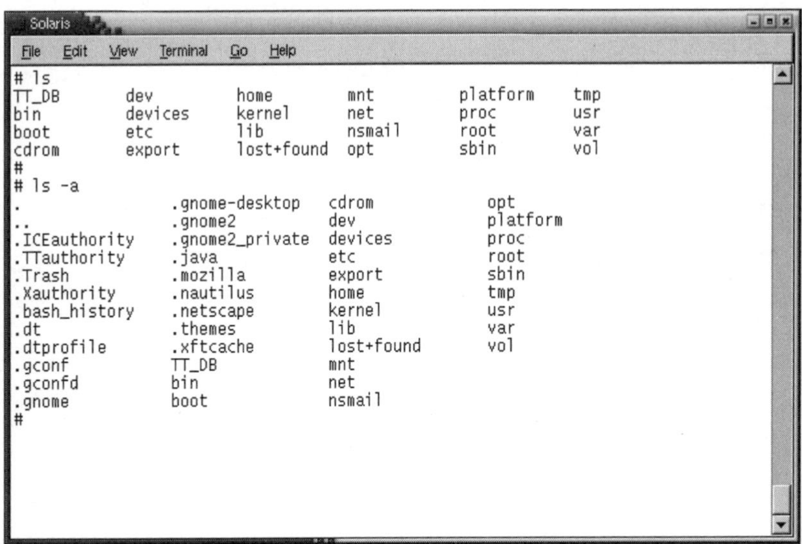

Figure 4-5

One of the most common problems you run into in using the `ls` *command is getting a permission-denied error when you try to list the contents of a directory as a non-root user. This error is typically caused by insufficient permissions (discussed later in this chapter).*

File Types

In the `ls -l` example (Figure 4-4), every file line began with a `d`, `-`, or `l`. These characters indicate the type of file that's listed. There are other file types (shown by their `ls -l` single-character representation in the following table), but these three are the most common.

File Type	Description
-	Regular file, such as an ASCII text file, binary executable, or hard link (links are discussed in the following section)
b	Block special file (block input/output device file used for transferring data from or to a device such as a physical hard drive)
c	Character special file (raw input/output device file used for transferring data from or to a device such as a physical hard drive)
d	Directory file (file that contains a listing of other files and/or directories contained within the directory)
l	Symbolic link file (discussed in the following section)
p	Named pipe (a mechanism for interprocess communications)
s	Socket (used for interprocess communication)

Links

A link in Unix is similar to a shortcut in Microsoft Windows. To comprehend links, you need to understand inodes. Every file in Unix has a number, called an inode, associated with it. Unix doesn't use the filename to refer to the file; it uses the inode. An inode is unique to a partition, so two completely unrelated files can have the same inode if they're in different partitions. That's much like your driver's license number (inode), which is unique in your state (partition). A driver in another state can have the same driver's license number that you do, but the two of you can be uniquely identified based on your states.

Links are extremely useful in many ways, such as enabling you to alias a command, program, or file to a more common name. You can also use links to create "copies" of a file without wasting storage space by duplicating the actual content.

There are two types of links: hard and soft (also called symbolic). A hard link cannot span file systems (physical file systems such as hard drives), and the file linked is exactly the same as the original file. In inode reference, the file that you are linking to will have the same inode number as the link name, which is why you cannot a hard link across different file systems. All changes made to either the file hard-linked to or the file resulting from the hard link are reflected in both. To create a hard link, use the command:

`ln` *file_name link_name*

A hard link has the same inode as the original file, as shown by the `ls -i` command.

A soft (symbolic) link can span file systems or even different computer systems. It will have a unique inode number assigned to it, and if the link is removed, the original file remains. To create a symbolic link, use the command:

`ln -s` *file_name link_name*

If you look back at Figure 4-4, you'll see an `l` in the file-type position and a `->` next to the filename of the second file in the `ls -l` output. These indicate a link. The directory named `bin` shows `./usr/bin` after the `->`. This means the directory is really located in `/usr/bin`. Links are often used to make it easier to find files, to create convenient shortcuts to other files, to group collections of files, and to call files or directories by other names. Although directories typically show a `d` type in the first column of `ls -l` output, a file that links to a directory shows a file type of `l` because it is not really a directory, but a link to a directory.

When creating soft links, always use absolute paths instead of relative paths for maximum portability. (Portability is being able to use a script on multiple types of Unix systems.)

Modifications to any of the links or to the original file that is linked to will be seen no matter how you reference the file (by the *`hard_link`*, the *`soft_link`*, or the original filename). When moving or deleting a file that has links to it, you must be cognizant of any soft links on the system because you could break them. For instance, say you have the `sales_forecasts.txt` file in a directory that contains your sales forecasts for the year, but you want others to be able to look at it by using a soft link from a different file system. You could create a soft link called `steves_sales_forecasts.txt` in a shared directory so that others could easily locate and access it. You could also create the hard link `my_sales_forecasts_2005.txt` in your home directory (assuming it is on the same file system) so you could easily reference the file when you wanted to. If you change the name of the original file (`sales_forecasts.txt`), the hard-linked file (`my_sales_forecasts_2005.txt`) will still point to the correct file because hard links use the inode as the reference and the inode doesn't change when the filename changes. The soft-linked file `steves_sales_forecasts.txt`, however, will no longer point to the correct location because soft links use the filename as the reference. If you change the name of any of the links (soft or hard), they will still point to the proper location because the original file doesn't change.

One last word on modifying files with links: If you delete the original file that has links to it (`sales_forecasts.txt`) and then re-create the file with different data but the same name (`sales_forecasts.txt`), the hard link will no longer work because the inode of the file has changed, but the soft link will still work because it refers only to the name of the file.

Try It Out — Create Links

Links can be difficult to understand initially, but trying them out should clarify linking for you.

1. Use the `cd` command to navigate to your home directory:

```
$ cd ~
```

2. Use the `touch` command to create a file called `original_file`:

```
touch original_file
```

This will be the base file that you will link to using both hard and soft (symbolic) links.

3. Run the `ls -l` command to see the file you just created, with output similar to the following:

```
$ ls -l
-rw-r--r--    1  username   usergroup    0  Jan 16 16:19 original_file
$
```

Notice the number of links to the file is 1 (second column), meaning this is the only link to the inode. (The file size is 0—column before Jan—meaning this file contains no data.)

4. Use the `ln` command to create a hard link to `original_file`, naming the link `hard_link`:

```
$ ln original_file hard_link
$
```

If you try to create a hard link between files on different file systems, you will receive an error something like `ln:/hard_link is on a different file system.`

5. Run `ls -l` again. You should see the following two files (in addition to the rest of your home directory files) in similar output:

```
-rw-r--r--    2  username   usergroup    0  Jan 16 16:19 hard_link
-rw-r--r--    2  username   usergroup    0  Jan 16 16:19 original_file
```

Notice the number of links to the file is 2 (second column), meaning this is one of two links to the inode (the original file). The date last modified (Jan 16 16:19) is also the same for both files even though you didn't modify `original_file`.

6. Run the `ls -i` command to show the files' inode numbers. You will see that the inode numbers for the files are identical:

```
$ ls -i
116 hard_link
116 original_file
$
```

7. Now use the `ln -s` command to create a soft link to `original_file` called `soft_link`:

```
$ ln -s original_file soft_link
```

8. Use the `ls -l` command to show the files again. The output should be similar to the following:

```
$ ls -l
-rw-r--r--   2  username   usergroup   0  Jan 16 16:19 hard_link
-rw-r--r--   2  username   usergroup   0  Jan 16 16:19 original_file
-rw-r--r--   1  username   usergroup  13  Jan 16 16:30 soft_link -> original_file
$
```

Notice that `soft_link` shows a different number of links (1) and a different modification time (16:30) than `original_file` and `hard_link`. It also has extra output showing where the link goes (`-> original_file`) because it is linking to another file system, and is not a direct link to the same inode.

9. Use the `ls -i` command to view all of the files' inode numbers. You can see that `soft_link`'s inode is not the same as `original_file`'s and `hard_link`'s.

```
$ ls -i
116 hard_link
116 original_file
129 soft_link
$
```

10. Use the `cat` command (discussed later in this chapter) to view the contents of each of the files and confirm that no text or data exists in them:

```
$ cat original_file

$ cat hard_link

$ cat soft_link

$
```

11. To see how changing the original file affects the linked files, use the `echo` command and output redirection to add the line `"This text goes to the original_file"` to `original_file`:

```
$ echo "This text goes to the original_file" >> original_file
```

This command echoes the text you type and then appends (>>) the output to the end of the file `original_file`. *Because there's no other data in the file, the append command puts the new line in at the beginning of* `original_file`.

12. Run the `ls -l` command to see the difference in the file sizes of the original file and the links, even though you added data only to `original_file`.

```
$ ls -l
-rw-r--r--    2  username   usergroup    36  Jan 16 16:52 hard_link
-rw-r--r--    2  username   usergroup    36  Jan 16 16:52 original_file
-rw-r--r--    1  username   usergroup    13  Jan 16 16:30 soft_link -> original_file
$
```

You can see that the size and modification time of `hard_link` and `original_file` have changed, while the `soft_link` file remains the same. If you view the contents of the files with the `cat` command, you see that the all three files have exactly the same contents:

```
$ cat original_file
This text goes to the original_file
$ cat hard_link
This text goes to the original_file
$ cat soft_link
This text goes to the original_file
$
```

13. To see how changing the hard-linked file affects the original file, use the `echo` command and output redirection to add the line `"This text goes to the hard_link file"` to the `hard_link` file:

```
$ echo "This text goes to the hard_link file" >> hard_link
```

14. Run `ls -l` and view the output. Both `original_file` and `hard_link` have changed modification times and sizes, while `soft_link` has not:

```
$ ls -l
-rw-r--r--    2  username   usergroup   73   Jan 16 17:11 hard_link
-rw-r--r--    2  username   usergroup   73   Jan 16 17:11 original_file
-rw-r--r--    1  username   usergroup   13   Jan 16 16:30 soft_link -> original_file
```

15. Now use `cat` to show the contents of the files again. See how each has changed:

```
$ cat original_file
This text goes to the original_file
This text goes to the hard_link file
$cat hard_link
This text goes to the original_file
This text goes to the hard_link file
$ cat soft_link
This text goes to the original_file
This text goes to the hard_link file
$
```

If you use an `echo` command to add a line of text to the `soft_link` file, you will modify the original file, which will cause the `hard_link` file to update as well.

16. Use the `echo` command and output redirection to add the line `"This text goes to the soft_link file"` to the `soft_link` file:

```
$ echo "This text goes to the soft_link file" >> soft_link
```

17. Using the `cat` command to show the contents of the files, you get the following output:

```
$ cat original_file
This text goes to the original_file
This text goes to the hard_link file
This text goes to the soft_link file
#cat hard_link
This text goes to the original_file
This text goes to the hard_link file
This text goes to the soft_link file
$ cat soft_link
This text goes to the original_file
This text goes to the hard_link file
This text goes to the soft_link file
$
```

How It Works

These links all refer to the same file, but the way they appear on the system differs. Both soft links and hard links can point to the same file, and editing them will modify the contents of the original. The primary differences between a hard link and a soft link are how they behave when the original file is removed and how they are used when the link is on a file system different from the linked-to file.

File and Directory Permissions

The permissions of a file are the first line of defense in the security of a Unix system. The basic building blocks of Unix permissions are the read, write, and execute permissions, which are described in the following table:

Permission	Applied to a Directory	Applied to Any Other Type of File
read (r)	Grants the capability to readthe contents of the directory or subdirectories.	Grants the capability to view the file.
write (w)	Grants the capability to create, modify, or remove files or subdirectories.	Grants write permissions, allowing an authorized entity to modify the file, such as by adding text to a text file, or deleting the file.
execute (x)	Grants the capability to enter the directory.	Allows the user to "run" the program.
-	No permission.	No permission.

Here's example output from the `ls -l` command that includes one file and one directory:

```
$ ls -l /home/mikec
-rwxr-xr-- 1 mikec    users    1024         Nov 2 00:10  myfile
drwxr-xr--- 1 mikec    users    1024         Nov 2 00:10  mydir
```

The permissions for each are the second through the tenth characters from the left (remember the first character identifies the file type). The permissions are broken into groups of threes, and each position in the group denotes a specific permission, in this order: read, write, execute. The first three characters (2–4) represent the permissions for the file's owner (mikec in this example). The second group of three characters (5–7) consists of the permissions for the group to which the file belongs (users in the example output). The last group of three characters (8–10) represents the permissions for everyone else ("others" in Unix parlance). The following table elaborates on the permissions shown for `myfile` in the example `ls -l` output:

Characters	Apply to	Definition
`rwx` (characters 2–4)	The owner (known as user in Unix) of the file	The owner of the file (mikec) has read (or view), write, and execute permission to the file.
`r-x` (characters 5–7)	The group to which the file belongs	The users in the owning group (users) can read the file and execute the file if it has executable components (commands, and so forth). The group does not have write permission—notice that the - character fills the space of a denied permission.

Characters	Apply to	Definition
`r--` (characters 8–10)	Everyone else (others)	Anyone else with a valid login to the system can only read the file—write and execute permissions are denied (`--`).

The - is a placeholder to provide the proper separation for easier reading. If user sallyb belongs to the users group and wants to view `myfile`, she can do so because the group has read and execute permissions on that file. If she is not the owner and does not belong to the users group, she can view the file only if the "others" group ("everyone else") has read permission. In this example, everyone else has read permission, so sallyb can view the file.

Directory permissions differ slightly, as the table at the beginning of this section shows. Read allows the contents of the directory and subdirectories to be read; write enables creation, modification, and deletion of files and subdirectories; and execute allows entry to the directory.

Changing Permissions

To change file or directory permissions, you use the `chmod` (change mode) command. There are two ways to use `chmod`: symbolic mode and absolute mode. Applying permissions with `chmod`'s absolute mode requires a numerical representation of the permissions, which is more efficient and is how the system views permissions. Permissions applied with `chmod`'s symbolic mode use the familiar `rwx` format and are easier to understand for most new users.

Using chmod in Symbolic Mode

The easiest way for a beginner to modify file or directory permissions is to use the symbolic mode. The first set of file permissions (characters 2–4 from the `ls -l` command) is represented with the `u`, for user; the second set (characters 5–7) is by `g`, for group; and the last set (characters 8–10) is represented by an `o`, for everyone else (other). You can also use the `-a` option to grant or remove permissions from all three groups at once.

With symbolic permissions you can add, delete, or specify the permission set you want by using the operators in the following table. The example file, `testfile`, has original permissions of `rwxrwxr--`.

chmod operator	Meaning	Example	Result
+	Adds the designated permission(s) to a file or directory.	`chmod o+wx testfile`	Adds write and execute permissions for others (permission character set 9–10) on `testfile`.
-	Removes the designated permission(s) from a file or directory.	`chmod u-x testfile`	Removes the file owner's capability to execute `testfile` (`u` = user or owner).

Table continued on following page

chmod operator	Meaning	Example	Result
=	Sets the designated permission(s).	chmod g=r-x testfile	Sets permissions for the group to read and execute on testfile (no write).

Here's an example using testfile. Running ls -l on testfile shows that the file's permissions are rwxrwxr--:

```
$ ls -l
-rwxrwxr-- 1 toms    users    1024         Nov 2 00:10   testfile
```

Then each example chmod command from the preceding table is run on testfile, followed by ls -l so you can see the permission changes:

```
$ chmod o+wx testfile
$ ls -l
-rwxrwxrwx 1 toms    users    1024         Nov 2 00:10   testfile
$ chmod u-x testfile
$ ls -l
-rw-rwxrwx 1 toms    users    1024         Nov 2 00:11   testfile
$ chmod g=r-x testfile
$ ls -l
-rw-r-xrwx 1 toms    users    1024         Nov 2 00:12   testfile
$
```

Here's how you could combine these commands on a single line:

```
$ chmod o+wx,u-x,g=r-x testfile
```

Using chmod with Absolute Permissions

The second way to modify permissions with the chmod command is to use a number to specify each set of permissions for the file. Each permission is assigned a value, as the following table shows, and the total of each set of permissions provides a number for that set.

Number	Octal Permission Representation	Permission Reference
0	No permission	---
1	Execute permission	--x
2	Write permission	-w-
3	Execute and write permission: 1 (execute) + 2 (write) = 3	-wx
4	Read permission	r--
5	Read and execute permission: 4 (read) + 1 (execute) = 5	r-x
6	Read and write permission: 4 (read) + 2 (write) = 6	rw-
7	All permissions: 4 (read) + 2 (write) + 1 (execute) = 7	rwx

The numbers from each set are stated together to form the file permissions. For example, if the file owner (user) has read (4), write (2), and execute (1) permissions (4 + 2 + 1 = 7), the group has read permission (4), and everyone else has no permissions (0), the permissions for the file would be 740. If you want to change the `myfile` file's permissions to those examples, use this command:

```
chmod 740 myfile
```

following the syntax of the `chmod` command, `chmod` *`permission filename`*.

To change `testfile` permissions (which were just changed to `-rw-r-xrwx` with `chmod` symbolic permissions) back to the original, you'd run this command:

```
$ chmod 774 testfile
```

Then run `ls -l` to verify:

```
$ ls -l /home/toms
-rwxrwxr-- 1 toms    users    1024          Nov 2 00:10  testfile
```

If you used 043 instead of 774 in the `chmod` command, the new permissions would be:

```
$ ls -l /home/toms
----r---wx 1 toms    users    1024          Nov 2 00:10  testfile
```

Permissions are a complex topic and are extremely important to the security of your system. Chapter 12 discusses the security implications of permissions in more depth.

Viewing Files

After you have traversed the file system and found the file you are looking for, you probably want to view that file. There are many ways to do that in Unix, from using interactive editors (such as vi, which is discussed in Chapter 7) to using some of the commands introduced in this section. The commands discussed here enable you to view a file quickly and move on without having to open a separate program. These commands have other functionality, but for this chapter, the focus will be on their file-viewing capabilities.

To view a file with all the output to the current terminal screen, use the command `cat` *`filename`*. This can be a problem in a long file because `cat` by itself simply dumps the contents of the file, not allowing you to pause the output—you'd have to read very fast! The `more` command can help. It runs the same way as `cat`, but the output requires you to press the space bar or an arrow key to move the file forward, enabling you to view a screenful of output at a time. With the `more` command you can also press **Enter** to move forward a single line at a time. The `less` command is more powerful because you can move forward and backward within the file using the vi movement keys (discussed in Chapter 7) or the arrow keys. You have to press **q** to quit these file views. Here are examples of the `more` and `less` commands:

```
more /etc/syslog.conf

less /etc/syslog.conf
```

The head and tail commands are interesting because they enable you to view the beginning (head) or the end (tail) of a file. Here's how to use them:

```
head /etc/syslog.conf

tail /etc/syslog.conf
```

These commands show you only the first 10 or the last 10 lines of a file by default. If you want to see more or fewer lines, you can specify it with the `-n x` argument, using the number of lines you want in place of *x*. Here are sample commands to see the first 15 or last 15 lines of a file, respectively:

```
head -n 15 /etc/syslog.conf

tail -n 15 /etc/syslog.conf
```

An important option for the tail command is -f (for follow). This option continuously scans the input file instead of simply showing the number of lines indicated. To review the /var/log/syslog file (system log file for many Unix systems) in real time as events are occurring, for example, you could run:

```
tail -f /var/log/syslog
```

The output would show you the contents of /var/log/syslog as they were being written to the file until you press the **Ctrl+C** key combination to stop the loop. This is very useful for watching files, especially log files, as they grow.

Creating, Modifying, and Removing Files

To copy a file within the file system, you can use the cp command. Here's how you'd copy the file /etc/skel/cool_file to another location:

```
cp /etc/skel/cool_file /home/danl/cool1
```

You must have the appropriate permissions to copy, move, or modify a file. Typically you will require at least read permission on the source file (file to copy) and write access to the destination directory and/or file for the copy to occur.

This command creates an exact duplicate of /etc/skel/cool_file in the /home/danl directory with the name of cool1.

The cp command is good for copying files, but to move a file from one location to another without copying, you use the mv (move) command with similar syntax. For example, here's how to move the /etc/skel/cool_file from its original location to /home/danl and rename it cool1:

```
mv /etc/skel/cool_file /home/danl/cool1
```

The mv command can also simply change the name of a file or directory. To change the name of the /home/danl/cool1 file to /home/danl/login_script, for example, you'd execute the following command:

```
mv /home/danl/cool1 /home/danl/login_script
```

The mv command works on directories, too, so you can move an entire directory from one location to another. If danl changed his username to danl12, you could change the home directory name using:

```
mv /home/danl /home/danl12
```

To create a blank file, you can use the touch command. If you use touch on an existing file, the last modified information is adjusted, but if you use it with a new filename, a blank file is created. Here's how:

```
touch filename
```

This is useful when you want to create a blank file for testing or other purposes.

Deleting Files

Of course, there will be times when you want to completely delete a file. Then you can use the rm (remove) command. Here's how to remove (delete) /etc/skel/cool_file from the system:

```
rm /etc/skel/cool_file
```

The rm command has very powerful options, the primary two being -f and -r. The -f option forces rm to remove a file without asking if it is OK; it will make the command occur with no output and will just take action. The -r option will have the rm command descend into any subdirectories of a directory specified as an argument to the rm command. If a file is specified for deletion with the rm command, the rm command will not descend into any directories (it descends into a directory only when a directory is named for deletion).

You should also be very careful typing arguments of the rm command, especially when using the -f (force) and -r (recursive, or descend into subdirectories), because you could remove or destroy your system. For example, if you're logged in as root, want to delete a file called /tmp/remove_file, and type:

```
rm -rf / tmp/remove_file
```

The accidental space between the / and tmp would cause the / file system to be deleted, completely obliterating your system. The rm command by itself, with no switches, does not remove directories, but the rm command with the -rf switches removes directories and their subdirectories. Make sure you know exactly where in the directory structure you are (use the pwd command) before using rm and, when possible, use the absolute path to ensure you know exactly what you are deleting. Here's an example: Your file system is getting full and you have to make room on the system right away. You run the ls -l command on the /var/log/archives directory (you have backups of everything, of course) and decide to remove any extra logs on the system. You go to your root terminal that you thought you ran the ls -l command in and run the following command:

```
rm -rf *
```

It turns out you were in the wrong terminal window — you were currently in the / directory. If you were logged in as root, you would completely remove all system files and render your system unusable because the command you ran would recursively remove (-r) all files (*) on the system without prompting you at all (-f).

Making and Removing Directories

The `mkdir` and `rmdir` commands deal specifically with directories. `mkdir` creates a new directory in which to store files and other directories. Its syntax is `mkdir` *`directory_name`*. To create a directory called `testdir`, for example, you would use the command:

```
mkdir testdir
```

The `testdir` directory is stored in your current working directory. If you want to place it in a different directory, you need to use the absolute path. Here's how you'd create the directory `testdir` in the `/tmp` directory:

```
mkdir /tmp/testdir
```

To remove a directory, use the syntax `rmdir` *`directory_name`*. To remove the `testdir` created in the preceding example, use the command:

```
rmdir /tmp/testdir
```

As with `rm`, you can cause significant damage by not being aware of where you are in the file system and by running commands as the root user, although the consequences aren't quite as severe because of limitations in the `rmdir` command.

> `rmdir` *removes completely empty directories only, providing some safeguards against accidentally deleting directories containing files and other directories.*

Basic File System Management

Like any storage medium, file systems can fill up to capacity, creating tremendous problems if not managed properly. The first way to manage your partition space is with the `df` (disk free) command. (Partitions were discussed earlier in the chapter.) The command `df -k` (disk free) displays the disk space usage in kilobytes, as shown in Figure 4-6.

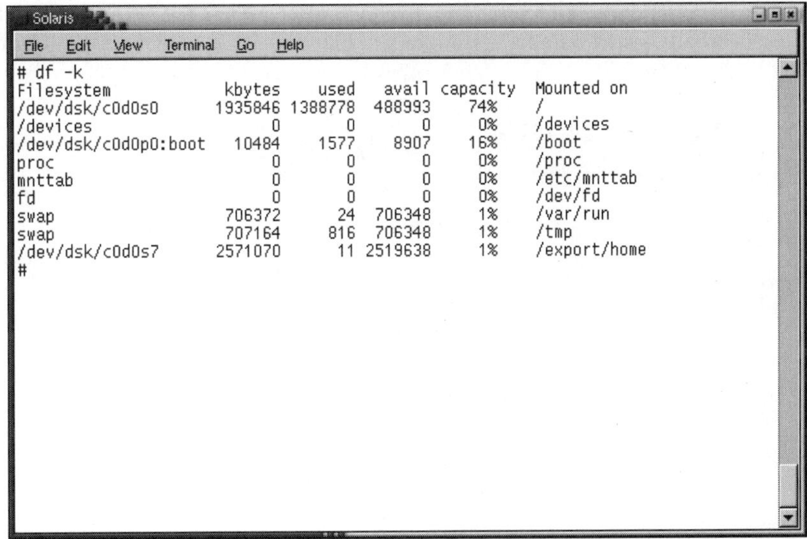
Solaris
File Edit View Terminal Go Help
df -k
Filesystem kbytes used avail capacity Mounted on
/dev/dsk/c0d0s0 1935846 1388778 488993 74% /
/devices 0 0 0 0% /devices
/dev/dsk/c0d0p0:boot 10484 1577 8907 16% /boot
proc 0 0 0 0% /proc
mnttab 0 0 0 0% /etc/mnttab
fd 0 0 0 0% /dev/fd
swap 706372 24 706348 1% /var/run
swap 707164 816 706348 1% /tmp
/dev/dsk/c0d0s7 2571070 11 2519638 1% /export/home
#

Figure 4-6

Some of the directories, such as `proc` and `fd`, show 0 in the kbytes, used, and avail columns as well as 0% for capacity. These are special (or virtual) file systems, and although they reside on the disk under `/`, by themselves they do not take up disk space. The `df -k` output is generally the same on all Unix systems. Here's what it usually includes:

Column	Description
Filesystem	The physical file system (`fdX (X=floppy drive number)` = floppy drive, `/dev/dsk/c0t0d0s0` represents a partition on a disk drive, and so forth).
kbytes	Total kilobytes of space available on the storage medium.
used	Total kilobytes of space used (by files).
avail	Total kilobytes available for use.
capacity	Percentage of total space used by files.
Mounted on	What the file system is mounted on. In Figure 4-6, the `/` (root) file system is mounted on `/dev/dsk/c0d0s0` and has only 26% of its total allocated space available. Mounts are discussed later in the chapter.

The avail and capacity columns are important to track because you don't want your `/` (root) or `/tmp` partitions to fill up, because that will cause serious problems. Every portion of the file system is its own entity; the `/` file system is on its own separate physical partition (or device), as is `/export/home` (the usual location for users' home directories on Sun Solaris's version of Unix). Even if `/export/home` becomes full, the root and other partitions will not, because they are their own entities (discussed in the following section).

You can use the -h (human readable) option to display the output in a format that shows the size in easier-to-understand notation as shown in the bottom half of Figure 4-7 (the -h option is not available on all versions of Unix.).

```
# df -k
Filesystem            kbytes    used   avail capacity  Mounted on
/dev/dsk/c0d0s0      1935846 1388778  488993    74%    /
/devices                   0       0       0     0%    /devices
/dev/dsk/c0d0p0:boot   10484    1577    8907    16%    /boot
proc                       0       0       0     0%    /proc
mnttab                     0       0       0     0%    /etc/mnttab
fd                         0       0       0     0%    /dev/fd
swap                  706372      24  706348     1%    /var/run
swap                  707164     816  706348     1%    /tmp
/dev/dsk/c0d0s7      2571070      11 2519638     1%    /export/home
#
# df -h
Filesystem             size   used  avail capacity  Mounted on
/dev/dsk/c0d0s0        1.8G   1.3G   478M    74%    /
/devices                 0K     0K     0K     0%    /devices
/dev/dsk/c0d0p0:boot    10M   1.5M   8.7M    16%    /boot
proc                     0K     0K     0K     0%    /proc
mnttab                   0K     0K     0K     0%    /etc/mnttab
fd                       0K     0K     0K     0%    /dev/fd
swap                   690M    24K   690M     1%    /var/run
swap                   691M   816K   690M     1%    /tmp
/dev/dsk/c0d0s7        2.5G    11K   2.4G     1%    /export/home
#
```

Figure 4-7

The du (disk usage) command enables you to specify directories to show disk space usage on a particular directory. This command is helpful if you want to determine how much space a particular directory is taking.

```
$ du /etc
10      /etc/cron.d
126     /etc/default
6       /etc/dfs
...
```

The -h option makes the output easier to comprehend:

```
$ du -h /etc
  5k    /etc/cron.d
 63k    /etc/default
  3k    /etc/dfs
...
```

One other command you should be familiar with is fsck (file system check). Unix generally uses a superblock to track the file system, including the size of the file system, free blocks available, and other relevant information. When the system does not shut down gracefully (such as when it's powered off while still in multiuser mode) or when the system crashes, errors are introduced into the block. These errors could include the system's marking of blocks as free (meaning they can be written to) when they are actually in use (which can cause serious data corruption), inode size errors, and other administrative problems. These cause inconsistencies in the superblock that require repair. The `fsck` command attempts to repair them. Because of the potentially disastrous issues surrounding this command, extreme care should be taken when running it, so refer to its man page for more information.

Making File Systems Accessible

A file system must be mounted in order to be usable by the system. When you boot up your system, the root directory and any other files you name in `/etc/fstab` or `/etc/dfstab` (or any file that identifies the way that mounts are handled, which differs by Unix variant) are mounted for the system to use. These mounts generally don't require user intervention and are usually not visible to the end user. Mounting a file system means that you are presenting the file system to the system for use. If you want to use a CD-ROM drive (cdrom) in Unix, for example, the system must mount it to the root file system so that you can navigate the drive. The cdrom may attach to the root file system via the `/mnt` directory or the `/cdrom` directory. On some systems (Mac OS X, for instance), this happens automatically; on other systems, you have to issue commands to make the file system available. Take a look at the example file system in Figure 4-8.

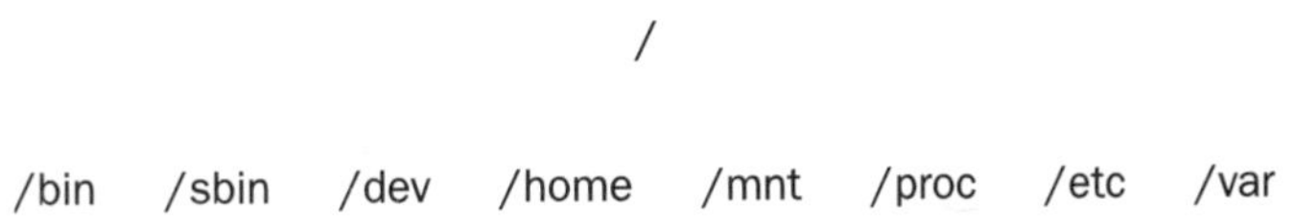

/

/bin /sbin /dev /home /mnt /proc /etc /var

Figure 4-8

The `/mnt` directory, by Unix convention, is where temporary mounts (such as CD-ROM drives, remote network drives, and floppy drives) are located. A file called `fstab` (the filename varies based on Unix version) identifies all the different file systems that should be mounted during boot-up. For instance, if you wanted to use a CD-ROM drive, you would need to tell Unix that the new file system had been added to the primary file system because you would probably want to use more than one CD-ROM drive over the course of your use of Unix. You do not generally want to have a removable device be part of the boot-up mounts, because this can cause problems if the device is removed. You need to identify this new file system to Unix so that it can understand how to interoperate with the medium, and you also need to identify where on the file system it will be attached (what directory). You use the `mount` command, described later in this chapter, to add the CD-ROM drive, and through the options passed, you can have this file system available as needed. After you mount this file system, the new file system hierarchy will include `cdrom` under the `/mnt` directory, as shown in Figure 4-9.

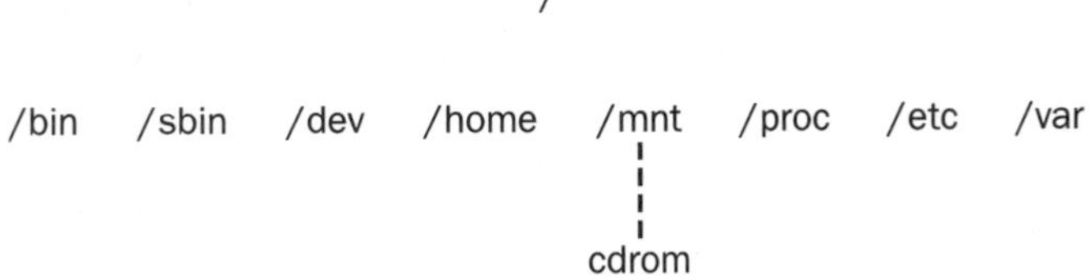

Figure 4-9

To see what is currently mounted (available for use) on your system, use this command:

```
mount
```

The resulting output is similar to that shown in Figure 4-10.

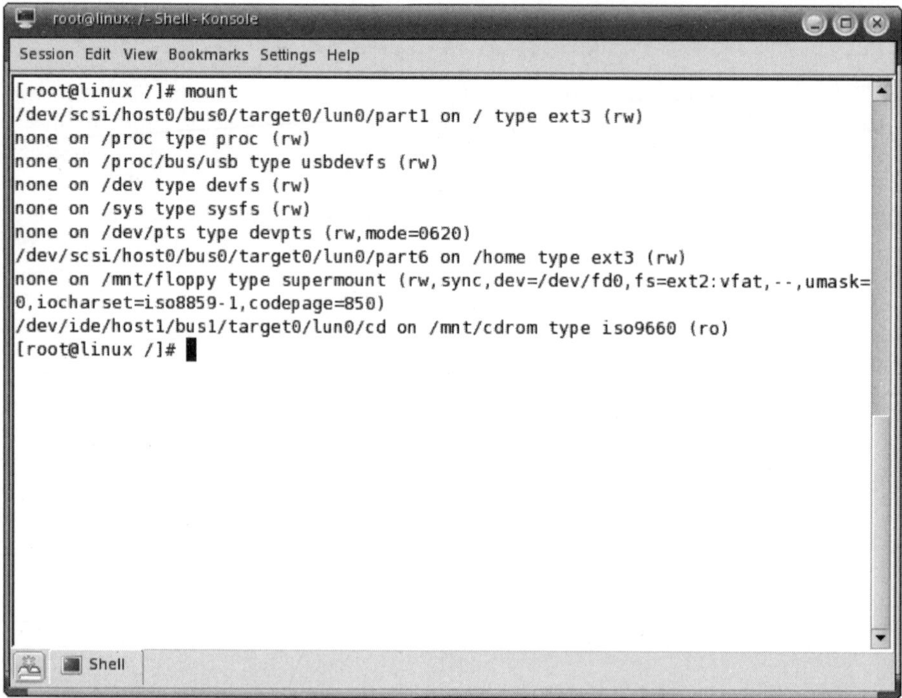
root@linux: / - Shell - Konsole
Session Edit View Bookmarks Settings Help
[root@linux /]# mount
/dev/scsi/host0/bus0/target0/lun0/part1 on / type ext3 (rw)
none on /proc type proc (rw)
none on /proc/bus/usb type usbdevfs (rw)
none on /dev type devfs (rw)
none on /sys type sysfs (rw)
none on /dev/pts type devpts (rw,mode=0620)
/dev/scsi/host0/bus0/target0/lun0/part6 on /home type ext3 (rw)
none on /mnt/floppy type supermount (rw,sync,dev=/dev/fd0,fs=ext2:vfat,--,umask=
0,iocharset=iso8859-1,codepage=850)
/dev/ide/host1/bus1/target0/lun0/cd on /mnt/cdrom type iso9660 (ro)
[root@linux /]#
Shell

Figure 4-10

The format for output from the `mount` command is typically broken up into the following columns:

Column	Description
Device to be mounted	Actual device name; for instance, this is a SCSI CD-ROM.
Mountpoint	Location of the new directory in the file system.
Type of file system	The file system type—such as msdos, hfs, and iso9660—tells the system how to work with the storage medium.
Mount options	Mount options associated with the type of file system.
Dump options	Used to back up the system (discussed further in Chapter 18).
`fsck` options	For identifying the order of file systems checks during boot.

For example, take a look at the last line of output from the mount command in Figure 4-10:

```
/dev/ide/host1/bus1/target0/lun0/cd on /mnt/cdrom type iso9660
(ro,nosuid,nodev,umask=0, iocharset=iso8859-1,codepage=850,user=beginningunix
```

The device to be mounted is `/dev/ide/host1/bus1/target0/lun0/cd`—that's the actual name; it's a SCSI CD-ROM device. The mountpoint is `/mnt/cdrom`, and the type of file system is iso9660, which is a CD-ROM. The options for the device are `ro` (read only), which means you can't write to the CD-ROM; `nosuid` (no set user ID or set group ID); `nodev` (don't interpret character or block special devices for this file system); `umask` (discussed in Chapter 6); `iocharset` (for converting 8-bit to 16-bit characters); `codepage` (for converting FAT and VFAT filenames); and `user` (the username—beginningunix in this example), who can mount the file system as needed. There are no dump or `fsck` options for this device.

File systems can be mounted automatically or manually, depending on the Unix system you're using, so you may not need to mount them manually. You can run the `mount` command to see what file systems are mounted, and if a needed file system isn't in the output list, then it was not automatically mounted (assuming no one mounted it between boot and the time you run the `mount` command). If you need to mount a file system, you can use the `mount` command with the following syntax:

mount -t *file_system_type device_to_mount directory_to_mount_to*

If you want to mount a CD-ROM to the directory `/mnt/cdrom`, for example, you can type:

```
mount -t iso9660 /dev/cdrom /mnt/cdrom
```

This assumes that your CD-ROM device is called `/dev/cdrom` and that you want to mount it to `/mnt/cdrom`. Refer to the `mount` man page for more specific information or type **mount -h** at the command line for help information. After mounting, you can use the `cd` command to navigate the newly available file system through the mountpoint you just made.

To unmount (remove) the file system from your system, use the `umount` (note spelling: only one n) command by identifying the mountpoint or device. For example, to unmount `cdrom`, use the following command:

```
umount /dev/cdrom
```

The `mount` command enables you to access your file systems, but on most modern Unix systems, the automount function makes this process invisible to the user and requires no intervention.

Summary

The concept of file systems is important because you use them for storing and using applications in your Unix system. This chapter discussed how to navigate a file system, what the different types of files are, how permissions work at a rudimentary level, how to view files quickly, and how to work with directories. The chapter also covered basic file system management and making file systems accessible to the user.

Exercise

Write a command that will set the file permissions of the file `samplefile` to read, write, and execute for the owner of the file, and read and execute permissions for the group and for others, using absolute mode (sometimes referred to as octal mode).

Customize Your Working Environment

An environment variable controls a particular aspect of the Unix environment. That is, environment variables affect the look and feel of your computing experience, as well as many underlying actions that you might never notice. You can use environment variables to change almost every aspect of the Unix experience.

This chapter explains environment variables in more detail and shows you some of the more common ones. In particular, it focuses on *shells*, the programs that translate your keystrokes into commands that the operating system can recognize and accept. There are many Unix shells available today, and the array can be somewhat confusing. You'll explore the differences and receive suggestions on adopting the shell that will work best for you.

Environment Variables

Unix is incredibly flexible. This can be a delight or a horror, depending on what you're trying to do. For most users, the learning curve is steep. However, you can cut away a lot of trouble if you spend some time defining your environment before you move too deeply into the Unix experience!

The PS1 Variable

Unix behavior can be changed dramatically depending on the value assigned to a particular environment variable. For example, the environment variable `PS1` controls the top-level *command prompt*, or string of characters before the cursor. You see this prompt when you open a terminal window or after you log in to the console on your machine. The prompt can contain almost anything you want it to, as long as you define the environment variable with the appropriate value.

The following example assumes that you are using either the Bourne or the bash shell environment, which is usually the case with a default installation. If you issued the command:

```
PS1=">"
```

the top-level command prompt in that shell would appear as:

```
>
```

with the cursor following the > character. Pretty simple, yes? What if you issued the command:

```
PS1="I am ready to do your bidding, Bob!"
```

As you can probably guess, the resulting prompt would look like this

```
I am ready to do your bidding, Bob!
```

and would immediately be followed by the cursor. While this sort of thing is amusing, it can quickly grow tiresome. A more useful prompt contains information about your working directory, which is your current location within the entire file system. This information is critical when you are trying to determine the path of a particular file. (To learn more about the path, see "Understanding the Path" later in this chapter.)

Try It Out Configure the Bash Prompt

There are a number of ways in which you can configure your prompt in the bash shell, using the `PS1` environment variable. (Although the format differs, the `PS1` variable is used in other shells as well.) One useful configuration displays the working directory in the prompt. To set the value of `PS1` so that it shows the working directory, issue the command:

```
PS1="[\u@\h \w]\$"
```

How It Works

The result of this command is that the prompt displays the user's username, the machine's name (hostname), and the working directory. (It's useful to include the username so that you can tell whether you're logged in as yourself or as another user, especially if you're the sole system administrator.) Here's an example result:

```
[dave@linux1 /etc]$
```

There are quite a few escape sequences that can be used as value arguments for `PS1`; try to limit yourself to the most critical so that the prompt does not overwhelm you with information.

Escape Sequence	Function
`\t`	Current time, expressed as HH:MM:SS.
`\d`	Current date, expressed as Weekday Month Date (or Day).
`\n`	Newline.
`\s`	Current shell environment.
`\W`	Working directory.
`\w`	Full path of the working directory.

Escape Sequence	Function
`\u`	Current user's username.
`\h`	Hostname of the current machine.
`\#`	Command number of the current command. Increases with each new command entered.
`\$`	If the effective UID is `0` (that is, if you are logged in as root), end the prompt with the `#` character; otherwise, use the `$`.

Other Environment Variables

Shells take an assortment of environment variables. In addition, should you want to delve deeply into shell scripting, you can create your own environment variables to serve particular functions in your scripts. For example, you might create a set of variables that defines prompts for your users based on how much disk space they have used. This is not a standard shell variable, but it's easy to think of situations where it might be useful, especially if you have a teenager prone to downloading vast amounts of music or video files and clogging up the family hard drive!

To learn more about shell scripts — text files used to automate various shell functions — see Chapters 13 and 14.

Environment variables also differ based on the shell environment you've chosen. While most shells have variables that fulfill the same purposes, you might find them under slightly different names in different shells, or the variable with an identical name might take a different syntax in another environment. In "Configuring Your Shell" later in this chapter, you'll take a look at some of these unique environment variables.

Some users work with Unix for many years without doing much to their environment variables. Other users dive right in, not feeling fully at home until every possible variable is tinkered with and configured to the finest degree. Most of us fall somewhere in the middle, configuring a favorite text editor or mail client, perhaps changing the prompt, and making a few other small changes that help create a more familiar and comfortable computing environment.

Understanding the Path

As you learned in Chapter 4, every element on your Unix machine is considered to be a file. That is, the operating system treats all commands and executable programs in the same manner that it treats an actual file. This is a tough concept for some folks to grasp, especially if you come from a purely GUI environment such as Microsoft Windows. However, in the long run, treating everything like a file makes it easier to administer a Unix system.

The root directory is known by the character `/`.

The thing to remember about Unix and the way it handles files is that each file, whether it be command, program, or static document, has a unique location. This location is called its *full path name*, and it specifies the file's unique place within the entire file system. For example, the command `ls` (used to list files) usually has the full path name `/bin/ls`. This means that the `ls` command is usually stored in the `/bin` directory, which is stored in the first level of directories below the root directory. The full path name compresses the specific file tree into a single line, but you can also think of the path name as representing this progression:

```
/
    bin
      ls
```

Using full path names has its advantages. In particular, it's a great way to learn your file system and to remember a file's specific location. However, full path names can be rather tedious in regular use, especially if you're working with programs and documents that are stored deep within a nested directory. Imagine that you are writing a new program and that this program's executable file is located in a subdirectory of your home directory. To execute this file, you'd have to type a full path name like this:

```
/users/home/susan/MyProg/prog
```

In the process of writing and debugging your program, you might type this command hundreds of times. That's a lot of wasted keystrokes and physical effort, not to mention that it increases the possibility of typing errors.

Another problem with full path names is that you might want to use a particular program but you don't know where it's located on this particular system. For example, the oldest of old-school Unix types still use an e-mail program simply called `mail`. This program could be found in `/bin/mail` or at `/usr/bin/mail` or even somewhere completely nonstandard, all depending on how the system administrator decided to structure the file system. If you've just installed a new flavor of Unix and used the default settings, the installer might have put `mail` someplace that you weren't expecting. The end result is that you spend a lot of time and effort searching through the file system so that you can issue the correct full path name and, eventually, get into your e-mail.

The PATH Environment Variable

There is a common solution to all of these problems. The `PATH` environment variable contains a list of directories where executable files might be located. If a directory is listed in the `PATH` variable's value, that directory's name does not need to be typed to invoke an executable file that resides in it. For example, if the mail program is stored in `/usr/bin/` and `/usr/bin/` is part of `PATH`'s value, you can simply type **`mail`** at the command prompt to invoke the program, instead of using the complete path `/usr/bin/mail`.

In Unix terminology, to invoke a program is to call it into operation.

The value of the `PATH` variable is usually set at the system-wide level in a configuration file such as `/etc/profile`. Most standard Unix systems have certain common directories listed there as a matter of course. In addition, the installation procedures for many large software packages (such as the Mozilla Web browser) automatically add directories to the path so that they can be easily found.

You can add your own values to the `PATH` variable. When you invoke a shell environment, the shell's configuration files — both global and user-specific — are executed, and any additional values that you want to add to the `PATH` variable's value can be added to the shell configuration file.

In the Bourne and bash shells, the format for appending values to the `PATH` variable is this:

```
PATH=$PATH:new value
```

So, if a user called joe wants to add his home directory `/home/joe` to the path, he would do so in this manner:

```
PATH=$PATH:/home/joe
```

Multiple directories can be added as a colon-separated list:

```
PATH=$PATH:/home/joe:/home/joe/myprog:/home/joe/myprog/bin
```

In addition, the user can add the command:

```
export PATH
```

to the initialization file. This causes the new values of the variable to be available outside of that particular iteration of the shell. This is useful for people using multiple shells or using graphical interfaces and the like.

While most users do not need to worry about the order in which directory names are added to the value of `PATH`, there are times when the order is important. For example, assume that you have two programs, each in a different directory but both having the same name. If you invoke the program by issuing its name at the command prompt, the shell will look at the files in the `PATH` directories in order. As soon as the shell finds the correct program, the program will start, no matter whether it's the program you intended to invoke. To invoke the other program with that name first, you need to issue the complete path name at the prompt.

The dollar sign at the beginning of the `PATH` *statement alerts the shell that the new directory, or value, is to be appended to the current value of* `PATH` *rather than replacing it. If you issue the command as* `PATH=PATH:/usr/sbin`, *for example, the value of* `PATH` *will include the relative directory PATH as well as the full path name* `/usr/sbin`. *If you issue the command as* `PATH=$PATH:/usr/sbin`, *the* `/usr/sbin` *directory will be added to the directories already included in* `PATH's` *value.*

If you have recently changed the value of `PATH` *and suddenly cannot invoke programs with the simple command name, you may have missed the* `$` *while issuing the command. You will need to determine and reconfigure the correct value for PATH.*

Relative and Absolute Paths

When working with full path names, it's important to understand the difference between *relative* and *absolute* paths. In a Unix environment, all paths are named relative to the root directory, `/`. Thus, as previously explained, `/bin` is a subdirectory of `/`, and `/bin/appdir` is a subdirectory of `/bin`, making `appdir` a third-level directory. The full path name `/bin/appdir` is also an absolute path name, because it contains all the elements of the tree structure from `/` to the ultimate destination.

However, you don't need to use the absolute path name every time you want to move through the file system. All you need to know is the destination and the starting point—your current working directory. If you followed the directions earlier in this chapter, you already have the current working directory conveniently displayed in your prompt.

Assume that the current working directory is `/bin`. To move to the `appdir` subdirectory using the `cd` (change directory) command, you could issue the absolute path, as in

```
cd /bin/appdir
```

But you're already in `/bin`, so why add extra keystrokes? Just issue the command:

```
cd appdir
```

A directory name given without an absolute path is always assumed to be relative to the current directory. If, for example, the `appdir` directory contained a subdirectory called `dir1`, you could move there from `/bin` with the command

```
cd appdir/dir1
```

Note that there's no slash preceding the relative path.

The relative path works regardless of the number of levels in the path. If your working directory is `dir1`, the relative path:

```
dir2/dir3/dir4
```

still means:

```
/bin/appdir/dir1/dir2/dir3/dir4
```

The deeper you delve into the file system, the more useful the relative path becomes.

Moving around the File System

Apart from the use of absolute and relative path names, Unix uses some shorthand notations for common directory functions. These conventions make it easier to understand your location in the file system as a whole.

- The current directory is represented by a single dot (`.`). If you want to specify a file in the current directory (for example, if it is an executable file, but not in `PATH`), you can reference it as `./myfile`.
- Likewise, the parent directory of the current directory is represented by a double dot (`..`). If the current directory is `/bin`, and you issue the command `cd ..`, you move to the root directory, `/`.
- A user's home directory is represented by the tilde (~). No matter where you are in the file system, the command `ls ~` produces a listing of the files stored in your home directory.

Choosing a Shell

Although many Unix systems may seem barebones and identical, there are subtle variations that affect your ultimate user experience. One of the most basic configurations is the choice of a *shell environment*. A shell is a program that lies between you (the user) and the kernel of the operating system. When you issue commands or type at the prompt, you interact with the shell. In turn, the shell translates your commands and keystrokes into something the kernel can understand. The kernel responds, and then the shell presents the output to you.

On a typical Unix system, several shells are installed by default and are available to you. Generally, shell choice is a matter of personal preference. When a system administrator creates a new user account, she assigns a default shell. The user can change the shell at a later point if the default is unacceptable, but the vast majority of users stick with the default shell whether it is the most appropriate environment for them or not. If you are your own system administrator, choosing a shell is simple; just set the one you want when you create your account, as described in Chapter 3.

Why would you want to change your shell environment? Perhaps you don't like the prompt style in a particular shell. You might have years of experience with a particular programming language and want an environment that structures commands in a similar fashion. You could be fascinated with the automation possibilities of shell scripting and want a shell that makes this process as easy as possible. You might change shells like shoes, using one for certain kinds of work and another for different purposes. It's easy to change between shells, whether temporarily or permanently.

Changing a Shell Temporarily

It's easy to change the shell environment for a single user session, or even for a mere two or three commands, and then return to your regular shell of choice. To do so, simply issue the desired shell's name as a command. For example, if your default shell is bash and you want to use tcsh, simply type:

```
tcsh
```

at the shell prompt. If the directory where tcsh is stored is not part of the value of your `PATH` environment variable, however, you will need to issue the full path name, usually:

```
/bin/tcsh
```

That's all it takes! When you're ready to return to your default shell (bash, in this example), just type:

```
exit
```

at the shell prompt. This is the best way to try out new shells or to switch between shells for specific purposes. Even if you log out while in the new shell environment, your default value will apply when you log in again.

The only downside is that you must issue the proper command every time you want to use the new shell in a new session. If you have bash set as your default shell and yet find that you end up doing most of your work in tcsh, you might prefer changing the default shell environment, as shown in the next section. For those users who work in a number of shells in one session, however, invoking particular shells only as needed is a quicker way to manage the environment.

Changing the Default Shell

If you have a favorite shell that is not the default shell on your account, you have two options: change the shell each time you log in, using the method described in the previous section, or change the default shell permanently. For the latter, you change the value of the variable that controls shell selection, so that the new shell is invoked each time you log in. That state will persist until you change the default shell again.

To change the default shell, use `chsh`, the command to change shell. At the command prompt, type:

```
chsh
```

You are prompted for your password and for the new shell's name. Enter this information, and the new shell is established as the default. To switch shells between the new and old versions, you still need to enter the shell name as a separate command.

`chsh` *is not valid on every system. You might try the* `passwd` *program with the* `-e` *or* `-s` *flags, as in* `passwd -e` *or* `passwd -s`. *If these also fail, contact your system administrator for help.*

Which Shell?

While most users understand the need for a shell environment, many are stymied by the range of shell options. There are a number of Unix shells, some of which are used extensively and some of which are of interest or use only to their creators. Each of these shells has its own pluses and minuses, and you can drive yourself crazy trying to figure out which one shell will be the ultimate solution for your particular situation.

Relax! Most Unix users end up with a small number of shells that they use for different purposes. Your main shell will be the one you are most comfortable with, but you might want to work with a different shell for programming, or even use a particular shell for games or to otherwise blow off some steam and relax. This section introduces the most popular Unix shells and shows you the basics of each and why you might want to give each one a try.

Bourne Shell

No matter what Unix variant you use, you've probably got a version of the Bourne shell somewhere on the system. Bourne was the original Unix shell, and has changed little over the years. In fact, the most prevalent Bourne tutorial on the Web is one that was originally written in 1978 for Bourne version 4.3. The only major difference between the original and the current Bourne documentation is that the newer files have been formatted with HTML.

You can find this tutorial, written by Steve Bourne himself, at `http://steve-parker.org/sh/bourne.shtml`.

Depending on your perspective, you may find the Bourne shell to be an elegant, lean environment, or you may think it's painfully lacking in modern convenience and ease. Whether or not you choose to use Bourne on a regular basis, take the time to become familiar with its rudiments. Should you be in a situation where your machine is locked down to the bare minimums — such as with a rescue disk — Bourne may be the only shell environment available to you. It would be better to know how to use it before such a crisis occurs.

That said, many system administrators like to use Bourne for shell scripting. Bourne, like all shells, is a command language as well as a user environment, and shell scripts can be an easy way to automate many ordinary administrative routines without having to build complex programs and learn new programming languages. There is a vast amount of information on Bourne shell scripting available in books and online. While newer shells with more features make ongoing user interaction easier, Bourne still holds its own in the world of streamlined shell scripting.

Invoke the Bourne shell with the `sh` command. The default Bourne prompt ends with the `$` symbol, followed by the cursor; if you are logged in as root, you see the # character instead of the `$`. The Bourne shell parses two configuration files as it starts:

- `/etc/profile` — A global configuration file for Bourne-family shells.
- `.profile` — A file, stored in your own home directory, containing the specific configurations you want for shell activity in your own account. This file is also for Bourne-family shells.

Learn more about using these files in "Configuring Your Shell" later in this chapter.

Ash

Some systems may run the ash shell instead of true Bourne. Originally created by the NetBSD development team, ash is a lightweight Bourne clone that takes up a lot less disk and memory space than Bourne. It's particularly useful for machines with less memory or smaller drives. Although it lacks some of the standard Bourne features, such as a history file of recently issued commands, it is a completely functional shell environment. Should you be running a bare-bones Unix box that doesn't have a lot of room for fancy software, especially if you're running a BSD variant, consider installing ash. You can download ash packages or source code from most online software repositories if you didn't get them as part of your operating system.

Bourne Again SHell

Although the original Bourne shell is on almost every Unix system in the world, it's not always the friendliest shell on the disk. Enter bash, which is Bourne-like but not a Bourne clone. The bash shell was originally written as the shell environment for the GNU operating system, a Unix-like operating system that includes only royalty-free code (and therefore cannot technically be called a Unix variant — in fact, GNU stands for "GNU's Not Unix"). To meet the philosophical demands of the GNU project, developers built a shell that mimicked sh's scripting capabilities, and they called it the Bourne Again SHell, or bash.

Bash was originally intended as a drop-in replacement for Bourne, but it has been continuously developed over the past several years and now includes many features — ranging from user-interface tools to a more advanced scripting language — that are not found in the original Bourne shell.

Most Bourne shell scripts will run under bash with no modifications. As a result of the changes in bash's native language, however, the reverse is not always true. You may need to do some tinkering before you can run bash scripts in a pure Bourne environment.

The bash shell is extremely popular, especially among those who originally learned to script in the Bourne shell but wanted better user-interface tools, and has been ported to almost all Unix variants. You probably have a bash shell on your Unix machine, and it might even be the default shell environment. It is certainly worth a try, even if you don't want to do a lot of shell scripting. The multiple features of this shell are attractive to users at any level:

- Bash offers environment variables to configure every aspect of your user experience within the shell.
- The command history enables you to scroll back through previous commands, whether to save keystrokes in repeating a command or to identify the source of a problem.
- Bash offers built-in arithmetic functions, both integer arithmetic commands at the command line and arithmetic expressions for your shell scripts.
- Wildcard expressions help you find the exact name of a program or see all the files with a particular string in the filename across the system. You can also use wildcards with commands to execute an operation on multiple files.
- Command-line editing lets you use Emacs and vi (text editors) commands to make edits at the prompt without opening a file.
- Bash has a long list of built-in commands that make machine administration much easier, many of which can be used both at the command line and within a script. (Learn more from the bash manual page, which you can find by issuing the command `man bash` at the command prompt.)

Korn Shell

The Korn shell, invoked with the `ksh` command, is another member of the Bourne shell family. This shell is also extremely popular and has adherents as devoted as those who prefer bash. However, the line between the two shells is somewhat blurry because bash incorporates many features of the Korn shell, including arithmetic functions and command-line editing configurable to resemble Emacs or vi.

If you plan to do a lot of shell programming, the Korn shell may be a good choice for you. It has a good selection of programming features, including the capability to build menus for your shell scripts and the use of *array variables*. Array variables are indexed lists of multiple values for a single variable. The combination of advanced arithmetical calculations and arrays means that Korn shell users can build shell scripts with surprising sophistication. In fact, the newest version of ksh has functions found in a variety of popular programming languages, including Tcl, Icon, AWK, and Perl, but with an easier interface.

You may not have the Korn shell available on your default installation. You can download the latest version from AT&T at `http://research.att.com/sw/download`. FAQs and installation help are available at `http://kornshell.com`, along with sample scripts and extensions to use with Tcl or Motif scripts.

For some users, the open source nature of a program is a critical component of software choice. The Korn shell has not always been open source, although AT&T now releases it as such. If you would prefer a ksh clone that is a true open source shell environment, consider pdksh, the Public Domain Korn Shell. Unfortunately, because pdksh is a volunteer project, it does not have the same development schedule as the Korn shell, so the current release is less feature-rich than the current ksh release. Still, if you're serious about maintaining a 100 percent open source machine, give pdksh a try. Learn more at `http://web.cs.mun.ca/~michael/pdksh/`.

Z Shell

The Z shell (zsh) is a relative newcomer to the Unix world, having only been on the scene since about 1990. Still, 14 years is a long time in the world of computer science, and zsh is a mature shell environment, currently at version 4.2.0. Of all the Bourne-related shells, the Z shell is most like the Korn shell. In fact, Korn users will find the migration to Z almost seamless. That said, the Z shell bears similarities to almost every major shell environment now available. The configuration options are stupefying, and if you are willing to put in the time, you can probably get the Z shell to behave in whatever super-specific way you desire.

Although the Z Shell does many of the things found in the C shells, be aware that it is built on a Bourne base and thus tends toward sh syntax and procedure.

The Z shell is stuffed full of features and options. If a user, somewhere, has wanted to do something in a shell, it's probably possible under Z. The advantage, obviously, is that Z can do a great many things. The disadvantage lies with you—you may not want a shell that has so many options or functions. Think of zsh as a top-of-the-line automobile, sewing machine, or PDA that has every bell and whistle on the market. If you spend 90 percent of your time commuting 10 miles to work on the same road, you don't need all the fancy off-road or child-friendly items. If you spend that 90 percent taking your kids into the backcountry, however, you'll probably push the limits of the car a lot further. Even if you only fantasize about those off-road trips, you might want to have the gear for the possibilities. The Z shell is like that.

Depending on the age of your operating system packages, you may not have the latest version of the Z shell; version 4.2 was released in August 2004. Visit `http://zsh.org` *and select the mirror site most convenient for you. All mirrors host the latest Z shell packages, along with documentation and links to important online documents, like the FAQ and the user guide.*

C Shells

Fluent in C? Need a shell environment that understands those C-flavored commands? The C shells csh and tcsh might be the right shells for you. At the basic user level, there's not a huge difference between the C shells and those related to the Bourne shell. Once you begin to work with environment variables and shell scripts, however, you'll quickly begin to see a divergence between the two shell families.

The programming syntax used in the C shells is derived from the C programming language. Not surprising, C devotees are usually also C shell devotees. If you're used to working with C syntax, these shells will be a breeze for you, especially as you move into shell scripting. If you are unfamiliar with C, you might find yourself quite confused in some situations where the C syntax differs from traditional sh-style commands. For example, Bourne-based shells use this syntax to define an environment variable:

```
VARIABLE = value
```

In the C shells, environment variables are defined with the command:

```
setenv VARIABLE value
```

Thus, the Bourne-style command `EDITOR="pico"` would be expressed as `setenv EDITOR pico` in a C shell.

More than once we've heard from frustrated users who can't seem to get their shells to behave properly. In most cases, the user has somehow gotten himself into a shell of a different family, whether by invoking the shell or through the default software decisions made by a system administrator. If you're trying to issue Bourne-style commands and they don't work, chances are that you're in a C-type shell. The opposite is also true; if you're trying to set a variable using `setenv` and it won't stick, you're probably in a Bourne-type environment. To get to the shell you want to use, invoke it with the appropriate command or ask your system administrator to install the shell package if it is not already on the system.

The basic C shell, csh, has multiple basic functions, including filename completion, wildcard substitution, and some useful administrative tools such as job control and history substitution. Tsch, an enhanced version of csh, offers even more flexibility. Under tcsh, you find configurable command-line editing, command completion, an excellent method of directory parsing, and a large number of environment variables specific to the shell. With tcsh, you can also use the arrow keys on your keyboard to traverse the command history, a function that is common in more modern shells but isn't available by default in the older shell environments.

You probably have one or both of the C shells in your Unix default installation. If you need to download or upgrade your C shells, visit your distribution's download site for C packages and source code. You can also check `http://tcsh.org` *for tcsh packages and documentation.*

Perl Shells

Because Perl is such a popular programming language, it's not surprising that a few enterprising Perl wranglers have attempted to build Perl shells. These efforts are ongoing, but haven't yet resulted in a reliable shell that can serve as a sturdy replacement for one of the shells listed above. Still, if you like hacking Perl, you might enjoy having a Perl-based shell on your machine to take advantage of Perl's interpreter and regular expression rules. There are two Perl-based shells in somewhat active development:

- psh — The Perl shell psh is now in version 1.8. You can download the current version at `http://gregorpurdy.com/gregor/psh/`.
- Zoidberg — A modular Perl-based shell that is far more experimental. It is not yet up to a 1.0 release, so it's definitely beta software. However, the concept is intriguing, melding the convenience of Perl modules with a regular shell environment. Learn more at `http://zoidberg.student.utwente.nl/index.plp`.

Available Shells

Not every system has every shell installed on it. Most systems generally have at least one variant of the Bourne shell: the actual Bourne shell (sh), the GNU Bourne Again SHell (bash), or the generic public domain Bourne clone (ash). No matter which Bourne variant is installed on your machine, it's likely linked to the name sh, which can be used as the command to invoke a Bourne work-alike shell environment.

In addition, many Unix default installations include some flavor of C shell: either csh, the original C shell, or tcsh, the GNU work-alike. Search through the `/bin` directory and other likely locations to see whether you have additional shell options, such as ksh, the Korn shell. You may even find rarer shells such as the Z and Perl shells. You probably won't find these on many stock systems, but you may want to download the packages and give them a try.

Shells for Fun

Really want to waste some time in the shell environment? Consider the odd subculture of *game shells*, shells written to emulate popular text-based Unix games like adventure or multiuser dungeon games (MUDs). These shells aren't designed for actual work, but common Unix commands invoke particular actions on the part of the game characters.

There are three shells written to emulate the adventure game: advshell, advsh, and nadvsh. Advshell is the original, written as a sh script. Advsh is written in C, and nadvsh (the New Adventure Shell) is written for bash, ksh, and zsh. These shells don't require additional libraries and tend to run cleanly. For more information, check out the project homepages:

- Advshell and advsh: `http://ifarchive.org/if-archive/shells/`
- Nadvsh: `http://nadvsh.sourceforge.net/`

Perhaps you're not much of an adventure player, or you've devoted far too many hours to your favorite hack 'n' slash MUD to learn something new. The mud-shell might be right up your alley! This shell is written in Perl and is actually comprehensible as a regular shell environment, albeit one in which you might be eaten by a grue. Learn more at `http://xirium.com/tech/mud-shell/`.

Configuring Your Shell

After you've selected a shell environment, you will probably want to configure it. There are four main elements of shell configuration, and you may use any or all of them in any combination to make your environment perfect for you:

- Run control files
- Environment variables
- Aliases
- Options

In this section of the chapter, you learn more about each of these elements and see samples that illustrate their use.

Run Control Files

Run control files are executed as soon as the shell boots up, whether at the moment you log in to your account or the moment at which you invoke the shell with a command issued at the prompt. When the shell starts, it parses all applicable run control files. The first run control file that the shell checks is a global configuration file. Depending on the shell, more than one global configuration file may be used, with one file defining global settings, one controlling the login shell, and possibly another defining subshell processes. After the global configuration file or files are parsed, the shell then parses any existing personal configuration files stored in your user account. As with global configurations, you may have more than one level of personal configuration file.

The following table shows the various run control files for popular Unix variants. Files in this table are both global and personal run control files.

Different versions of Unix call their shell initialization files differently. The examples in this text may not match your system's methods exactly. Consult your local shell documentation if you have a question.

Shell	Configuration File	File Purpose
bash	/etc/bashrc	Global configuration.
	/etc/profile	Global configuration for login shells.
	~/.bash_profile	User's personal configuration file for login shells.
	~/.bashrc	User's personal configuration file for all subshells.
	~/.profile	User's personal configuration file for all login shells. This file is read if ~/.bash_profile does not exist.
sh & ash	/etc/profile	Global configuration.
	~/.profile	User's personal configuration.
ksh & pdksh	/etc/profile	Global configuration.
	~/.profile	User's personal configuration.
zsh	/etc/zshenv	Global first configuration file.
	/etc/zprofile	Global login shell configuration.
	/etc/zshrc	Global second configuration file.
	/etc/zlogin	Global login shell configuration.
	/etc/zlogout	Global cleanup file.
	$ZDOTDIR/.zshenv	User's personal first configuration file.
	$ZDOTDIR/.zprofile	User's personal login shell configuration.
	$ZDOTDIR/.zshrc	User's personal second configuration file.
	$ZDOTDIR/.zlogin	User's personal login shell configuration.
	$ZDOTDIR/.zlogout	User's personal cleanup files.
psh	~/.pshrc	User's configuration file. (There is no global configuration file under the Perl shell.)
csh & tcsh	/etc/csh.cshrc	Global configuration.
	~/.csh.login	User's personal login configuration.

Readers interested in the Z shell are encouraged to read the documentation carefully. `$ZDOTDIR` *is a variable that controls where the user's personal files are. If it is undefined, the user's home directory will be used.*

Global Configuration Files

When the shell environment begins to run after your initial login, the first configuration it parses is the global configuration file, should one be required for the default shell. `/etc/profile` is a Bourne family shell configuration file containing global settings that affect every account on the machine. This file usually controls the way in which files are exported, the default terminal type, and the messages that indicate new e-mail has arrived for a particular user. `/etc/profile` is also used to create a *umask*, the default set of permissions that apply to new files at the time each file is created.

On a well-configured system, only those with root access can modify `/etc/profile`. Remember that every setting in this file affects every user of Bourne family shells, and that this file is invoked before a given user's personal preferences file. It's usually best to keep `/etc/profile` lean and controlled so that logins don't take forever to finish. `/etc/profile` files running under Unix variants look remarkably similar even with individual configurations. Following are a few examples of `/etc/profile` from different flavors of Unix to show you the similarities and differences.

Ash /etc/profile

The ash `/etc/profile` file is basic and doesn't define many global settings:

```
PATH="/bin:/usr/bin:/sbin:/usr/sbin:/usr/local/bin:/usr/X11R6/bin"
exec `set -o vi`
ulimit -c 0
if [ `id -gn` = `id -un` -a `id -u` -gt 14 ]; then
umask 002
else
umask 022
fi
USER=`id -un`
PS1="# "
LOGNAME=$USER
HISTSIZE=1000
HISTFILE="$HOME/.history"
EDITOR=mp
INPUTRC=/etc/inputrc
TERM=linux
NNTPSERVER="news.comcast.net"
# GS_FONTPATH="/usr/X11R6/lib/X11/fonts/Type1"
export PATH PS1 USER LOGNAME HISTSIZE INPUTRC EDITOR TERM NNTPSERVER
```

Note the short value of `PATH`, which includes only the common binary directories.

Red Hat Linux /etc/profile

This `/etc/profile` comes from a Red Hat Linux machine that uses bash as the default shell:

```
# /etc/profile

# System wide environment and startup programs
# Functions and aliases go in /etc/bashrc

if ! echo $PATH | /bin/grep -q "/usr/X11R6/bin" ; then
  PATH="$PATH:/usr/X11R6/bin"
fi
```

```
ulimit -S -c 1000000 > /dev/null 2>&1
if [ `id -gn` = `id -un` -a `id -u` -gt 14 ]; then
        umask 002
else
        umask 022
fi

USER=`id -un`
LOGNAME=$USER
MAIL="/var/spool/mail/$USER"

HOSTNAME=`/bin/hostname`
HISTSIZE=1000

if [ -z "$INPUTRC" -a ! -f "$HOME/.inputrc" ]; then
        INPUTRC=/etc/inputrc
fi

export PATH USER LOGNAME MAIL HOSTNAME HISTSIZE INPUTRC

for i in /etc/profile.d/*.sh ; do
        if [ -x $i ]; then
                . $i
        fi
done

unset I
```

As you can see in line 4, aliases and other functions are stored in the `/etc/bashrc` file, another global configuration file specific to bash. The file is laid out much like a shell script, with sections that contain if-then programming constructs. However, it's still a relatively simple global configuration file.

A Cross-Unix Generic /etc/profile

If you work on a number of Unix variants and dislike having to remember all the different quirks of each flavor's command-line environment, check out the generic `/etc/profile` at `http://bluehaze.com.au/unix/eprofile`. It creates a common command-line environment across Solaris, SunOS, HP-UX, Linux, and Irix: that's every major commercial Unix plus Linux. Pretty impressive!

The `/etc/profile` file itself would cover nine pages in this book, so it isn't included here. However, it's well worth looking at, if only for ideas. It is particularly well-commented, with good explanations for every block of code and hardly anything extraneous. In short, this file is an excellent introduction to `/etc/profile` and its myriad uses. Check it out.

/etc/bashrc

If you decide to run bash (the Bourne Again SHell), you may want to configure an additional global run control file, `/etc/bashrc` (or `/etc/bash.bashrc`, depending on your Unix variant). Like `/etc/profile`, `/etc/bashrc` defines particular characteristics of a bash user session. It controls the default configuration for all users of the bash shell on the system, and therefore should have permissions set so that only an administrator can edit it.

The /etc/bashrc file can look quite different depending on the flavor of Unix in question and the controls already placed in /etc/profile. Many administrators store the main configurations in /etc/profile and keep /etc/bashrc quite short, with only bash-specific edits. For example, here is the /etc/bashrc file from a BSD installation:

```
# System-wide .bashrc file for interactive bash(1) shells.
PS1='\h:\w \u\$ '
# Make bash check it's window size after a process completes
shopt -s checkwinsize
```

This file has only two functions: defining the bash prompt and checking window size. Everything else about shell environments on this system is controlled by /etc/profile so that those values will apply no matter what shell is in use.

On a Red Hat Linux system, /etc/bashrc looks a little different:

```
# /etc/bashrc
# System wide functions and aliases
# Environment stuff goes in /etc/profile

# by default, we want this to get set.
# Even for non-interactive, non-login shells.
if [ "`id -gn`" = "`id -un`" -a `id -u` -gt 99 ]; then
        umask 002
else
        umask 022
fi

# Here's where I ask you to put the "umask 022" line to override previous

# are we an interactive shell?
if [ "$PS1" ]; then
  if [ -x /usr/bin/tput ]; then
    if [ "x`tput kbs`" != "x" ]; then # We can't do this with "dumb" terminal
        stty erase `tput kbs`
    elif [ -x /usr/bin/wc ]; then
       if [ "`tput kbs|wc -c `" -gt 0 ]; then # We can't do this with "dumb"
terminal
         stty erase `tput kbs`
       fi
    fi
  fi
  case $TERM in
    xterm*)
     if [ -e /etc/sysconfig/bash-prompt-xterm ]; then
       PROMPT_COMMAND=/etc/sysconfig/bash-prompt-xterm
     else
       PROMPT_COMMAND='echo -ne
"\033]0;${USER}@${HOSTNAME%%.*}:${PWD/$HOME/~}\007"'
     fi
     ;;
    screen)
       PROMPT_COMMAND='echo -ne
"\033_${USER}@${HOSTNAME%%.*}:${PWD/$HOME/~}\033\\"'
       ;;
```

```
        *)
            [ -e /etc/sysconfig/bash-prompt-default ] &&
                PROMPT_COMMAND=/etc/sysconfig/bash-prompt-default
        ;;
      esac
      [ "$PS1" = "\\s-\\v\\\$ " ] && PS1="[\u@\h \W]\\$ "

      if [ "x$SHLVL" != "x1" ]; then # We're not a login shell
            for i in /etc/profile.d/*.sh; do
                if [ -r "$i" ]; then
                    . $i
                fi
            done
      fi
    fi
    # vim:ts=4:sw=4
```

As with the first version of /etc/bashrc, this file is used only for bash-specific functions, and the file contains a commented-out line that directs the reader to /etc/profile for general environment settings. In particular, this file is primarily concerned with the type of environment in this particular shell iteration, so that appropriate prompts and functions are available to the user. The file responds differently to interactive and non-interactive (that is, it is invoked as a dumb terminal) shells.

Personal Run Control Files

The shell also parses personal run control files after it is invoked. However, not every user has a personal run control file that defines additional configurations for her individual shell environment. For example, if you're looking for a personal run control file defined in the table at the beginning of this section and you can't find it, it may not exist. Such files are not created until they are needed. Common settings in personal run control files include more entries in the PATH variable's value, preferred terminal settings and colors, font sizes, aliases, and so forth.

Environment Variables

As explained at the beginning of this chapter, environment variables can be used to configure almost every element of a given shell's behavior. Whether you configure a great number of variables by hand or let the graphical configuration tools of your desktop interface define variable values for you, you probably have a lengthy listing of variables with settings specific to your user account.

You can see the variables defined in any shell on your system with the set command. Simply type **set** at the command prompt and press **Enter** to see output that lists all the variables currently defined on your system and their values. If a particular variable is not listed in the output, it just has not yet been defined. Assign a value, and the variable will appear in your next output from set.

The output from set *shows you the values of all environment variables defined in the current shell: the values from* /etc/profile, *the values from your personal* ~/.profile *configuration file, any variables you or other users have defined by hand, and any variables defined by a program as it operates.*

To illustrate the different kinds of variables that Unix shells use, the following sections show the `set` command issued in three shells: tcsh, bash, and zsh. As you look at the output from each command, you can see the differences among these shells and their emphasis on configuration through environment variables.

Tcsh Environment Variables

As you can tell from the output, the following tcsh session is running on a Mac OS X machine. Mac OS X is based on FreeBSD, and you might be surprised at the Unix experience you can get in a Terminal window! The variables set for tcsh here are quite limited; the `PATH` is short, the prompt is generic, and there aren't too many unusual variables shown in the output:

```
% set

addsuffix
argv    ()
cwd     /Users/joe
dirstack        /Users/joe
echo_style      bsd
edit
gid     20
group   staff
history 100
home    /Users/joe
killring        30
loginsh
owd
path    (/bin /sbin /usr/bin /usr/sbin)
prompt  [%m:%c3] %n%#
prompt2 %R?
prompt3 CORRECT>%R (y|n|e|a)?
promptchars     %#
shell   /bin/tcsh
shlvl   1
status  0
tcsh    6.12.00
term    xterm-color
tty     ttyp1
uid     501
user    joe
version tcsh 6.12.00 (Astron) 2002-07-23 (powerpc-apple-darwin)
  options 8b,nls,dl,al,kan,sm,rh,color,dspm,filec
```

You can also use the `setenv` command under tcsh to define environment variables.

Bash Environment Variables

Here is a selection from the environment variables set for bash on the same machine. Note that the output is longer, showing that bash has more bash-specific variables defined in this installation (the `/etc/profile` file is the same for both the tcsh and the bash outputs shown in these examples).

```
$ set
BASH=/bin/bash
BASH_VERSINFO=([0]="2" [1]="05b" [2]="0" [3]="1" [4]="release" [5]="powerpc-apple-
darwin7.0")
BASH_VERSION='2.05b.0(1)-release'
COLUMNS=80
DIRSTACK=()
EUID=501
GROUP=staff
GROUPS=()
HISTFILE=/Users/joe/.bash_history
HISTFILESIZE=500
HISTSIZE=500
HOME=/Users/joe
HOST=Joseph-Merlinos-Computer.local
HOSTNAME=Joseph-Merlinos-Computer.local
HOSTTYPE=powermac
IFS=$' \t\n'
LINES=24
LOGNAME=joe
MACHTYPE=powerpc
MAILCHECK=60
```

Zsh Environment Variables

Finally, the Z shell environment variables defined on a Red Hat Linux machine are:

```
$ set
BASH=/bin/bash
BASH_ENV=/home/joe/.bashrc
BASH_VERSINFO=([0]="2" [1]="04" [2]="21" [3]="1" [4]="release" [5]="i386-redhat-
linux-gnu")
BASH_VERSION='2.04.21(1)-release'
COLORS=/etc/DIR_COLORS
COLUMNS=80
DIRSTACK=()
EUID=501
GROUPS=()
HISTFILE=/home/joe/.bash_history
HISTFILESIZE=1000
HISTSIZE=1000
HOME=/home/joe
HOSTNAME=surimi.nigiri.org
HOSTTYPE=i386
IFS='
'
INPUTRC=/etc/inputrc
LANG=en_US
LESSOPEN='|/usr/bin/lesspipe.sh %s'
LINES=24
```

The complete Z shell output is much longer than that from tcsh or bash. As mentioned earlier, Z shell is a feature-heavy shell environment with a vast amount of configurability. That level of flexibility is reflected in the length of the variable listing.

Aliases

A great way of customizing your working environment is the *alias*. An alias is simply a way of substituting one term for another. Aliases are created, unsurprising, with the `alias` command.

For example, if you are prone to making typographical errors, you might want to require a confirmation prompt before deleting files. You can do that by using the command `rm -i`. However, if you've conditioned yourself to use the `rm` command without the `-i` flag and you find yourself deleting files that needed to be saved, you might create an alias to stop the problem. You can do this by aliasing the `rm` command to the string `rm -i`. The new function can be invoked by typing the regular `rm` command.

To create an alias, use this format:

```
alias rm = "rm -i"
```

The general syntax is:

```
alias command = string
```

If you do this from the command line, the alias will be available only in the current iteration of the shell. That is, you will lose the alias if you start a new shell or when you log out. To have the alias always available to you, place the command in your personal shell configuration file.

Aliases function differently in C shell variants than in Bourne variants. For example, the preceding alias command would be issued as ***alias rm 'rm -i'****, which uses single quotes and dispenses with the equal sign, in C shells. Consult your shell documentation if you're having trouble setting aliases.*

Options

Not all shell functions need to run all the time. If your machine's memory is limited, you may want to turn off some of the optional shell elements to streamline the process. Different shells have different options, but all are invoked by issuing the shell command with the added option, as in:

```
shellname -option
```

The following table shows some selected options found in popular shells. You can learn more about the specific options available for your chosen shell by consulting the shell's manual page (found by typing **man *shellname*** at the command prompt).

Shell	Option	Function
bash	`-norc`	The `.bashrc` file will not be read when the shell starts or a user logs in.
	`-rcfile` *`filename`*	Another specified file will be read instead of `.bashrc` at login.

Table continued on following page

Shell	Option	Function
	`-nolineediting`	The command-line editing feature will not function during this session.
	`-posix`	Only functions that comply with the POSIX standard will function during this session.
csh/tcsh	`-e`	The shell exits if a command causes an error.
	`-f`	The shell starts without reading `.cshrc` or `.tcshrc`.
	`-s`	Take commands from the standard input only.
	`-t`	Execute a single command and then exit the shell.
ksh	`-n`	Parse commands (read and check for syntactical errors) but do not execute them.
	`-f`	Disable filename expansion (also known as *globbing*).
	`-r`	Start the shell in restricted mode, which does not permit changing working directory, redirecting output, or changing basic variable values.
	`-C`	Prevents use of the > redirection operator to overwrite existing files.
zsh	`-c`	Takes an argument to the `zsh` command as the first command to execute, rather than waiting for input once the shell has booted.
	`-v`	Verbose option (found in most shells) that prints commands to the standard output while they are processing.

Dynamic Shared Library Paths

As a programmer, you will almost certainly need to use some of the standard libraries that have been built by others over the years. These libraries contain functions that have become standard for programmers to use in designing their own code. On most Unix systems, these libraries are included as part of the basic installation. Indeed, much of Unix itself is built around code that depends on library functions.

This being the case, you must be able to locate libraries already installed on the system and to make your own libraries available for programs running outside your personal account. On GNU-based systems, there are a few configuration files that contain lists of directories to be searched for libraries, functioning like a library-specific version of the `PATH` variable. Most commonly (on GNU/Linux systems, anyway) the file is located at `/etc/ld.so.conf`. FreeBSD systems may have it under `/var/run/ls.so.hints` and `/var/run/ld-elf.so/hints`.

Apple's Mac OS X, although FreeBSD-based, does not use these files.

LD_LIBRARY_PATH

Should you want to use a nonstandard location for a library file, `LD-LIBRARY_PATH` is the appropriate environment variable to use. It works much the same way as `PATH`, taking a colon-separated list of directories as its value. This variable is evaluated before the various configuration files are read; if any libraries with identical names exist in more than one directory, the one in `LD_LIBRARY_PATH` takes precedence over the one named in the configuration file.

> `LD_LIBRARY_PATH` *does not work on all Unix systems. It works on GNU-derived systems and on FreeBSD, but on HP-UX, the function is served by the* `SHLIB_PATH` *variable. On AIX, it's* `LIBPATH`.

A number of commentators regard the `LD_LIBRARY_PATH` variable and its analogs as bad things, at least as commonly implemented. The reasons for this generally revolve around security issues and the fact that `LD_LIBRARY_PATH` can cause confusion if not handled properly. To get a sense of this debate before you decide whether to implement this variable, visit `www.visi.com/~barr/ldpath.html`.

Despite the legitimate security concerns, there are valid uses for this variable. The most common reason to use `LD_LIBRARY_PATH` is for testing. Suppose that you're working on a program called myprog, which uses the `libmyprog` library. You have a working version of `mylib` installed at `/usr/lib/libmyprog.so.3.`, but you want to test your program against a new version of the library. You might install the new library at `/usr/lib/test/libmyprog.so.3.` and set `LD_LIBRARY_PATH` to have the value `/usr/lib/test/`. When you run the program, the new version of the library is loaded instead of the old one. After you have finished testing, you can reset the variable to a null value, assign a new version number to the library, and recompile the program with instructions to link to the new version.

LD_DEBUG

Another useful environment variable is `LD_DEBUG`. This variable causes the C loader to print out verbose information about what it's doing. The variable takes several options as values, which can be seen by setting the value of the variable to `help` and then running a program. Programmers will find the `files` and `libs` options particularly helpful because they show the libraries accessed during the debug process. For example:

```
$ export LD_DEBUG=help
$ ls
Valid options for the LD_DEBUG environment variable are:

  bindings   display information about symbol binding
  files      display processing of files and libraries
  help       display this help message and exit
  libs       display library search paths
  reloc      display relocation processing
  statistics display relocation statistics
  symbols    display symbol table processing
  versions   display version dependencies

To direct the debugging output into a file instead of standard output
a filename can be specified using the LD_DEBUG_OUTPUT environment variable.
$
```

Summary

After you've installed a version of Unix and gotten everything in working order, it's time to configure your installation so that it suits your needs. Unix is an incredibly flexible operating system, and almost every element of the user experience is configurable. One of the basic user configurations involves selecting a shell environment, which acts as a translator between your input and the operating system's kernel. You choose a shell and then configure it to your taste with multiple tools.

The basic steps in configuring the user environment to your liking are these:

- Review the shells already installed on your system and decide whether one is sufficient or whether you need to download and install new packages.
- Read the documentation for your new shell. Shells tend to be documented exhaustively, from the basic manual pages to thick books at your local computer bookstore. It's usually sufficient to start with the man pages and some Web searching, but if you find yourself intrigued by subtle configurations or shell scripting, read further in this book or pick up something devoted solely to your shell of choice.
- Review the configuration files established by default when the shell was installed. Is the `/etc/profile` file sufficiently personalized? Remember that you need to be logged in as root to edit global configuration files.
- Configure your prompt so that it's informative and easy to understand.

Exercises

1. Edit the shell prompt to display the date and your user ID.
2. You have installed a new program on your machine, but when you type the command, the program does not run. What is the most likely problem?
3. Assume that you want the changes made in Exercise 1 to be permanent. How do you accomplish this?

Unix Commands In-Depth

Think back to your first computer. Was it a Macintosh? A PC running some version of Windows? If your computing life started in the world of graphical interfaces, you may find Unix to be somewhat bewildering. However, if you can remember writing tiny BASIC programs on a Commodore 64 or an Amiga, you might think that Unix is a welcome throwback to the days when the monitor showed nothing but a command prompt.

Long before there were any such things as computer desktops, windows, icons, or mice, there were text-based terminals and command lines. In fact, Unix was the first operating system that was machine-independent — before Unix, each machine needed its own personalized operating system that handled its particular mechanical quirks. Imagine how hard it must have been to develop a common operating system in the days before mass-produced computers! Since its earliest days, Unix has primarily used a command-line interface: a simple prompt, followed by a cursor, using only text. In this kind of environment, there is only one mode of interacting with the machine, and that's via commands.

Of course, Unix machines now offer graphical interfaces. Under some Unix variations, the graphical interface is the default user environment. However, you can always work in a text-only mode on a Unix machine. In fact, should there be a malfunction or a crash, the text-only environment may be the only one available to you.

Commands are executable programs. Sometimes they are stand-alone programs, and sometimes they are functions that are built into the shell. In either case, a command enables the user to request some sort of behavior from the machine. That behavior can be as simple as listing the contents of a directory or as complex as running a long chain of scripts that set the basic parameters within which the machine will run. Although you've used some of these commands already in the first few chapters of this book, this chapter delves into the concept of Unix commands and shows you the basic administrative commands that you'll use frequently. You'll also see some ways to combine commands for output of greater complexity and interest. You'll revisit some of these commands in later chapters, where you'll have more opportunity to try them out.

Anatomy of a Command

A Unix command can be broken down into two parts: the command itself and the arguments appended to it. Most command names are the same as the string of letters that invokes that operation. For example, the `ls` command is used to list the contents of a directory. If you type **ls** at the command prompt, the contents of the working directory (that is, the directory in which you are currently located) print to the screen:

```
$ ls
Games Mail resume.txt
```

Whatever happens when you issue the command by itself at the prompt is called the command's *default behavior*. Commands are far more powerful than the default behavior might imply, however. With the use of arguments, you can influence the behavior or output of the command. An argument adds additional information that changes the way in which the command executes. Consider the command:

```
ls /etc
```

Here, the command itself is `ls`. The added `/etc` portion is an argument that changes the direction of the command, which will now print the contents of the `/etc` directory. On a Linux system, the output might look like this:

```
$ ls /etc
a2ps.cfg        gshadow                makedev.d         rc6.d
a2ps-site.cfg   gshadow-               man.config        rc.d
adjtime         gtk                    mc.global         rc.local
alchemist       host.conf              mesa.conf         rc.sysinit
aliases         HOSTNAME               mime-magic        redhat-release
aliases.db      hosts                  mime-magic.dat    resolv.conf
anacrontab      hosts.allow            mime.types        rmt
at.deny         hosts.deny             minicom.users     rpc
auto.master     hotplug                modules.conf      rpm
auto.misc       identd.conf            modules.conf~     samba
bashrc          im                     modules.devfs     screenrc
CORBA           im_palette.pal         motd              securetty
cron.d          im_palette-small.pal   mtab              security
cron.daily      im_palette-tiny.pal    nmh               sendmail.cf
cron.hourly     imrc                   nscd.conf         sendmail.cf.rpmsave
cron.monthly    info-dir               nsswitch.conf     services
crontab         init.d                 openldap          sgml
cron.weekly     initlog.conf           opt               shadow
csh.cshrc       inittab                pam.d             shadow-
csh.login       inputrc                paper.config      shells
default         ioctl.save             passwd            skel
devfsd.conf     iproute2               passwd-           smrsh
dhcpc           isdn                   pbm2ppa.conf      snmp
dhcpcd          issue                  pine.conf         sound
DIR_COLORS      issue.net              pine.conf.fixed   ssh
dumpdates       krb5.conf              pnm2ppa.conf      sudoers
esd.conf        ldap.conf              ppp               sysconfig
exports         ld.so.cache            printcap          sysctl.conf
fdprm           ld.so.conf             printcap.local    syslog.conf
filesystems     lilo.conf              printcap.old      termcap
```

```
fstab           localtime        profile        updatedb.conf
fstab.REVOKE    login.defs       profile.d      vfontcap
ftpaccess       logrotate.conf   protocols      wgetrc
ftpconversions  logrotate.d      pwdb.conf      X11
ftpgroups       lpd.conf         rc             xinetd.conf
ftphosts        lpd.perms        rc0.d          xinetd.d
ftpusers        ltrace.conf      rc1.d          yp.conf
gnome           lynx.cfg         rc2.d          ypserv.conf
gpm-root.conf   mail             rc3.d
group           mailcap          rc4.d
group-          mail.rc          rc5.d
```

Using this argument made it possible for the user `ned` to view the contents of `/etc` without leaving his home directory (see the command prompt in the first line of the code block, which indicates the working directory).

Chapter 5 explains how to show the working directory in your command prompt.

This type of argument is known as a *target* because it provides a target location for the command to work upon. There are other kinds of arguments as well, known variously as options, switches, or flags. These tend to be specific to a given command, and information about the arguments that work with a specific command can be found on that command's manual page. Learn more about man pages in the next section of this chapter, "Finding Information about Commands," and in Chapter 2.

Arguments can influence the form of a command's output as well as its operation. For example, if you were to issue the preceding command as:

```
ls -l /etc
```

the `ls` command would show the directory listing for `/etc` in long format, which provides additional information about the files being listed. Here is partial output for the `ls -l /etc` command:

```
$ ls -l /etc
total 1780
-rw-r--r--    1 root      root          15221 Feb 28  2001 a2ps.cfg
-rw-r--r--    1 root      root           2561 Feb 28  2001 a2ps-site.cfg
-rw-r--r--    1 root      root             47 Dec 28  2001 adjtime
drwxr-xr-x    4 root      root           4096 Oct  1  2001 alchemist
-rw-r--r--    1 root      root           1048 Mar  3  2001 aliases
-rw-r--r--    1 root      root          12288 Sep  8  2003 aliases.db
-rw-r--r--    1 root      root            370 Apr  3  2001 anacrontab
-rw-------    1 root      root              1 Apr  4  2001 at.deny
-rw-r--r--    1 root      root            210 Mar  3  2001 auto.master
-rw-r--r--    1 root      root            574 Mar  3  2001 auto.misc
-rw-r--r--    1 root      root            823 Feb 28  2001 bashrc
drwxr-xr-x    3 root      root           4096 Apr  7  2001 CORBA
drwxr-xr-x    2 root      root           4096 Mar  8  2001 cron.d
drwxr-xr-x    2 root      root           4096 Oct  1  2001 cron.daily
drwxr-xr-x    2 root      root           4096 Oct  1  2001 cron.hourly
drwxr-xr-x    2 root      root           4096 Oct  1  2001 cron.monthly
-rw-r--r--    1 root      root            255 Feb 27  2001 crontab
drwxr-xr-x    2 root      root           4096 Oct  1  2001 cron.weekly
```

```
-rw-r--r--    1 root     root          380 Jul 25  2000 csh.cshrc
-rw-r--r--    1 root     root          517 Mar 27  2001 csh.login
drwxr-x---    2 root     root         4096 Oct  1  2001 default
```

See how much more information the `-l` argument provides? The lengthy output now shows you a lot of useful data, including each file's permissions, owner, and creation date.

Flags are usually—but not always—preceded by a dash, or hyphen. The `tar` command, for example, takes its flags without a prepended dash. Multiple flags can be used simultaneously, and there is generally some flexibility as to how they are formatted. Just be careful that you don't use so many arguments that the output is difficult to understand.

In addition to accepting multiple arguments at one time, some commands require multiple targets. Consider the `cp` command, which makes a copy of a specified file. To use it, you must define both the file being copied and the file that is the copy. For example, the command

```
cp /etc/profile /home/joe/profile
```

makes a copy of the `/etc/profile` file and names it `/home/joe/profile`. In this format, `/etc/profile` is known as the *source*, and `/home/joe/profile` is known as the *destination*. Not all commands require both a source and a destination, and, in some programs, leaving out one or the other might cause the command to assume a source or destination. Always make sure you understand the default behavior of a command before you use it.

Try It Out — Use Arguments to `ls`

Try this exercise to understand the flexibility of the Unix command syntax. Using the `ls` command previously described, add the `-a` option to include hidden files in the directory listing; hidden files are those with filenames that begin with a dot, as in `.bashrc`.

1. At the command prompt, issue the command:

   ```
   ls -l -a /etc
   ```

2. Issue the command:

   ```
   ls -la /etc
   ```

3. Compare the output of the two commands. They are the same.

How It Works

A command produces the same output whether its arguments are combined or added independently.

Finding Information about Commands

Because Unix commands can be so complex, it's good that there is a source of information already on your computer to help you navigate the labyrinth of command syntax and arguments. Unix offers several ways to access information about commands, from simply identifying related files to lengthy informational files.

In this section, you learn three of the most important commands for learning more about the programs on your machine.

If you don't have a particular manual page installed on your machine, you may find it in the collection at `http://unixhelp.ed.ac.uk/alphabetical`.

man

As you learned in Chapter 2, Unix manual pages (or man pages) are the best way to learn about any given command. Find a particular manual page with the command `man` *`commandname`*. Manual pages may be brief, like this one:

```
$ man apropos
apropos(1)                                                apropos(1)

NAME
       apropos - search the whatis database for strings

SYNOPSIS
       apropos keyword ...

DESCRIPTION
       apropos  searches a set of database files containing short
       descriptions of system commands for keywords and  displays
       the result on the standard output.

SEE ALSO
       whatis(1), man(1).

                           Jan 15, 1991                        1

(END)
```

Other manual pages go on for screen after screen. No matter how long they are, manual pages follow the basic format illustrated in this example. The manual page provides the name, function, syntax, and optional arguments for a given command.

info

Some programmers include an additional set of help documents, known as *info pages*, with their packages or programs. You can access these pages with the `info` command, such as:

```
$ info info
File: info.info,  Node: Top,  Next: Getting Started,  Up: (dir)

Info: An Introduction
*********************

   Info is a program for reading documentation, which you are using now.

   To learn how to use Info, type the command `h'.  It brings you to a
programmed instruction sequence.
```

```
* Menu:

* Getting Started::            Getting started using an Info reader.
* Advanced Info::              Advanced commands within Info.
* Creating an Info File::      How to make your own Info file.


--zz-Info: (info.info.gz)Top, 16 lines --All-----------------------------------
Welcome to Info version 4.0. Type C-h for help, m for menu item.
```

If info pages are not installed on your system, you will not be able to use the `info` *command.*

Info pages are generally found with GNU software or software produced by the Free Software Foundation. While programmers almost always create basic man pages for their programs, not everyone creates the more detailed info pages. It's worth trying the `info` command, though, to see if an info page exists for the program you want to learn more about.

Be aware that `info` *often triggers the Emacs text editor to display the info pages. If you're not familiar with Emacs, it might be quite confusing to navigate through the pages. You can always exit the Emacs editor by typing* ***C x C c****. If that doesn't work, just press the* ***Q*** *key and you should exit the info viewer.*

apropos

Looking for a specific file or a manual page that doesn't come up when you think you've typed the right command name? The `apropos` command may be useful to you. It is used with keywords to find related files. Its syntax is simple—just issue the command:

```
apropos keyword
```

Here's another example:

```
$ apropos gzip
gunzip [gzip]          (1)   - compress or expand files
gzip                   (1)   - compress or expand files
zcat [gzip]            (1)   - compress or expand files
zforce                 (1)   - force a '.gz' extension on all gzip files
```

The `apropos` output does not tell you where the files are stored in the file system, but it's a good way to find out whether particular packages or commands are installed on your machine before you go searching for them. To find one of these packages, use the `whereis` command, as in `whereis gunzip`. You will see output like this:

```
$ whereis gunzip
/usr/gunzip   /usr/bin/gunzip   /usr/share/man/man1/gunzip.1.gz
```

If `apropos` *does not work for you, you may need to issue the command* `catman -w`*. When that command has completed, try using* `apropos` *again.*

Command Modification

Unix commands are not limited to the functions performed when the command name is typed at the prompt. You can use a number of different tools to enhance or alter the function of a command, or to manage the command's output. This section explores some of the most popular ways to modify Unix commands.

Metacharacters

One of the more interesting aspects of using a command-line interface is the capability to use special characters called *metacharacters* to alter a command's behavior. These characters are not part of the commands themselves but are features of the shell that enable the user to create complex behaviors.

The syntax presented here is based on the Bourne and Bourne-derived shells. Most of the features described in this section are basic to Unix but may be implemented differently in different shells. If you're having trouble with metacharacters, make sure you check your shell's documentation to verify the appropriate syntax.

The most popular metacharacters are known as *wildcards*. These are special characters that can be used to match multiple files at the same time, increasing the likelihood that a command will find the desired filename or target on the first try. There are three wildcards that are most often used:

- `?` matches any one character in a filename.
- `*` matches any character or characters in a filename.
- `[ ]` matches one of the characters included inside the `[ ]` symbols.

You can use these wildcards in combination with a command to locate multiple files, or to find a file when you can't quite remember its full name. For example, suppose that the working directory contains the files:

```
date help1 help2 help3 myprog.f myprog.o
```

You can add wildcards to the target argument of the `ls` command to find any or all of these files in a single search. The following table shows the various combinations of files that would display, depending on the wildcard used.

Argument + Wildcard	Files Matched
`help?`	help1 help2 help3
`myprog.[fo]`	myprog.f myprog.o
`*`	date help1 help2 help3 myprog.f myprog.o
`*.f`	myprog.f
`help*`	help1 help2 help3

Wildcards are also useful when you are looking for files of a particular type. Many who work in *heterogeneous environments* (that is, a network with Unix, Windows, and Macintosh machines) transfer files created with Microsoft Office among multiple machines on the network. Use wildcards to identify all the Word files in the working directory with the following command:

```
ls *.doc
```

Others who work in a heterogeneous environment use pure text files as a common language readable on all platforms in all sorts of text editors and word processors. If all the text files in the working directory are identified with the suffix `.txt`, you could list only those files with the command:

```
ls *.txt
```

If you tend to use both `.txt` and `.text` as suffixes for text files, wildcards are even more helpful. Issue the command as:

```
ls *.t[ex]*
```

and the output lists all the text files in the directory, regardless of the particular suffix used to name the files.

If you use asterisks as the first or last character in a wildcard search, you might get many more results than you expect because the search would also locate temporary and system files. Should you get such a large number of results that you can't deal with them comfortably, refine your wildcard and redo the search.

Metacharacters are an important aspect of regular expressions. You'll learn more about them in Chapter 8.

Input and Output Redirection

To function, every command needs a source of input and a destination for output. These attributes are programmed into the commands as a default behavior and are known as that command's *standard input* and *standard output*. In the vast majority of cases, the standard input is the keyboard, and the standard output is the screen — specifically, the Terminal window, if you're using a graphical interface.

In some cases, the standard input and output are defined otherwise. If this is the case for your machine, you probably already know it. If you sit down at an unfamiliar machine and it has no keyboard, or the output does not appear on the monitor when you expect it, find the machine's administrator and inquire about the input and output settings. You might be attempting to work on a machine of critical importance that has had its inputs and/or outputs configured to keep stray users from messing things up for everyone.

While changing the standard input and output permanently is possible, it's not usually a good idea. However, you can change the input and output for individual actions. This is known as *redirection*, and it's a great way to streamline a sequence of tasks. With redirection, you can force a particular command to take input from a source other than the keyboard, or to put the output somewhere besides the monitor. For example, you might want to set up a program to run without your having to be at the keys to invoke it, and then to dump its output into a text file that you can peruse at your leisure.

Input and output redirection uses the < and > characters to define the temporary input and output sources. Suppose that you want to use `ls` to find the contents of a directory, but you want the output captured in a text file rather than printing to the screen. To do so, create a file named `lsoutput` and then issue the command:

```
ls > lsoutput
```

The > character takes the output of `ls`, which would normally go to the screen, and writes it to the `lsoutput` file. (If the specified file does not already exist, the > operator will create it.)

Be careful when you redirect output. If, for example, the preceding command were issued twice, the second command would overwrite the contents of the `lsoutput` file and destroy the previous data. If you want to preserve the previous data, use the >> operator, which appends the new data to the end of the file. If the specified file doesn't exist, or is empty, >> acts just like >. Depending on your typing skill, it may be safer to build the habit of using >>.

In the same way that > redirects the output of a command, < can be used to change the input. This function is normally used to build a chain of commands, so that the output of Command A is used as the input for Command B. It's a great way to automate administrative functions. For example, assume that you want to alphabetize a list of terms contained in a file called `terms`. You can use the `sort` command in combination with the input redirection operator <, as in:

```
sort < terms
```

In this instance, the `sort` command will take its input from the `terms` file rather than from the standard input.

Input and output redirection can also be combined. For example, the command

```
sort < terms > terms-alpha
```

will sort the items in the `terms` file and then send the output of the sort into a new file called `terms-alpha`. As you can see, the complexity of input and output redirection is limited only by the basic logic of the operation.

A handy tool for programmers, the output redirection operator can be used to redirect only the error messages produced by a command. This is done by adding a 2 (in the Bourne-derived shells) to the operator.

The Bourne shells use 0, 1, and 2 as file descriptors for output redirection; those readers familiar with C programming will recognize 0 as stdin (standard input), 1 as stdout (standard output), and 2 as stderr (standard error).

If you're working on a program called myprog., for example, and you want to see the error messages that occur when you run the program, you can issue the following command in your working directory:

```
myprog 2> errfile
```

You'd run the program by typing its name at the command prompt, and then open the `errfile` file in a text editor to see the error messages generated by myprog. If `errfile` doesn't exist, the program generated no errors.

Pipes

A *pipe* is an operator that combines input and output redirection so that the output of one command is immediately used as the input for another. The pipe is represented by the vertical line character (|), which is usually a shift character located somewhere near the Return or Enter key on your keyboard. Suppose you want to list the contents of a directory, but the directory's listing is so long that many of the entries scrolled off the screen before you can read them. A pipe gives you a simple way to display the output one page at a time, with the following command:

```
$ ls -l /etc | more
total 1780
-rw-r--r--    1 root     root        15221 Feb 28  2001 a2ps.cfg
-rw-r--r--    1 root     root         2561 Feb 28  2001 a2ps-site.cfg
-rw-r--r--    1 root     root           47 Dec 28  2001 adjtime
drwxr-xr-x    4 root     root         4096 Oct  1  2001 alchemist
-rw-r--r--    1 root     root         1048 Mar  3  2001 aliases
-rw-r--r--    1 root     root        12288 Sep  8  2003 aliases.db
-rw-r--r--    1 root     root          370 Apr  3  2001 anacrontab
-rw-------    1 root     root            1 Apr  4  2001 at.deny
-rw-r--r--    1 root     root          210 Mar  3  2001 auto.master
-rw-r--r--    1 root     root          574 Mar  3  2001 auto.misc
-rw-r--r--    1 root     root          823 Feb 28  2001 bashrc
drwxr-xr-x    3 root     root         4096 Apr  7  2001 CORBA
drwxr-xr-x    2 root     root         4096 Mar  8  2001 cron.d
drwxr-xr-x    2 root     root         4096 Oct  1  2001 cron.daily
drwxr-xr-x    2 root     root         4096 Oct  1  2001 cron.hourly
drwxr-xr-x    2 root     root         4096 Oct  1  2001 cron.monthly
-rw-r--r--    1 root     root          255 Feb 27  2001 crontab
drwxr-xr-x    2 root     root         4096 Oct  1  2001 cron.weekly
-rw-r--r--    1 root     root          380 Jul 25  2000 csh.cshrc
-rw-r--r--    1 root     root          517 Mar 27  2001 csh.login
drwxr-x---    2 root     root         4096 Oct  1  2001 default
--More--
```

Here's the same output from `ls -l /etc` that you saw earlier in this chapter, but this time it's limited to a single screen's worth of files because the output is piped through the `more` command. (Learn more about `more` in the "Common File Manipulation Commands" section later in this chapter.)

> *Pipes, redirection, and all the other features in this section can be combined in near-infinite combinations to create complex chains of commands. For example, the command*
>
> ```
> sort < terms > terms-alpha | mail fred
> ```
>
> *would perform the sort operation described previously, and then mail the contents of the* `terms-alpha` *file to a user named fred. The only limitation to these combinations is the user's ingenuity.*

Command Substitution

Command substitution is yet another way of using the output of one command as an argument to another. It is a more complex operation than simply piping the output through a second command, but it can be used to create command strings of some sophistication. Consider the command:

```
ls $(pwd)
```

In this case, the command pwd is the first command to run; it outputs the name of the working directory. Its value is sent as an argument for the ls command. The output returned by this command would be the directory listing for the current working directory.

The astute reader will note that this example has much the same effect as the ls *command itself, but it is a useful illustration of command substitution in operation.*

Yes, this command has much the same effect as:

```
pwd | ls
```

The output is the same, but there are some differences in the behind-the-scenes way that it's carried out. The construction using the $ operator is distinctive in that the command in parentheses is executed in a *subshell* — that is, a new instance of the shell is spawned, the command is evaluated, the subshell closes, and the result is returned to the original shell.

If you have special environment conditions set up that might not transfer to a subshell (a manually set PATH *value, for example), the subshell might not inherit this condition. In such a case, the command may fail.*

Instead of using the $() construction, you can also use backticks. For example,

```
ls `pwd`
```

accomplishes exactly the same thing as ls $(pwd). Another alternative is to use curly braces, as in:

```
ls ${pwd}
```

The difference here is that the command in the curly braces is executed in the current shell, and no subshell process is spawned. (Curly braces do not work on all Unix variants.)

Working with Files and Directories

The most common Unix commands are those used to manage files and directories. You might find yourself issuing one of these commands hundreds of times a day as you go about your business. In this section, you learn the two most popular file management commands and the various arguments that go along with them.

ls

Earlier in this chapter, you learned to use the ls command to list the contents of a directory. The output of ls can be simple or extremely lengthy and complex. Both results are valuable, depending on the kind of information you need about directory contents. The ls command takes the syntax:

```
ls [options] [directory]
```

If you don't specify a directory, ls assumes that you want to know about the contents of the current working directory. You can use ls to get information about any directory on the system, however, as long as its permissions allow you to read the contents. (Permissions are discussed later in this chapter.)

The `ls` command offers a number of arguments that can shape the output to provide the information you need. The following table shows some of the most commonly used options. If these are not the arguments you need, consult the `ls` manual page with the command `man ls`.

Argument	Function
`-l`	Lists directory contents in long format, which shows individual file size, permissions, and other data.
`-t`	Lists directory contents sorted by the timestamp (time of the last modification).
`-a`	Lists all directory contents, including hidden files whose name begins with the `.` character.
`-i`	Lists directory contents including inode or disk index number.
`-R`	Lists directory contents including all subdirectories and their contents.

cd

The `cd` command is something that you will use frequently. It's the command used to move through the file system. It takes the syntax:

```
cd directory
```

If you issue the command without a directory destination, `cd` automatically moves you to your home directory. This is particularly useful when you've been exploring the file system and find yourself nested deep within another directory structure; just type `cd` at the command prompt and you'll return to familiar ground immediately.

Common File Manipulation Commands

After you've found the file you're looking for, there are a number of things you can do to it. This section introduces several commands used to manipulate individual files, whether they are programs, documents, or other elements treated as files by the Unix operating system.

The commands available to you depend on the Unix distribution you are using, as well as the installation choices made by your system administrator.

cat

If you want to see the contents of a given file, there's no easier way than the `cat` command, which prints the contents of a specified file to the standard output, usually the monitor. It takes the following syntax:

```
cat [options] file(s)
```

If you simply issue the command as `cat filename`, the contents print to the screen, scrolling if the file is longer than the screen length. Use a pipe to send the output through `more` or `less` (discussed in the following section) if it is too long to view in one screen. The following table shows a number of options for the `cat` command.

Argument	Function
-n	Numbers the output's lines
-E	Shows a $ character at the end of each line
-s	Collapses sequential blank lines into one blank line
-t	Displays nonprinting tabs as ^I
-v	Shows all nonprinting characters

One particularly helpful use of the `cat` command is to concatenate multiple files into one larger new file, making it easier to read the content of these files at one time. Do this with the command:

```
cat file1 file2 file3 >> newfile
```

Note the use of the redirection operator >> in this command.

more/less

The `more` and `less` commands are virtually identical. They are used to break up command output or file contents into single-screen chunks so that you can read the contents more easily. Both `more` and `less` can move forward through a file, although only `less` can be used to move backward. The commands take the same syntax:

```
more filename
less filename
```

When you have finished viewing the current screen of output, press the spacebar to advance to the next screen. If you are using `less` to view the output or file, you can use the B key to move back one screen.

If you've found the information you're looking for but you haven't scrolled through the entire file yet, just press Q in either `more` *or* `less`*. You'll return to the command prompt.*

mv

The `mv` command is used to move a file from one location to another. It takes the syntax:

```
mv old new
```

where *`old`* is the current name of the file to be moved to the location defined as *`new`*. If the value of *`new`* is simply a new filename, the file is renamed and remains in the current directory. If the value of *`new`* is a new directory location, the file is moved to the new location with the existing filename. If the value of *`old`* is a directory, the entire directory and its contents will be moved to the location specified as *`new`*.

Depending on the settings on your system, if `new` *is an existing file or directory, its contents will be overwritten by the contents of* `old`*. Be careful when reusing file and directory names.*

cp

Like the `mv` command, `cp` is used to create new files or move the content of files to another location. Unlike `mv`, however, `cp` leaves the original file intact at its original location. `cp` uses the syntax

```
cp file1 file2
```

where *`file1`* is the original file and *`file2`* is the destination file. If you use the name of an existing file as the destination value, `cp` overwrites that file's contents with the contents of *`file1`*.

rm

The `rm` command is used to delete a file. It uses the syntax:

```
rm [options] filename
```

This command can be quite destructive unless you are careful when you issue it, especially if you use wildcards. For example, the command `rm conf*` deletes all files beginning with the characters `conf`, whether you wanted to delete those files or not. The following table shows some common options for `rm`.

Argument	Function
`-i`	Forces interactive mode, prompting you to confirm each deletion
`-r`	Forces recursive mode, deleting all subdirectories and the files they contain
`-f`	Forces force mode, ignoring all warnings (very dangerous)

Be aware that combining certain options—especially the `-r` and `-f` flags—can be dangerous. The command `rm -rf *.*` would remove every single file from your file system if issued from the root directory, or every file from your home directory if issued from there. Don't do this.

touch

The `touch` command is used to update the *timestamp* on the named file. The timestamp shows the last time the file was altered or accessed. `touch` uses the syntax:

```
touch filename
```

If the filename issued as an argument does not exist, `touch` creates it as an empty file.

wc

Use the `wc` command to determine the length of a given file. `wc` uses the syntax:

```
wc [options] filename
```

By default, the output shows the length in words. The following table shows the options available for `wc`.

Argument	Function
`-c`	Shows number of individual characters (bytes) in the specified file
`-l`	Shows number of lines in the specified file
`-L`	Shows the length of the longest line in the specified file

File Ownership and Permissions

One of the distinguishing features of Unix is that it was designed from its earliest days to be a multiuser system. In contrast, it is only in recent years that other operating systems have created true multiuser functionality on a single machine. Because of its multiple-user design, Unix must use mechanisms that enable users to manage their own files without having access to the files of other users. These mechanisms are called *file ownership* and *file permissions*.

File Ownership

Any Unix user can own files. Generally, the files that the user owns are ones that he created, or which were created as a result of some action on his part. The exception to this, of course, is the *superuser*, also known as *root*. The superuser can change the ownership of any file, whether he created it or not, with the `chown` command. For example, if the superuser gives the command

```
chown jane /home/bill/billsfile
```

the ownership of the file `/home/bill/billsfile` is transferred to the user jane. Won't Bill be surprised when that happens?

Username versus UID

By now you're familiar with the idea of a username, the name you use when you log in to a Unix machine. The name is assigned to you by the system administrator (or yourself, if you're your own system administrator). In addition to a username, every user has a numerical ID number known as a user ID or UID, which is how the user is known to the system. Typically, these numbers are assigned automatically, although they can be specified when an account is created. The number itself is arbitrary, even though many systems require that ordinary users have UID numbers above 500.

The superuser always has UID 0.

For purposes other than logging in, the username and UID are basically synonymous. For example, the command

```
chown jane /home/bill/billsfile
```

could just as easily be rendered as

```
chown 503 /home/bill/billsfile
```

assuming that Jane's UID is 503. You don't need to know your UID for normal purposes, but it can come in handy.

Groups

In addition to a UID, you also have at least one group ID, or GID. As with the UID, the operating system uses GIDs rather than the group names to manage groups. Every user belongs to at least one group, and may belong to several more. Groups contain users who share certain permissions for certain activities. You may belong to a group that has the same name as your username. The superuser may add you to other groups depending on the access you need to certain files or directories.

Groups can also own files, and file ownership can be transferred from one group to another. To do so, use the `chgroup` (change group) command:

```
chgroup groupname filename
```

As with `chown`, you can substitute the GID for the group name.

File Permissions

The concept of file permissions is related to the concept of file ownership. As the owner of a file, a user has a right to decide who can access a file, and what kind of access others can have. File permissions are somewhat confusing to the Unix novice, but they are a critical part of maintaining a safe and secure machine, so this section reviews what you learned about permissions in Chapter 4.

Permissions should be as restrictive as possible. As long as legitimate users can use the file in intended ways, every other avenue of access should be locked down.

There are three kinds of file permission:

- Read (file can be viewed)
- Write (file can be edited)
- Execute (file can be run as a program)

Likewise, there are three categories of users to whom these permissions can be applied:

- User (owner of that particular file)
- Group (group to which the file is assigned)
- All (all users and groups)

When you define permissions for a given file, you must assign a type of permission to each category of users. If you are writing a program, you probably want to give yourself read, write, and execute permission. If you are working with a team, you might want to have your system administrator create a group for the team. You can then give the team read and execute permissions so they can test your program and make suggestions but not be able to edit the file. Without write permission for the team, changes must go through you.

If you're going to create a group to grant read and execute permissions to a specific set of users, be sure to deny the same permissions to all users not in the group.

How to Read a Permissions List

How do you tell what permissions a file has? Simple, just use the `ls -l` command, and the permission information is printed as part of a directory listing. For example, here's a partial listing of the `/etc` directory shown earlier in the chapter (from left to right, the columns show file permissions, UID, username, group name, file size, timestamp, and filename):

```
-rw-r--r--    1 root     root         1048 Mar  3  2001 aliases
-rw-r--r--    1 root     root        12288 Sep  8  2003 aliases.db
-rw-r--r--    1 root     root          370 Apr  3  2001 anacrontab
-rw-------    1 root     root            1 Apr  4  2001 at.deny
```

The string of characters on the left displays all the permission information for each file. The permission information consists of nine characters, beginning with the second character from the left. The first three characters represent the permission for the user, the second three for the group, and the final set of three represents permission for all.

```
-rwxrwx---
```

The preceding expression shows that the user and the group have read, write, and execute permission. The string

```
-rw-rw-r--
```

shows that the user and the group have read and write permission, and all other users have only read permission.

Changing Permissions

The permissions on a file can only be changed by the file's owner or the superuser. Permissions are changed using the `chmod` (think "change mode") command. `chmod` can be used in two ways: symbolic or absolute. These methods are discussed in Chapter 4.

umask

When you create a file, it has a default set of permissions. On most systems, any file you create will have read and write permissions for you, and no permissions for your group or other users. Like everything else in Unix, this behavior is configurable.

The default permission scheme is controlled by the `umask` command. Like `chmod`, `umask` takes a numerical value as its argument. Unlike `chmod`, however, the value given to `umask` represents the permissions that are to be *denied*. That is, the `umask` value gives permission to everything except that which is specified.

To put this in concrete terms, suppose that you want to give all newly created files the permission mode 644, which gives the owner read and write permission, and read permission to both group and all as described in Chapter 4. Simply take that number and subtract it from 666, the default octal base for files, to get the proper argument for `umask`:

```
umask 022
```

This command will cause all new files to be created with permission mode 644. The effect of `umask` is limited to the shell in which it's invoked. To make the effect persist, put it in your `.profile` file.

Executable Files

As mentioned earlier, programs are just files that are executable. It may seem an obvious point, but all you really need to do to make a file executable is to give execute permission on the file to anyone who you want to be able to run it. Not to belabor the obvious, but it's very common for people to create a program on a Unix machine, and then wonder why it won't run. Making the file executable is a crucial step in the process.

First, use the `ls -l` command to check the current permissions on the file. If you do not have execute permissions for this file, use `chmod` to change the permissions. Remember, though, that you must be the file's owner to change the file's permissions. If you are not the owner, you must find the file's owner and have that person issue the `chmod` command to give you access.

If you have superuser access, you can force the permissions change without asking the owner. This isn't particularly friendly, though. If you must make these changes, it's a good idea to inform users that you've changed permissions on their files.

If you're still having trouble invoking an executable file, you may have run into another common problem faced by programmers unfamiliar with Unix—an incorrect `PATH` value. Chapter 5 introduced the concept of the `PATH` environment variable. If the directory containing the executable file is not part of your `PATH` variable's value, you must give the full path name of the executable file to run it. Should you want to make the program available to users other than yourself, it may be a good idea to move the executable to a directory that is in the global `PATH` variable's value, as defined by your system administrator. After the `PATH` issues have been resolved, you'll just need to type the program's name at the prompt to run it.

Maintaining File System Quotas

One of the problems that continually confront Unix administrators is that of disk space. Anybody who's owned a computer for any length of time knows how files can proliferate to the point where they eat up all available disk space. As you can probably guess, this problem is multiplied many times on a multi-user system. With multiple users, each user's space-hogging tendencies combine to create one giant disk-space-eating monstrosity. What can you do?

Luckily, there's a built-in solution on most Unix systems: disk quotas. A quota is a limit on the amount of disk space each user is allotted. Most Unix systems have some sort of quota system available, but they differ in their implementations. Should the default quota system on your machine not be sufficient, you can purchase commercial software robust enough for vast numbers of greedy file-swapping users.

The first step in implementing quotas is to enable them for the file system. On most systems, this requires a change to the file system control file (usually `/etc/fstab`). Different systems will have different formats for enabling quotas in this file. Under Linux, for example, the `/etc/fstab` file might look like this:

```
LABEL=/          /            ext3    defaults        1 1
LABEL=/boot      /boot        ext3    defaults        1 2
none             /dev/pts     devpts  gid=5,mode=620  0 0
LABEL=/home      /home        ext3    defaults,usrquota,grpquota 1 2
none             /proc        proc    defaults        0 0
none             /dev/shm     tmpfs   defaults        0 0
```

```
/dev/hda2           swap            swap     defaults          0 0
/dev/cdrom          /mnt/cdrom      udf,iso9660 noauto,owner,kudzu,ro 0 0
/dev/fd0            /mnt/floppy     auto     noauto,owner,kudzu 0 0
```

The `usrquota` and `grpquota` options added to the line for the `/home` file system indicate that quotas are in effect for those directories. Directories without those options do not have quotas enabled.

Other Unix flavors have different formats, so consult your system's documentation to find the correct syntax.

After you've added the quota options to the appropriate directory lines in `/etc/fstab` or made other configurations as required by your system, the file system must be remounted. If your system is a personal computer that only you (or just a few people) are using, you can simply reboot the machine. If you're enabling quotas across a larger network, you may need to manually unmount (`umount` command) and then remount (`mount` command) the file system.

If you have multiple users on your system, you may want to schedule this operation for a low-traffic time, such as late at night. You will also need to kick any logged-in users off the system.

Quotas are now enabled in the defined directories. To get the quotas working, you need to create a quota file in the top-level directory of the file system. The file defines the limits the quotas enforce. As with the `/etc/fstab` file, different flavors of Unix use different methods to do this. Under Linux, you can use the `quotacheck` command:

```
quotacheck -acug /home
```

This command implements four separate arguments:

- `-a`—All mounted local file systems in the `/etc/mtab` file are checked to see if quotas are enabled.
- `-c`—Quota files should be created for each file system with quotas enabled.
- `-u`—`quotacheck` checks for user quotas.
- `-g`—`quotacheck` checks for group quotas.

Under other systems, you may have to create the quota files by hand. A common procedure might look something like this:

```
cd /home
touch quotas
chmod 600 quotas
```

This creates the `quotas` file and makes it writable only by the superuser. Although any user can issue the `chmod` command on files the user account has permissions for, only the superuser can `chmod` files to root level permissions.. Only the root user should be allowed to set quotas on the system.

With the quota files set up, use the `edquota` command to set the quotas. For example, to edit the quota for the user jeff, you'd give the following command:

```
edquota jeff
```

This opens a quota file for the user jeff. The file opens in your text editor (more about text editors in Chapter 7) and looks something like this:

```
Disk quotas for user jeff (uid 506):
Filesystem     blocks        soft        hard      inodes      soft      hard
/dev/hda3      440436           0           0       37418         0         0
```

Blocks show the amount of data in Jeff's account, and inodes show the number of individual files. Replace the zeroes under "soft" and "hard" with the soft and hard limits you want to give this user. A *soft* limit can be exceeded, but the user will get a warning; a *hard* limit cannot be exceeded. Exit the editor, and the user's quota is set.

A block is 512 bytes of data. Be sure to do the math before you set quotas so that you are limiting users to the true amount of disk space you want to allot.

Summary

Whether or not you use a graphical interface for most of your work, you can always manage a Unix machine from the command line. Commands invoke programs that modify elements of the user experience, enable you to work with documents and executable code, and perform administrative tasks. In this chapter, you learned about several command families:

- Commands that find information
- Commands that channel input and output in non-standard ways
- Commands that help you work with the file system
- Commands that change and move existing files
- Commands that define and change file ownership and permissions
- Commands that set and enforce disk quotas

Exercise

Create a command that will list the contents of each subdirectory of the `/home` directory beginning with the letter k, count the number of files found, and save that number in a file called `k-users-files`.

7 Editing Files with Vi

There are many ways to edit files in Unix, including the use of early line-based text editors such as ed (EDitor) and ex (EXtended) and the use of screen-oriented text editors such as Emacs (Editor MACroS) and vi (VIsual editor). Line editors allow you to edit a file only line by line; screen editors enable you to edit lines in context with other lines in the file. Vi is generally considered the de facto standard in Unix editors because:

- It's usually available on any Unix system. Once you have learned how to use it, there is no learning curve when you're working on another Unix system, which allows for faster recovery or adjustments of files.
- Vi implementations are very similar across the board (from Linux, to Mac OS X, to Sun Solaris, and so on).
- It requires very few resources.
- It is more user friendly than ed or ex.

Vi is pronounced "vee eye." There is a popular joke about a newbie (someone new to Unix or to computers in general) asking a more seasoned Unix veteran when the Seven (VII) editor would be coming out because Six (VI) seemed outdated.

Nearly everyone who uses Unix will need to know how to use vi at one time or another, especially in situations with limited resources (where no graphical user interface [GUI] is present or where minimal resources are available). Vi can be intimidating to new users, especially those who are used to graphically oriented word processors. Vi is purely a functional text editor, and no fancy formatting can be accomplished through vi by itself, although you can use it in conjunction with a text formatter such as LaTeX (`http://directory.fsf.org/text/doc/LaTeX.html`).

This chapter teaches you to use vi, from the basics to more advanced text manipulation functions.

Using Vi

When you begin using vi, it can seem to be a cold, unhelpful environment, but once you're familiar with the basics, it's not at all unfriendly. There are several ways to start ("open an instance of") vi, all of which you type in a console window:

Command	Description	Results
`vi`	Start vi without any filename arguments.	Vi starts with an empty palette. You must save to a new file before exiting.
`vi` *`filename`*	1. Use an existing filename as the argument. 2. Use a new filename as the argument (file doesn't exist until saved in vi).	1. The existing file opens in vi. When you save it, the file is updated with the changes you make. 2. When you save this file, you create a new file with the filename specified in the argument.
`vi -R` *`filename`* or `view` *`filename`*	Open the file in read-only mode.	The file is read-only (changes can't be saved); great for practicing your vi commands on a file.

Figure 7-1 shows the editor started with command `vi` *`filename`* (`vi testfile`).

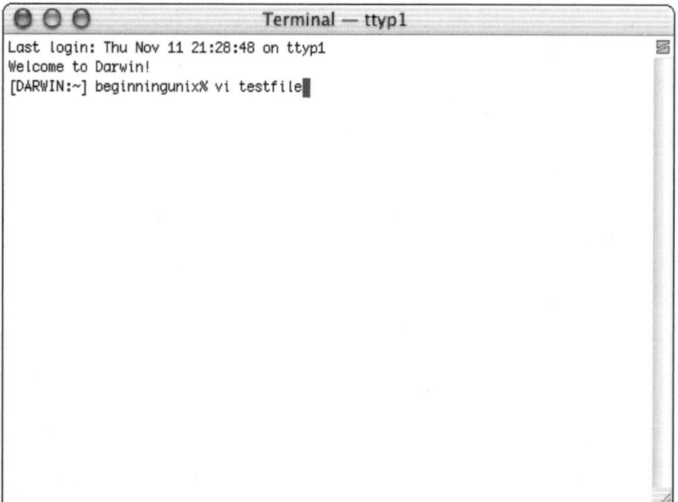

Figure 7-1

Whenever you start vi—whether by itself, with an existing filename, or with a new filename—you begin in command mode. Figure 7-2 shows a new file open in vi.

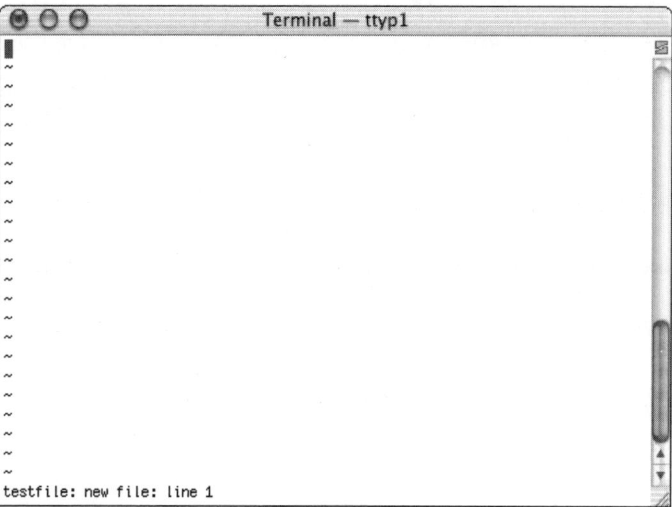

Figure 7-2

You will notice a tilde (~) on each line following the cursor. A tilde represents an unused line (no line feed or text of any kind). If a line does not begin with a tilde and appears to be blank, there is a space, tab, newline, or some other nonviewable character present. As Figure 7-2 shows, there's not much information on most versions of vi (some do provide minimal information or direction on what to do next); the only information is in the status line at the bottom of the screen, which displays the filename and the line the cursor is on. Like a lot of things in Unix, the information provided may vary from system to system. Your implementation of vi may have more or less information.

Figure 7-3 shows how to start vi with an argument of a file that exists (`/etc/services`).

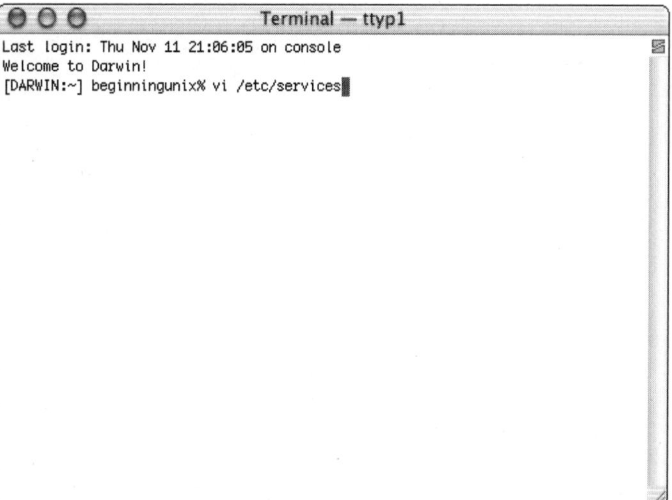

Figure 7-3

If you receive a permission-denied error or read-only indicator when trying to open a file with vi, either that file has protections beyond what you can access or you started vi in read-only mode.

*Non-text files, such as binary files, can create problems for the user in vi, such as displaying garbage—output that is unreadable. If you run into a file with unexpected results (nonreadable, for example), simply type **:q!** to exit the file without making any modifications to the file.*

There are two modes in vi:

- Command mode—Enables you to perform administrative tasks such as saving files, executing commands, moving the cursor, cutting (yanking) and pasting lines or words, and finding and replacing. In this mode, anything that's typed—even a single character—is interpreted as a command.
- Insert mode—Enables you to insert text into the file. Everything that's typed in this mode is interpreted as input.

Vi always starts in command mode. To enter text, you must be in insert mode. How do you get there? Simply type **i**. There are other ways to get into insert mode, and they're described later in the chapter. To get out of insert mode, press the **Esc** key, which will put you back into command mode.

*If you are not sure which mode you are in, press the **Esc** key twice, and then you'll be in command mode. In fact, just to be safe, you can always press **Esc** twice to get into command mode.*

Moving within a File

To move around within a file without affecting your text, you must be in command mode (press **Esc** twice). The most basic movement is from character to character. Here are some of the commands you can use to move around one character at a time:

Command	Result
`k`	Up one line
`j`	Down one line
`h`	Left one space
`l`	Right one space

You can use the standard arrow keys available on most keyboards to move around in a file, but it's recommended that you know the keys specified in the table because the arrow keys do not work on all platforms for which vi is available.

If you want to move more than one character or line within the file, you can put the number of movements you want to make prior to pressing the movement key. For example, if you want to move 10 lines down in a file, you can type **10j** (while in command mode) and your cursor will move 10 lines down from the current line. Here's another example; assume you have the following line in a file:

```
The quick brown fox jumped over the lazy dog.
```

If the cursor is at the first T in this sentence, and you type **10l**, the cursor will move 10 characters to the right (including spaces) — to the b in brown. If the cursor is on the f in fox and you type **6h**, the cursor will also move to the b in brown, 6 characters to the left.

Vi is case-sensitive, so you need to pay special attention to capitalization when using commands.

There are many other ways to move within a file in vi. Remember that you must be in command mode (press **Esc** twice). Here are some of them:

Command	Description	Result
`0`	Zero	Positions cursor at beginning of line
`$`	Dollar sign	Positions cursor at end of line
`w`	Lowercase w	Positions cursor to the next word (words are groups of characters separated by a space, tab, or punctuation mark)
`b`	Lowercase b	Positions cursor to previous word
`(`	Left parenthesis	Positions cursor to beginning of current sentence (sentences are identified by the punctuation marks followed by two spaces
`)`	Right parenthesis	Positions cursor to beginning of next sentence
Ctrl+F	Press Ctrl and F keys at the same time	Scrolls forward one full screen
Ctrl+B	Press Ctrl and B keys at the same time	Scrolls backward one full screen
`G`	Uppercase G	Positions the cursor on the last line of the file (you can use `xG` to represent a line number to go to as well; for instance, `4G` will move the cursor to line 4)
`:x`	Colon followed by a number (replace *x* with the number)	Positions the cursor on line number represented by *x* (for example, `:4` will move to line 4 of the file)

Let's take a look at some examples of using these keys to move around a file. Figure 7-4 shows a file (`/etc/syslog.conf`) open on a Mac Os X system in a vi session.

In the `/etc/syslog.conf` file, the `*` represents zero or more occurrences, as explained in Chapter 8. As in most Unix files, the `#` sign at the beginning of a line represents a comment that isn't read by the system, but is intended for the person viewing the file.

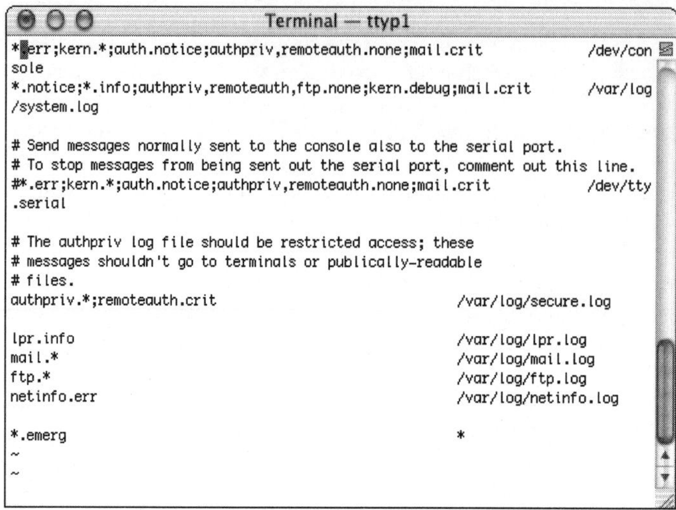

Figure 7-4

In this file, the cursor is on the first line, second character (`.`). Because the sizes of terminal windows vary, the beginning of a new line can be confusing. In this example, the word "sole" on a line by itself appears to be a new line, but in actuality the next new line begins with the asterisk (`*`) following "sole"; you want to keep this in mind when you use the line movement command. This is easier to visualize when you turn on line numbers. You can do so by using the `:set nu` option while in command mode (see Figure 7-5). The `:set nu` command numbers each new line (including blank lines) — the numbering is not part of the actual file, but definitely helps you see which line is which. The command to remove the line numbers is `:set nonu`.

```
Terminal — ttyp1
      1 *.err;kern.*;auth.notice;authpriv,remoteauth.none;mail.crit
/dev/console
      2 *.notice;*.info;authpriv,remoteauth,ftp.none;kern.debug;mail.crit
/var/log/system.log
      3
      4 # Send messages normally sent to the console also to the serial port.
      5 # To stop messages from being sent out the serial port, comment out this
 line.
      6 #*.err;kern.*;auth.notice;authpriv,remoteauth.none;mail.crit
/dev/tty.serial
      7
      8 # The authpriv log file should be restricted access; these
      9 # messages shouldn't go to terminals or publically-readable
     10 # files.
     11 authpriv.*;remoteauth.crit                          /var/log/secure.
log
     12
     13 lpr.info                                            /var/log/lpr.log
     14 mail.*                                              /var/log/mail.lo
g
     15 ftp.*                                               /var/log/ftp.log
     16 netinfo.err                                         /var/log/netinfo
.log
```

Figure 7-5

*While you are in insert mode, pressing the **Enter** key starts a new line. If you enter text with 5,000 words before pressing the **Enter** key, those 5,000 words are considered a single line.*

If you type **$** while in command mode in the file shown in Figure 7-5, the cursor will move to the end of line 1 and, assuming there are no spaces after the word `/dev/console`, it will be positioned on the e in console. If you type **0** (zero) while in command mode, the cursor will be positioned at the * (asterisk) of line 1. Now that you are back at the beginning of the line, type **w** and the cursor will move to the e in err. The cursor moves to this position because the commands `w` and `b` (lowercase) move word by word, counting each punctuation mark as a word. Uppercase `W` and `B` accomplish the same thing except that punctuation is not counted. If you type **W**, the cursor will move to the next word, so it will be positioned on the first `/` in `/dev/console` in the first line. You can also put a number before these commands to move the cursor that many positions. For instance, if you want to move forward 6 blocks of text, you type **6w**.

Remember that all commands in vi are case-sensitive. Typing a command key in the wrong case can result in unexpected output.

To identify the cursor's current location, use the key combination **Ctrl+G**. The line and character position of the cursor are displayed in the status line at the bottom of the screen, as shown in Figure 7-6. This is important in case you want to return to the line after you progress through the file.

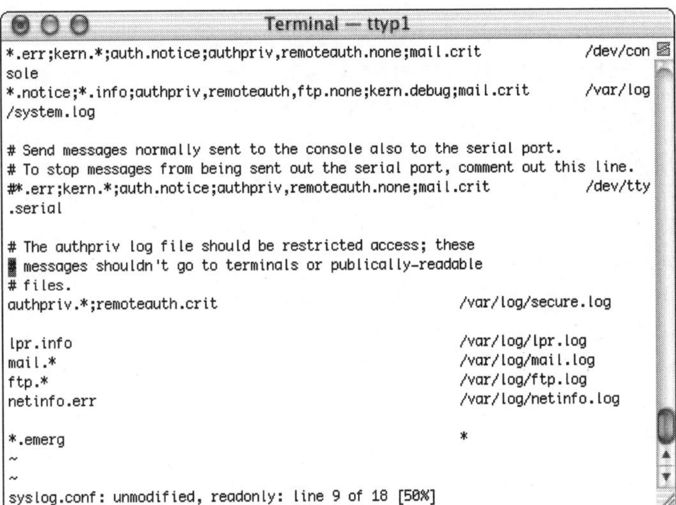

Figure 7-6

Here's the status line from Figure 7-6:

```
syslog.conf: unmodified, readonly: line 9 of 18 [50%]
```

It says that the `syslog.conf` file is currently being viewed and has not been modified in any way (including spaces). The file is opened read-only, which means that the file cannot be saved with the same name, overwritten, or modified based on current file permissions. The cursor is positioned on line 9, and there are 18 total lines in the file. The cursor is at the 50% mark of the file.

The vi status bar shows the full path of a file that's opened outside of its current directory. For instance, if the file in this example were opened from `/home` *instead of* `/etc` *(where it resides), the filename would show the full path* `/etc/syslog.conf`.

You can use the `line-numberG` command to return to a specific line number. If you were at the end of the file and wanted to return to the line where the cursor is shown in Figure 7-6, for example, you'd type **9G** while in command mode.

The Ctrl+G combination shows different output depending on the platform on which vi is used. For instance, Figure 7-7 shows the same command (Ctrl+G) used on a Linux system.

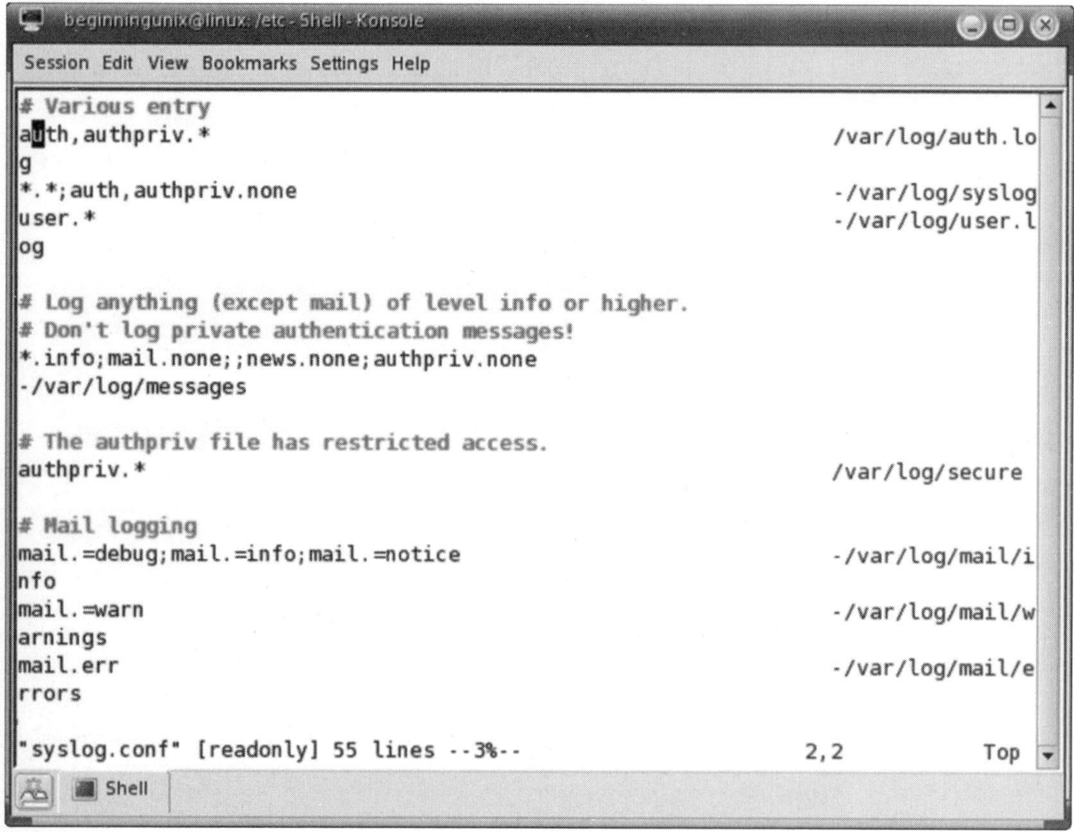

Figure 7-7

Here's the status line from the bottom of Figure 7-7:

```
"syslog.conf"  [readonly]  55 lines  --3%--                2,2        Top
```

It shows that the file `syslog.conf` is open read-only and has 55 lines. The cursor is located 3% into the file, at line 2, character 2 (2,2). (The file's complete path would display if the file were opened in a directory other than its own.)

Searching Files

Sometimes there's a particular portion of a file that you want to find. In those cases, you can do a simple search. To initiate the search, press **Esc** twice to get into command mode and type **/**, followed immediately by the characters for which you want to search, and then press **Enter** or **Return**. For example, to search for the string end, you'd type **/end** and then press **Enter** or **Return**. This search finds the character string regardless of where it is in the word, so if you were searching for the word *end*, you might not find it, because the cursor would move to the first instance of the search criteria in the file, possibly *end* by itself, but also perhaps susp*end*, dep*end*, *end*eavor, f*end*er, and so on. If you type spaces in the search, these are taken into account as well, so that typing **/ end** will find a word beginning with *end*. If you want to search backward from the current cursor position (toward the beginning of the file), type a **?** (question mark) instead of a **/**.

If there are multiple instances of the search characters you are looking for, you can type a lowercase **n** after each find to search in the same direction (forward or backward) or an uppercase **N** after each to search in the opposite direction of your current search.

Exiting and Saving a File

After you've read or edited your files, you'll want to exit vi. The most commonly used exit commands are `:q!` and `:wq`. To exit vi without saving your changes, go into command mode and type **:q!**. If you want to save the file and exit vi, go into command mode and type **:wq**. The following are the major commands for exiting and saving files (remember to press **Esc** twice to ensure you are in command mode):

Command	Description	Result
`:q`	Colon lowercase q	Quits vi editor. If changes were made, vi either asks if you want to exit without saving or informs you that changes were made and does not exit.
`:w`	Colon lowercase w	Writes (saves) the current file. If you are editing an existing file and you don't have the proper permissions to write to the file, it is not saved and you receive an error message (as you do if the file is opened in read-only mode).
`:wq`	Colon lowercase w and q	Write the file and then quit (same issues with permissions as `:w`).
`:q!` or `:w!` or `:wq!`	Preceding commands followed by exclamation mark	The ! tells vi to do the command without any of the protections of asking if you want to overwrite an existing file or asking if you want to save the file before exiting, for example. If you don't have write access to a file and you use the `:wq!` combination, vi will fail to write and quit successfully, and you will lose your edits.

Table continued on following page

Command	Description	Result
`ZZ`	Two uppercase Zs	Writes the file and exits (same as `:wq`).
`:x`	Colon lowercase x	Writes the file and exits.
`:w` *`filename`*	Colon, lowercase w, space, filename (use an actual filename in place of *`filename`*)	Writes the file as *`filename`*. This saves your file with your changes to another file, which means that you can save changes to a file that you don't have permissions for. You write the new file to a directory for which you do have permissions, such as your home directory. This option must be used if you started vi without a filename argument; otherwise you lose all data in the file.
`:e!`	Colon lowercase e followed by exclamation mark	Opens the last successfully written version of the file (without saving any current changes). This is great for recovering from multiple mistakes made since your previous write without having to quit and restart vi.

If you use `:w` *`filename`* to save your edits to a file other than the one you were originally editing, be aware that you are left in the original file, not the one you saved your work to. For example, if you open `/etc/syslog.conf` and make changes, but don't want to save all the changes before double-checking the file, you can save the altered file to `/tmp/syslog.conf` with the `:w /tmp/syslog.conf` command. If you then make more changes to the open file and save the file with the `:wq!` command, all those changes are saved in `/etc/syslog.conf`.

Vi also lets you append the file you have created to another file using the redirection characters >>. For example, if you want to append your current file to `/tmp/testfile2`, simply issue `:w >> testfile2` and the contents of the current file are added to the end of `testfile2` file. The `testfile2` file must already exist for this command to work.

Editing Files

All of the previous sections covered commands that can be run in command mode, which doesn't allow you to edit your files. To edit the file, you need to be in the insert mode, as mentioned earlier in the chapter. There are many ways to enter insert mode from the command mode:

Command	Description	Result
`i`	Lowercase i	Inserts text before current cursor location
`I`	Uppercase I	Inserts text at beginning of current line
`a`	Lowercase a	Inserts text after current cursor location

Command	Description	Result
`A`	Uppercase A	Inserts text at end of current line
`o`	Lowercase o	Creates a new line for text entry below cursor location
`O`	Uppercase O	Creates a new line for text entry above cursor location

Most commands in vi can be prefaced by the number of times you want the action to occur. For example, `2O` creates two new lines above the cursor location.

These commands are entered while in command mode to begin the process of entering text into vi. Typing a lowercase **i** simply puts you into insert mode, with the text input occurring before the location of the cursor. Let's look at some examples using the following sentences (which will be used throughout this section):

```
Sentence one.
The quick brown fox jumps over the lazy dog.
Sentence three.
```

If the cursor is on the character r in the word brown in the second sentence, and you type the letter **i** in command mode, any letters you type after that will go between the b and the r in brown. Say that after you enter insert mode, you type the letters **newtext**. Here's what the example sentence will look like:

```
The quick bnewtextrown fox jumps over the lazy dog.
```

If you type the letter **a** instead of **i** while in command mode, text insertion will begin after the r and before the o in brown, and the example sentence will look like this:

```
Sentence one.
The quick brnewtextown fox jumps over the lazy dog.
Sentence three.
```

If you use the `o` command to enter the same text from the same starting point, the result will be:

```
Sentence one.
The quick brown fox jumps over the lazy dog.
newtext
Sentence three.
```

The `O` command from the same starting point will result in:

```
Sentence one.
newtext
The quick brown fox jumps over the lazy dog.
Sentence three.
```

Using the `I` or `A` will allow you to insert text at the beginning (before "The") or at the end (after "dog.") of the current line, respectively. You remain in insert mode until you press the **Esc** key.

Deleting Characters

Deletion of characters, lines, and words within vi requires its own set of commands. Here are the most common:

Command	Description	Result
x	Lowercase x	Deletes the character under the cursor location (or starting with the character under the cursor if the command is preceded by a number)
X	Uppercase X	Deletes the character before the cursor location (or starting with the cursor if the command is preceded by a number)
dw	Lowercase dw	Deletes from the current cursor location to the next word (or multiple words if preceded by a number)
D	Uppercase D	Deletes from the cursor position to the end of the current line
dd	Lowercase dd	Deletes the line the cursor is on

Using the same example sentence, with the cursor over the r in the word brown:

- The `x` command deletes the letter r.

```
Sentence one.
The quick bown fox jumps over the lazy dog.
Sentence three.
```

- The `X` command deletes the letter b:

```
Sentence one.
The quick rown fox jumps over the lazy dog.
Sentence three.
```

- The `dw` command removes from the letter under the cursor to the beginning of the next word:

```
Sentence one.
The quick bfox jumps over the lazy dog.
Sentence three.
```

- The `D` command deletes from the letter under the cursor through the end of the line (until a new line):

```
Sentence one.
The quick b
Sentence three.
```

- The `dd` command deletes the entire line, leaving:

```
Sentence one.
Sentence three.
```

These are commands that can be prefaced with the number of times you want the action to occur. For instance, using the original example and beginning with the cursor on the r in brown, the command `2x` deletes 2 characters:

```
Sentence one.
The quick bwn fox jumps over the lazy dog.
Sentence three.
```

A `2dw` command results in:

```
Sentence one.
The quick bjumps over the lazy dog.
Sentence three.
```

A `2D` command deletes from the r under the cursor through the following line so that you're left with:

```
Sentence one.
The quick b
```

Some of these options work a little differently in the various implementations of vi. If one of the commands in this chapter doesn't work as expected, refer to the man page for vi.

A `2dd` command leaves only the first sentence:

```
Sentence one.
```

In vi, commands can be combined to form complex actions. The command sequence `ddO`, for example, deletes the current line and then opens a newline for your new text. With your cursor on the r in brown in the example sentences, in command mode, type **ddO** and then type **Now is the time for all good men to come to the aid of the party.** Here's the result:

```
Sentence one.
Now is the time for all good men to come to the aid of the party.
Sentence three.
```

The two separate vi commands run together, deleting the line the cursor is on (`dd`) and opening a newline (`O`).

Change Commands

You also have the capability to change characters, words, or lines in vi without deleting them. Here are the relevant commands:

Command	Description	Result
`cc`	Two lowercase c's	Removes contents of the line, leaving the text you type in.
`cw`	Lowercase c and lowercase w	Changes the word the cursor is on from the cursor to the end of the word. This command also puts you into insert mode. If you want to change the whole word, your cursor must be positioned on the first character in the word.
`r`	Lowercase r	Replaces the character under the cursor. Vi returns to command mode after the replacement is entered.
`R`	Uppercase R	Overwrites multiple characters beginning with the character currently under the cursor. You must use Esc to stop the overwriting.
`s`	Lowercase s	Replaces the current character with the character you type. Afterward, you are left in insert mode.
`S`	Uppercase S	Deletes the line the cursor is on and replaces with new text. After the new text is entered, vi remains in insert mode.

Let's see how these commands work. Here are the example sentences again:

```
Sentence one.
The quick brown fox jumps over the lazy dog.
Sentence three.
```

The `cc` command gets the same result as the command sequence `ddO`. With your cursor on the r in brown in the example sentences, in command mode, type **cc** and then type **Now is the time for good men to come to the aid of the party.** Here's the result:

```
Sentence one.
Now is the time for all good men to come to the aid of the party.
Sentence three.
```

The `cw` command is the same as the command sequence `dwi`, except that a blank character will exist after the deletion. Assuming that your cursor is still on the b in brown, compare the result of the two in the following lines:

```
The quick b fox jumps over the lazy dog.
The quick bfox jumps over the lazy dog.
```

The first line uses `cw`, and the second uses `dwi`. The `cw` command throws you into insert mode so that you can change the text at that point. For example, if you type **cw lue**, the result is a fox of a different color:

```
Sentence one.
The quick blue fox jumps over the lazy dog.
Sentence three.
```

The `r` command enables you to replace the character under the cursor with whatever single character you type next. If you type **r** in command mode in the example sentence, and then type **5**, the result will be:

```
The quick b5own fox jumps over the lazy dog.
```

The `R` command allows you to replace characters (beginning with the one under the cursor) with the new text you type—each character you type replaces an original character. Type **R**, and then type **555 1234**, and here's the result:

```
The quick b555 1234 jumps over the lazy dog.
```

The lowercase `s` works the same as the `R`, except it deletes the letter under the cursor and then begins overwriting.

Advanced Commands

There are some advanced commands that simplify day-to-day editing and allow for more efficient use of vi. Here are some of the most useful:

Command	Description	Result
`J`	Uppercase J	Joins the current line with the line below it
`yy`	Two lowercase y's	Yanks (copies) the current line
`yw`	Lowercase y and lowercase w	Yanks (copies) the current word from the character the cursor is on until the end of the word
`p`	Lowercase p	Puts the yanked text after the cursor
`P`	Uppercase P	Puts the yanked text before the cursor

Use the `J` command to join two lines together. With the example sentences (and the cursor on the r), the result of `J` will be:

```
Sentence one.
The quick brown fox jumps over the lazy dog.  Sentence three.
```

Adding a number before the `J` command may or may not join more lines, depending on your vi implementation.

The yank command is one of the most useful commands when editing large files. Yanking is akin to using the copy command in graphical editors. Type **yy** with the cursor on the r in brown, and the entire line is copied into memory. Move the cursor to the line preceding where you'd like the yanked text to appear, and type **p**. The copied line appears on the line after the cursor's current line. For example, I ran the `yy` command while the cursor was on the r in brown. I placed the cursor on the line that says "Sentence three" and typed **p**, with the following result:

```
Sentence one.
The quick brown fox jumps over the lazy dog.
Sentence three.
The quick brown fox jumps over the lazy dog.
```

When yanking and pasting, you will lose what is held in the yank buffer if you enter a delete command, because the buffer will fill with whatever was deleted. You can use movement or insertion commands and not lose the yank buffer. This behavior may differ on some versions of Unix, particularly versions of Solaris.

The `yw` command copies only the portion of the word from the character under to cursor to the end of the word, and you can prepend a number that equals the number of words to be copied. If you use 2yw, for example, and then move the cursor to the S in "Sentence one." and enter the `p` command, you'll get the following:

```
Srown fox entence one.
The quick brown fox jumps over the lazy dog.
Sentence three.
```

Using the `P` command results in the following:

```
rown fox Sentence one.
The quick brown fox jumps over the lazy dog.
Sentence three.
```

These are very powerful commands. Work with them a bit to get more comfortable with the output they give you.

Try It Out Use Commands in Vi

Create a new file, enter some text, and try out some of the commands you've learned.

1. Open a new file called `beginning_unix_testfile` in the `/tmp` directory:

   ```
   vi /tmp/beginning_unix_testfile
   ```

2. You are in command mode. Change to insert mode by typing **i**.
3. Type the following, making sure to press **Enter** at the end of each line:

   ```
   The quick brown fox jumps over the lazy dog.
   Sentence two.
   Sentence three.
   Sentence four.
   Vi will never become vii.
   Sentence six.
   ```

4. Press **Esc** to go into command mode.
5. Type **1G** to move to the first line, and then type **4l** to position the cursor over the q in quick.
6. Type **cw**, which removes the word `quick` and puts you into insert mode.

7. Type the word **slow**, and then press **Esc**. Now your file should look like this:

```
The slow brown fox jumps over the lazy dog.
Sentence two.
Sentence three.
Sentence four.
Vi will never become vii.
Sentence six.
```

8. Type **2j** to move down two lines. The cursor will be on the last e in `Sentence` on line 3.

9. Type **r** and then type **E**. The sentence should look like this:

```
SentencE three.
```

10. Type **k** once to move up one line. Type **2yy** to copy two lines.

11. Type **4j** to move to the last line, and then type **p** to paste the text from the buffer. Here's the result:

```
The slow brown fox jumps over the lazy dog.
Sentence two.
SentencE three.
Sentence four.
Vi will never become vii.
Sentence six.
Sentence two.
SentencE three.
```

12. Press **Esc** and then type **q!** to exit the file without saving the output.

How It Works

This exercise has given you the opportunity to try out some of the vi commands you've learned so far in this chapter. Here are the key points to your success with vi:

- You must be in command mode to use commands. (Press **Esc** twice at any time to ensure that you are in command mode.)
- You must be careful to use the proper case (capitalization) for all commands.
- You must be in insert mode to enter text.

There are quite a few commands, as you've noticed, and the command tables in this chapter are a good reference while you learn your way around vi.

Help!

There are a lot of commands to use in vi, so don't be surprised if you can't remember all of them or what they do. In command mode, you can always type **man vi** at the command line (console) to get the full online manual page, including information on the different vi modes and other pertinent information.

If you make a major mistake and want to quit the file, simply type **:q!** to exit from the file without saving. Alternatively, use `:w` *`filename`* to save the file with another name — in case you want to look it over to determine what mistakes you made. In this instance, none of your changes are written to the original file.

If you made a lot of corrections and don't want to lose some of your previous edits, the undo commands `u` and `U` can be useful. The `u` command undoes the last edit, so that if you accidentally deleted 3,000 lines with `3000dd`, for example, you could type **u** in command mode and the deleted 3,000 lines would be put back in place. The `U` command restores the current line, so that if you accidentally deleted "The quick," you could type **U** in command mode and the line would revert to its original "The quick brown fox jumps over the lazy dog."

> *Some versions of vi allow unlimited undo commands while others keep an undo in a buffer only until the next command that requires the buffer, such as another yank or delete command. There are ways to save to the buffer, but that is beyond the scope of this chapter. Refer to the online man page for vi for more information on buffer manipulation.*

Another common issue involves system messages that show up in the middle of a file that you're editing. As you can imagine, these messages can cause you some confusion by appearing while you are editing text. For example, say you're editing the `/etc/syslog.conf` file shown in Figure 7-8.

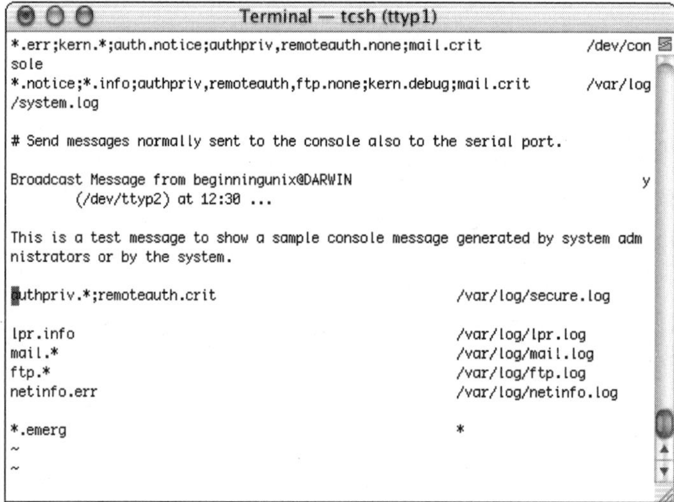

Figure 7-8

See the "Broadcast Message..." lines? Those are not part of the file — it's a system message that's popped up in the middle of the editing project. Use the key combination **Ctrl+L** to remove the messages and return to the original text.

Running Commands

Vi has the capability to run commands from within the editor. To run a command, you only need to go into command mode and type **:!** ***command***. For example, if you want to check whether a file exists before you try to save your file to that filename, you can type **:! ls** and you will see the output of `ls` on the screen. When you press any key (or the command's escape sequence), you are returned to your vi session. This can be very helpful when you don't want to interrupt your vi session but you need the output of a command.

Be aware that if you give someone root capabilities to vi (such as with `sudo`), even if you specify the file, that person can run commands using the `:!` sequence, presenting a serious security vulnerability. Never give the capability to run root or any other interactive editor with `sudo`, RBAC, and so on.

Replacing Text

Vi's substitution command (`:s/`) enables you to quickly replace words or groups of words within your files. The syntax for the command is `:s/`*`characters to be replaced`*`/`*`what to replace with`*`/`. For instance, to replace an occurrence of "misspelled" with "spelled correctly," you'd use the command:

```
:s/misspelled/spelled correctly/
```

Well, things aren't always as easy as they first appear. The file shown in Figure 7-9, for example, has 84 instances of the word misspelled.

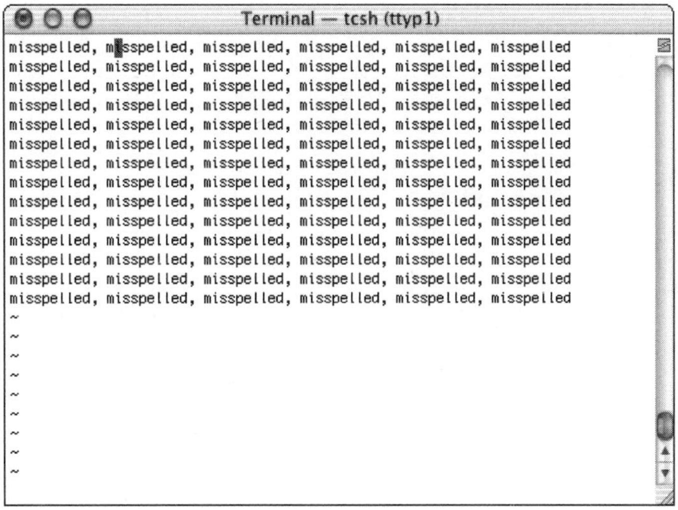

```
Terminal — tcsh (ttyp1)
misspelled, misspelled, misspelled, misspelled, misspelled, misspelled
misspelled, misspelled, misspelled, misspelled, misspelled, misspelled
misspelled, misspelled, misspelled, misspelled, misspelled, misspelled
misspelled, misspelled, misspelled, misspelled, misspelled, misspelled
misspelled, misspelled, misspelled, misspelled, misspelled, misspelled
misspelled, misspelled, misspelled, misspelled, misspelled, misspelled
misspelled, misspelled, misspelled, misspelled, misspelled, misspelled
misspelled, misspelled, misspelled, misspelled, misspelled, misspelled
misspelled, misspelled, misspelled, misspelled, misspelled, misspelled
misspelled, misspelled, misspelled, misspelled, misspelled, misspelled
misspelled, misspelled, misspelled, misspelled, misspelled, misspelled
misspelled, misspelled, misspelled, misspelled, misspelled, misspelled
misspelled, misspelled, misspelled, misspelled, misspelled, misspelled
misspelled, misspelled, misspelled, misspelled, misspelled, misspelled
~
~
~
~
~
~
~
~
~
```

Figure 7-9

Note that the cursor is on the first line. Enter the command `:s/misspelled/spelled correctly/`, and you get the result shown in Figure 7-10.

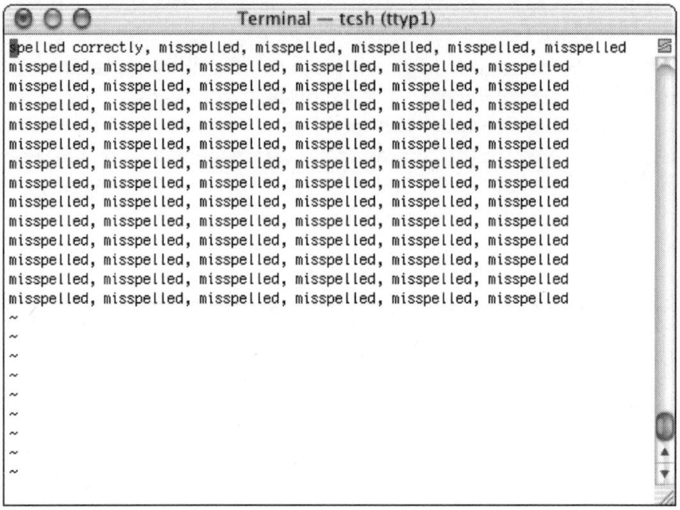

Terminal — tcsh (ttyp1)

```
spelled correctly, misspelled, misspelled, misspelled, misspelled, misspelled
misspelled, misspelled, misspelled, misspelled, misspelled, misspelled
misspelled, misspelled, misspelled, misspelled, misspelled, misspelled
misspelled, misspelled, misspelled, misspelled, misspelled, misspelled
misspelled, misspelled, misspelled, misspelled, misspelled, misspelled
misspelled, misspelled, misspelled, misspelled, misspelled, misspelled
misspelled, misspelled, misspelled, misspelled, misspelled, misspelled
misspelled, misspelled, misspelled, misspelled, misspelled, misspelled
misspelled, misspelled, misspelled, misspelled, misspelled, misspelled
misspelled, misspelled, misspelled, misspelled, misspelled, misspelled
misspelled, misspelled, misspelled, misspelled, misspelled, misspelled
misspelled, misspelled, misspelled, misspelled, misspelled, misspelled
misspelled, misspelled, misspelled, misspelled, misspelled, misspelled
misspelled, misspelled, misspelled, misspelled, misspelled, misspelled
~
~
~
~
~
~
~
~
~
```

Figure 7-10

Not exactly the result you wanted, is it? Only the first instance of misspelled was changed because that's how substitution works: the first instance found on the same line as the cursor is changed. To change every instance on a line, run:

```
:s/misspelled/spelled correctly/g
```

The `g` stands for globally, and in Unix that means on the line containing the cursor. The result of this command is that all occurrences on the cursor's line are changed, as shown in Figure 7-11.

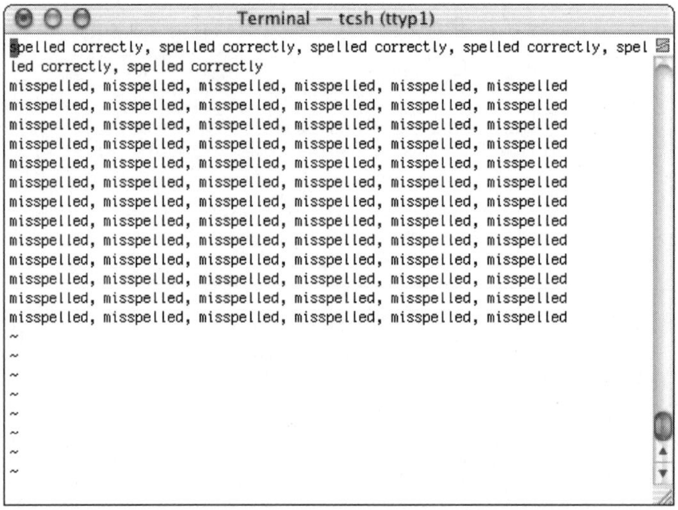

Terminal — tcsh (ttyp1)

```
spelled correctly, spelled correctly, spelled correctly, spelled correctly, spel
led correctly, spelled correctly
misspelled, misspelled, misspelled, misspelled, misspelled, misspelled
misspelled, misspelled, misspelled, misspelled, misspelled, misspelled
misspelled, misspelled, misspelled, misspelled, misspelled, misspelled
misspelled, misspelled, misspelled, misspelled, misspelled, misspelled
misspelled, misspelled, misspelled, misspelled, misspelled, misspelled
misspelled, misspelled, misspelled, misspelled, misspelled, misspelled
misspelled, misspelled, misspelled, misspelled, misspelled, misspelled
misspelled, misspelled, misspelled, misspelled, misspelled, misspelled
misspelled, misspelled, misspelled, misspelled, misspelled, misspelled
misspelled, misspelled, misspelled, misspelled, misspelled, misspelled
misspelled, misspelled, misspelled, misspelled, misspelled, misspelled
misspelled, misspelled, misspelled, misspelled, misspelled, misspelled
misspelled, misspelled, misspelled, misspelled, misspelled, misspelled
~
~
~
~
~
~
~
~
```

Figure 7-11

If you want to change the spelling on a number of consecutive lines, specify the line numbers in the following syntax:

```
x,ys//characters to be replaced/what to replace with/
```

where *x* is the number of the first line of changes and *y* is the number of the last line. To replace every instance of "misspelled" with "spelled correctly" in lines 2 through 8, you could try the following command:

```
:2,8s/misspelled/spelled correctly/
```

The result is shown in Figure 7-12 (the `.set nu` option has been turned on to show the line numbers, which are not saved with the file).

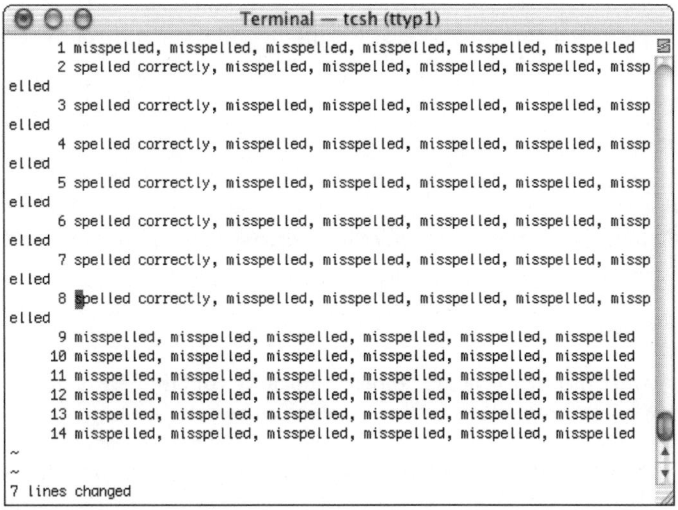

```
Terminal — tcsh (ttyp1)
     1 misspelled, misspelled, misspelled, misspelled, misspelled, misspelled
     2 spelled correctly, misspelled, misspelled, misspelled, misspelled, missp
elled
     3 spelled correctly, misspelled, misspelled, misspelled, misspelled, missp
elled
     4 spelled correctly, misspelled, misspelled, misspelled, misspelled, missp
elled
     5 spelled correctly, misspelled, misspelled, misspelled, misspelled, missp
elled
     6 spelled correctly, misspelled, misspelled, misspelled, misspelled, missp
elled
     7 spelled correctly, misspelled, misspelled, misspelled, misspelled, missp
elled
     8 spelled correctly, misspelled, misspelled, misspelled, misspelled, missp
elled
     9 misspelled, misspelled, misspelled, misspelled, misspelled, misspelled
    10 misspelled, misspelled, misspelled, misspelled, misspelled, misspelled
    11 misspelled, misspelled, misspelled, misspelled, misspelled, misspelled
    12 misspelled, misspelled, misspelled, misspelled, misspelled, misspelled
    13 misspelled, misspelled, misspelled, misspelled, misspelled, misspelled
    14 misspelled, misspelled, misspelled, misspelled, misspelled, misspelled
~
~
7 lines changed
```

Figure 7-12

That didn't do the job the way you anticipated, did it? Only the first instance of "misspelled" on each line was replaced. To change every instance of "misspelled" to "spelled correctly" on lines 2 through 8, you've got to put the `g` at the end of the command, like this:

```
:2,8s/misspelled/spelled correctly/g
```

To replace every instance of "misspelled" in the entire file, here's the command you need:

```
:1,$s/misspelled/spelled correctly/g
```

This replaces every instance from the first line (1) to the end of the file ($). You need the `g` at the end, remember, or only the first instance of "misspelled" on each line will change.

If you don't want to accept all substitutions blindly, you can add the confirm command `c` to the very end of the command sequence:

```
:1,$s/misspelled/spelled correctly/gc
```

The result is that you are asked to confirm every change by typing **yes** or **no**.

Metacharacters—characters that have special meaning in Unix—can be used to specify certain sequences. The `*`, for example, represents zero or more occurrences. To replace all instances of "particular" and "particularly" with "essential," use the following command:

```
:1,$s/particular*/essential/g
```

Metacharacters are discussed in depth in Chapter 8.

The \ (backslash) specifies that the metacharacter after it will mean the exact character. To replace every instance of * with hello, here's the command to use:

```
:1,$s/\*/hello/g
```

The last set of expressions to be discussed in this section are the \< and \>, which match characters at the beginning or end of a word respectively. To find all instances of "the" at the beginning of a word (such as "theater") but not when it occurs anywhere else (such as "lathe" or "scathed") and replace them with "none," you can type:

```
:1,$s/\<the/none/g
```

This replaces the word "the" with "none," replaces instances of "the" with "none" in "theater" (which becomes "noneater"), and leaves "bathed" and "lathe" as before.

These are some of the basic expressions that can be used; you'll learn about others in Chapter 8.

Versions of Vi

The original version of vi is often emulated, so that most people are not using it at all but are using another version. For instance, most Unix systems run Vim, which is vi improved, although most users don't realize it because Vim is set up to run like vi unless a `.vimrc` file is set. The following list describes many of the vi incarnations offered now, but the original vi is still available on most systems. Learning the original is beneficial in case the other versions are not installed.

- Vim—Vi IMproved. The most-used version of vi in the Unix world. It has all the features of vi, plus some major improvements, including syntax highlighting and multiple levels of undo. If you are using vi on a modern system, you are most likely using Vim. More information is available at `http://vim.org`.
- Elvis—An updated version of vi with some extra features. You'll find more information at `http://elvis.vi-editor.org`.

- Vile — Vi Like Emacs. It tries to bring the best of both vi and Emacs together. More information is available at `http://dickey.his.com/vile/vile.html`.
- Nvi — BSD version of vi. More information is available at `www.bostic.com/vi`.

You'll find many other versions of vi listed at the vi lovers' home page, `http://thomer.com/vi/vi.html`.

Summary

This chapter covered the use of vi from the ground up, including:

- Using keys (commands) to move within a file
- Searching for words or strings of text
- Saving files and exiting vi
- Editing files (insert mode)
- Searching for and replacing text in files
- Using metacharacters in searching and replacing

You've got the basics of editing files with vi now. Before you move on to Chapter 8, in which you'll learn about regular expressions, solidify your new vi knowledge by doing the following exercises.

Exercises

1. How can you be absolutely sure what mode you are in when using vi?
2. How do you search for the word "computer" in a file while in command mode? How would you continue the search in the opposite direction?
3. How would you copy 5 lines of text and then insert them 10 lines down?
4. How would you replace the word "person" with "human" across an entire file, even if it existed multiple times on the same line?

Advanced Tools

In Chapter 6, you learned basic Unix commands and how they work. Now you'll build on that knowledge and expand your command library. This chapter tackles advanced commands and regular expressions (formulas for matching strings that follow specific patterns). Regular expressions are important, and they're also quite challenging when you're just learning about them. Don't worry, though, because this chapter provides a good foundation for your learning.

Regular Expressions and Metacharacters

A regular expression is a syntactical set or phrase that represents a pattern of text or strings. Regular expressions enable you to represent a varying array of characters with a much smaller set of predefined characters. They often include metacharacters — characters that represent another set or group of characters or commands.

No discussion of regular expressions and metacharacters is useful without examples, so create a file called `/tmp/testfile` that you can use as you work your way through this chapter: Here's what to put in the file (note the capitalization and punctuation):

```
Juliet Capulet
The model identifier is DEn5c89zt.
Sarcastic was what he was.
No, he was just sarcastic.
Simplicity
The quick brown fox jumps over the lazy dog
It's a Cello? Not a Violin?
This character is (*) is the splat in Unix.
activity
apricot
capulet
cat
celebration
corporation
cot
cut
cutting
```

```
dc9tg4
eclectic
housecat
persnickety
The punctuation and capitalization is important in this example.
simplicity
undiscriminating
Two made up words below:
c?t
C?*.t
cccot
cccccot
```

Save the file; you'll use it throughout this chapter. Ready to explore metacharacters?

Understanding Metacharacters

Metacharacters are useful in reducing the amount of text used with commands and for representing groups of text with a minimal set of characters. The following list describes shows some of the more common metacharacters. The results shown in each case represent output from your `testfile` if the example search were run on it. The matching characters in the result list are boldfaced to make it easier to see the match.

If you have used Microsoft Windows or MS-DOS operating systems, you may be familiar with wildcards, which are somewhat similar to metacharacters. Do not confuse wildcards (available through the shell) with metacharacters, though, because they are interpreted differently and can produce unexpected results if you try to use them interchangeably.

- . — **Description**: Dot or period. Represents one character.

  Example: Find any instances of the letter c and the letter t with exactly one character between them:

  ```
  c.t
  ```

  Results from `testfile`:

Simpli**cit**y	**cut**	simpli**cit**y
apri**cot**	**cut**ting	**c?t**
cat	d**c9t**g4	cc**cot**
cot	house**cat**	cccc**cot**

- `[]` — **Description**: Square brackets. Result will match any one of the characters inside them.

  Example: Find any instances of the letter c and the letter t with only one of the letters in the square brackets between them:

  ```
  c[aeiou]t
  ```

  Results from `testfile`:

Simpli**cit**y	**cot**	simpli**cit**y
apri**cot**	**cut**	c**cot**
cat	house**cat**	cccc**cot**

- `*` — **Description**: Asterisk (splat). Represents zero or more occurrences of other characters.

  Example: Find any instances of the letter c and the letter t with zero or more characters between them.

```
c*t
```

  Results from `testfile`:

```
Juliet Capulet
The model identifier is DEn5c89zt.
Sarcastic, was what he was.
No, he was just sarcastic.
Simplicity
The quick brown fox jumps over the lazy dog
It's a Cello? Not a Violin?
This character is (*) is the splat in Unix.
activity
apricot
capulet
cat
celebration
corporation
cot
cut
cutting
dc9tg4
eclectic (also eclectic; same word so only one instance shows)
housecat
persnickety
The punctuation and capitalization is important in this example.
simplicity
undiscriminating
c?t
c?*.t
cccot
cccccot
```

- `[^ insert_character(s)]` — **Description**: Square brackets with a caret between them. Do not match any of the characters following the caret.

  Example: Find any instances of the letter c and the letter 5 with none of the characters inside the brackets between them.

```
c[^aeiou]t
```

  Results from `testfile`:

```
dc9tg4
c?t
```

- `^insert_character` — **Description** Match the sequence only if it is at the beginning of the line.

  Example: Find any instances of the exact string ca at the beginning a line:

```
^ca
```

Results from `testfile`:

```
capulet
cat
```

Without the ^, the output would be instances of ca anywhere on the line:

Results from `testfile`:

```
Sarcastic was what he was.
No, he was just sarcastic.
capulet
cat
housecat
The punctuation and capitalization is important in this example.
```

- `^[`*`insert_character(s)`*`]` — **Description**: Caret preceding a bracketed sequence. Match any one character inside brackets; match sequence at the beginning of the line.

  Example: Find all instances of the letter c at the beginning of the line, any one of characters in the brackets, and the character t.

```
^c[aeiou]t
```

  Results from `testfile`:

```
cat
cot
cut
cutting
```

  If the ^ were not in the syntax, the output would be instances of c[aeiou]t anywhere on the line:

```
Simplicity
apricot
cat
cot
cut
cutting
housecat
simplicity
cccot
cccccot
```

- `$` — **Description**: Dollar sign. Match the occurrence at the end of the line only.

  Example: Find the character c and the character t at the end of the line, with zero to any combination of characters in between:

```
c*t$
```

  Results from `testfile`:

```
Capulet      cat      c?t
DEn5C89zt    cot      c?*.t
```

apri**cot**	**cut**	cc**cot**
capulet	house**cat**	cccc**cot**

- \ — **Description**: Blackslash. Removes special meaning from the character immediately following, so that a ? is taken literally rather than as a metacharacter.

  Example: Find all instances of the character c, a literal ?, and the character t:

  ```
  c\?t
  ```

  Results from `testfile`:

  c?t

- ? — **Description**: Question mark. Represents zero or one character (not to be confused with *, which matches zero, one, or many characters). Not available with all programs in Unix.

  Example: Find all instances of the character c and the character t with zero or one character between them:

  ```
  c?t
  ```

  Results from `testfile`:

  ```
  Simplicity
  eclectic
  activity
  housecat
  apricot
  The punctuation and capitalization is important in this example.
  cat
  simplicity
  cot
  c?t
  cut
  cccot
  cutting
  cccccot
  dc9tg4
  ```

- `[a-z]` — **Description**: Full lowercase alphabet designation inside brackets. Match all occurrences of any single letter.

  Example: Match all instances of the character c and the character t with a single instance of a letter a through z between them.

  ```
  c[a-z]t
  ```

  Results from `testfile`:

Simpli**cit**y	**cut**	simpli**cit**y
apri**cot**	**cut**ting	cc**cot**
cat	house**cat**	cccc**cot**
cot		

- `[0-9]` — **Description**: Matches single instances of all numbers 0–9.

  Example: Find all instances of the letter c and the letter 5 with any single instance of a number between 0 and 9 between them.

```
c[0-9]t
```

  Results from `testfile`:

```
dc9tg4
```

- `[d-m7-9]` — **Description**: Matches a single occurrence of any character d through m or 7 through 9. This illustrates how these commands can be grouped.

  Example: Find all instances of the letter c and the letter t with a single instance of any of the letters c through t or a single instance of any number 0 through 4.

```
c[c-t0-4]t
```

  Results from `testfile`:

```
Simplicity      dc9tg4
apricot         cccot
cot             cccccot
simplicity
```

The metacharacters listed here are commonly used and generally available with most commands. Not all metacharacters or regular expressions work with every program, and sometimes only a subset of metacharacters is supported within a program. Read the man page for the command you are going to use to determine its support for the metacharacters.

Metacharacters and regular expressions are typically used with the following commands (although there are others):

```
awk        fgrep
ed         less
emacs      more
expr       sed
grep       vi
egrep
```

Regular Expressions

Regular expressions can be extremely simple or very complex, depending on the program they are used with and what you are looking for. They can include metacharacters or regular characters. A regular expression is the syntax used to match something, and metacharacters enable you to expand a more complex group of regular characters with a smaller subset of predefined characters. The following regular expression is a very simple one that that would match any single character between the brackets:

```
c[a-n]n
```

A regular expression can be as complicated as the following:

[0-9][0-9][0-9]\.[0-9][0-9][0-9]\.[0-9][0-9][0-9][0-9]

This would match the standard format for a U.S. telephone number (for instance, 555.555.0000). Notice that the \ (backslash) escapes the . (period) so that the period represents a literal period and not what the period metacharacter typically means (one or more characters).

Learning to use regular expressions and metacharacters can be a long and involved process, but understanding these basics will assist you in doing what is needed on your Unix system. A full discussion of regular expressions is beyond the scope of this book, but *Beginning Regular Expressions* by Andrew Watt (Wiley, ISBN 0-7645-7489-2) is a good reference for learning more about this important topic.

Using SFTP and FTP

SFTP (Secure File Transfer Protocol) and FTP (File Transfer Protocol) are the two major protocols for transferring files between Unix systems. The syntax of the `sftp` and `ftp` commands is similar to those of `telnet` and `ssh` in that you initiate the command and then identify where you want to log in. For instance, to `sftp` to the Mac OS X machine named darwin (remote machine with an IP address of 192.168.1.58), you'd type:

```
sftp 192.168.1.58
```

or

```
sftp darwin
```

The output will look much like Figure 8-1.

For `ftp`, you'd type:

```
ftp 192.168.1.58
```

or

```
ftp darwin
```

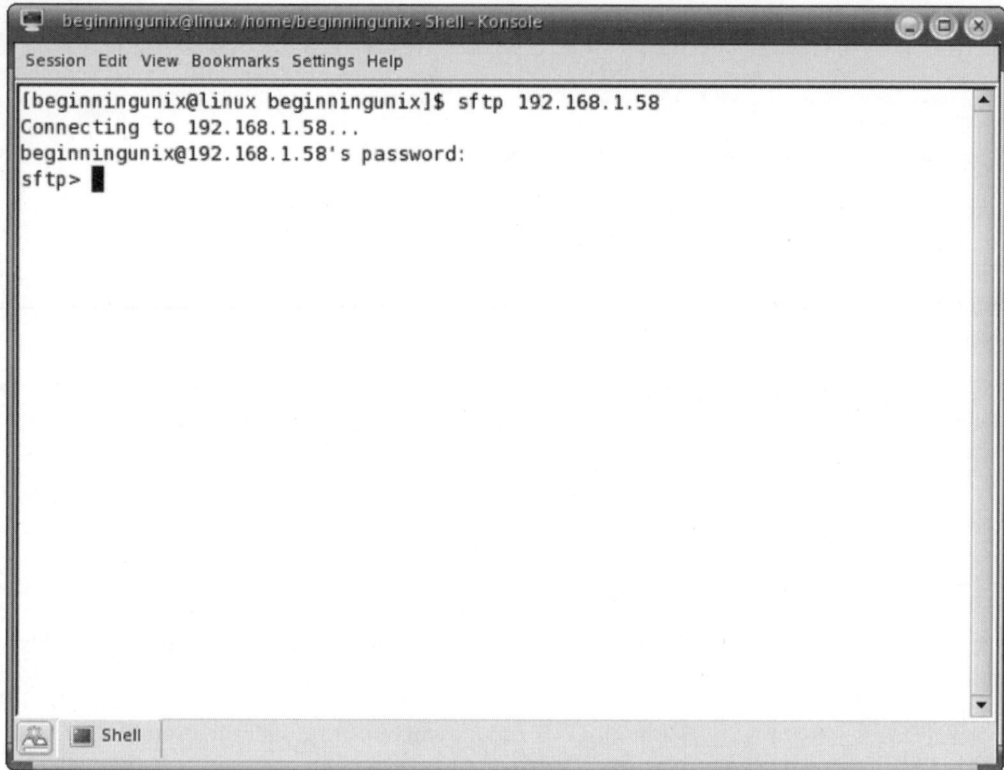

Figure 8-1

If you typed the latter, the output would be similar to:

```
$ ftp darwin
connected to darwin
Name (darwin:beginningunix): beginningunix
331 Password required for beginningunix
Password:
230-
   Welcome to Darwin!
230 User beginningunix logged in.
Remote system type is Unix
Using binary mode to transfer files.
fpt>
```

Figure 8-2 shows the output of the `ftp 192.168.1.58` command. You can see that's it's pretty much the same, except that the machine's IP address is used instead of its name (darwin).

For the `ftp darwin` example, here's the sequence of events that occurs, beginning with the initial command:

```
$ ftp darwin
```

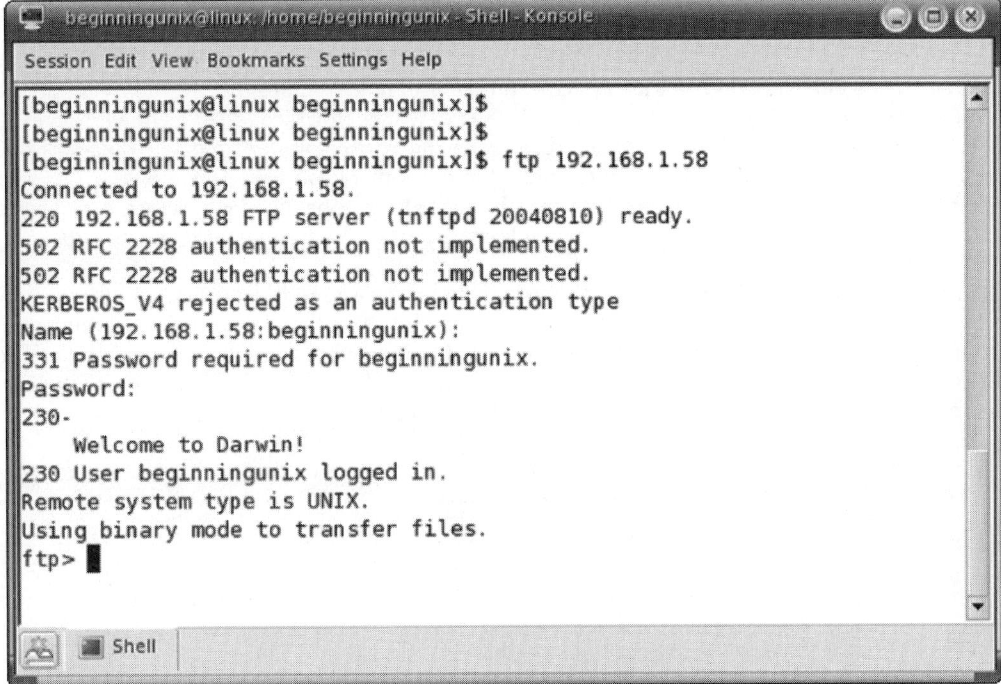

Figure 8-2

You do not have to use the name of the machine to connect, as you know. You could use its IP address instead, as Figure 8-2 illustrates.

The system announces the successful connection to the remote machine:

```
connected to darwin
```

You're connected but have not been authenticated, so you are prompted for your username. Type it after the colon, and then press **Enter** or **Return**. (Pressing **Enter** or **Return** without typing your username allows your default username — the one that you are logged in as on the local system — to be provided to the remote machine. You can see the default name in the parentheses after Name. Often, the default name is the same as your remote-machine username.). Then you are prompted for your password. You must enter your correct system password for the remote system (it may or may not be the same as your password for the local system).

```
Name (darwin:beginningunix): beginningunix
331 Password required for beginningunix
Password:
```

With your credentials accepted, the remote machine provides you with introductory information:

```
230-
    Welcome to Darwin!
230 User beginningunix logged in.
```

```
Remote system type is UNIX.
Using binary mode to transfer files.
```

The fourth line indicates this is a Unix system, and the fifth line indicates that the binary mode is the default download type. Binary mode means that the file will be downloaded at the lowest-level computer representation possible, using 1s and 0s, which is the core computer language. Binary downloading is the safest form, but sometimes takes longer than the other download type, ASCII, which typically consists of letters and symbols on the keyboard. The ASCII-type download is acceptable for text files, but binary mode is best for binary-file, executable-program, and compressed-file downloads.

After you have `sftp`'d or `ftp`'d into a Unix system, you receive a modified prompt, `sftp>` or `ftp>` respectively. When you are `sftp`'ing or `ftp`'ing, you are not using the typical shell environment you would if you had logged in interactively and are therefore limited to a specific set of commands. You are also limited to a specific set of commands for the movement of files. Type **help** and press **Enter** or type **?** and press **Enter** to see a list of the commands, as shown in Figure 8-3.

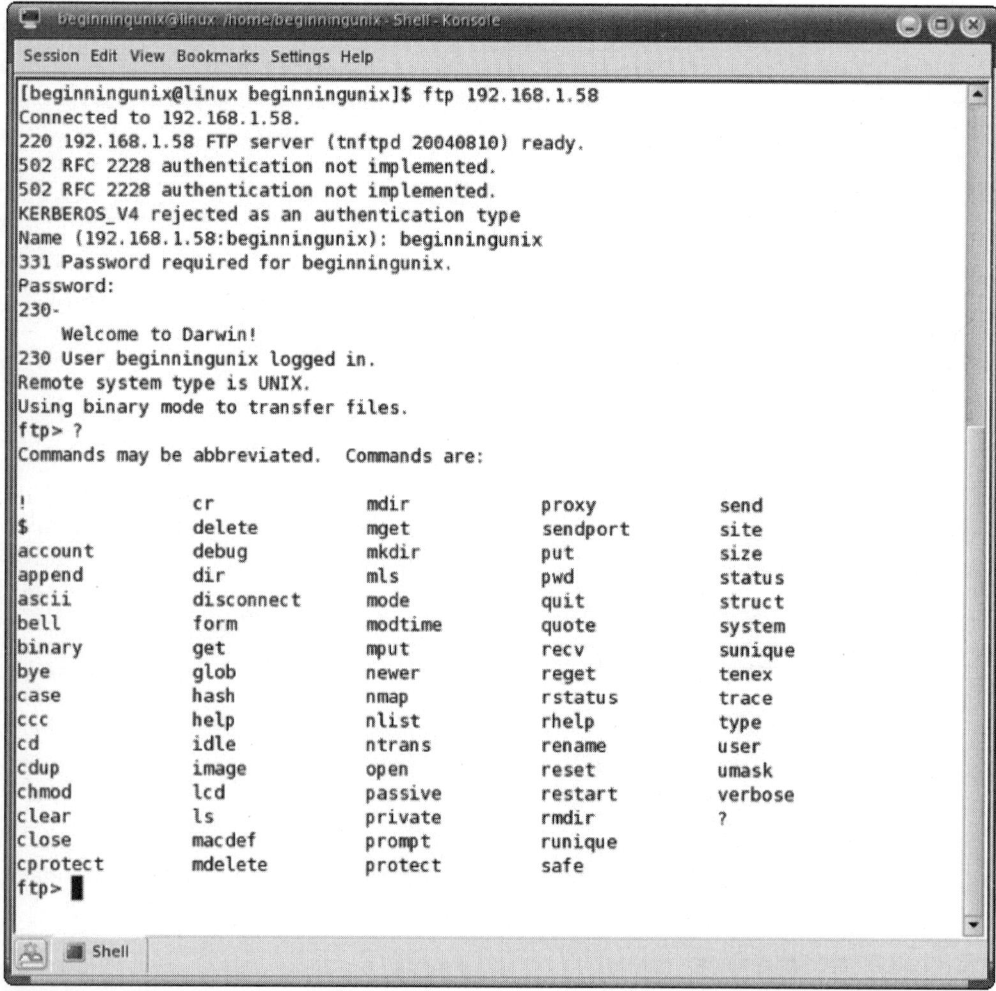

Figure 8-3

To see more specific information about a command, type `help command`. Following are some of the commands available during sftp/ftp sessions (you learned about some of these commands — `rmdir`, `mkdir`, `pwd`, `cd`, and `ls` — in Chapter 4):

Command	Description	Available in SFTP	Available in FTP
`ascii`	Changes the transfer type to ASCII (good for text files).	No	Yes
`binary`	Changes the transfer type to binary (good for binary files).	No	Yes
`bye`	Ends the ftp session.	Yes	Yes
`cd`	Changes directory; used to traverse through the file system.	Yes	Yes
`dir` or `ls`	Shows the contents of a directory.	`ls`, yes; `dir`, no	Yes
`get`	Retrieves file from remote server.	Yes	Yes
`hash`	Turns on hash sign (#) to indicate download progress (default is for each # sign to equal 1024 bytes).	No	Yes
`help`	Shows list of commands.	Yes	Yes
`?`	Shows list of commands (same as `help`).	Yes	Yes
`lcd`	Changes the current local directory to that indicated.	Yes	Yes
`pwd`	Shows the current working directory.	Yes	Yes
`mdelete`	Deletes files on remote server.	No	Yes
`mget`	Retrieves files from remote server.	No	Yes
`mkdir`	Creates a directory on the remote server.	Yes	Yes
`more`	Shows the contents of a file.	No	Yes
`mput`	Copies a file from the local machine to the remote machine.	No	Yes
`put`	Copies a file from the local machine to the remote machine.	Yes	Yes
`rmdir`	Removes a directory on remote server	Yes	Yes
`size`	Shows the size of a file on the remote system.	No	Yes
`system`	Shows the operating system of the remote machine.	No	Yes

After logging in to the remote FTP server, use the `cd` (change directory) command to move around the file system:

```
ftp> cd /home/myfiles
```

To retrieve a file from a remote FTP or SFTP server, use the `get` command. Here's an example of how to retrieve the file `/home/myfiles/myfile.txt` from the remote ftp server (darwin):

```
ftp> get myfile.txt
200 PORT command successful
150 Opening Binary mode data connection for 'myfile.txt' (722 bytes).
226 Transfer complete.
722 bytes received in 0.036 seconds (19 Kbytes/s)
221 Thank you for using the FTP service on Darwin
ftp>
```

The first line contains the `get` command followed by the name of the remote file (`myfile.txt`) that will be retrieved and put into the current directory on the local system. The remote system then reports that the command was successful (`200 PORT command successful`). The third line shows that the download is beginning and that file is 722 bytes in size. The system reports that the transfer is complete, and then tells you the details: how long it took to download the file and at what speed. The sixth line is a simple pleasantry, thanking you for using the system.

If you had typed the command `hash` *before using the* `get` *command, you would have seen a succession of hash marks (*`#`*) indicating the progression of the download, which for long files can assist in determining that the FTP session has not stalled.*

You are returned to a command prompt (`ftp>`) so that you can execute other FTP commands. In this example, the `quit` command terminates the FTP session, ending your connection to the remote machine and returning you to the local system, as indicated by the `$` prompt:

```
ftp> quit
$
```

The `sftp` command operates in almost an identical manner as `ftp` and provides similar output, but it also affords the capability to set up secure, password-free logins and other functionality. The primary difference between FTP and SFTP is that FTP does everything unencrypted or in plain text, whereas SFTP uses encryption, which hides the information and data being transferred between machines. All you do is use `sftp` instead of `ftp` to initiate the connection. Your session would have the `sftp>` prompt instead of the `ftp>`. SFTP offers many more advantages over FTP; you can read more about them at `www.openssh.org`.

More Advanced Commands

You'll find yourself using the commands introduced in this section because they add a great deal of functionality to your work on Unix.

grep

`grep` is one of the most useful commands in Unix. It searches files for a sequence you specify and then prints the results. This may seem trivial, but you may find yourself using this command daily, searching for and within files.

Grep stands for global regular expression print, which is from an ed (pre-vi) editor's set of commands that was initiated with the `g/re/p` *command. That command sequence was used so often that it was decided to create a separate command with the functionality to search and print. The consolidated command is* `grep`.

The command structure for grep is:

`grep` *string_to_search_for file_to_search*

A simple `grep` would be a search for the word *root* in the `/etc` directory and its subdirectories:

```
grep root /etc/*
```

This would result in significant output because, as you might guess, there are many files that contain the word *root*. `grep` supports the use of most of the metacharacters previously described, depending on your version of the command.

`grep` also has a `-v` argument, which enables you to search for everything but a named string. To search `/etc/passwd` for all accounts except the *root* string, you'd type:

```
grep -v root /etc/passwd
```

The output would show the contents of the `/etc/passwd` file that didn't contain the string *root*.

`grep` also can be combined with other commands, as this example shows:

```
cat /etc/passwd | grep root
```

This produces the same output as the preceding command would without the `-v` option, but it demonstrates how you can use `grep` to search for specific characters from the output of another command. The `grep` command can be combined with almost any other command to create useful output.

find

The `find` command is used for finding files in the directory structure. The syntax for `find` is:

`find` *path_to_look_in options*

To find the file `passwd` in the `/etc` directory, you can use the `-name` option:

```
find /etc -name passwd
```

The resulting output shows any matches it finds within the directory and subdirectories of the specified path.

The `find` command comes with many options. The following table describes those most frequently used:

Option	Description
`--help`	Shows help information for the `find` command.
`--maxdepth` *n*	Descends the directory structure to *n* depth. For instance, to search only the directory listed and no subdirectories, you would use `--maxdepth 0`.
`--mindepth` *n*	Descends a minimum of *n* subdirectories.
`--mount`	Prevents searches over other file systems (such as those that are remotely mounted). Searches that span many different file systems tax network resources.

There are other options to use in searching for files; refer to the man pages for more information. The following table lists some of the tests (arguments that refine the output) available for the `find` command. These tests do not work without the `find` command and options.

Test	Description
`+`*n*	Searches for anything greater than the number *n*.
`-`*n*	Searches for anything less than the number *n*.
n	Searches for anything exactly matching the number *n*.
`-amin` *n*	Searches for files that were last accessed *n* minutes in the past.
`-atime` *n*	Searches for files that were last accessed *n* days ago (e.g., `atime 1` searches for a file accessed 1 day ago).
`-fstype` *type*	Searches for the specified file system *type*. Options include `nfs`, `ufs`.
`-gid` *n*	Searches for files with a gid (numeric group ID) equal to *n*.
`-group` *group_name*	Searches for files that have a group name equal to *group_name*.
`-name` *filename*	Searches for files named *filename*. You can use metacharacters to make the search easier.
`-perm` *mode*	Searches for files with permissions set exactly to *mode* (absolute or symbolic).
`-size` *n*	Search for files with the size specified as *n*. You can use `c` for bytes and `k` for kilobytes if you want the output in a format other than the default 512-byte blocks. To find a 2-kilobyte file, you'd use `-size 2k`.
`-type` *file_type*	Searches for files of *file_type*. The options are `b` for block device, `c` for character device, `d` for directory, `p` for named pipe, `f` for regular file, `l` for symbolic link, and `s` for socket.
`-uid` *n*	Searches for file that has the uid (user ID) *n* attached.
`-user` *username*	Searches for files that have *username* attached.

There are many other options available, including some for specially formatted output and some to use regular expressions. For example, to find all files on the system owned by the user beginningunix in the /home directory (and all of its subdirectories), you would use a command similar to:

```
find /home -user beginningunix
```

Say that your system administrator contacted you to make some space in your home directory. You have a lot of files in your home directory, and you aren't sure which files may be causing the problem. To search for files larger than 2,000,000 kilobytes (approximately 2 gigabytes), you can use the following command to show all files that meet that criterion:

```
find /home/beginningunix -size +2000000k -print
```

As most Unix commands do, find has many options; refer to the man page to determine if there are options that would suit your particular needs.

sort

The sort command is a powerful little utility that enables you to sort the output of a command or file in a specified order. The options for sort are described in the following table:

Option	Description
-d	Sorts via dictionary order, ignoring non-alphanumerics or blanks.
-f	Ignores case when sorting.
-g	Sorts by numerical value.
-M	Sorts by month (i.e., January before December).
-r	Provides the results in reverse order.
-m	Merges sorted files.
-u	Sorts, considering unique values only.

The sort command can be quite useful; you'll see why if you try it out with its options.

Try It Out Sort a File

1. Create a file called /tmp/outoforder with the following text:

```
Zebra
Quebec
hosts
Alpha
Romeo
juliet
unix
XRay
xray
```

```
Sierra
Charlie
horse
horse
horse
Bravo
1
11
2
23
```

2. Sort the file by dictionary order:

```
sort -d /tmp/outoforder
```

The results are:

```
1
11
2
23
Alpha
Bravo
Charlie
Quebec
Rome
Sierra
XRay
Zebra
horse
horse
horse
hosts
juliet
unix
xtra
```

Notice that the strings beginning with an uppercase letter have come before any of the lowercase words.

3. The word horse is in the file three times. To remove the extra instances of it in your sort, you can use:

```
sort -du /tmp/outoforder
```

How It Works

If you sort using a file as the input as you did here, the sort does not overwrite or adjust the contents of the input file. After running these two commands on the `/tmp/outoforder` file, the order of the file is the same it originally was. That's because the `sort` command sends the output to standard output (usually the screen). To have the command write to a file, you need to use the > or >>, the write to or append to file operators.

Some new users use `sort` and then redirect the output back into the input file. This removes the contents of the file or creates other possibly undesirable effects, so be sure not to try this.

The `sort` command becomes more powerful when combined with other commands such as `grep` to provide a structured, orderly output that can be parsed by the user.

tee

The `tee` command enables you to split the output of a command to multiple locations. For instance, if you need to see the output of a command on the screen, but you also need to have the output written to a file for later use, you can use `tee`. To run this command, you simply need to define a command and then identify where you want the output file to go. Here's an example:

```
ps -ef | tee /tmp/troubleshooting_file
```

shows the output of the `ps` command on the screen and also writes it to `/tmp/troubleshooting_file`, where it can be viewed later. To append to the file instead of overwriting, you use the `-a` option:

```
ps -ef | tee -a /tmp/troubleshooting_file
```

You can specify as many files as you want after the `tee`, and the output will go to each file.

script

The `script` command enables you to record your entire interactive login session. It captures and places in a file every keystroke you make (and its output) from the time you start it until you end it. `script` is especially useful for troubleshooting problems or using the contents of a session for later review. To use `script`, you simply need to type it with the `-a` option and a filename:

```
script -a /tmp/script_session
```

Without the -a option, the specified file, if it already exists, will be overwritten.

Everything you type after the `script` command is recorded in the file you indicate, `/tmp/script` in this example. If you don't indicate a filename, the command creates a file called `typescript` in the directory you start the command in. When you have completed your scripting session, type `exit` to end it. Be careful not to leave the script session running, because the file you create can begin taking up a significant amount of space, to the point of filling up your file system.

wc

The `wc` command enables you to print a count of the total number of newlines, characters, or words within a file. It has the options described in the following table:

Option	Description
`-c`	Shows the count of characters in the file.
`-l`	Shows the count of newlines in the file.
`-w`	Shows the count of words in the file.

To show the count of words in a file called `/tmp/countfile`, for example, you'd use the following command:

```
wc -w /tmp/countfile
```

The resulting output will show the count of words in the specified file. The other options work in a similar manner.

Using `wc` without any of the options provides all of the results: characters, newlines, and words.

Summary

In this chapter, you learned the basics of using metacharacters and regular expressions, and you were introduced to the `sftp` and `ftp` commands. You also explored some of the more advanced Unix commands, including `grep`, `find`, and `sort`.

As you continue to use Unix, your toolbox will continue to grow. Most things you need to accomplish on a Unix system have a command associated with the task, and it is highly recommended you use the man pages in conjunction with the man page searching option to find tools you need for further advancement.

Exercises

1. Demonstrate how to use the `grep` command to find the service `telnet.d` in the `/etc/inetd.conf` file.
2. You know there's a huge (more than 5 million kilobytes) file in the `/tmp` directory that was last accessed four days ago. You can't remember the filename. How would you search for it?

Advanced Unix Commands: Sed and AWK

As you build your skills in the Unix environment, simple commands may not offer all the functions you need. Most programmers rely on advanced Unix commands to work with scripts and programs, no matter what language they are using. In this chapter, you learn more about two powerful commands that can bring a new level of flexibility and ease to your programming and general Unix work:

- sed: a text editor that works on full streams of text
- AWK: an output formatting language

The commands `sed` and `awk` are somewhat unusual as common Unix commands go. Rather than providing a mechanism to navigate directories or create or delete files, these two commands perform operations primarily on existing text. This text can be the contents of an administrative file, such as `/etc/passwd`; the output from another command, such as `ls`; or the contents of an actual text file that you've created with a text editor—perhaps a program or a lengthy text file, such as the chapter of a book.

The `sed` and `awk` commands find their roots in the old line editor, `ed`. Almost nobody uses `ed` anymore, but it can still be found on most Unix systems. (It's probably on yours! At the very least, code to install `ed` is probably on your installation disks or included in your installation download.) `ed` is a command-line program for editing text files, written in the early days of computing. In those days, a terminal screen could not display multiple lines of output, so you could work on only one line at a time of any given file, no matter how large or complex. The `ed` editor was devised to work within this restriction, offering a number of commands used to navigate through files, perform editing operations, and locate specific lines of files, then perform a specified task on those lines.

> *If you are interested in the* `ed` *editor, try typing* `ed` *at the command prompt to see whether it is currently installed on your system (Type* `q` *to quit* `ed`*). Because it is such a basic program, the* `ed` *man page is the best way to learn more about this editor: Type* `man ed` *at the prompt. If you do not have the man page installed, you can read it on the Web at* `http://unixhelp.ed.ac.uk/CGI/man-cgi?ed`

Sed

The sed command does much the same thing as ed. The main difference is that sed performs these actions in a noninteractive way. Sed is a stream editor (thus the name), and it is designed to work on a specified stream of text according to rules set by the user beforehand. This text stream is usually the output of a previous operation, whether instigated by the user or part of a list of commands that run automatically. For example, the output of the ls command produces a stream of text—a directory listing—that can be piped through sed and edited. In addition, sed can work on files. If you have a group of files with similar content and need to make a particular edit to the contents of all these files, sed will enable you to do that very easily. For example, have a go at the following "Try it Out" section, in which you combine the contents of two files while at the same time performing a substitution for the name "Paul" in both files.

Try It Out Work with Sed

Editing commands for sed can be provided at the command line:

1. Create two files, each with a list of first names, in vi:

```
% vi names1.txt
Paul
Craig
Debra
Joe
Jeremy

% vi names2.txt
Paul
Katie
Mike
Tom
Pat
```

2. At the command line enter and run the following command:

```
% sed -e s/Paul/Pablo/g names1.txt names2.txt > names3.txt
```

3. Display the output of the third file to discover the resulting list of names:

```
% cat names3.txt
Pablo
Craig
Debra
Joe
Jeremy
Pablo
Katie
Mike
Tom
Pat
%
```

How It Works

The sed utility reads the specified files and/or the standard input and modifies the input as directed by a list of commands. The input is then written to the standard output, which can be redirected if need be.

In this example, the `sed` command is searching for all instances of the name Paul in the two files provided in the command-line argument and replacing them with the name Pablo. After the search and replace has been completed, the output is redirected from standard out to a new file called `names3.txt`. Notice the trailing `g` in the command, `s/Paul/Pablo/g`:

```
% sed s/Paul/Pablo/g names1.txt names2.txt > names3.txt
```

This specifies that sed should look globally. Without that trailing `g`, if the name Paul happened to be on the same line twice, only the first would be substituted.

Note that while only one line from each file was affected by substitution, all the lines from both files are displayed, in the order they are processed, in the output from sed. The original files are unchanged; only the output, or in this example the file created from the output, contains the substitution of Pablo for Paul.

Using the -e Option

Multiple commands may be specified by using the `-e` option:

```
% sed -e 's/Paul/Pablo/; s/Pat/Patricia/' names1.txt names2.txt
Pablo
Craig
Debra
Joe
Jeremy
Pablo
Katie
Mike
Tom
Patricia
%
```

The `-e` option is necessary when supplying more than one editing command as a command-line argument to sed. Note that while enclosing the instructions in single quotes is not required (they weren't used in the first sed example), they should be used in all cases. Enclosing the instructions in quotes helps the user visualize what arguments are related to editing and what arguments are related to other information, such as which files to edit. Moreover, the enclosing single quotes will prevent the shell from interpreting special characters or spaces found in the editing instruction.

There are three ways for providing a series of editing instructions for sed to process at the command line. One way is to use the semicolon, such as in the previous example, to separate editing instructions.

Another is to precede each individual editing argument with the `-e` switch, like this:

```
% sed -e 's/Paul/Pablo/g' -e 's/Pat/Patricia/g' names1.txt names2.txt
```

A third option is to use the multiple-line entry capability of the shell, if available. The following is how that would appear within the Bash shell environment, but not C shell:

```
% sed '
> s/Paul/Pablo/
> s/Pat/Patricia/ names1.txt names2.txt'
Pablo
Craig
Debra
Joe
Jeremy
Pablo
Katie
Mike
Tom
Patricia
```

Sed Files

Of course, no matter which of the three methods just described is used, none are practical when it comes time to enter a long list of editing commands for sed on the command line. To provide a large series of commands, sed has the capability to read a file full of commands that contains the editing instructions as a single command-line argument. This is done using the `-f` option.

The file denoted with the `-f` argument simply specifies a text file with a series of actions to be performed in sequence. Most of these actions could be done manually from within vi: replacing text, deleting lines, inserting new text, and so on. The advantage is that all editing instructions are in one place and are executed on a single pass. In the following "Try It Out," you'll put together a collection of commands that will edit two files and place the results into a third file for safekeeping.

Try It Out Use Sed with Multiple Commands

1. Locate the two text files with a list of names from the previous example. Or simply create a new list of names:

```
pdw% vi names1.txt
Paul
Craig
Debra
Joe
Jeremy

% vi names2.txt
Paul
Katie
Mike
Tom
Pat
```

2. Create a new file with vi called `edits.sedscr` and list a series of editing instructions for sed:

```
% vi edits.sedscr
```

```
s/Pat/Patricia/
s/Tom/Thomas/
s/Joe/Joseph/
1d
```

3. Invoke sed:

```
% sed -f edits.sedscr names1.txt names2.txt > names3.txt
```

The result is the following output in the `names3.txt` file:

```
Paul
Craig
Debra
Joseph
Jeremy
Paul
Katie
Mike
Thomas
Patricia
```

How It Works

When you use multiple commands in a file, enter one per line. Each command is individually executed by sed, in the order it is listed within the file. Again, the original files are unchanged; only the output contains the results of sed executing the script file.

As with a previous example, this example redirects the output to a file. In most cases, unless redirecting the output of sed to another program, this is the preferred use of handling output from sed—capturing it in a file. This is done by specifying one of the shell's I/O redirection symbols followed by the name of a file:

```
% sed -f edits.sedscr names1.txt > names3.txt
```

Notice that the output is not redirected to the original file but to a new file that will be created after sed generates its response.

Sed Commands

The sed editor set consists of 25 commands. Some of the most useful ones include the following:

Command	Name	Description
`xa\ text`	Append	Appends text following the command to each line matching the given line address (*x*). Replace *x* with the number (address) of the line to which you want to append `text`.
xd	Delete	Deletes the addressed line, or lines. That is, these lines are not sent to standard output.

Table continued on following page

Command	Name	Description
`xq`	Quit	Quits when address is encountered. The addressed line first is written to output along with any text appended to it by previous append or read commands, then sed quits processing the file.
`xr` *`file`*	Read file	Reads contents of file and appends after the given line address.
`xs/pattern/replacement text/flags`	Substitution	Substitutes replacement for pattern on each addressed line. If additional information about how the substitution is to be executed, such as if the substitution is to be made globally, on all occurrences of the matching pattern, or only for a range of matches, a flag is provided to modify the behavior of the substitution command.
[reg ex pattern] `w` *`file`*	Write files	Appends contents of pattern space to file. This command creates the file if it does not exist; if the file exists, its contents are overwritten each time the script is executed. Multiple write commands that direct output to the same file append to the end of the file.

While these representative commands note a preference for line addresses when editing files, the line address is optional with any command. Instead of a line address, a pattern described as a regular expression surrounded by slashes, a line number, or a line-addressing symbol can be used. For example, the substitution commands used in the previous examples listed a pattern to match instead of a line address:

```
s/Joe/Joseph/
```

If a line address is used, most sed commands can accept processing one or more lines at a time. To handle more lines, line addresses that indicate a range of lines need to be entered separated by a comma: Here are a few examples:

```
# Delete the first and second lines
1,2d
# Delete lines 2 to 5
2,5d
# append the text to the first and second lines
1,2a\ Hello World!
# read the given file and append to after the second line
2r append_file.txt
```

However, a few commands, such as quit, accept only a single-line address. This makes sense because a sed script cannot be applied to a range of lines — sed can only quit once.

```
# Quit at the 100th line
100q
```

Multiple commands executed on the same address can be grouped together by surrounding the list of commands in braces:

```
# Delete the last line and quit
${d
  q
}
```

The first command can be placed on the same line with the opening brace, but the closing brace must appear on its own line. Also, notice the indentation of the commands inside the braces; spaces and tabs at the beginning of lines are also permitted to allow for easier comprehension when reviewing a list of commands to see what's being done at each step. If the line address of the last line within a file is not known, it can be specified using the dollar sign (`$`), as in this example.

For the sake of readability by any user, placing multiple commands on the same line is highly discouraged because `sed` scripts are difficult enough to read even when each command is written on its own line.

AWK

Sed works much like editing commands manually in any type of text editor, so it's a good choice for editing text in a file or from other commands in a noninteractive, batch environment. But sed does have some shortcomings, such as a limited capability to work on more than one line at a time, and it has few rudimentary programming constructs that can be used to build more complicated scripts. So there are other solutions when it comes to scripting complex text processing; AWK, which offers a more general computational model for processing a file, is one of them.

A typical example of an AWK program is one that transforms data into a formatted report. The data might be a log file generated by a Unix program such as `traceroute`, and the report might summarize the data in a format useful to a system administrator. Or the data might be extracted from a text file with a specific format, such as the following example. In other words, AWK is a pattern-matching program, akin to sed.

Try It Out Use AWK

Try out this one `awk` command at the command line:

```
%awk '{ print $0 }' /etc/passwd
```

The results will look something like the following, depending on the entries in the `/etc/passwd` file:

```
root:x:0:0:root:/root:/bin/bash
bin:x:1:1:bin:/bin:/sbin/nologin
sync:x:5:0:sync:/sbin:/bin/sync
shutdown:x:6:0:shutdown:/sbin:/sbin/shutdown
halt:x:7:0:halt:/sbin:/sbin/halt
mail:x:8:12:mail:/var/spool/mail:/sbin/nologin
nobody:x:99:99:Nobody:/:/sbin/nologin
sshd:x:74:74:Privilege-separated SSH:/var/empty/sshd:/sbin/nologin
apache:x:48:48:Apache:/var/www:/sbin/nologin
webalizer:x:67:67:Webalizer:/var/www/usage:/sbin/nologin
```

```
ldap:x:55:55:LDAP User:/var/lib/ldap:/bin/false
mysql:x:27:27:MySQL Server:/var/lib/mysql:/bin/bash
pdw:x:500:500:Paul Weinstein:/home/pdw:/bin/bash
%
```

How It Works

AWK takes two inputs: a command, set of commands, or a command file and a data or data file. As with sed the command or command file contains pattern-matching instructions for which AWK is to use as a guideline for processing the data or data file.

In this example, AWK isn't processing any data but is simply reading the /etc/passwd file's contents and sending the data unfiltered to standard out, much like the cat command. When AWK was invoked, it was provided with the two pieces of information it needs: an editing command and data to edit. The example specifies /etc/passwd as input file for data, and the edit command simply directs AWK to print each line in the file in order. All output is sent to standard out (which can be directed elsewhere), a file, or another command.

Extracting with AWK

The real working power of AWK is in extracting parts of data from a larger formatted body.

Using the /etc/passwd file again, the following command takes two of the fields from each entry in the /etc/passwd file and creates a more human-friendly output:

```
% awk -F":" '{ print "username: " $1 "\t\t\t user id:" $3 }' /etc/passwd
```

The results will be something similar to this:

```
username: root          user id:0
username: bin           user id:1
username: sync          user id:5
username: shutdown      user id:6
username: halt          user id:7
username: mail          user id:8
username: nobody        user id:99
username: sshd          user id:74
username: apache        user id:48
username: webalizer     user id:67
username: ldap          user id:55
username: mysql         user id:27
username: pdw           user id:500
%
```

By default AWK associates a blank space as a delimiter for the incoming data; to change this association the -F switch is used to denote a different field separator — the colon, for example, is the field separator in the /etc/passwd file. So the quotation marks around the colon, directly following the -F switch denote the delimiter that is in use.

This example also uses a print command to provide a structure to the output:

```
print "username: " $1 "\t\t\t user id:" $3
```

All the text to be printed as noted is wrapped in double quotation marks. The `$1` and `$3` are variables that contain the data AWK is filtering. AWK initializes a set of variables every time it process a file; `$1` is the variable that contains the text up to the first delimiter; `$2` is the second field, and so on, so this command calls for the contents of the first (`$1`) and third (`$3`) fields. Variable `$0` would be the whole line.

The AWK editing command consists of two parts: patterns and commands. Patterns are matched with the line from the data file. If no pattern is provided, AWK matches any line and the command is always executed. The preceding example has no pattern to match before determining whether the command is to be executed, so AWK executes the command for each and every line.

Working with Patterns

Patterns in AWK work just like patterns in sed; they consist of a string of text or one or more regular expressions contained within slashes (`/`). Here are a couple of example patterns:

```
# String example
/text pattern/
# Reg Ex example match any lowercase chars
/[a-z]/
```

The commands that follow the pattern rules provide instructions on what AWK is to do when a pattern match evaluates as true. Commands may contain several instructions, each separated by a semicolon (;). Common AWK instructions include `=`, `print`, `printf`, `if`, `while`, and `for`.

These instructions behave like similar instructions in other programming languages, providing the capability to assign values to variables (`=`), print output (`print` and `printf`), or execute segments of code given a certain set of conditions (`if`, `while`, and `for`). Conditional statements provide for the capability to refine pattern matching.

In the preceding example, the first and third fields are printed in between text that identifies the values for the user reading the output. The statement `printf` denotes that the output is going to have its own format and allows for the use of escape sequences such as the `\t`, which simply denotes spacing of the output, specifically that the output should be spaced by a tab; the example called for two tabs.

Other commonly used escape sequences include those shown in the following table.

Escape Sequence	Function
`\f`	Form feed, new page
`\n`	New line (\012 or \015)
`\r`	Carriage return, overprint
`\v`	Vertical tab
`\'`	Single quotation mark
`\"`	Double quotation mark
`\\`	Backslash

Table continued on following page

Escape Sequence	Function
\0	Null (character value 000)
\a	Alert, bell
\b	Backspace
\040	Space
\ddd	Octal notation
\xddd	Hexadecimal notation

Pattern matching, with either exact strings or regular expressions, is at the heart of both sed and AWK. So it makes sense that understanding how it works and what power that regular expressions bring to it are important aspects of maximizing the benefit of tools such as sed, AWK, and even Perl. (Perl is discussed in Chapter 17.)

Programming with AWK

AWK, unlike sed, is actually a full-fledged, structured, interpreted programming language for pattern matching. That might sound intimidating, but it isn't once the basics are understood.

What it does mean is that AWK is a lot more robust when it comes to developing rules for matching patterns of data with regular expressions. Just think of the rules as a series of steps or commands for breaking apart the data. As with sed, more then a handful of commands can be placed within a file for better overall management. In the following "Try It Out," you place commands from the previous "Try It Out" example into a file that AWK can then use as a collection of steps for processing data.

Try It Out Use an AWK File

1. Use vi to enter the following and save the file as `print.awk`:

```
BEGIN {
  FS=":"
}
{ printf "username: " $1 "\t\t\t user id: $3 }
```

2. Execute `awk` as follows:

```
% awk -f print.awk /etc/passwd
```

The resulting output is just as the previous example:

```
username: root          user id:0
username: bin           user id:1
username: sync          user id:5
username: shutdown      user id:6
username: halt          user id:7
```

```
username: mail          user id:8
username: nobody        user id:99
username: sshd          user id:74
username: apache        user id:48
username: webalizer     user id:67
username: ldap          user id:55
username: mysql         user id:27
username: pdw           user id:500
%
```

How It Works

The script as executed performs the same function as the previous example; the difference here is the commands reside within a file, with a slightly different format.

Because AWK is a structured programming language, there is a general format to the layout of the file:

1. Beginning commands, which are executed only once at the beginning of the file, are set into a block starting with the word `BEGIN`. The block is contained in braces exactly as the example shows:

```
BEGIN {
  FS=":"
}
```

2. Pattern-matching commands are blocks of commands that are executed once for each and every line in the data file. Here's an example:

```
{ printf "username: " $1 "\t\t\t user id: $3 }
```

3. Ending commands, a block of commands first denoted by the word `END`, are executed only once, when the end of file is reached. While the "Try It Out" example contains no commands with an `END` block, a possible `END` block for this example might look something like this:

```
END {
  Printf "All done processing /etc/passwd"
}
```

The only code in the example's `BEGIN` block is the definition of the delimiter, the colon. This is akin to the `-F` switch used at the command line in the previous example. In this example, the delimiter is assigned to a variable, `FS`, which AWK will check when executing the main pattern-matching block of code.

`FS` (field separator) is one of several standard variables that AWK uses. Others include:

- `NF` — Variable for providing a count as to the number of words on a specific line.
- `NR` — Variable for the record being processed. That is, the value in NR is the current line in a file `awk` is working on.
- `FILENAME` — Variable for providing the name of the input file.
- `RS` — Variable for denoting what the separator for each line in a file is.

AWK variables are typeless. That is, unlike other programming languages where the content of the variables has to be predefined — for example, is the variable a numeric value that can be manipulated by the rules of mathematics or a string of alphanumeric characters that are evaluated by a different set of rules — AWK allows any value to be entered without first providing a data type. In other words, numbers or character strings can be assigned to variables and AWK tries to make some sense out of what is present within the variable.

The main section of the program, the pattern-matching commands for each data line, is executed in order from the top line down. Lines from the data file are read and evaluated one by one, from the top of the file down as well.

When the AWK program is reading and evaluating a data file, the commands see only the current single line from the data file at a time and all AWK program variables. The whole line is subject to pattern matching and is automatically loaded into special variables such as `$0`, `$1`, and so on.

The `END` block, as with the `BEGIN`, provides a set of commands that are to be executed only once, when the end of the incoming data has been reached. The last example did not include an `END` segment. `BEGIN` and `END` segments are not necessary for all AWK programs. They are helpful, however, in setting up and cleaning up a working environment from which the bulk of the programming can work within.

> *The versions of AWK available on some systems do not allow* `BEGIN` *or* `END` *commands, but set all variables to zero or space when the execution of the program starts. Make sure you consult the documentation on your system before attempting anything ambitious.*

In any case, the point for `BEGIN` and `END` segments is that AWK is a stateless programming environment. That is, AWK treats each new input line in a similar way. Beginning and ending blocks as well as variables and conditional instructions enable the programmer to create a set of states that allows some lines of data to be treated in different ways than other lines of data. This is important because most real tasks need a set of states to filter data in a useful manner.

Summary

The editor sed and programming language AWK enable you to perform powerful text manipulation and editing tasks at the command line. You can use them separately or together to manage the contents of multiple Unix file types. Sed and AWK offer a variety of features, including the capability to:

- Use output from one program as input for text manipulation functions
- Sort and extract information from a lengthy file, displaying only the desired data
- Use sophisticated pattern-matching functions
- Globally replace multiple pattern strings with a single command

Exercises

Create the following file to use for these exercises. Name it `addresses.txt`:

```
Roger Longtwig:35 Midvale Ave.:Austin, TX:35432
Brad Brookstone:1044 E. 32nd St.:NY, New York:10001
Richard Smack:845 Pleasant Ter.:Dauberville, CT:06239
Django Steinbart:10 E. Point Way:Atlanta, GA:30374
Cliff Claymore:111 S. Main St.:Clevenger, IA:55472
```

1. Create a command that will sort these by ZIP code into a file called `addresses-sorted.txt`.
2. Create a sed script that will replace any street abbreviation (such as St. or Ave.) or cardinal abbreviation (N., S., E., W.) with the full word.
3. Create a command that will reverse the "NY, New York" in the second line to "New York, NY".

Job Control and Process Management

This chapter covers starting and stopping processes, sending signals to running programs, viewing information on running processes, shell job control, and more. These essential functions enable the Unix user to manage multiple processes from the command prompt, as well as to understand the ongoing functions of a multiuser operating system. You'll learn how to identify and control system and user processes with basic Unix tools.

What Is a Process?

A *process*, in simple terms, is an instance of a running program.

As covered in Chapter 2, the parent of all processes, `init`, is started when the operating system boots. Historically, it is process ID number 1. As other programs are started, each is assigned a unique process identifier, known as a *PID*.

Behind the scenes, a fork library call or an execve system call is used to start the new program. A *fork* is produced when the current running program is copied to make a *child*, an exact copy of the running program. The forked program has a new PID and a different parent process ID (of course), and the child's resource utilizations are all reset. For example, by default, the forked child and its parent share file descriptors and can share open files.

In contrast to forking a process, you can replace the current running process with a new process. The Unix shell includes a built-in command called `exec` that replaces the running shell with a new program. (Behind the scenes, this uses the execve system call.) For example, typing `exec date` will run the `date` program, and the original shell will be closed.

Normally, process IDs are assigned in a sequential order. As processes stop, the previously unavailable PIDs can be used again. Usually, PIDs are in the 1 to 32768 range. Some systems have 64-bit PIDs and a larger range. On a sample NetBSD workstation that has been up for 50 days, you might see 117 processes with PIDs ranging from 0 through 27152.

Some systems assign a pseudo-random process ID in an attempt to stop malicious programs from guessing PIDs to exploit temporary file race conditions. (A race condition is when different programs attempt to do something before the other; for example, a malicious program may attempt to create a symlink using a guessed filename to an important file before another program uses the filename.) Nevertheless, if the security issue exists, randomness probably doesn't matter since many process IDs can be guessed anyway.

To see the PID assigned to your shell, look at the `$` shell variable. For example:

```
% echo $$
23527
```

This output, 23527, is the process ID of the running command line shell.

Starting a process is as simple as typing a command at the Unix shell prompt or starting a program from a menu. The software contains executable code for your platform. The file system attributes indicate whether the file is an executable and who has permission to execute it (the owner of the file, the members of group that owns the file, or everyone). You can use the `ls` long listing (`ls -l`) to see these file modes.

The `file` command, found on most Unix systems, can also tell you if a file is an executable. For example, on a NetBSD 1.6.x system, you might issue this command:

```
$ file /bin/ls
/bin/ls: ELF 32-bit LSB executable, Intel 80386, version 1 (SYSV), for NetBSD,
statically linked, stripped
```

On a Mac OS X box, `file` shows:

```
$ file /bin/ls
in/ls: Mach-O executable ppc
```

On a Linux system, you might see:

```
$ file /bin/ls
/bin/ls: ELF 32-bit LSB executable, Intel 80386, version 1 (SYSV), for GNU/Linux
2.0.0, dynamically linked (uses shared libs), stripped
```

Give the `file` command a try by running it with the filenames of all types of Unix files as the arguments and see what it tells you. You should see brief descriptions of the file types.

Shell Scripts

You can also have executable files that can be executed as they are written, rather than being written in programming code. When such a program is loaded, the first characters of the file indicate what type of executable format it is. The magic characters `#!` (often called a *sh-bang*) tell the kernel to run the program listed after the `#!`, including setting command-line arguments as required. The file then becomes the input to be used by the now-running interpreter.

Try It Out Making a Simple Shell Script

Use that well-known example of a shell script, "Hello World," to explore the concept of making a simple shell script.

1. Open a text editor.
2. Enter these two lines into an empty file:

```
#!/bin/cat
Hello World
```

3. Save the file as `cat.script` and exit the editor.
4. Make the file executable with this command:

```
chmod a+x cat.script
```

5. Run the file:

```
./cat.script
```

You can also use the full path to the command to run it. The output will simply be the file itself, because `cat` displays it.

How It Works

As you can tell from this simple example, the sh-bang program doesn't even have to be a real programming language interpreter, but in most cases, it is used by `/bin/sh` and for Perl scripts. Many examples of shell scripting are covered throughout this book. For more details on getting started with shell scripting, see Chapter 13.

What Processes Are Running?

It is easy to see your own processes by running the `ps` (process status) command. Issued without any arguments, `ps` displays your own processes that are associated with a terminal. The `ps` tool is very useful for quickly seeing what processes you and others on your same system have running. It also can be used to see which processes are using up your memory or overworking your CPU.

For example, on a Linux 2.6.x system, you might get this output:

```
$ ps
  PID TTY          TIME CMD
18358 ttyp3    00:00:00 sh
18361 ttyp3    00:01:31 abiword
18789 ttyp3    00:00:00 ps
```

The following is from a NetBSD 1.6.x system:

```
$ ps
  PID TT STAT    TIME COMMAND
  2205 p1 IWs+  0:00.00 bash
```

```
17404 p2 Ss+    1:59.69 ssh -l reed montecristo
26297 p3 Ss     0:00.04 bash
26316 p3 R+     0:00.00 ps
```

This example is from a Mac OS X 10.3 box:

```
$ ps
  PID  TT  STAT      TIME COMMAND
29578 std  Ss     0:00.03 -bash
29585 std  S      0:00.00 sleep 1000
```

Notice in these default examples that `ps` displays the process ID, the terminal that process is attached to (like `ttyp3` or `p2`), the accumulated user plus system time for the process, and the command (and some arguments) for that process.

The NetBSD example also shows the run state for those processes (in the STAT column). The running state of the process is identified by the first letter. The following table shows some of the common states.

State	Function
I	Idle, sleeping for more 20 seconds
D	Waiting for disk or other uninterruptible wait
R	Runnable, active use
S	Sleeping for less than 20 seconds
T	Stopped or traced process
Z	Zombie process; a dead or defunct process

Depending on the Unix system and the type of `ps` *command installed, you may have different or additional state identifiers. Be sure to read the* `ps(1)` *man page for details.*

In the preceding `ps` output examples, the `W` state means the process is swapped out. The small `s` state means it is a session leader. The plus sign (+) means that that process has use of that terminal.

ps Syntax

The `ps` command is one of a few commonly used Unix tools that have different syntax and different output format on different Unix flavors. The two common `ps` tool formats are the BSD (or Berkeley) `ps` implementation, as available on *BSD and Mac OS X systems, and the Unix System V implementation, like that found on Solaris systems. Most Linux systems provide a `ps` tool that accepts both `ps` tool formats. In fact, the `ps` tool provided with the `procps` suite for Linux systems conforms to the Single Unix Specification version 2 and also mimics `ps` for IBM S/390, AIX, Digital Unix, HP-UX, IRIX, SCO, SunOS, and Unix98.

The main difference in the `ps` syntax is the usage of the dash character to prefix options. The standard BSD `ps` options do not use a dash with the `ps` command line options. For example, to output the process status of your current shell using a BSD-style `ps`, issue the command:

```
ps $$
```

To do the same with a System V style `ps`, use:

```
ps -p $$
```

Give it a try to figure out what syntax your `ps` uses. (Perhaps it supports both.)

Process States

In the Linux `ps` example shown earlier, the output did not show information about process states. To have `ps` output this extra information, using the BSD `ps` syntax, you can use the `u` argument:

```
$ ps u
USER        PID %CPU %MEM   VSZ   RSS TTY      STAT START   TIME COMMAND
reed      18358  0.0  0.7  2460   668 ttyp3    S    Sep13   0:00 -sh
reed      18361  0.0 11.6 32936 10756 ttyp3    S    Sep13   6:12 abiword
reed      19736  0.0  0.8  2508   784 ttyp3    R    18:12   0:00 ps u
```

As you can see, it reports the user running the process, the process ID, the percentage of the CPU the process has been using over the past minute, the percentage of the real memory, the virtual memory size in kilobytes, the physical memory used, the terminal it is connected to, the states, when the process was started, the amount of CPU time used by process (since it was started), and the command name.

Similar information can be shown using the System V `ps` style with the `-l` switch. The following example is on a Solaris system:

```
$ ps -l
 F S   UID   PID  PPID  C PRI NI     ADDR     SZ    WCHAN TTY      TIME CMD
 8 S   511   366   360  0  50 20        ?    332        ? pts/2    0:01 bash
 8 S   511   360   358  0  40 20        ?    136        ? pts/2    0:00 sh
 8 O   511 11820   366  0  50 20        ?    138          pts/2    0:00 ps
```

The first field (F) is no longer used and is included for only historical purposes. The second field (S) is the state.

It is important to note that the command name could be modified. Some processes change their reported command name to show status information about the running process. For example, a POP3 server may use the command name field to show what it is currently doing. The initial command name may show the actual filename of the POP3 daemon software, and the changed name may indicate who is currently retrieving e-mails.

System Processes

By default, your system should have several processes running (or in other run states). For example, an ordinary workstation might have 76 processes, and 53 processes running. This is easy to see by issuing the command `ps ax | wc -l` and then subtracting one for the line that contains the `ps` header.

The `a` argument for `ps` causes it to report information about processes for all users. The `x` argument tells `ps` to display information about processes without a controlling terminal.

System processes are programs running behind the scenes handling many essential maintenance aspects for your system. Normally, system processes do not have a TTY (teletype) in use. Many of these processes are often called *daemons*, and they do routine work. The following is an example of system processes running on a Linux system:

```
$ ps ax
  PID TTY        STAT   TIME COMMAND
    1 ?          S      0:00 init [3]
    2 ?          SW     0:00 [migration/0]
    3 ?          SWN    0:00 [ksoftirqd/0]
    4 ?          SW<    0:00 [events/0]
    5 ?          SW<    0:00 [khelper]
    6 ?          SW<    0:00 [kacpid]
   20 ?          SW<    0:00 [kblockd/0]
   21 ?          SW     0:00 [khubd]
   31 ?          SW     0:00 [pdflush]
   32 ?          SW     0:00 [pdflush]
   33 ?          SW     0:13 [kswapd0]
   34 ?          SW<    0:00 [aio/0]
  618 ?          SW     0:00 [kseriod]
  646 ?          SW<    0:00 [ata/0]
  647 ?          SW     0:00 [khpsbpkt]
  670 ?          SW     0:00 [kjournald]
  788 ?          SW     0:00 [kjournald]
  793 ?          S      0:00 /usr/sbin/syslogd
  797 ?          S      0:00 /usr/sbin/klogd
  816 ?          S      0:00 /usr/sbin/sshd
  829 tty1       S      0:00 /sbin/agetty 38400 tty1
  830 tty2       S      0:00 /sbin/agetty 38400 tty2
  831 tty3       S      0:00 /sbin/agetty 38400 tty3
```

The following is a list of system processes running on a Solaris system. It uses the `-e` switch to output information on every process:

```
$ ps -e
   PID TTY      TIME CMD
     0 ?        0:02 sched
     1 ?        0:18 init
     2 ?        0:00 pageout
     3 ?        8:06 fsflush
   314 ?        0:00 sac
   224 ?        0:00 utmpd
   315 console  0:00 ttymon
    47 ?        0:00 sysevent
    54 ?        0:00 picld
   130 ?        0:00 rpcbind
   191 ?        0:00 syslogd
   179 ?        0:00 automoun
   153 ?        0:00 inetd
   205 ?        0:00 nscd
   213 ?        0:00 powerd
   166 ?        0:00 statd
   203 ?        0:00 cron
   169 ?        0:00 lockd
```

```
  318 ?        0:00 Xsun
  317 ?        0:00 ttymon
  307 ?        0:02 vold
  257 ?        0:00 sendmail
  245 ?        0:00 afbdaemo
  237 ?        0:00 smcboot
  238 ?        0:00 smcboot
  239 ?        0:00 smcboot
  258 ?        0:00 sendmail
  319 ?        0:01 mibiisa
  290 ?        0:00 snmpdx
  295 ?        0:00 dtlogin
  299 ?        0:00 dmispd
  322 ?        0:00 dtlogin
  302 ?        0:00 snmpXdmi
  320 ?        0:00 sshd
  323 ??       0:00 fbconsol
  335 ?        0:00 dtgreet
```

This last example shows the system processes on a Mac OS X box:

```
$ ps ax
  PID  TT  STAT      TIME COMMAND
    1  ??  Ss     0:00.02 /sbin/init
    2  ??  Ss     1:48.08 /sbin/mach_init
   78  ??  Ss     0:01.30 /usr/sbin/syslogd -s -m 0
   84  ??  Ss     0:02.28 kextd
  106  ??  Ss     0:00.58 /usr/sbin/configd
  107  ??  Ss     0:00.14 /usr/sbin/diskarbitrationd
  112  ??  Ss     0:02.74 /usr/sbin/notifyd
  128  ??  Ss     0:00.01 portmap
  142  ??  Ss     0:04.01 netinfod -s local
  144  ??  Ss     2:56.96 update
  147  ??  Ss     0:00.00 dynamic_pager -F /private/var/vm/swapfile
  171  ??  Ss     0:00.00 /usr/sbin/KernelEventAgent
  172  ??  Ss     0:00.40 /usr/sbin/mDNSResponder
  176  ??  Ss     0:00.68 /System/Library/CoreServices/coreservicesd
  177  ??  Ss     0:00.14 /usr/sbin/distnoted
  187  ??  Ss     0:00.88 cron
  192  ??  Ss     0:01.21 /System/Library/CoreServices/SecurityServer -X
  199  ??  S      0:00.00 /usr/libexec/ioupsd
  200  ??  Ss     1:37.85 /System/Library/Frameworks/ApplicationServices.framew
  203  ??  Ss     0:00.63 /System/Library/Frameworks/ApplicationServices.framew
  210  ??  Ss     0:04.15 /usr/sbin/DirectoryService
  228  ??  Ss     0:17.88 /usr/sbin/lookupd
  254  ??  Ss     0:00.02 /usr/libexec/crashreporterd
  279  ??  Ss     0:00.01 nfsiod -n 4
  287  ??  Ss     0:00.02 rpc.statd
  291  ??  Ss     0:00.00 rpc.lockd
  306  ??  Ss     0:12.81 /usr/sbin/cupsd
  310  ??  S      0:00.00 rpc.lockd
  319  ??  Ss     0:00.05 xinetd -inetd_compat -pidfile /var/run/xinetd.pid
  328  ??  Ss     0:01.30 slpd -f /etc/slpsa.conf
  334  ??  Ss     0:00.03 mountd
  337  ??  Ss     0:00.00 nfsd-master
```

```
  338  ??  S       0:11.83 nfsd-server
  345  ??  Ss      0:22.02 /usr/sbin/automount -f -m /Network -nsl
  348  ??  Ss      0:00.01 /usr/sbin/automount -f -m /automount/Servers -fstab -
  355  ??  Ss      0:00.00 /usr/sbin/postfix-watch
 4560  ??  Ss      0:00.65 /System/Library/CoreServices/loginwindow.app/Contents
 4561  ??  S       0:00.53 /System/Library/Frameworks/ApplicationServices.framew
 4565  ??  Ss      0:00.17 /System/Library/CoreServices/pbs
 4570  ??  S       0:00.86 /System/Library/CoreServices/Dock.app/Contents/MacOS/
 4571  ??  S       0:09.84 /System/Library/CoreServices/SystemUIServer.app/Conte
 4572  ??  S       0:03.95 /System/Library/CoreServices/Finder.app/Contents/MacO
 4581  ??  S       0:07.51 /Applications/Utilities/NetInfo Manager.app/Contents/
 4612  ??  Ss      0:00.18 /System/Library/CoreServices/loginwindow.app/Contents
 4614  ??  S       5:29.32 /System/Library/CoreServices/SecurityAgent.app/Conten
 4615  ??  S       0:00.18 /System/Library/Frameworks/ApplicationServices.framew
15147  ??  Ss      0:00.27 /usr/sbin/sshd -I
```

In the preceding examples, a terminal (TTY) is not associated with most of the system processes. This is noted by a question mark in the TTY field. Also note that the output may be truncated to fit the console width. Using the BSD `ps`, you can add two `ww` options for extra-wide output.

Process Attributes

Each process has an environment with various attributes such as command-line arguments, user environment variables, file descriptors, working directory, file creation mask, controlling terminal (console), resource limitations, and a lot more. Many of the attributes are shared with the parent process.

The kernel also knows about, and can report, numerous other process attributes. On a NetBSD box, the kernel keeps track of around 85 different attributes for each process. Some examples include reporting the process ID of its parent, the real and effective user and group IDs, the time the process was invoked, and resource utilization, such as memory usage and total time spent executing the program. A real user or group ID is generally the user and group that initially started the program. The effective user or group ID is when a process is running with different (such as enhanced) permissions. (You can read more about this later in this chapter in the "SETUID and SETGID" section.)

To view the various process attributes, you can use the `ps -o` switch, which is available for both styles of `ps`. It is used for defining the output format. For example, to output the process IDs, parent PIDs, and the size of the processes in virtual memory of your own running processes, issue the command:

```
ps -o user,pid,ppid,vsz,comm
```

The following are commonly used output format fields:

Field	Definition
user	Effective user ID of the process
pid	Process ID
ppid	Process ID of the parent

Field	Definition
pcpu	Percentage of CPU time used
rss	Real memory size in kilobytes
pmem	Percentage of rss to physical memory
vsz	Kilobytes of the process in virtual memory
tty	Controlling terminal name
state (or s)	Process state
stime	Time started
time	Accumulated user and system CPU time
command (or comm)	Command name

Be sure to review your `ps(1)` *manual to see what output formats are available.*

Stopping Processes

Ending a process can be done in several different ways. Often, from a console-based command, sending a **CTRL + C** keystroke (the default interrupt character) will exit the command. But sometimes the interrupt character may be trapped or ignored.

The standard tool for killing a process is `kill`. Technically, the `kill` command does not kill a command, but sends a special signal to the process. Signals are used for simple communication between processes. Programmers frequently write their software to handle signals in different ways, such as to tell the software to reload its configuration, reopen log files, or enable debugging output. Some signals may be used to tell the software that a network connection is closed, an illegal or problematic memory access was attempted, there are hardware errors, or some other event has occurred. Over 30 signals are available.

If your system has developer manual pages, you can learn more about signal programming under the C language by reading the `signal(3)` *and* `sigaction(2)` *man pages.*

The default signal for the `kill` command is SIGTERM (for *terminate*). It is possible that the software you're trying to stop is written to cleanly back up files or close down its work when it receives this TERM signal, but don't count on it.

To use the `kill` command, just place the process ID of the process to signal as the command line argument. For example, to send the default SIGTERM signal to the process ID 5432, run the command:

```
kill 5432
```

Be very careful with the `kill` *command. Use the correct PID or you may accidentally close or signal the wrong program, which may make your system unstable or unusable.*

You can also choose the signal by name by prefixing the signal name with a dash, such as:

```
kill -SIGTERM 5432
```

The SIG part of the signal name is optional.

To list the possible signal names, run `kill` with the `-l` switch:

```
$ kill -l
HUP     INT     QUIT    ILL     TRAP    ABRT    EMT     FPE     KILL    BUS
SEGV    SYS     PIPE    ALRM    TERM    USR1    USR2    CLD     PWR     WINCH
URG     POLL    STOP    TSTP    CONT    TTIN    TTOU    VTALRM  PROF    XCPU
XFSZ    WAITING LWP     FREEZE  THAW    CANCEL  LOST    XRES    RTMIN   RTMIN+1
RTMIN+2 RTMIN+3 RTMAX-3 RTMAX-2 RTMAX-1 RTMAX
```

With some shells, the `kill` command is already built-in. To use the independent `kill` tool instead of the built-in `kill`, you can run it with the full path name, as in `/bin/kill` (or `/usr/bin/kill` depending on your system).

Signals can also be identified by a signal number. The bash shell's built-in `kill` command lists the signals with their signal numbers, for example:

```
$ kill -l
 1) SIGHUP       2) SIGINT       3) SIGQUIT      4) SIGILL
 5) SIGTRAP      6) SIGABRT      7) SIGEMT       8) SIGFPE
 9) SIGKILL     10) SIGBUS      11) SIGSEGV     12) SIGSYS
13) SIGPIPE     14) SIGALRM     15) SIGTERM     16) SIGURG
17) SIGSTOP     18) SIGTSTP     19) SIGCONT     20) SIGCHLD
21) SIGTTIN     22) SIGTTOU     23) SIGIO       24) SIGXCPU
25) SIGXFSZ     26) SIGVTALRM   27) SIGPROF     28) SIGWINCH
29) SIGINFO     30) SIGUSR1     31) SIGUSR2     32) SIGPWR
```

If you attempt to kill a process and it does not die, you can try using the unignorable SIGKILL signal. This signal can't be handled by individual programs. As mentioned earlier, programs may be written to exit cleanly, so don't use `kill -9` as your first choice or you may close the program with files or tasks in an inconsistent state.

The `kill` command doesn't use command names as arguments. Although this may seem like an inconvenience, it does make sense—you would not want to kill the wrong program if you have several processes running with the same command name. The normal way to find the PID of the command you want to kill is with the `ps` command. The `ps` output can be piped through `grep` to list only matching processes. For example, to find the process ID of the FireFox Web browser, you might issue this command:

```
$ ps auxww | grep firefox
reed    29591  0.0 16.2 40904 21224 ??  SNs    20Nov04  314:57.03
/usr/pkg/lib/firefox-gtk2/firefox-bin /home/reed/lynx_bookmarks.html
reed    14929  0.0  0.4   100   480 pj  DN+    3:23PM     0:00.01 grep firefox
```

The `grep` output also shows the `grep` line itself. You could kill that FireFox process with the command `kill 29591`.

If using a System V `ps` *tool, use the* `ps -ef` *or* `-el` *switches.*

Many Unix systems provide tools called `pgrep`, `pkill`, and `killall` that can be used with command names instead of using PIDs. On Solaris and System V systems, `killall` means "kill all." It is used by `shutdown` to terminate all active processes. On other systems, `killall` is used to send signals to processes by name. Be careful when using `killall`. On Linux systems, this dangerous tool is called `killall5`.

A safer tool is `pkill`. The `pkill` command is used like the `kill` command but instead of using the PID as the argument to the signal, the command name is used. To kill the FireFox browser, for example, you could run:

```
pkill firefox
```

The argument to `pkill` is a simple regular expression for matching. Also, the `pgrep` tool can be used to simply list the process IDs as `pkill` would see them, without sending any signal. (The `pkill` tool defaults to sending the SIGTERM signal.)

The `pkill` command can be dangerous because it may match more than you expect. Use the `pgrep` command to test first. Be sure to read your system's `pgrep` (and `pkill`) man pagse to see its specific options.

Some systems have a `pidof` command that is similar to `pgrep` but doesn't do a substring match.

The Process Tree

A process tree displays the lineage of your different processes, placing a child process with its parent. Note that only one parent process exists per child process but that each parent can have multiple children. For example, here is a sample Linux process tree:

```
$ pstree
init-+-3*[agetty]
     |-events/0-+-aio/0
     |          |-ata/0
     |          |-kacpid
     |          |-kblockd/0
     |          |-khelper
     |          `-2*[pdflush]
     |-gconfd-2
     |-kdeinit-+-artsd
     |         |-firefox-bin---firefox-bin---3*[firefox-bin]
     |         |-3*[kdeinit]
     |         `-kdeinit---sh---ssh
     |-8*[kdeinit]
     |-khpsbpkt
     |-khubd
     |-2*[kjournald]
     |-klogd
     |-kseriod
     |-ksoftirqd/0
     |-kswapd0
     |-migration/0
     |-sshd---sshd---sshd---sh---pstree
     |-syslogd
     `-xdm-+-X
           `-xdm---startkde---kwrapper
```

The example clearly shows that `init` is the parent of all processes. Also interesting in the output is the `pstree` child, because it shows the parent and grandparents.

A nice process tree program can be written with AWK and shell scripts, or with Perl scripting. A simple `pstree` *command is available at* `www.serice.net/pstree/`. *Another* `pstree` *implementation is available in the* `psmisc` *suite from* `http://psmisc.sourceforge.net/`. *Also, the* `ps` *command from the* `procps` *suite provides a* `--forest` *switch that outputs a nice ASCII reproduction of the process tree.*

Zombie Processes

Normally, when a child process is killed, the parent process is told via a SIGCHLD signal. Then the parent can do some other task or restart a new child as needed. However, sometimes the parent process is killed. In this case, the "parent of all processes," `init`, becomes the new PPID (parent process ID). You can often see this indicated by a process ID of 1 as the PPID of some other process.

When a process is killed, a `ps` listing may still show the process with a `Z` state. This is a *zombie*, or defunct, process. The process is dead and not being used. In most cases, in a few moments it will actually be gone and your `ps` output won't show it. In some rare cases, like with old Unix kernels combined with buggy software, you may find that some processes just won't die even if you send a -SIGKILL signal to them.

If a process is hung, first try sending it a couple of -SIGTERM signals. If you wait and then verify that the process has not yet quit, try sending a -SIGKILL signal. If you find that the process stubbornly refuses to die, you may need to reboot your system.

The top Command

The `top` command is a very useful tool for quickly showing processes sorted by various criteria. It is an interactive diagnostic tool that updates frequently and shows information about physical and virtual memory, CPU usage, load averages, and your busy processes. The `top` command is usually found on *BSD, Linux, and Mac OS X systems. It can also be downloaded at `www.groupsys.com/topinfo/` in versions suitable for various other Unix systems.

Here's an example of `top` running under a Solaris system:

```
load averages:  0.19,  0.24,  0.12;  up 3+19:01:58                    06:14:02
37 processes:  36 sleeping, 1 on cpu
CPU states: 99.7% idle,  0.0% user,  0.2% kernel,  0.0% iowait,  0.0% swap
Memory: 512M real, 381M free, 26M swap in use, 859M swap free

   PID USERNAME LWP PRI NICE  SIZE   RES STATE    TIME    CPU COMMAND
     1 root       1  59    0 1232K  368K sleep    0:17  0.00% init
   358 root       1  59    0 4520K 2696K sleep    0:13  0.00% sshd
   307 root       2  59    0 2648K 2000K sleep    0:01  0.00% vold
   366 jreed      1  59    0 2672K 1984K sleep    0:01  0.00% bash
 16492 jreed      1  59    0 1760K 1184K cpu      0:00  0.00% top
   318 root       1  59    0  122M   11M sleep    0:00  0.00% Xsun
   335 root       1  59    0 7912K 4864K sleep    0:00  0.00% dtgreet
```

```
  322 root       1  59    0 6488K 2832K sleep    0:00  0.00% dtlogin
  205 root      18  59    0 3264K 2528K sleep    0:00  0.00% nscd
  302 root       2  59    0 3560K 2368K sleep    0:00  0.00% snmpXdmid
  295 root       1  59    0 5008K 2048K sleep    0:00  0.00% dtlogin
  179 root       3  59    0 3728K 1992K sleep    0:00  0.00% automountd
  319 root       7  59    0 2400K 1960K sleep    0:00  0.00% mibiisa
  299 root       2  59    0 3144K 1936K sleep    0:00  0.00% dmispd
  257 root       1  59    0 4424K 1864K sleep    0:00  0.00% sendmail
```

Some older versions of Solaris and SunOS do not provide the `top` command. It can be downloaded from a third party, such as `www.sunfreeware.com`, or installed from source.

The following output shows `top` running on a Mac OS X box:

```
Processes:  60 total, 2 running, 58 sleeping... 126 threads             06:14:04
Load Avg:  0.00, 0.00, 0.00      CPU usage:  0.0% user, 4.2% sys, 95.8% idle
SharedLibs: num =  115, resident = 34.0M code, 3.52M data, 9.45M LinkEdit
MemRegions: num =  3065, resident = 23.8M + 7.87M private, 52.0M shared
PhysMem:   106M wired, 93.8M active,  106M inactive,  306M used, 1.20G free
VM: 3.52G + 80.7M   256370(0) pageins, 0(0) pageouts

  PID COMMAND      %CPU   TIME    #TH #PRTS #MREGS RPRVT  RSHRD  RSIZE  VSIZE
17705 gconfd-2     0.0%  0:00.91   1    13     47   792K  1.95M  2.75M  28.3M
17700 bash         0.0%  0:00.61   1    13     18   228K   964K   664K  18.2M
17699 sshd         0.0%  0:01.90   1     9     42   256K  1.69M   636K  30.2M
17697 sshd         0.0%  0:00.35   1    15     39   100K  1.69M  1.41M  30.0M
15361 bash         0.0%  0:00.33   1    12     17   192K   948K   844K  18.2M
15358 sshd         0.0%  0:01.02   1     9     39   112K  1.69M   468K  30.0M
15147 sshd         0.0%  0:00.27   1    15     39   100K  1.69M  1.41M  30.0M
 9960 top          7.3%  0:00.36   1    17     26   268K   492K   648K  27.1M
 4615 ATSServer    0.0%  0:00.18   2    44     50   392K  4.03M  1.81M  60.3M
 4614 SecurityAg   0.0%  5:29.32   1    62     88  1.29M  13.8M  10.7M   144M
 4612 loginwindo   0.0%  0:00.18   3   110     90  1008K  2.97M  3.05M   127M
 4581 NetInfo Ma   0.0%  0:07.51   2    78    103  1.86M  8.79M  15.8M   154M
 4572 Finder       0.0%  0:03.95   1    99    123  3.46M  16.9M  21.8M   169M
 4571 SystemUISe   0.0%  0:10.05   1   169    113  1.80M  8.38M  17.0M   154M
 4570 Dock         0.0%  0:00.86   2    76    100   612K  8.95M  10.6M   143M
 4565 pbs          0.0%  0:00.17   2    47     39   516K  1.36M  4.28M  43.8M
```

Different implementations of `top` provide different information and have different keystrokes for interactive behavior. Generally, the `top` command shows the process with the most CPU activity at the top of the list. This is customizable.

> *View the manual page for your* `top` *command or, if your* `top` *supports it, press the question mark (?) while running* `top` *for help. Press the **Q** key to quit* `top`.

The previous examples of `top` output show the load average over 1, 5, and 15 minutes. You can also run the `uptime` or `w` commands to display the load averages:

```
netbsd3$ uptime
 4:21AM  up 139 days, 17:11, 5 users, load averages: 0.22, 0.22, 0.24
```

The *load average* shows the average number of jobs in the run queue for the past minute, 5 minutes, and 15 minutes. It is an indicator of active processes. This information can be used to quickly determine whether your system is busy.

> *The load average information is specific to your operating system release and your hardware. You cannot accurately compare load averages from different systems to evaluate performance. For example, a NetBSD system running on an Alpha hardware architecture with a load average of 10 may feel and behave faster than a Linux system on a standard x86 architecture with a load average of 3.*

It is very common to see a load average of 0.00 or near zero even on a moderately used system.

The /proc File System

The `/proc` file system is a dynamically generated file system that can be used to retrieve information about processes running on your system. Depending on the Unix system, the `/proc` file system can also be used to retrieve and set other kernel-level configurations. Linux and Solaris systems provide `/proc` file systems. `/proc` file systems are also available for other Unix systems but are usually not mounted by default.

The `/proc` file system contains a directory entry for active processes named after the PID. These directories contain files that provide various attributes about the process. For example, the following is the directory listing of a `/proc` file system for a personal shell process on a Solaris box:

```
$ ls -l /proc/$$
total 5402
-rw-------   1 jreed    build    2736128 Dec 16 12:06 as
-r--------   1 jreed    build        152 Dec 16 12:06 auxv
-r--------   1 jreed    build         32 Dec 16 12:06 cred
--w-------   1 jreed    build          0 Dec 16 12:06 ctl
lr-x------   1 jreed    build          0 Dec 16 12:06 cwd ->
dr-x------   2 jreed    build       8208 Dec 16 12:06 fd
-r--r--r--   1 jreed    build        120 Dec 16 12:06 lpsinfo
-r--------   1 jreed    build        912 Dec 16 12:06 lstatus
-r--r--r--   1 jreed    build        536 Dec 16 12:06 lusage
dr-xr-xr-x   3 jreed    build         48 Dec 16 12:06 lwp
-r--------   1 jreed    build       2112 Dec 16 12:06 map
dr-x------   2 jreed    build        544 Dec 16 12:06 object
-r--------   1 jreed    build       2568 Dec 16 12:06 pagedata
-r--r--r--   1 jreed    build        336 Dec 16 12:06 psinfo
-r--------   1 jreed    build       2112 Dec 16 12:06 rmap
lr-x------   1 jreed    build          0 Dec 16 12:06 root ->
-r--------   1 jreed    build       1472 Dec 16 12:06 sigact
-r--------   1 jreed    build       1232 Dec 16 12:06 status
-r--r--r--   1 jreed    build        256 Dec 16 12:06 usage
-r--------   1 jreed    build          0 Dec 16 12:06 watch
-r--------   1 jreed    build       3344 Dec 16 12:06 xmap
```

Here is the `/proc` entry for `init` on a Linux box:

```
$ sudo ls -l /proc/1
total 0
-r--------    1 root     root            0 Dec 20 04:41 auxv
-r--r--r--    1 root     root            0 Dec 20 02:11 cmdline
lrwxrwxrwx    1 root     root            0 Dec 20 04:41 cwd -> /
-r--------    1 root     root            0 Dec 20 04:41 environ
lrwxrwxrwx    1 root     root            0 Dec 20 04:00 exe -> /sbin/init
dr-x------    2 root     root            0 Dec 20 04:41 fd
-r--r--r--    1 root     root            0 Dec 20 04:41 maps
-rw-------    1 root     root            0 Dec 20 04:41 mem
-r--r--r--    1 root     root            0 Dec 20 04:41 mounts
lrwxrwxrwx    1 root     root            0 Dec 20 04:41 root -> /
-r--r--r--    1 root     root            0 Dec 20 02:11 stat
-r--r--r--    1 root     root            0 Dec 20 04:41 statm
-r--r--r--    1 root     root            0 Dec 20 02:11 status
dr-xr-xr-x    3 root     root            0 Dec 20 04:41 task
-r--r--r--    1 root     root            0 Dec 20 04:41 wchan
```

The `/proc` file system can be used to see what file descriptors are in use by processes, what the command name is, what executable is actually running, what environment variables are defined, and more.

SETUID and SETGID

Programs can run with enhanced capabilities when the files have set-user-ID-on-execution or set-group-ID-on-execution modes set. If a program is owned by the root user and the set-user-ID mode bit is set, it will have enhanced (root) privilege when it's run by a regular user. For example, look at these `setuid` or `setgid` tools on a Mac OS X box:

```
-r-xr-sr-x  1 root  operator   23336 23 Sep  2003 /bin/df
-r-sr-xr-x  3 root  wheel      41480 25 Sep  2003 /usr/bin/chsh
-r-sr-xr-x  1 root  wheel      37704 23 Sep  2003 /usr/bin/crontab
-r-xr-sr-x  1 root  kmem       24320 23 Sep  2003 /usr/bin/fstat
-r-sr-xr-x  1 root  wheel      39992 25 Sep  2003 /usr/bin/passwd
-rwxr-sr-x  1 root  postdrop  140556 25 Sep  2003 /usr/sbin/postqueue
```

This output is in normal `ls` long-listing format (such as `ls -l`). The user and group execute bits shown with a small letter `s` indicate they are setuid or setgid, respectively.

This output shows there are a number of useful administrative tools that operate under the SETUID and SETGID umbrellas:

- The `setgid df` command runs as the operator group so it can look at disk devices that are not readable by everyone but are readable by members of the operator group.
- The `setuid chsh` and `passwd` tools run as the root user, so a regular user can update the user database. This software is written so that the users can modify only their own entries.

- The `setuid crontab` command runs with root privileges, so it can create, edit, or remove the user's own `crontab` from the `crontabs` directory, usually at `/var/cron/tabs/`.
- The `setgid fstat` tool runs as the `kmem` group so it can read from the `/dev/kmem` device, which is not readable by the world but is readable by `kmem` group members. The `/dev/kmem` device is used to retrieve various system data structures useful for troubleshooting, debugging, and performance analysis.
- The `setgid postqueue` tool runs with `postdrop` group privileges so it can view and manage Postfix e-mail queue files. (Postfix is a mail transfer agent that is not installed by default on all Unix systems. See `www.postfix.org` for more information.

There are many other examples of SETUID and SETGID software used on a daily basis. You can use the `find` tool to list this software on your system. Give the following command a try:

```
sudo find / -perm -4000 -print
```

This command lists all the files that have the set-user-ID-on-execution bit set.

As you may imagine, SETUID and SETGID software can potentially cause security issues. For example, software that doesn't correctly check its input could be abused to run other commands or access other files with enhanced privileges. SETUID or SETGID software should be carefully written and audited. Most Unix systems do not allow `setuid` (or `setgid`) scripts because of several techniques for taking advantage of a shell script and its environment. Some systems do offer `suidperl`, which can be used for creating `setuid` Perl scripts. (See Chapter 17 for information on getting started with Perl.)

The main way to utilize `setuid` and `setgid` functionality safely is to use fine-grained groups that own the directories and/or files (including devices) to which a user needs read or write access. For example, the user databases could be split up into many separate files with some allowing permission for the specific user to modify.

Shell Job Control

The Unix command-line shell can be used to run programs in the background so you can run multiple programs at a time. It also can be used to suspend commands and restart suspended commands. To tell the shell to run a given command in the background, simply append an ampersand to the end of the command line. For example, to run `sleep` in the background, issue the command:

```
$ sleep 60 &
[1] 16556
$
```

This command runs `sleep` for 60 seconds. The `sleep` tool basically waits a set amount of time and then exits successfully. By using the ampersand, the next command-line shell prompt is displayed and is usable immediately for running other commands.

The example output is from the BASH shell. The number 1 in brackets is the job number, And the 16556 is the process ID. This is displayed by the shell, not by the `sleep` command.

Most shells have a built-in `jobs` command that can be used to show your running shell jobs:

```
$ jobs
[1]+  Running                    sleep 60 &
```

A command running in the background is not waiting for console input, but may possibly be outputting text to the console. A command running in the foreground can have full interaction.

You can move a job from the background to the foreground by running the built-in `fg` command. If you have multiple jobs, you can set the job number as the `fg` argument, as in:

```
$ fg 1
sleep 60
```

Once you bring a command to the foreground, your shell's prompt does not display until the process is ended, and you can't run another command until then.

The shell also enables you to suspend a currently running foreground process by pressing the suspend keystroke combination **Ctrl + Z** by default. Using the `sleep` command is an easy way to practice using job control. Here's an example of pressing **Ctrl + Z** after running `sleep`:

```
$ sleep 60
^Z
[1]+  Stopped                    sleep 60
$ jobs
[1]+  Stopped                    sleep 60
$ bg %1
[1]+ sleep 60 &
$
```

The ^Z (**Ctrl + Z**) keystroke stopped job number one. It can be unsuspended by using `fg` or the built-in `bg` command. In this example, `bg` was used to run it in the background.

Shell jobs can also be killed (or signals can be sent to shell jobs). Most shells have a built-in `kill` command where you use a percent sign to reference a job number instead of a PID. For example, `kill %1` would send the terminate signal to the job number one. Be sure to use the percent sign if you're using shell jobs, or you may end up sending the signal to the wrong process.

A process can also be suspended by sending signal 18 (SIGTSTP) to it, and then unsuspended by sending signal 19 (SIGCONT):

```
$ sleep 120 &
[2] 15695
$ kill -18 %2
 [2]+  Stopped                    sleep 120
$ kill -19 %2
$ jobs
[2]+  Running                    sleep 120 &
netbsd
$
```

Using `kill` to suspend and unsuspend processes may be useful when you don't have a way to press **Ctrl + Z** to suspend.

Summary

This chapter covered several simple but essential tools for process management. Processes are simply loaded programs associated with a unique process ID. Processes are often known as parents and children — the created process (the newly started program) is called the child.

- Process information can be listed with the `ps` and `top` tools and by viewing the `/proc` file systems (on operating systems that provide `/proc`).
- The `ps` and `top` tools can be used for performance reporting and troubleshooting.
- Signals are a way to communicate between processes.
- The `kill` command is the standard tool for sending signals to processes; and its default is to send a termination signal.
- Unix shells provide a simple way to run multiple programs in the background simultaneously by adding an ampersand (`&`) to the end of the command line.

Running Programs at Specified Times

It is no wonder that the first digital computers were designed to handle repetitive tasks most people would find difficult or uninteresting. This is what computers excel at. This method of computing, known as batch computing, is still with us today, and the value of the digital computer, no matter what operating system, is cut severely if the computer system is solely dependent on an interactive mode, constant action and reaction from a user or users. This chapter explores some of the fundamental tools available on a Unix system for running programs at scheduled times—the first step in taking full advantage of digital computers.

Of course, you can't run anything at a scheduled time without a clock, so this chapter first explains how to set a system clock, how it relates to the clock embedded on the hardware, and how to synchronize the clock with other systems on a network.

This chapter also examines common tools such as crontab used to schedule and run programs and scripts on a Unix system, and provides working examples of how system automation can help save a user from unnecessary repetition and boredom.

System Clock

Most computer systems actually have two 24-hour clocks: a hardware clock and a system clock. The battery-powered hardware clock is embedded within the computer hardware. It's designed to keep track of time when the system is not turned on. The system clock is its software counterpart, created when the system initializes. It is set from the hardware clock.

On most Unix systems, the hardware clock is set to keep Universal Time (UTC), also called Greenwich Mean Time (GMT), instead of the time of day in the system's actual time zone. The system can be configured to keep track of UTC time and to adjust for the offset between UTC and the local time, including daylight saving time.

For example, when a Unix-based system such as Linux boots, one of the initialization scripts runs the program `hwclock`, which copies the current hardware clock time to the system clock. This is an important first step because it is from the system clock (also known as the kernel clock or software clock) that the Unix system gets the current time and date.

UTC does not change as daylight saving time comes into effect in various time zones (and not all places participate in daylight saving time).

Most system clocks store and calculate time as the number of seconds since midnight January 1, 1970, UTC, regardless of whether the hardware clock is set to UTC. To allow the clock to increment 1 second at a time, Unix simply counts seconds since New Year's Day 1970. All changes in denoting the time are done by library functions linked into the system or applications that convert between UTC and local time at runtime.

An advantage to storing time in this fashion is that there was no inherent Y2K problem with Unix-based systems. The disadvantage is that the Y2K problem has simply been postponed, because the number of seconds since the January 1, 1970 UTC, known as the Unix epoch, are stored on a signed 32-bit integer on a 32-bit system and sometime in the year 2038, the number of seconds since the beginning of the Unix epoch will be larger then a 32-bit integer.

Another advantage is that system tools such as `date` or applications such as ntpd adjust on-the-fly to the local time conditions so that the format used to display the current time can be adjusted on a system, application, or user level. Consider a situation in which a user is accessing the system from a different time zone. If he chooses, he can set an environment variable, `TZ`, to adjust all dates and times to appear correctly for his specific time zone and not the time zone where system is physically located.

The system clock is an important part of the overall system. Without it, a number of programs and functions such as automation would not work. Setting the system clock or hardware clock requires superuser (root) privileges. In the following examples, the `sudo` command is used to grant temporary superuser status to the privileged user for changing the clock settings.

Checking and Setting the System Clock with Date

To check or set the system clock, `date` is the command-line tool to use. Given no arguments, the command returns the current date and time:

```
% date
Sun Oct 31 23:59:00 CST 2004
```

The command outputs the relevant time zone, too. In this example, it denotes that this specific system clock is synchronized for central standard time.

To set the current time and date to, say, a minute and half into the New Year, January 1, 2006, 00:01:30, the `date` command needs the proper arguments in the format of CCYYMMDDhhmm.ss, where CCYY is the four-digit year (2006); MMDD is the two-digit month and two-digit day (0101); and hhmm.ss is the two-digit hour (24-hour notation), two-digit minute, and two-digit second (0001.25):

```
% sudo date 200601010001.30
Sun Jan  1 00:01:30 CST 2006
```

Syncing Clocks on Linux with hwclock

There are a number of methods for setting the hardware clock of a given system. One common way is to configure the clock when setting up other hardware initialization settings in the hardware's built-in software. However, because the software interface varies from hardware platform to hardware platform, another method is to set the system clock first, and then synchronize (sync) the hardware clock to the system clock setting.

The `hwclock` command is for querying and setting the hardware clock. With no arguments, it displays the current setting:

```
$ /sbin/hwclock
Tue 30 Nov 2004 02:50:43 PM CST  -0.600758 seconds
```

The `hwclock` command is not located in the user's path of executable programs because many systems, including various Linux distributions, place commands such as `hwclock` with other programs that are intended to be used only by root in a directory called `/sbin`. As noted before, setting the hardware clock, which is one of the main functions of this command, is intended only for superuser accounts such as root. Thus, to even query the date the hardware clock is set to, a typical user of a Linux distribution will need to include the path to the `hwclock` command as well as the command itself.

To sync the hardware clock with the system clock, the `hwclock` command requires the switch `--systohc`:

```
$ sudo /sbin/hwclock --systohc
```

If the hardware clock is to be set to UTC, an additional switch, `--utc`, is needed to complete the command.

Syncing the System Clock with NTP

Another common tool for keeping the clocks in order is syncing the system with an outside system, using the Network Time Protocol (NTP). As the name implies, this requires a networked system. It looks for the current time at another trusted system running a NTP server. Moreover, if the system always has a network connection at boot time, the system can skip syncing with the hardware clock all together and use `ntpdate` (often included with the ntpd package on Linux systems) to initialize the system clock from a network-based time server. It doesn't matter whether the time server is remote or on a local network.

Here's an example of how to use the tool:

```
$ sudo ntpdate
10 Dec 19:35:39 ntpdate[3736]: step time server 17.254.0.27 offset -11.081510 sec
```

The ntpd program is the standard for synchronizing clocks across a network, and it comes with a list of public time servers to which a system can connect using the NTP. NTP not only provides a method for transmitting the current time but also takes into account the delay in transition, providing an additional level of accuracy. Moreover, NTP uses a trust level to determine what server has an authoritative time. The lower the number, the better the trustworthiness, so a level 1 clock is best because it's set by an accurate and trusted time source. Most systems—Apple, Linux, Windows—provide one or two public NTP servers to which systems can sync if no other local or network server is available. These tend to be level 2 servers.

To synchronize the system clock using NTP, first find one or more NTP servers to use. Check with a network administrator or server provider, who may have set up a local NTP server for this purpose. There are a number of online lists of publicly accessible NTP servers, such as the listing at `http://ntp.isc.org/bin/view/Servers/WebHome`. In worst case, check whether your Unix system provider offers a public NTP server with which you can connect. Always make sure you understand the usage policy for any server and ask for permission if required.

On a number of Unix-type systems, NTP is configured in the `/etc/ntp.conf` file:

```
server ntp.local.com prefer
server time.apple.com

driftfile /var/db/ntp.drift
```

The `server` options specify which servers are to be used; each server is listed on an individual line. If a server is specified with the `prefer` argument, as with `ntp.local.com`, that server is preferred over any other listed servers. A response from a preferred server is used unless it differs significantly from the responses of other listed servers.

Additional information can be provided in the `ntp.conf` file if needed. For example, a `driftfile` option specifies a file that stores information about the system clock's frequency offset. This is used by `ntpd` to automatically compensate for the clock's natural drift, should `ntpd` be cut off from all external time sources for a period of time.

Any Unix system can be an NTP server for other systems using ntpd.

Scheduling Commands to Run in the Future

To put the system clock to good use and to automate tasks, all Unix systems provide two key tools — `cron` and `at` — for running commands, applications, and scripts at specified times.

Routine Execution with Cron

The cron program enables Unix users to execute commands, scripts, and applications at specified times and/or dates. Cron uses a Unix daemon (called crond) that needs to be started only once, usually when the system boots, and lies dormant until it is required. When is the `cron` daemon required? The daemon, called `crond`, is required when the time comes to run a specified command, script, or application from one of the config files, or crontabs.

Starting and Using Cron

To start `cron` from the command line, simply enter the following command:

```
$ sudo crond
$
```

The process automatically goes into the background; unlike most applications, `cron` doesn't require the `&` argument to force it there.

However, on most Unix distributions, `crond` is automatically installed and will run at startup. Use the `ps` (process status) command to check that the daemon is running:

```
$ ps auwx | grep cron
root       2068  0.0  0.0  2168  656 ?       S    Nov02   0:00 crond
pdw       24913  0.0  0.0  4596  568 pts/3   R    02:08   0:00 grep cron
```

Once the cron daemon is up and running, it can be put to extensive use.

Try It Out — Schedule Backup of Important Documents

Each user on a Unix system has a home directory that stores all documents, applications, and system options for personal use. The information in this directory can be valuable and irreplaceable, and many go to great lengths to keep it safe. An important step in keeping valuable data safe is to keep a backup copy. Of course, remembering to routinely back up any item can be challenging, even in the best of times, let alone in the course of any given day with plenty of distractions at work or at home. Sounds like a perfect use of cron, doesn't it?

Follow these steps to schedule backup for one of your directories:

1. Take a look at your home directory and determine which documents are important and where they reside. Depending on personal organization habits, the directory might look something like this:

```
$ ls
bin  Desktop  docs  downloads  Mail  tmp
$
```

2. Of the directories containing information, choose one for this exercise. `docs` is always a good one—its contents generally should be backed up—and that's what is used in the example.
3. Create a new subdirectory within your home directory called backups.

```
$ mkdir backups
$
```

4. Open the cron configuration file `/etc/crontab` in a text editor. (You need superuser privileges to open and edit the file.)

```
$ sudo vi /etc/crontab
```

The contents of the file will look something like this:

```
SHELL=/bin/bash
PATH=/sbin:/bin:/usr/sbin:/usr/bin
MAILTO=root
HOME=/

# Adjust the time zone if the CMOS clock keeps local time, as opposed to
# UTC time.  See adjkerntz(8) for details.
1,31 0-5 * * * root adjkerntz -a

# run reports on network usage
```

```
*/5 * * * * root /usr/local/bin/mrtg /usr/local/etc/mrtg/mrtg.conf

# routine maintenance for Weinstein.org
0,30 * * * * cd /home/pdw/public_html/weinstein.org; make tabernacle 2>&1
>/dev/null

# seti@home client for pdw
0  1,5,9,13,17,21 * * * cd /usr/local/bin/setiathome; ./setiathome -nice 19 >
/dev/null 2> /dev/null
```

5. At the end of the file, add the following lines:

```
# Copy docs directory to a local backup directory every hour
# Entered by (your name) on (today's date). Version 1.0
0 * * * * userid cp -r ~~username/docs ~username/backups
```

At the top of the next hour change into the backups directory and do a detailed directory listing:

```
$ ls -l
total 1
drwxr-xr-x  0 userid userid 4096 Feb  8 14:00 docs
$
```

How It Works

Open `/etc/crontab` in a text editor again to understand the magic of cron. The first few lines are pretty straightforward; they set up the environment for cron to do its job:

```
SHELL=/bin/bash
PATH=/sbin:/bin:/usr/sbin:/usr/bin
MAILTO=root
HOME=/
```

Here's an explanation of each entry:

- `SHELL` — The shell cron will run under.
- `PATH` — The directories that will be in the search path for cron. That is where to find most of the programs installed on the system from which cron will probably be invoked at the scheduled time.
- `MAILTO` — Who gets mailed the output of each command, if a command cron is running has output. If no user if specified, the output will be mailed to the owner of the process that produced the output.
- `HOME` — The home directory for the cron application.

The second part of the crontab file defines the conditions for when and what, the details of which are set up in a space-separated series of fields. There are normally seven fields in an entry:

```
0 * * * * userid cp -r ~~username/Mail ~~username/backups; cp -r ~~username/docs
~username/backups
```

Each entry is generally preceded by comment lines (each starting with a #) that describe or otherwise identify the entry. These are discussed in the "Properly Documenting the Crontab File" section, coming up next.

Here's a rundown on the fields:

1. **Minute:** The minute of the hour on which the command will run. The value in this field is a number from 0–59. This example runs on the hour, so the minute value is 0.
2. **Hour:** The hour on which the command will run. This entry is specified using the 24-hour clock. That is, the value must be between 0–23, with 0 equating to midnight. An asterisk (*) indicates every hour, as in the example.
3. **Day of month:** Day (1–31) the command is to run. If the command is to be executed on the 19th of each month, for example, the value for this field would be 19. An asterisk (*) indicates every day, as in the example.
4. **Month:** The month in which a specified command will run. The value may be specified numerically, 1–12 or as the name of the month, Jan–Dec, using the first three characters only. (Case does not matter; sep is the same as Sep.) An asterisk (*) indicates every month, as in the example.
5. **Day of week:** Day of week for a command to run. The value can be numeric, 0–7, or the name of the day, Sun–Sat, using the first three characters only. (Case does not matter; thu is the same as Thu.) If numeric, both 0 and 7 equate to Sunday.
6. **User:** The user who runs this command.
7. **Command:** The command to be invoked. This field may contain multiple words or commands—whatever it takes to get the job done.

Properly Documenting the Crontab File

Comments are a useful feature in any configuration file and should be used to the fullest extent possible. They enable you to document what you add or modify in the file. A # symbol precedes a comment—anything to the right of the #, and on the same line, is part of the comment. So while it's possible to begin a comment anywhere on the line, it's good practice in these files to keep comments on lines by themselves, as the example in the previous section illustrated:

```
# Copy docs directories to a local backup directory every hour
# Entered by (your name) on (today's date). Version 1.0
```

There is some important information that should always be communicated in the comments, including:

- Name of the person who added/modified the entry
- How to contact that person if anything goes wrong
- Date when the entry was added or modified
- The purpose of the entry (or of its modification), specifying the files it acts on

Remember, documentation is effective only if it remains current. Up-to-date documentation can be useful for building additional scheduled routines, understanding normal administration routines, and helping in disaster recovery, among other things. Running a computer system can be a complex job, but the work is made a little easier when everything is properly documented.

Building Complex Schedules

What if the copy commands should be executed at multiple hours, but not every hour? Not to worry, multiple events can be scheduled within a field by separating all instances with commas and no space between. The following example will run the script on the first minute of every other hour, starting at midnight.

```
1 0,2,4,6,8,10,12,14,16,18,20,22 * * * userid cp -r ~~username/docs ~username/backups
```

If both the day of month and day of week fields are specified, the command will execute when either event happens. This example will run the command at midday every Monday and on the 16th of each month:

```
* 12 16 * 1 userid cp -r ~~username/docs ~username/backups
```

It produces the same result as both of these entries put together:

```
* 12 16 * * userid cp -r ~~username/docs ~username/backups
* 12 * * userid  cp -r ~~username/docs ~username/backups
```

To schedule a backup Monday through Friday only, try this:

```
* * * * 1-5 userid cp -r ~~username/docs ~username/backups
```

Besides providing a list (as the first complex examples showcase) or range (as the in last example) of values for a value of time, the crontab file syntax also provides a way to enter step values. Think of step values as stepping stones. A person can step on every stone on a path or every second stone on a path. For example, if a shell script that backs up important data during the course of a day is to run every 5 hours, a step value of 5 can be entered. In this example the syntax would be "*/5" with the "*" representing every possible hour and the "/5" representing each hour to step:

```
* */5 * * * userid cp -r ~~username/docs ~username/backups
```

Moreover, steps can also be combined with a list. So, if the backup script is to be invoked every other day in the middle of the month, the command would look like the following, where a range of dates in the middle of the month (`10-16`) is provided and a step value (`/2`) denotes to step ahead 2 days before executing the command again:

```
* 12 10-16/2 * * userid cp -r ~~username/docs ~username/backups
```

This is the same as the following list example:

```
* 12 10,12,14,16 * * userid cp -r ~~username/docs ~username/backups
```

Reports and Log Rotation on Linux

Another common use for cron is housekeeping of system logs and generating productive usage reports. For example, there are a number of reporting scripts in four `/etc` subdirectories of most Linux distributions: `cron.hourly`, `cron.daily`, `cron.weekly`, and `cron.monthly`. The scripts in these directories are run either hourly, daily, weekly, or monthly, respectively, by cron.

Here is a sample directory listing for `/etc/cron.daily` on a Red Hat Enterprise Linux system:

```
$ ls
00-logwatch    inn-cron-expire    rhncheck       sysstat
00webalizer    logrotate          rpm            tmpwatch
0anacron       makewhatis.cron    slocate.cron   tripwire-check
$
```

`00webalizer` is an example of a shell script for processing Web server logs and may look something like this:

```
#! /bin/bash
# update access statistics for the Web site

if [ -s /var/log/httpd/keplersol.com-access_log ] ; then
     /usr/bin/webalizer -cQ /etc/webalizer.keplersol.conf
fi

if [ -s /var/log/httpd/weinstein.org-access_log ] ; then
     /usr/bin/webalizer -cQ /etc/webalizer.weinstein.conf
fi

exit 0
```

In Chapter 13 you learn how shell scripts work, how to read them, and how to create them; for now, just know that this script verifies that the log files exist and then, using configuration files created for the webalizer program, processes those logs, generating reports that can be viewed at a location predefined within the configuration file.

The following crontab entry denotes that these routine reports will be executed using the root user's permissions. That is, these scripts will be run as if user root invoked the `run-parts` command with the argument specifying the directory whose collection of scripts is to be executed. The `run-parts` command runs all of the scripts within that directory.

Here is an example of the crontab file covering the four log subdirectories:

```
01 * * * * root run-parts /etc/cron.hourly
02 4 * * * root run-parts /etc/cron.daily
22 4 * * 0 root run-parts /etc/cron.weekly
42 4 1 * * root run-parts /etc/cron.monthly
```

As you can tell, the `cron.hourly`, `cron.daily`, `cron.weekly`, and `cron.monthly` directories are processed every month (* in the month field). The monthly directory is done only on the first day of the month, at the 4:42 a.m. The weekly directory scripts are executed on Sunday (0 in the day field). The daily directory runs at 4:02 a.m. every day (* in day field). The scripts in `/etc/cron.hourly` run on the first minute of every hour, every day of every week of every month (* in all of those fields).

Managing Output from Cron

As noted previously, the output from cron is mailed to the owner of the process, or to the user specified in the `MAILTO` variable. However, if the output should be mailed to someone else instead, you can use the Unix pipe to just pipe the output to the `mail` command. Note that the mail command is invoked using the `-s` switch, which sets the subject of the e-mail being sent to the string that is provided following the switch:

```
0 * * * * userid cp -r ~username/docs ~username/backups | mail -s "Backup Script Output"
username
```

The output also could be redirected to a log file:

```
0 * * * * userid cp -r ~username/docs ~username/backups >> log.file
```

This example redirects the output of the copy command to a log file, which can be useful in some instances.

Controlling Access to Cron

Cron gives administrators the capability to specify who may and may not use it. This is done by the use of `/etc/cron.allow` and `/etc/cron.deny` files. These files work the same way as other daemons' `allow` and `deny` files. To prevent a user from using cron, just put his username in `cron.deny`; to enable a user to use cron, place his username in the `cron.allow`. To prevent all users from using cron, add the line `ALL` to the `cron.deny` file.

If there is neither a `cron.allow` nor a `cron.deny` file, the use of cron is unrestricted.

crontab

Because Unix is a multiuser operating system, a number of applications such as cron have to be able to support many users. For security reasons, it would be unwise to provide all users access to `/etc/crontab` where they can easily see what critical routines are being run and when. Far better is for each user to have his or her own `crontab` file, which can be created, edited, and removed by the command `crontab`. This command creates an individual `crontab` file and is often stored in `/var/spool/cron/crontabs/`*`user`*, although it may be found elsewhere (perhaps `/var/spool/cron/`*`user`* or `/var/cron/tabs/`*`user`*) depending on the Unix flavor being used.

Here are the command arguments for `crontab`:

Argument	Description
`-e`	Edits the current `crontab` or creates a new one
`-l`	Lists the contents of the `crontab` file
`-r`	Removes the `crontab` file

The command `crontab -e` will cause the user's crontab file to load in the editor specified in the `EDITOR` or `VISUAL` environment variable.

A user's personal `crontab` follows exactly the format of the main `/etc/crontab` file, except that the `MAILTO` variable needn't be specified because the default entry is the process owner, which is generally the user.

One-Time Execution with at

To schedule a command, series of commands, or script to run at a specific time, but only once, use `at` instead of `cron`. `at` is the method for scheduling one-time execution of events by atd and is intended for scheduling specific jobs under precise circumstances. In other words, to rotate logs every Saturday `at` is not appropriate — that's what `cron` if for — but if on Thursday afternoon a meeting gets scheduled for Friday morning and you want to make sure nothing disastrous happens to a critical document you'll need for it, you may want to make sure a backup copy is made at the end of the business day. That job is perfect for `at`. To see how it works, select one of your documents and try it out.

Try It Out Perform a One-Time Backup of an Important Document

1. Locate your document and check the current date as in the following:

```
$ ls
important_report.swx
$ date
Thu Dec  9 14:53:06 CST 2004
```

2. Type the `at` command followed by the time you want the job to occur:

```
$ at 17:00
```

3. Type the copy command (`cp`), the name of file you want to copy, and the location of the file in which you want to place the backup copy on the file system, and then press **Enter**:

```
at> cp important_report.swx ~username/backups
```

4. Press **Ctrl + D** to exit the `at` shell; you should see something akin to the following:

```
job 1 at 2004-12-10 17:00
$
```

Use the `atq` command to double-check that the job has been scheduled. To delete a command before it has been executed, use the `atrm` command:

```
$ atq
1       2004-12-10 17:00 a username
$
```

To delete a command before it has been executed, use the `atrm` command:

```
$ atrm 1
```

How It Works

The first step was to locate the document in question. This is because the working directory, the environment — except for the variables `TERM` and `DISPLAY`, and the umask — are retained by `at` from the time of invocation.

`at` reads a command or series of commands from standard input or a specified file. The command or commands collected by `at` are executed at a time in the future also specified to `at`. The commands are executed using either the shell set by the user's environment variable `SHELL` or `/bin/sh`.

at allows for fairly complex time specifications. In its most basic form, at accepts times in the HH:MM format. If that time is already past in the current day, the next day is assumed, so no specific date is given. Hours can be 0–24, or they can be 0–12 a.m./p.m. (no space between number and am/pm), and you can also specify midnight, noon, or, for those in the United Kingdom, teatime (4 p.m.). Here are some examples of various at times:

```
$ at 17:45
$ at 5pm
$ at 5:15pm
$ at noon
$ at teatime
```

You can denote the day the job will run by giving a date in the form MMDD or MMDDYY. The date specification must follow the time specification:

```
$ at teatime 010105
```

Times can also be relative to a specific time. That is, you can do a countdown-type argument that says how much time, in minutes, hours, days, or weeks from the specific time a scheduled job needs to be executed. The following will carry out a command 5 minutes from when the at command was invoked:

```
$ at now + 5 minutes
```

Or to run a job 2 hours from now, you'd use:

```
$ at now + 2 hours
```

To run a job at 4 p.m. 3 days from now, you'd use:

```
$ at 4pm + 3 days
```

Or to run a job 1 week from now, you'd use:

```
$ at 1 week
```

In any case, the next step for creating an event is to provide a command or series of commands for at to execute at the defined time. You'll recall that in the first example the command for copying the important documents was input at the command line, also known as from standard input:

```
at> cp important_report.swx ~username/backups
```

The command can also come from a file. To do so, use the -f switch, followed by the file in which the commands reside:

```
$ at 17:00 -f ~jdoe/bin/backup
job 3 at 2004-12-10 17:00
$
```

Controlling Access to at

As with cron, a Unix administrator can control which users are allowed to use `at`. One method of access control is to simply create an `/etc/at.allow` file. In this way the `at` daemon will limit access to those users listed within the `at.allow` file, denying access to everyone else.

Another method of access control is to create an `/etc/at.deny` file, which is done by default on most Unix systems. An `/etc/at.deny` file works in the opposite way as an `/etc/at.allow` file. It controls who cannot use `at` — the users listed in the file are denied permission, and everyone else can use the command.

The question of which access control method, and thus which file to use, `/etc/at.allow` or `/etc/at.deny`, comes down to a question of your management style. If, as the administrator, you prefer to let people use things until they abuse the privilege, then use the default `/etc/at.deny`. If you believe that no one needs to use the `at` command unless directly granted the privilege, create and use `/etc/at.allow`.

If neither of these two files exists, only the superuser is allowed use of `at`. To allow everyone to use `at`, the administrator needs to create an empty `/etc/at.deny` file. (A note for the administrator: this is usually the default configuration.)

Summary

You now understand the two basic parts of system automation: having a valid system clock setting and running cron daemon with configuration information. Remember that there are a number of things to keep in mind when it comes to setting up commands, scripts, or applications to run at a specified time:

- The system clock is the operating system's timepiece.
- The hardware clock is important to setting the system clock at boot time.
- There are a number of ways to keep the system clock synced, including syncing with other computers on a network.
- Cron is the Unix application that keeps track of when a scheduled task is to be run.
- `crontab` is the configuration file for the cron daemon.
- Crontab is also the name of a command tool for editing `crontab` files for individual users.
- `at` is the Unix application that keeps track of when something is to be executed once, at a specific time.

Exercise

Create an entry for an individual user's `crontab` file that lists the user's directory and e-mails the output to the user every other day of the week.

Security

In the face of increased threats to computer systems, information security has grown to major importance in the world of computing. The menaces include external malicious attacks (from corporate espionage to hackers and crackers) and, if your system has users, internal security breaches (from disgruntled employees to unscrupulous visitors). Hardware, software, networks — the vulnerabilities are numerous. Unix security is as much philosophy as it is technical mastery. This chapter introduces the major security concepts and some commands you can use to make your systems more secure.

The Basics of Good Security

An age-old saying in computer security circles is that the only computer that is completely secure is one that is disconnected from any network, turned off, and embedded in a block of concrete. Of course, that's an exaggeration, but it does illustrate the point that no system is 100 percent secure. Security is not something that can be enabled by clicking one checkbox in the system, and it is not simply a matter of installing a software program and being done with it. Security is an ongoing journey, and one that can be fascinating.

Computer security is much like security in the real world. You probably have one or more locks on the front door of your house to discourage strangers from entering your home and helping themselves to your belongings. While you have made an effort to safeguard your home, you probably can imagine a situation in which your security measures could be overridden — in case of fire, for example, where firefighters would need to enter your home, perhaps by force. It is also likely that you have your savings secured in a bank. You may also store your valuables in a safe deposit box, a place much safer than in your home. All of this is much like computer security, in that you decide what needs the absolute most protection, and what requires less protection.

There are three basic principles for protecting information security systems:

- Confidentiality — Information must be kept from those who do not have a need to know (keep private information private).
- Integrity — Information must be free from unauthorized changes or contamination.
- Availability — Information must be available to those who need access to it.

Assets Worth Protecting

Before you can begin to safeguard your system, you need to know what you are protecting. Although everyone has different specific types of data, and different needs, it's possible to create a very general listing of assets that are common to all computers and users in your company or organization. Take some time to identify and define these assets:

The amount of time, effort, and money you spend securing your system from attack should be based on the costs associated with the loss of your hardware, software, and information resources. For example, you wouldn't spend $10,000 dollars securing a system that if successfully attacked would lead to a loss valued at $100. Once you understand the value of what you are protecting, you can determine the appropriate level of resources to spend securing those assets in a meaningful and sensible manner.

Take some time to identify and define these assets:

- **Hardware** — The physical components of your computer system have value. If the system is located in an easily accessible place without any physical security in the form of locked doors, then it can be stolen. If someone can physically touch the computer system, he or she can potentially access all of the information it contains because the system can be booted off of alternative file systems (CD-ROMs, USB drives, and so forth), bypassing the primary operating system. An attacker could also insert network monitoring software to capture all the information passed over the network, a keylogger (stealth software that captures every keystroke you make), or many other means of assault. An attacker could also simply take the computer and remove the hard drive to gain access to the information the system holds.
- **Network connection** — Your network connection is an extremely valuable resource. Attackers can use your bandwidth (or network capacity) in various kinds of attacks against other systems. They also can use your network connection, effectively using your identity on the Internet (or at a minimum mask their identity), which to anyone on the outside would look like the attacks were coming from your location.
- **Data** — Everything that you use your computer for is stored in the system: your e-mail, address lists, personal files, and other things that you have personally created or modified. Any number of confidential documents are located in your computer. Think about how difficult it would be to recreate everything located on your hard drive if you had to. There's also the threat that someone can use that information to assume your identity, accessing your financial-planning program and e-mails.
- **Services** — If you use your computer to share information with any other users either in your department at work or with your family at home, it will be important to you that your system continues to provide those services without interruption. If you have a home-based business that relies on your Web server for marketing your product to customers, for example, you need to have the Web service running at all times, or you'll lose business.

Potential Issues

From viruses to data theft to denial-of-service attacks, there are plenty of things that can create havoc in your computer system. To protect against what you can and to minimize the impact of other events, it helps to have some idea what the potential dangers can be, as well as what you can do about them.

The following are the types of things that can go wrong, and those that you want to protect against and minimize the impact of:

- **User error**—By far the most common cause of data loss is from simple user error, especially on Unix systems, where a misplaced space or character can result in serious system modification without the confirmation that some other operating systems provide by default. (Unix was originally designed by and for programmers, and intentionally utilizes a terse command syntax at the shell level, which generally assumes proficiency on the part of the operator.)
- **Hardware failure**—Computers are mechanical devices, and while it is common to focus on the security of the software and operating system, the physical components are also necessary for operation. The power supply and hard drives are two components that can break. If either of these ceases to function, the result can range from partial to complete unavailability of the system.
- **Theft of hardware**—As previously mentioned, it is important to safeguard the physical computer. If the machine is not in a secure location, it can be stolen. All of the software security measures in the world will not protect your data if someone can simply remove the hard drive from the system and mount it on a system of his own.
- **Data manipulation**—If unauthorized access to your system is gained, any data on that system may be deleted, modified, or copied. If you are providing information via the Web, the data in your Web pages could be changed or deleted. Private files could be copied and shared with your competitors, or data can simply be deleted.
- **Theft of services**—If your system is compromised, your network bandwidth can be made available for others to access. For example, a hacker could create a folder on your system; fill it with copyrighted materials such as computer software, music, and movies; install an FTP server on your system; and then advertise that software. Unbeknownst to you, your machine would be providing services to an unintended audience.
- **Eavesdropping**—When you use your computer to communicate with other systems, such as by using e-mail or the Internet, third parties may be able listen in. This can be harmful in many ways, notably by exposing information that is meant to be confidential such as financial information and authentication information, including passwords and usernames on other systems.
- **Viruses**—There are other threats such as viruses, spyware, spam and other malicious software that spreads on the Internet. For the most part, these do not affect Unix systems. However, you should certainly be aware of the threat and use common sense when dealing with email containing attachments, especially from unknown parties. However, the risk of running into viruses is far lower in Unix than in operating systems because of Unix's security features as well as its many diverse implementations.

Securing Your Unix System

The rest of this chapter can help you run as secure a machine as possible, whether you are the sole user on the system or you maintain a system shared by multiple users. Think about security as a goal, not a destination—there will never be a point where it is done, and you can wash your hands of the matter. Always consider security in your approach to your systems and you will be ahead of the game.

Password Security

The basic authentication method for Unix host systems is a combination of a username and a password. In practice, your username is common knowledge because it's generally used in your e-mail address. It is often exposed by the system, both to local users via programs such as `who`, and to remote users via such methods such as `finger` and `rwho`. This makes it imperative for you to choose good passwords, keep those passwords secret, and change them with some regularity. Your password is the first line of defense against intruders entering your system at the operating system level. There are programs in common use that exist solely to attempt to guess passwords.

What makes a good password? A combination of things. For one, a good password is extremely difficult to guess or to be discovered by password-cracking tools. That means using no personally identifiable information such as your birth date or telephone number, pet names, sibling names, parents' names—in fact, stay away from names altogether, including sports teams, brand names, and so on. You also want to avoid using words that appear in a dictionary, as well as those that are jargon from a specific industry—especially an industry with which you are affiliated. Do not use common abbreviations. A good password consists of a combination of uppercase and lowercase letters as well as numbers and punctuation (nonalphanumerics).

One common suggestion is to take the first letter of each word in a phrase that is familiar to you—"Now is the time for all good men to come to the aid of their party," for example—and capitalize them to form a base for your password: NITTFAGMTCTTAOTP. Then take a portion of that sequence—use at least eight characters—and replace some of the letters with numbers and nonalphanumerics. In this example, you could use the beginning of the sequence, NITTFAGM, and replace the I with a 1 and the F with a 4 to get N1TT4AGM. Have fun with the case, such as n1tT4aGm, and add punctuation, for a final password of n1tT4-aGm&. (Of course, you shouldn't use this password now that it has been published, but it's a good example of the process of creating a strong password.)

No matter how you create a strong password, make sure that you can memorize it. Do not write the password down. That's worth repeating: Do not write your password anywhere. People who write down their passwords and leave them near their computers reduce security as much as having a weak password in the first place. If you absolutely must write down the password, keep it in a safe location, physically on you; still, it's highly recommended that you do not write it down.

Password Discovery Programs

Software that attempts to guess passwords through the use of multiple dictionaries and common sequences has existed for quite some time. It tries many passwords one right after another until it finds a match. This technique is called a brute force attack. As computers get faster and faster, this software gets more and more sophisticated (and quicker) at discovering passwords. A password such as theSafe9a55w0Rd once would have taken years to crack or discover, but now it could be done in a matter of days. That's why passwords must be changed frequently (typically 60–90 days) to achieve the best level of security. By changing your password frequently, you most likely will have changed a password that may have been discovered before the attacker has a chance to use it.

Two of the most popular password discovery programs are Crack and John the Ripper. John the Ripper is a more modern implementation that compiles on almost all modern operating systems. Both programs operate in a similar fashion, working against the system password file (usually `/etc/passwd` or `/etc/shadow`), trying passwords until finding a match. System administrators and security professionals often utilize these tools to determine the password strength of their user accounts. If you decide to use these tools to audit system passwords, you must first have the system owner's permission in writing or you could face severe criminal or civil penalties.

Do not use any tools described in this chapter without thoroughly understanding the implications of their use and the potential legal ramifications of using them without proper authorization from the owners of the system on which you want to use them. These software programs are valuable tools in a system and security administrator's toolkit because they enable you to determine potential system weaknesses before an attacker can. Remove these tools after using them so that no unauthorized person can use them to attack your systems.

If you have obtained the proper permissions for the system owners to run John the Ripper, you can download it at `http://openwall.com/john`. Full instructions on the installation and use of this program are available at the Web site.

Limiting Administrative Access

As you learned in Chapter 3, the root user—superuser—has absolute control over the system, including the capability to modify other users' accounts or the system with impunity. The supremacy of this account necessitates that the it be afforded a higher level of protection than other accounts. When malicious entities are attacking a system, they almost always attempt to gain access to the root or superuser account because of its unlimited power.

UID 0

The root user has the userid (UID) of 0. The root user account should be afforded the highest security, including the strongest password possible. If this account is compromised, the system is untrustworthy for data storage at the minimum and the complete domain of a malicious entity in the worst case. To protect your system, use the root account only when it is absolutely necessary, such as for system administration. You can accomplish this best by never directly logging into the root user account from the initial system startup. Instead, log in as a regular (nonprivileged) user and then use the `su` command to switch users to the root account for the time you need it. For example, to see the encrypted password string in `/etc/shadow` for the root user, `su` to the root user, run the command you need, and then log out of the root user account, like this:

```
jdoe@ttyp1[~]$ su - root
root@ttyp1[~]# cat /etc/shadow | grep root
exit
logout
jdoe@ttyp1[~]$
```

By not using the root account for day-to-day activities, such as Web browsing or text editing, you prevent the possibility of running a program you download off the Internet as the root user, which could lead to system compromise. You also avoid a litany of other possible scenarios in which the root user account could be exposed to malicious users.

Additionally, check `/etc/passwd` on a regular basis to ensure that no users other than the true root user have a UID of 0 (field three). For example, say you ran `cat` on `/etc/passwd` and showed the following:

```
root:x:0:0:root:/root:/bin/bash
badguy:x:0:100:/home/badguy:/bin/bash
```

Users root and badguy both have full root privileges on the system based on their UIDs (0). If you find any users other than root with a UID of 0, research the validity of that entry immediately because it could potentially be a malicious hacker who has gained access to your system.

Another security measure to consider is not allowing users to directly log into the system as the root user from a remote console. Every Unix system handles this differently, so consult your system documentation for information about how to disable remote root logins.

Root Management Options

Traditionally, administrative tasks are completed by using the `su` (switch user) command, which enables a user to become root by entering the password assigned to the root account. This is frowned upon for many reasons. Most importantly, the root account generally has no accountability when a system has multiple users, all of whom are familiar with the root password; if one of them uses `su` to become root, and then carries out a command, that action is simply logged as a command executed by the user root, who generally has the long-form name of System Administrator. That is not helpful in the case of error, when you're trying to track down exactly who was logged into the system and who executed specific commands.

Here's where the `sudo` or (SuperUser Do) command helps you out, enabling you to track use of privileged commands and providing some protection against giving out the root password to others for system maintenance. It allows flexible delegation of administrative tasks, enabling you to authorize individual users to perform explicit actions that would generally require UID 0. The user uses `sudo` with his or her own username. The user simply precedes the command he orshe wants to execute with `sudo`, such as `sudo shutdown`. The user is then prompted for his or her own password, and the action proceeds, and is logged (if logging has been configured), including the ID of the user who executed the command. This logging occurs for both successful and unsuccessful access attempts.

`sudo` is far superior to `su` for several reasons, notably:

- Enhanced logging — Each action is verbosely logged (with command arguments) using the configurable syslogd, including username.
- Flexible configuration — Sudo enables you to grant administrative access to individual users and groups.
- Granular access control — Sudo enables you to grant individual users and groups access to only the explicit administrative commands that you choose.

Setting up Sudo

Most versions of Unix include sudo, but if you don't have the package or source code, you can download the latest version from `http://courtesan.com/sudo/`. After installing sudo, you generally have three files whose locations vary depending on how sudo was installed:

- `sudo` — The binary program that's called when you use the `sudo` command. It is not modifiable in its binary form.
- `visudo` — A binary program that enables you to safely edit the sudo configuration file `sudoers`.
- `sudoers` — The plain text file that you edit to modify or add permissions.

When sudo is invoked, it reads the sudoers file, which generally is located in the /etc. You use visudo to edit /etc/sudoers because it locks the file for editing and also performs a basic syntax check on the file before committing changes.

Here's a basic /etc/sudoers file:

```
# sudoers file.
#
# This file MUST be edited with the 'visudo' command as root.
#
# See the sudoers man page for the details on how to write a sudoers file.
#

# Host alias specification
Host_Alias              LINUX_SERVERS=linux1,linux2, 192.168.1.3
# User alias specification
User_Alias              ADMIN=jdoe
# Cmnd alias specification
Cmnd_Alias              READLOG=/usr/bin/less /var/log/lastlog, \
               /usr/bin/less /var/log/system.log, \
               /usr/bin/less /var/log/mail.log
# User privilege specification
ADMIN                   LINUX_SERVERS=READLOG
```

The configuration file has five sections. The first three allow you to create aliases, which can be used later in the file's fourth section, user privilege. There are three kinds of aliases: host, user, and command. By defining aliases, it becomes easy to manage specific users and commands. In the example file, the user alias ADMIN contains the user jdoe. If you want a new administrator, simply add his or her name to the alias, and he or she will have access to the same commands as the other admins—individual programs need not be configured. The same logic goes for the command aliases. The fifth section, "Defaults specification," is where you can set up the default behavior of sudo (for more information, see the sudo man page.)

The host alias is especially useful because it allows the same sudoers file to be used on multiple machines, through the use of Network File Services (NFS), although the commands and users on those machines may differ. This enables you to standardize administrative options across machines, which is always a good idea. The more you can standardize, the less falls thru the cracks, and the more secure your setup will be.

For more information regarding setting up sudo on your system, check the local man page (`man sudo`) or the sudo home page at `http://courtesan.com/sudo/`.

Try It Out — Use Sudo

John Smith, a system administrator just hired into the system administration group, needs to run some specific commands as the root user. John, whose username is jsmith, has to run the command `cat /etc/shadow` to verify that users were put into the system correct. He will run this command only on the linux5 system, which is the system on which the sudo command is located. As the sudo administrator, you must modify the sudoers file to give jsmith this access.

If you don't already have the sudo program on your system, download and install it (after obtaining proper permission if you don't own the system) as described in Chapter 19.

1. Log in as the root user and use the `visudo` command to edit your `sudoers` file:

   ```
   visudo
   ```

2. Your sample `sudo` file displays in the screen in a vi session. Here's an example:

   ```
   # sudoers file.
   #
   # This file MUST be edited with the 'visudo' command as root.
   #
   # See the sudoers man page for the details on how to write
     a sudoers file.
   #

   # Host alias specification
   # User alias specification
   # Cmnd alias specification
   # User privilege specification
   ```

3. To give John the access he needs, add the following entries in the appropriate sections (if you don't put it in the correct section, the commands still work but will be harder to manage):

   ```
   Host_Alias          Linux_System=linux5
   User_Alias          Administrator=jsmith
   Cmnd_Alias          CHECK_SHADOW=/bin/cat /etc/shadow
   Administrator       Linux_System=CHECK_SHADOW
   ```

   Your `sudoers` file would look similar to this:

   ```
     # sudoers file.
     #
     # This file MUST be edited with the 'visudo' command as root.
     #
     # See the sudoers man page for the details on how to write
       a sudoers file.
     #

     # Host alias specification
   Host_Alias          Linux_System=linux5
     # User alias specification
   User_Alias          Administrator=jsmith
     # Cmnd alias specification
   Cmnd_Alias          CHECK_SHADOW=/bin/cat /etc/shadow
     # User privilege specification
   Administrator       Linux_System=CHECK_SHADOW
   ```

4. Save your changes.

   Now the user jmith only needs to run the following command to view the contents of the `/etc/shadow` file as root:

   ```
   $sudo /bin/cat /etc/shadow
   ```

After trying this exercise, remove all the entries you added to `sudoers`. This prevents a user with the account of jsmith from being able to run the commands you just added. (Do not do this exercise on a live account.)

How It Works

In the `Host_Alias` section of `sudoers`, the `Linux_System` system alias is identified as `linux5`. In `User_Alias`, the `Administrator` alias is set to jsmith, the new administrator's username. In the `Cmnd_Alias` section, command aliases are set using absolute paths. The last line puts all the aliases together: `Administrator` is the user (`jsmith`) who can run the command; `Linux_System` is the system (`linux5`) on which the user can run the command; and the command that can be run is indicated by the alias `CHECK_SHADOW`, which equates to `/bin/cat /etc/shadow`.

Be aware that there are some commands with which sudo users can escalate their privileges. It is prudent to carefully consider which commands you provide sudo access to. In general, you should not give that access to the following:

- Commands that allow for shell escapes. If you give a user sudo access to vi, for example, the user can escape to a shell and have full access to the system as the root user. Other commands to be careful of are the `less` command and any custom-made programs.
- The `zip`, `gzip`, or other compression/decompression commands. These can be used to alter system files as the root user.

Use the absolute path to commands in `sudo`, or someone can write a malicious script and name it the same as a valid command.

You should generally not give users access to a shell directly with sudo because that enables them to navigate and modify the system as the root user.

Ensure that you are fully aware of a command's capabilities before you grant sudo access to it.

System Administration Preventive Tasks

There are a number of system administration tasks that can be called preventive. They are those that you do to help prevent your Unix system from being compromised. System administration tasks include system maintenance and cleaning. This section explores some of them.

Remove Unneeded Accounts

Unix system distributors often include a group of accounts that provide easy use of the system. Sometimes these accounts are very beneficial and are set up with adequate security, although older versions of Unix provide accounts by default that are not needed and can be compromised if not set up properly. Removing accounts you don't need is a good security measure.

For system accounts, set very strong passwords that are known to as few people as possible.

Review the `/etc/passwd` file (or other account files as appropriate) and identify accounts that you don't recognize. Carefully research the purpose of the unfamiliar system account—you may find that you do need the account for specific functionality. Before removing any unnecessary system accounts (described in Chapter 3), test your changes on a nonproduction system. If that's not an option, here's how you can disable the account:

1. Make a backup of the `/etc/shadow` and `/etc/passwd` files. If you make the copies on the system, ensure that the permissions are set to 700 and the files are owned by root.
2. Edit `/etc/passwd`, putting `/bin/false` as the shell entry while removing the current shell (`/bin/sh`, for example) for any system accounts you want to disable.
3. Edit `/etc/shadow`, entering a `*` in the encrypted password field.

These steps prevent the account from being logged into, because the user will not have a valid shell or password.

For accounts that are needed, use `sudo` to enable users to utilize the `sudo` command to `su` to the accounts instead of having users use the `su` command by itself. This will give you maximum visibility on who is using the accounts. By preventing direct logins, you can track who is logging into a group account in case there are any problems.

Patch, Restrict, or Remove Programs

Unix provides a lot of its functionality through programs that are included with the system. This gives users much needed flexibility, but also presents a problem in that malicious users/attackers can use the same software for less benign purposes. New vulnerabilities are found in software daily, and the vendors or community supporting the software release patches accordingly. To keep your system software up-to-date, you need to check your software vendors/developers' Web sites for patches often. And don't forget to patch your Unix system software.

Remove or restrict unneeded software from your system to prevent malicious users from using it in unintended ways and to reduce the administrative burden of patching it. One example is the gcc compiler, which is useful for building source code, but can be exploited by malicious users to compile dangerous programs such as password crackers or other software that can give them privileged access to computer systems. You may require gcc for compiling software, in which case you should severely restrict (with octal 700 permissions) access to the software, or if it is not needed, you should completely remove the program.

Before removing any software, test your changes on a nonproduction system. If you don't have a production system, rename the software (`gcc_old`, for example) and wait a period of time to make certain that it isn't needed for a specific application or purpose that may not have been immediately evident. If no problems occur, then remove the software.

Software also has dependencies that aren't always obvious, so using your system's built-in software or package management software (such as rpm for Linux or pkgrm for Solaris) will provide some protection from accidental deletion of crucial software. If you try to remove software without going through the package management software, you can create dependency issues (one program may depend on another program being previously installed). The built-in package management software will prevent or at least warn you before removing software that other programs may need to operate correctly.

Disable Unneeded Services

A *service* (described in more detail in Chapter 16) is a program that provides a specific function and can supply needed functionality for legitimate users, such as the telnet service that provides telnet functionality. Services also can be used by attackers to gain access to your system or to elevate their privileges. In most Unix systems, the `/etc/inetd.conf` file (`xinetd` files for Linux) contains a list of valid services available for users. To remove a service's functionality, you can comment out the line referring to the service in the file by putting a pound sign (#) in front of the service name and restarting the inetd or xinetd service. For example, to disable the telnet service on a Solaris system, you'd edit the `/etc/inetd.conf` file to comment out the line that says:

```
telnet  stream  tcp6   nowait   root  /usr/sbin/in.telnetd   in.telnetd
```

So that it looks like:

```
# telnet  stream  tcp6   nowait   root  /usr/sbin/in.telnetd   in.telnetd
```

Then you'd save the file and restart the inetd service from the command line like this:

```
#ps -ef | grep inetd
root     220    1    0    Nov  20    ?      0:00 /usr/sbin/inetd -s
#kill -HUP 220
```

Restarting the inetd service forces it to reread its configuration file (`/etc/inetd.conf`), facilitating your change.

You should remove rsh, finger, daytime, rstatd, ftp (if not needed), smtp and other software that are not specifically needed by the system for day-to-day operation. If you need the service at a later date, you can uncomment it by removing the # in its config file and restarting the inetd process as described previously.

Monitor and Restrict Access to Services

You can restrict access to remote services with TCP Wrappers. This small program enables you to intercept calls for specific services and then log access to those services as well as restrict access based on where the request is originating.

Download tcpd (TCP Wrappers Daemon) from `ftp://ftp.porcupine.org/pub/security/`. Compile the software as described in Chapter 19, and then edit your `/etc/inetd.conf` file to point to the tcpd wrappers daemon for the services tcpd supports (usually telnet, ftp, rsh, rlogin, finger, and some others). On a Solaris 10 system, for example, to use tcpd for the telnet service because you are required to run telnet, find the following line in `/etc/inetd.conf`:

```
telnet  stream  tcp6   nowait   root  /usr/sbin/in.telnetd    in.telnetd
```

Replace the portion that says `/usr/sbin/in.telnetd` with `user/sbin/tcpd` (or wherever you saved the tcpd binary from installation), so that the line looks like:

```
telnet  stream  tcp6   nowait   root  /usr/sbin/tcpd    in.telnetd
```

This allows tcpd to control the connection to in.telnetd service, including the logging of attempted access to the service. After you have installed tcpd, you can create two files:

- `/etc/hosts.allow`—Lists systems that are permitted to access services You specify the systems allowed to access the services. For example, to allow all users from 192.168.1.2 to access all services, you'd add the following entry:

```
ALL: 192.168.1.2
```

- `/etc/hosts.deny`—Lists systems that are not allowed to access services. A typical `/etc/hosts.deny` file includes the following entry, which denies everything not explicitly allowed in `/etc/hosts.allow`:

```
ALL: ALL
```

There are many different options for these files, and all changes should be tested on a nonproduction system before they are implemented. For more information, visit `http://www.cert.org/security-improvement/implementations/i041.07.html`.

Implement Built-in Firewalls

Most modern Unix systems include a built-in firewall for restricting access to the system based on criteria set by the system administrator. If your version of Unix includes or has a firewall program available, investigate its use and implementation. Linux, for example, has the very popular IPTables, Solaris has SunScreen, and the Mac OS X has Personal Firewall. These firewalls require knowledge of the system and the ability to determine system access requirements, so use them with great consideration. These programs are beyond the scope of this book, but you can find more information at:

- Linux IPTables—`http://netfilter.org/`
- Solaris SunScreen—`http://docs.sun.com/app/docs/coll/557.4`
- Mac OS X Personal Firewall—`http://download.info.apple.com/Apple_Support_Area/Manuals/servers/MacosxserverAdmin10.2.3.PDF`

Other Security Programs

There are a multitude of security programs available for the Unix operating system. Check out as many as you can to see how each might benefit your system. Here are a few programs to get you started (you should obtain permission from the system owner before using any of these programs):

- Tripwire—A file integrity checker that can determine whether a file has been changed. When properly configured, it can identify files that have changed on your system, which could be indicative of hostile activity, such as the change in the `/etc/passwd` file. Download the program at `http://tripwire.org` for the open-source version, or `http://tripwire.com` for the commercial version.
- Nessus—A vulnerability scanner that checks for at-risk services on your systems. It has an easy-to-use graphical user interface and can provide very detailed reports. More information is available at `http://nessus.org`.

- Saint — A vulnerability scanner with similar functionality as Nessus. More information is available at `http://saintcorporation.com`.
- NMAP — A port scanning tool to help you identify what ports or services are available on your system. More information is available at `http://insecure.org/nmap/`.
- Snort — A network intrusion detection tool that can also sniff network traffic or identify when potentially malicious activity is occurring on your network. More information is available at `http://snort.org`.
- GNUPG — Gnu Privacy Guard is a tool that enables you to encrypt files on your system to prevent others from accessing them without a special key. More information is available at `http://gnupg.org`.

Summary

Security is an ongoing process requiring diligence on the system owners' part. The information presented in this chapter is a very high-level, cursory overview of some of the fundamental aspects of Unix security. Every implementation of Unix has different security requirements and specialized configuration files. To truly secure your Unix system, you should refer to Web sites dealing specifically with your version of Unix as well as publications dedicated to the subject of security.

Exercise

Demonstrate how to set up a user with sudo access to switch users to the `backupuser` account on a single system with a hostname of `linux_backup`.

Basic Shell Scripting

In addition to being an environment for interacting with the computer, the shell can be used for programming. Shell programs, often called *scripts*, are used for a variety of purposes, most notably system administration. Shell scripts are simply a series of system commands stored in a single file. These commands are executed automatically and in order each time the file is invoked.

Think for a moment about the possibilities. Any program on the machine can be run from the shell, with input and output automatically redirected according to your desires. Once you get the hang of shell scripting, you can automate a vast range of jobs with a few simple scripts. Even better, the jobs that work best in shell scripts are the ones that are most irritating to do by hand, whether because they're boring or because they're repetitive.

This chapter introduces the basic concepts of shell scripting. The scripts are simple and may seem trivial, but they clearly illustrate the underlying mechanics that you need to master before you move on to subsequent chapters and the more advanced methods they contain.

Commenting and Documenting Scripts

Good documenting is critical for good programming. It's easy, especially on systems with multiple administrators, to have a bunch of scripts lying around on the disk. Most of these scripts are probably variations on the same concept, and it's likely that nobody knows much about any of them. Even on a single-user system, you may write scripts to do certain tasks, and then later open a file to see what's in it and not remember what the script does or why you wrote it in the first place.

The way around this — as with any type of programming — is good documentation. Shell scripts are self-contained documents, so the easiest and best way to document them is to use comments within the scripts themselves. Most programming languages have the capability to embed comments within programs, and the shells are no different.

In Unix shells, comment lines begin with a hashmark character (#). Anything that comes after the hashmark is taken to be a comment and is not interpreted as a command. Comments that span multiple lines must have a hashmark at the beginning of each line, as in:

```
# Here is a comment that
# spans multiple lines.
```

In addition, a hashmark can be inserted into the middle of a line, and everything to the right of it will be considered a comment:

```
some_command  # This is a comment explaining the command
```

The specific methods you use to add comments to your script are up to you. However, there are a few practices that will help keep you out of trouble:

1. **Put some basic information at the top of the script.** Include the name of the script, the date, and the overall purpose of the script. If the script is designed to accept command-line arguments, add a short section on the proper syntax for arguments. Include any notes or reminders that might shed light on anything unusual about the script.
2. **Keep a change log.** If you make changes to your script over time, keep a log of all the changes you make. Add each change to the top of the change log, so that the reader can see all changes made in reverse chronological order. When you do this, change the date at the top of the script so that the change log and actual script are in agreement.
3. **Comment each section.** Most scripts will have multiple sections. Each section should get a comment that explains what it does. There is no need to go into detail about *how* it does what it does (you should be able to communicate that with clear and lucid programming), but the purpose of the section should be explained in the comments.
4. **Identify any data that must be added by the user.** If the user of the script (whether it be you or someone else) needs to provide material for a section of a script, add a comment explaining the information that needs to be added and the format that that information needs to be in.

Although it's assumed that you've got some experience in reading scripts, it's useful to see good commenting in action (especially if you don't add comments to your own work on a regular basis). Here is an excerpt from the `/etc/rc.d/rc.sysinit` file on Red Hat Linux. This is the main script that controls how the machine is started, but its function isn't critical in this example. Just look at the comments.

```
# If a SCSI tape has been detected, load the st module unconditionally
# since many SCSI tapes don't deal well with st being loaded and unloaded
if [ -f /proc/scsi/scsi ] && grep -q 'Type:   Sequential-Access' \
   /proc/scsi/scsi 2>/dev/null ; then
      if grep -qv ' 9 st' /proc/devices ; then
            if [ -n "$USEMODULES" ] ; then
                  # Try to load the module.  If it fails, ignore it...
                  insmod -p st >/dev/null 2>&1 && modprobe \
                  st >/dev/null 2>&1
            fi
      fi
fi

# Load usb storage here, to match most other things
if [ -n "$needusbstorage" ]; then
      modprobe usb-storage >/dev/null 2>&1
fi

# If they asked for ide-scsi, load it
```

```
if grep -q "ide-scsi" /proc/cmdline ; then
      modprobe ide-cd >/dev/null 2>&1
      modprobe ide-scsi >/dev/null 2>&1
fi

# Generate a header that defines the boot kernel.
/sbin/mkkerneldoth

# Adjust symlinks as necessary in /boot to keep system services from
# spewing messages about mismatched System maps and so on.
if [ -L /boot/System.map -a -r /boot/System.map-`uname -r` ] ; then
      ln -s -f System.map-`uname -r` /boot/System.map
fi
if [ ! -e /boot/System.map -a -r /boot/System.map-`uname -r` ] ; then
      ln -s -f System.map-`uname -r` /boot/System.map
fi

# Now that we have all of our basic modules loaded and the kernel going,
# let's dump the syslog ring somewhere so we can find it later
dmesg > /var/log/dmesg
sleep 1
kill -TERM `/sbin/pidof getkey` >/dev/null 2>&1
} &
if [ "$PROMPT" != "no" ]; then
   /sbin/getkey i && touch /var/run/confirm
fi
wait
```

Notice that the comments before each section of code explain what each section does. Even if you have never run a Linux machine before, or you've never looked at initialization scripts, you should be able to follow this script's function by reading the comments. Consider your own scripts or programs. Could another programmer chosen at random understand your work and its purpose without actually running the program? If not, you may want to add more comments to make things clear.

A word of warning: You will be tempted at many turns to neglect comments. It may seem easy to skip them. After all, you might think, "I'm the only one who's going to use this, and I know what it does." This almost always turns out to be false, and you'll eventually find yourself going back over a script line by line to find a particular section, or to piece together the exact function of a particular block of code. Spending a few minutes commenting as you work on your script will save you lots of time and confusion down the road.

Getting Down to It

As mentioned at the beginning of this chapter, shell programs are essentially lists of commands that are executed sequentially. For example, you could write a basic script containing the commands:

```
pwd
ls
```

When you run this script, you'd get a report of the current working directory and its contents. Such a script may not be particularly useful, but you get the basic idea. The entire world of shell scripting begins with that simple concept.

Shell scripts have several required constructs that tell the shell environment what to do and when to do it. This section of the chapter introduces these constructs and shows you how to use them.

Invoking the Shell

Before you add anything else to your script, you need to alert the system that a shell script is being started. This is done using the *shebang* construct. For example,

```
#!/bin/bash
```

tells the system that the commands that follow are to be executed by the bash shell.

It's called a shebang because the # symbol is called a hash, and the `!` *symbol is called a bang. Unix programming is filled with idiosyncratic terms like these.*

To create a script containing these commands, you put the shebang line first and then add the commands:

```
#!/bin/bash
pwd
ls
```

Now, a script this simple doesn't need much in the way of comments, but this example does it anyway, so that it follows good practice:

```
# /home/joe/dirinfo
# 12/7/04
# A really stupid script to give some basic info
# about the current directory

#!/bin/bash
pwd
ls
```

In a nutshell, that's all there really is to scripting. All that remains is to save the file with the proper filename (in this case `/home/joe/dirinfo`, but any descriptive filename will work), and to make it executable. Once that's done, you can run the script merely by giving its filename at the command prompt.

Of course, if your home directory isn't part of your `PATH` *environment variable's value, you'll have to either add it or invoke the program by using its full path name.*

Of course, most scripts are more complex than this one. The shell is, after all, a real programming language, complete with variables, control structures, and so forth. No matter how complicated a script gets, however, it is still just a list of commands executed sequentially. If you get into trouble, you can usually keep your head if you just remember that.

It's good practice to store your own scripts in a separate directory so you can find them easily. Consider creating a `/bin` *subdirectory in your home directory to use for script storage.*

Variables

Variables in Unix operate in much the same way as variables in other programming languages. As you learned in Chapter 5, environment variable values can be assigned very simply, using the assignment operator (=) as in:

```
EDITOR="vi"
```

In this example, the variable named `EDITOR` is assigned the value `vi`. You can access the value of a variable by putting a dollar sign in front of the variable name:

```
echo $EDITOR
```

If typed at the command line, this command would output `vi`.

In the bash shell (which is what's being used in this chapter), variables are considered to be text strings by default. This can cause some problems for programmers new to the shell, who expect to be able to do mathematical calculations within shell programs.

It is possible to do math in bash, but it requires some extra work. You'll learn how to do that later in this chapter.

In bash, if you create a variable with the command `VAR="1"`, the value of `VAR` is the text character 1, rather than the numerical value 1. In other words, the variable's value is considered to be the *textual representation* of the number 1, rather than the *numerical value*. If you were to write the following code block

```
VAR=1
VAR=$VAR+1
echo $VAR
```

the output would be the text string `1+1` rather than the number 2.

Under some shells (bash versions above 2.0, for example), it's possible to declare variable types. Because simpler shells such as the regular Bourne Shell and its clone ash lack this capability, that function isn't included in this chapter. If you'd like to learn more about declaring variable types, see the bash 2 manual at `www.gnu.org/software/bash/manual/bash.html`

A variable's name, if preceded by the dollar sign, can be substituted into an expression, and the variable will be executed when the script is run. For example,

```
PERSON="Fred"
echo "Hello, $PERSON"
```

would produce the following output:

```
Hello, Fred
```

By convention, Unix variables are written in capital letters. This isn't required, but it does make it easy to find them in scripts. Variables can be named anything and can use letters, numbers, and certain symbols. However, there are certain special variables (discussed a little later in this chapter) that use numbers and nonalphanumerics in their names. As a rule, it's best to stick with alphanumerics and to keep numerals at the end of the variable's name. For example, VARIABLE3 would be okay, but 3VARIABLE might get you into trouble.

Reading Input from the Keyboard

In addition to assigning a variable within a script, you can assign a variable by reading its value from the keyboard. This is particularly useful when you want your script to respond differently depending on the input from a user or another command's output.

For example, you might write the simple script:

```
echo "What is your name?"
read PERSON
echo "Hello, $PERSON"
```

In this example, the `read` command takes the input from the keyboard and assigns it as the value of the variable `PERSON`.

Special Variables

Earlier, you were warned about using certain nonalphanumeric characters in your variable names. This is because those characters are used in the names of special Unix variables. These variables are reserved for specific functions. For example, the `$` character represents the *process ID number*, or PID, of the current shell. (The system uses PID numbers to keep track of running programs.)

If you were to type

```
echo $?
```

at a shell prompt, you'd get the exit status of the last command as the output. The following table shows a number of special variables that you can use in your bash scripts.

Variable	Function
?	The previous command's exit status.
$	The PID of the current shell process.
-	Options invoked at start-up of the current shell.
!	The PID of the last command that was run in the background.
0	The filename of the current script.
1-9	The first through ninth command-line arguments given when the current script was invoked: $1 is the value of the first command-line argument, $2 the value of the second, and so forth.
_	The last argument given to the most recently invoked command before this one.

Exit Status

The `?` variable represents the *exit status* of the previous command. Exit status is a numerical value returned by every command upon its completion. As a rule, most commands return an exit status of 0 if they were successful, and 1 if they were unsuccessful.

Some commands return additional exit statuses for particular reasons. For example, some commands differentiate between kinds of errors and will return various exit values depending on the specific type of failure. For most practical purposes, though, you can interpret 0 and 1 to mean success and failure (or true and false), respectively.

Flow Control

Sure, variables and other required programming constructs are interesting, but on the face of it, they may not seem to be particularly useful. One of the main reasons for variables in a shell script, however, is that they permit *flow control*. Flow control is crucial because it allows the program to evaluate conditions and take actions contingent on those conditions. In short, flow control allows programs to make decisions.

Flow control can generally be broken down into two types: conditional and iterative. Both types describe how scripts set conditions and how the scripts react when the given conditions are met or not met. The difference between the two types is more obvious once you begin to write code that involves them, because each type uses unique commands to perform their tasks.

Conditional Flow Control

Conditional flow control, as its name implies, is concerned with whether certain conditions are met. Conditional constructs enable the programmer to mark a section of code as being contingent upon a certain stipulation being met. In other words, that section of code will be executed only if the specified condition is met. If the condition is not met, the code will be skipped.

The if-then Statement

The heart of conditional flow control is the `if-then` statement. In general terms, an `if-then` statement looks like this:

```
if some_condition
then
     something happens
fi
```

The "something happens" part can be any block of code, from a single statement to a huge amount of code with a great deal of complexity.

As in many other programming languages, the code that is enclosed within the conditional construct is indented for ease of reading. The `if-then` *block is terminated with the word* `fi`*, which is just the word* if *spelled backward.*

Here is a short script that demonstrates the usage of an `if-then` statement:

```
#!/bin/bash

echo "Guess the secret color"

read COLOR
```

```
if [ $COLOR="purple" ]
then
   echo "You are correct."
fi
```

The line "You are correct." will only be output if the word guessed by the user is "purple".

Such constructs can quickly become quite complex. You can specify multiple conditions by adding an else clause to the `if-then` construct, as in this example:

```
#!/bin/bash

echo "Guess the secret color"

read COLOR
if [ $COLOR="purple" ]
then
   echo "You are correct."
else
   echo "Your guess was incorrect."

fi
```

In this example, the command enclosed inside the else clause will be executed if the condition in the original if clause was not met.

In addition, you can use an elif clause to specify a second condition:

```
#!/bin/bash

echo "Guess the secret color"

read COLOR
if [ $COLOR="purple" ]
then
   echo "You are correct."
elif [ $COLOR="blue" ]
   echo "You're close."
else
   echo "Your guess was incorrect."

fi
```

You can add as many elif clauses as you want. They are particularly useful for finely shaded responses from the script, or when you know that there are a limited number of possible input values, each of which requires a particular response.

The test Command

The `test` command is used to evaluate conditions. You'll notice that the preceding examples include square brackets around the conditions to be evaluated. The square brackets are syntactically equal to the `test` command. For example, the preceding script could have been written:

```
if ( test $COLOR="purple" )
```

This concept is important because the `test` command has a number of options that can be used to evaluate all sorts of conditions, not just simple equality. For example, use `test` to see whether a particular file exists:

```
if ( test -e filename )
```

In this case, the `test` command would return a value of true, or 0, if the file exists, and false, or 1, if it doesn't.

You can get the same effect by using square brackets:

```
if [ -e filename ]
```

The following table shows other options you can use with `test` or with square brackets:

Option	Test Condition
-d	The specified file exists and is a directory.
-e	The specified file exists.
-f	The specified file exists and is a regular file (not a directory or other special file type).
-G	The file owner's group ID matches the file's ID.
-nt	The file is newer than another specified file (takes the syntax *`file1 -nt file2`*).
-ot	The file is older than another specified file (takes the syntax *`file1 -ot file2`*).
-O	The user issuing the command is the file's owner.
-r	The user issuing the command has read permission for the file.
-s	The specified file exists and is not empty.
-w	The user issuing the command has write permission for the file.
-x	The user issuing the command has execute permission for the file.

With all these options, the command will return a value of either 1 or 0, depending on whether the implied statement is true or false.

Comparison Operators

Conditional flow control also enables you to make other kinds of comparisons. For example, to specify a condition where inequality rather than equality is desired, you could negate the equality by putting an exclamation point in front of it:

```
if [ $COLOR != "purple" ]
```

This condition would return true for any string other than purple. Comparison operators, shown in the following table, work in the same way that they do in simple arithmetic.

Operator	Example	Test Condition
=	string a = string b	Text string a is the same as text string b.
!=	string a != string b	Text string a is not the same as text string b.
>	string a > string b	Text string a is greater than text string b.
<	string a < string b	Text string a is lesser than text string b.

You might wonder how a text string can have a greater or lesser value than another text string, because letters don't normally have numerical values. In this case, however, they do have a value. Textual comparison is strictly alphabetical: a is greater than b, b is greater than c, and so forth. Thus, a string beginning with c, as in "cat," is greater than the string "dog."

Doing Math in the Shell

As mentioned earlier, variables in the shell are considered to be text strings by default. If you have assigned the value `1` to a variable, the variable holds the value of the *textual character* 1, and not the *numerical value* 1. This is a difficult distinction to grasp, and one that has led more than one novice shell programmer into frustration. As you might expect, this makes it more difficult to do math in the shell. For example, consider this block of code:

```
MYVAR=1
MYVAR=$MYVAR+1
print $MYVAR
```

The output of this code would be `1+1`, rather than 2.

Fortunately, there is a workaround. The `expr` command allows you to do simple arithmetic operations in the shell. With `expr`, you can rewrite the above sequence as:

```
MYVAR=1
MYVAR=`expr $MYVAR+1`
print $MYVAR
```

The `expr` command forces the text string 1 to be interpreted as the numerical value 1, and your code fragment now returns the output `2`. You can use the following operators to do arithmetic operations:

- + addition
- - subtraction
- * multiplication
- / division

The `expr` command has several other functions. See the command documentation for details.

Multiple Conditions

Conditional flow control allows you to require that multiple conditions be met before the script performs a given function. There are several logical operators that can be used to enforce these multiple conditional requirements. Suppose you want to meet two conditions before proceeding. You could do this:

```
if [ condition1 ]
then
   if [ condition2 ]
   then
      some action
   fi
fi
```

Or you could simplify it by using a logical `and` operator (`&&`):

```
if [ condition1 && condition2 ]
then
   some action
fi
```

There is also a logical `or` operator (||):

```
if [ condition1 || condition2 ]
then
   some action
fi
```

which is equivalent to:

```
if [ condition1 ]
then
   some action
elif [ condition2 ]
then
   the same action
fi
```

You may have noticed that these examples use indentation to show the various actions in a particular statement. This indentation, called nesting, is a typographical convention that makes it easier for humans to read code intended for machines. Although your scripts will function equally well without nesting, it's better for your sanity to develop the habit.

The case Statement

In addition to the `if-then` statement, conditional flow control uses the `case` statement. This is a type of conditional flow control that allows the programmer to create a list of alternatives that can be reacted to accordingly. The effect is much the same as an `if-then` statement with a number of `elif` clauses, but the results are somewhat more elegant. Here's the general format:

```
case expression in
   pattern1)
```

```
        action1
    ;;
    pattern2)
        action2
    ;;
    pattern3)
        action3
    ;;
esac
```

As with `if`*, the* `case` *statement is concluded with esac, which is just the word case spelled backward. Note also that each option's section is concluded with the double semicolon (*`;;`*).*

`case` statements are great for evaluating command-line arguments. Take a look at this script excerpt:

```
# See how we were called.
case "$1" in
  start)
        # Start daemons.
        action $"Starting NFS services: " /usr/sbin/exportfs -r
        echo -n $"Starting NFS quotas: "
        daemon rpc.rquotad
        echo
        echo -n $"Starting NFS mountd: "
        daemon rpc.mountd $RPCMOUNTDOPTS
        echo
        echo -n $"Starting NFS daemon: "
        daemon rpc.nfsd $RPCNFSDCOUNT
        echo
        touch /var/lock/subsys/nfs
        ;;
  stop)
        # Stop daemons.
        echo -n $"Shutting down NFS mountd: "
        killproc rpc.mountd
        echo
        echo -n $"Shutting down NFS daemon: "
        killproc nfsd
        echo
        action $"Shutting down NFS services: " /usr/sbin/exportfs -au
        echo -n $"Shutting down NFS quotas: "
        killproc rpc.rquotad
        echo
        rm -f /var/lock/subsys/nfs
        ;;
  status)
        status rpc.mountd
        status nfsd
        status rpc.rquotad
        ;;
  restart)
        echo -n $"Restarting NFS services: "
        echo -n $"rpc.mountd "
        killproc rpc.mountd
```

```
        daemon rpc.mountd $RPCMOUNTDOPTS
        /usr/sbin/exportfs -r
        touch /var/lock/subsys/nfs
        echo
        ;;
  reload)
        /usr/sbin/exportfs -r
        touch /var/lock/subsys/nfs
        ;;
  probe)
        if [ ! -f /var/lock/subsys/nfs ] ; then
          echo start; exit 0
        fi
        /sbin/pidof rpc.mountd >/dev/null 2>&1; MOUNTD="$?"
        /sbin/pidof nfsd >/dev/null 2>&1; NFSD="$?"
        if [ $MOUNTD = 1 -o $NFSD = 1 ] ; then
          echo restart; exit 0
        fi
        if [ /etc/exports -nt /var/lock/subsys/nfs ] ; then
          echo reload; exit 0
        fi
        ;;
  *)
        echo $"Usage: $0 {start|stop|status|restart|reload}"
        exit 1
esac
```

This sample is taken from the `/etc/rc.d/init.d/nfs` *script on Red Hat Linux. It is the script that controls the NFS (Network File System) service.*

Remember that the special variable `$1` represents the first command-line argument. The script gives seven possible options: `start`, `stop`, `status`, `restart`, `reload`, `probe` and `*`. The asterisk option will match anything. It is put last to catch anything that isn't one of the preceding options. If, for example, you called the script with the argument `flerbnert`, the script would simply print a message advising you of the allowed arguments, and then quit.

Iterative Flow Control

There are also a number of control structures that are *iterative* in nature. That is, they are designed so that a block of code will repeat itself, or *iterate*, until a certain condition is met.

The careful reader may argue that this is also a conditional situation. The important feature is the repetitive nature of these constructs.

The while Statement

The `while` statement causes a block of code to repeat as long as a certain condition is met. For example, consider the following:

```
#!/bin/bash

echo "Guess the secret color: red, blue, yellow, purple, or orange \n"
```

```
read COLOR

while [ $COLOR != "purple" ]
do
   echo "Incorrect. Guess again. \n"
   read $COLOR
done

echo "Correct."
```

In this example, the code between the `do` and the `done` will repeat as long as the value of `COLOR` is not purple.

The until Statement

The condition in the `until` statement is the opposite of that in the `while` statement. For example, you could rewrite the previous example this way:

```
#!/bin/bash

echo "Guess the secret color: red, blue, yellow, purple, or orange \n"
read COLOR

until [ $COLOR = "purple" ]
do
   echo "Incorrect. Guess again. \n"
   read $COLOR
done

echo "Correct."
```

Choosing a Shell for Scripting

You've got a number of options when it comes to choosing a shell for scripting. To a certain extent, the decision is purely one of personal preference. However, there are some important considerations to bear in mind:

1. Almost all Unix systems have their control scripts written in Bourne or bash. That in itself is a good reason to learn how to program in those two shells. The ability to read and, if necessary, modify or write new control scripts is very important if you are destined to spend any time running a Unix system.
2. The bash shell incorporates most of the best features of the Bourne, Korn, and C shells.
3. Many Unix administrators think the C shell is less than ideal for heavy-duty use. The idea was a good one: make a shell that used a C-like grammar. In theory, this ought to make it easy for C programmers to get up to speed on shell scripting. The problem is in the execution. The C shell is rife with bugs and bad design. Indeed, there is even a document available on the Web that goes into detail about why the C shell should never be used for programming: `www.faqs.org/faqs/unix-faq/shell/csh-whynot/`.

4. Other shells, such as `zsh`, Plan9 (`rc`), and so forth may be able to accomplish a certain task easier or better, but they are not widely installed on many systems. This means that you may have trouble if you need to switch systems, or if you want to share your scripts with others.
5. Most Unix people use the Bourne or bash shells more than any other. It's as much a matter of convention as anything else, but if you want to speak the lingua franca of Unix people, Bourne and bash are where it's at.

Summary

Shell scripts are an excellent way to automate strings of Unix shell commands. Scripts can take input from the keyboard (interactive with a user) or from output of other commands. Every script needs to have several basic components:

- Invocation of a specific shell environment
- Variables and their associated values
- A source of input

There are two main ways in which a shell script can use external input to modify its action: conditional flow control and iterative flow control. Several basic programming constructs can be used to manage script flow control:

- `if-then` statements
- the `test` command
- `case` statements
- `while` statements
- `until` statements

Exercises

1. Using if statements, write a script named `filescript.sh` that will:
    a. Take an argument from the command line. This argument should be a directory path. If no argument is given, the program will use the current directory as the default.
    b. List all text files in that directory (files whose names contain the suffix `.txt`).
    c. Along with listing the filenames, give the user the option to choose the file's size, permissions, owner, or group, or "all of the above" information to be displayed. Do this interactively.
2. Write the same program using `case` statements instead of if statements.

Be sure to comment appropriately.

Your scripts may vary from the solutions provided, but as long as they work, they're correct.

Advanced Shell Scripting

Chapter 13 has given you a foundation in the basic elements of shell scripting. At the moment, though, some of you may not be too impressed with what you can do with shell scripts. This chapter may change that! It discusses a whole range of more advanced script capabilities, which will make shell scripting a far more flexible and powerful tool in the Unix programmer's kit.

Taking a quick look back, you have learned how to choose the shell most appropriate to your needs, pass variables to your scripts, and dabble in a bit of flow control. This chapter builds on that knowledge, presenting a host of new operators, concepts, and functions, which can be used to in a wide variety of circumstances. It explores how to write and maintain secure scripts, as well as who should be allowed to execute scripts and what those scripts should be allowed to do. Topics such as restricted shells and secure wipes take the stage here.

Shells aren't limited to simple line-by-line commands. One of their more powerful features is the capability to create functions and libraries of functions. Consequently, this chapter looks at these topics and examines some of the associated topics, such as variable scope, which becomes important when dealing with more complex scripts.

Like any good programmer, you also need to think about how to debug your creations. Scripts are no different from any other language in this respect, and the chapter finishes by examining the various methods available to the conscientious shell scripter, including how to check for errors, what to do and where to look, and how to add stops.

By the end of this chapter, you will have the requisite knowledge to go ahead and become a scripting guru. However, like many things, shell scripting takes practice and a bit of cunning to find the best way to do things, so be sure that you spend some practice time building a wide variety of scripts and putting together a solid library to aid you in your work.

Advanced Scripting Concepts

Where and how you use scripts is really up to you, and limited only by your imagination. This section is intended to open your eyes to the flexibility and range of possibilities inherent in using scripts. Of course, it can't teach you to be exceptionally sneaky in your use of scripts, but it can give you the information that you need to do pretty much anything you can think of.

Scripts can be used to take input from somewhere, process the information, and send the results somewhere else—including other scripts. They have the capability to work with complex data types such as multidimensional arrays and can make use of their environment to perform work. Need to manage processes? That is no problem for shell scripts. Want to customize the way in which you interact with your command line or automate file-handling tasks? Think shell scripts!

You should be getting the feeling that shell scripts are pretty useful things. You'd be right—pretty much anything you don't want to do by hand over and over again is a good candidate for a shell script. With that said, there is still a lot of learning ahead of you, so it's time to get moving.

Input and Output Redirection

Why would you want to redirect input or output? There are actually quite a few reasons. What if, for example, you were running a script and wanted to save its output to a file, or better yet, what if you wanted the results of a program sent to another program? In one form or another, you'll need to redirect information at some stage, so learning how this is done is definitely worthwhile.

STDIN, STDOUT, and STDERR

Every time you open up a shell, Unix opens up three files for use by your program:

- `STDIN` (standard in)—This is generally your terminal's keyboard.
- `STDOUT` (standard out)—This is generally your terminal's monitor.
- `STERR` (standard error)—This also generally points to your terminal's monitor.

The important thing to remember here is that, by default, input comes from your keyboard and is printed to your screen. While this is the way most interaction is achieved, it is by no means the only way in which programs and files can interact. Redirection often involves associating a file with one of the standard input or output (IO) files and sending the desired information to the required file. (A few other ways to redirect IO are examined a little later.)

Redirection is pretty simple; Unix provides you with a few simple operators that handle the associations for you.

Redirection Operators

To redirect information as required, you are provided with the following operators.

Operator	Action
`>`	Redirects `STDOUT` to a file
`<`	Redirects `STDIN` to a file
`>>`	Appends `STDOUT` to a file.
`|`	Takes output from one program, or process, and sends it to another
`<< delimiter`	Associates the current input stream with `STDIN` until the specified delimiter is reached

The first two operators are pretty simple to use. For example, if you wanted to redirect output that would usually go to the screen (`STDOUT`), you could say something like this:

```
$ ls > fileList
```

The `ls` command usually prints directly to the screen, but in this example the output is redirected to `fileList`. Of course, you might not want `fileList` to be written over every time you send output to it. In that case, you could use >> to seek to the end of the target file and append the results there:

```
$ ls \some\other\directory >> fileList
```

Sometimes you will want to send output from one process directly to another process. To do so, use the pipe (|) operator like this:

```
$ ls | wc
```

In this example, the `STDOUT` of `ls` is sent directly to the `STDIN` of wc utility, which dutifully prints out its results to the screen (because its output isn't redirected elsewhere).

The final method of redirection examined here is << delimiter, which is used in a special type of document called a `HERE` file. Basically, this uses redirection to read from the given input until the delimiter is reached. One simple use of this would be to print multiple lines of output to the screen without using `echo` over and over:

```
Cat <<END
The cat
Sat on the
Mat.
END
```

The type of processing you can perform on a `HERE` document is really up to you, so play around with all of the redirection operators to get the hang of it.

One thing of interest before moving on is that the use of the > operator has a few modifier flags, which can be used to alter its behavior. For example, using > with `&` causes both `STDOUT` and `STDERR` to be redirected, as in the following:

```
$ ls >& fileList
```

In this case, any error messages would not print to the screen but would be sent to `fileList`.

Using `>!` forces file creation in append mode, or overwriting an existing file in normal mode, while using `>@` opens a file in binary mode instead of text mode.

You'll see more redirection in action in an example a little later on.

Command Substitution: Back Ticks and Brace Expansion

It's often quite important to capture the results of some command in a variable for use by your shell script. Back ticks are really useful for this sort of thing because they provide you with an inline method for executing a command and retrieving the results before the rest of your script executes.

For example, it is conceivable that you may wish to capture the number of lines in a given file so that your shell can then use this to determine a certain action. Using back ticks makes this a pretty simple task:

```
Lines=`wc -l textFile`
```

The variable `Lines` now contains the number of lines in the `textFile` file and can be used elsewhere in the shell script as needed. Shells also expand the contents of double-quoted strings, so double quotation marks also play a role in command substitution. Of particular interest here is brace expansion, which uses the format: `$(command)`, where `command` is any valid Unix command.

Accordingly, you could have achieved the same result as the preceding line by saying:

```
Lines="$(wc -l textFile)"
```

Remember to use quotation marks to help clarify what you mean in your commands. Use single quotation marks if you don't want any type of expansion to take place — in other words, you are enclosing a literal string. Otherwise, use double quotation marks if you do want variables to be substituted, and commands to be executed.

It's useful to note that the `$(command)` format supports nesting without having to escape the `$(` and `)` characters, so you can perform several operations in one go if necessary. Like this:

```
$ echo "Next year will be 20$(expr $(date +%y) + 1)."
```

Many people believe that nesting can get too complicated and can become confusing. Like anything, make sure you use it sensibly and you should be just fine. Let's move on.

Using Environment and Shell Variables

The variables you have seen so far are local variables, and available only to the shell to which they have been passed. Naturally, you don't want to be limited to running your scripts in isolation from the rest of your system, so there is often a need for scripts to interact with the environment in which they are running. To do this, they need to have access to environment and shell variables, which can be set by the user or are already available upon startup of the shell.

Environment variables are accessible not only to the shell itself but to any processes that it spawns. For example, if one shell creates a subshell, then any environment variables available to the parent shell are also available for use by the child shell. If you want the `PATH` environment variable to contain the `/bin` directory, you would say something like this:

```
export PATH=/bin
```

The `export` command is used to modify the shell environment. Without any options, it displays many of the shell environment variables. Checking for a man page for `mount` gives you the man page for your current shell.

For the remainder of your shell's life, and any and all child shells or processes started by the shell, the `PATH` variable will contain the `/bin` directory. You can export any type of variable to your environment like this:

```
export name=value
```

To look at which shell variables have been set for your environment, use the `set` command:

```
$ set
```

Depending on your system and which shell you are using, you will get differing results.

Shell variables are not set by the user but are set up when the shell initializes. The following table provides examples of the types of variables set up by the shell.

Variable	Contains
`CDPATH`	Path of shortcuts for cd (like `PATH`)
`COLUMNS`	Numbers of columns on the display
`EDITOR`	Path for editor
`HISTSIZE`	Number of commands in command history (default 500)

There are an almost infinite number of variables that you can set for your shell. In the bash shell, you can use the `set` command to see a list of all the current shell variables that are currently set. As you become more familiar with the shell and its variables, you can alter them to suit your needs.

Shell Functions

What are shell functions all about, and why do you need them? The simple answer is that for anything but the simplest script, using functions is a great way to keep your code structured. Functions enable you to break down the overall functionality of a script into smaller, logical subsections, which can then be called upon to perform their individual task when it is needed.

Using functions to perform repetitive tasks is an excellent way to create code reuse. Code reuse is an important part of modern object-oriented programming principles, and with good reason—it means that you don't have to write out the same bit of functionality over and over, which makes your life as a shell programmer a whole lot easier. It also makes your scripts a lot easier to maintain because all the functionality is encapsulated within (hopefully) clearly named functions.

It may help to think of a function as an embedded script within your main shell script. After all, there is very little difference between the two — a function simply executes within the context of its containing shell without creating a new process. A new shell script, of course, always starts its own process.

To declare a function, simply use the following statement:

```
name () { commands; }
```

The name of your function is `name`, and that's what you will use to call it from elsewhere in your scripts. The function name must be followed by parentheses, which are followed by a list of commands enclosed within braces.

Because functions can be used to perform pretty much any type of action that you can think of, it is often necessary to pass information to them for processing. The following "Try It Out" section takes a quick look at a function that takes some parameters.

Try It Out Pass Parameters to a Function

1. Type the following code and save the file as `~/bin/func.sh` (if you do not have a bin directory in your home directory, create one with the `mkdir` command discussed in Chapter 4):

```
#!/bin/bash

# func
# A simple function

repeat() {
    echo -n "I don't know $1 $2 "
 }

repeat Your Name
```

2. Make the script executable. (See the section on chmod in Chapter 4 for details).

```
chmod 755 ~/bin/func.sh
```

3. At the command line, run the script:

```
$ ~/bin//func.sh
```

The following should print to the screen:

```
I don't know Your Name
```

How It Works

The function `repeat` was declared with one `echo` command in the commands list. Once it has been declared, you can use the function from anywhere in the script. In this case, it was called it directly after the declaration, passing it two parameters: `Your` and `Name`:

```
repeat Your Name
```

Just as you saw in Chapter 13, a function can use special variables to access parameters. This is about as basic a function as you can get, and there is certainly a lot more you can do here. A key point here, though, is that a function must be declared before it is referenced within a script.

Returning Values

You'll often want a function to return some sort of result that can be used by the rest of your script. As you already know, scripts use `exit` to return a value, but for functions you use the `return` command. Because functions can be used in conditional statements, they are perfect for determining what actions to take, based on their return values. Alternatively, you can use return values to tell you whether errors have occurred or incorrect information has been passed to your function.

To explicitly set the exit status of a function (by default it is the status of the last command), use the following statement:

```
return code
```

`code` can be anything you choose here, but obviously you should choose something that is meaningful or useful in the context of your script as a whole. For example, if you are using your function to determine whether to execute an `if` block, you should return 0 or 1 to keep things clear.

Nested Functions and Recursion

One of the more interesting features of functions is that they can call themselves as well as call other functions. A function that calls itself is known as a *recursive function*, and can be used in a variety of situations that can be resolved by repeating an action over and over. A good example of this is finding the sums or factorials of numbers passed to a function.

For more complex situations, it is often necessary to use the functionality contained in one function from another, which is called nesting functions. The "Try It Out" section that follows shows you a simple example to demonstrate this.

Try It Out Use Nested Functions

1. Type the following script, and save it as `~/bin/nested.sh`:

```
#!/bin/bash

# nested
# Calling one function from another

number_one () {
  echo "This is the first function speaking..."
  number_two
}

number_two () {
  echo "This is now the second function speaking..."
}

number_one
```

2. Make the script executable.

```
chmod 755 nested.sh
```

3. Run the script from the command line using the following command:

```
$ ~/bin/nested.sh
```

Two messages should be echoing to your screen:

```
This is the first function speaking...
This is now the second function speaking...
```

How It Works

Run through the order of execution to get an idea of what happened here:

1. Function `number_one` is called.
2. `number_one` echoes its message to the screen.
3. `number_one` calls function `number_two`.
4. `number_two` echoes its message to the screen and exits.

Nested functions (sometimes known as *chaining*) are very powerful tools in the shell scripter's armory. They enable you to break large problems into smaller, more easily understood chunks, and then use those modular pieces of code to produce a neat and elegant solution.

Are there any downsides to scripting this way? Well, recursion is pretty resource-intensive and can lead to slow execution, so be wary of that. There is, however, one other thing you should really pay close attention to when working with functions, and that's scope.

Scope

The concept of scope is really not too hard to grasp, but if you're like me, you need to be on your guard wherever the specter of scope raises its head. Forgetting the effects of scope can lead to errant and unexpected results for the unsuspecting scripter.

There are two types of scope—global and local. If a variable has global scope, it means that it is accessible from anywhere within a script. This is not true for variables with local scope, which are accessible only in the block in which they were declared.

To get a better feel for how scope works, tackle the short example in the following "Try It Out."

Try It Out Work with Scope

1. Type the following script into a file and name it `~/bin/scope.sh`:

```
#!/bin/bash

# scope
```

```
# dealing with local and global variables

scope ()
{
  local lclVariable=1
  gblVariable=2
  echo "lclVariable in function = $lclVariable"
  echo "gblVariable in function = $gblVariable"
}

scope

# We now test the two variables outside the function block to see what happens

echo "lclVariable outside function = $lclVariable"
echo "gblVariable outside function = $gblVariable"

exit 0
```

2. Make the script executable.

```
chmod 755 ~/bin/scope.sh
```

3. Type the following in the command line to run the script:

```
$ ~/bin/scope.sh
```

You should receive the following output:

```
lclVariable in function = 1
gblVariable in function = 2
lclVariable outside function =
gblVariable outside function = 2
```

How It Works

The meat of this example occurs in the `scope` function. To make a variable local, you use the `local` keyword:

```
local lclVariable=1
```

This line sets the value of the local variable `lclVariable` to 1 and gives it local scope only. You then `echo` out the values of each of the variables within the function when you call it directly after the declaration.

This gives you the first two lines of your output, which is what you expect:

```
lclVariable in function = 1
gblVariable in function = 2
```

Finally, you try to `echo` out the values of the two variables declared within the `scope` function from the shell. As you can see, only the variable with global scope is visible to the shell — the `lclVariable` does not exist in the context of the shell, only that of the function.

Finally, it is difficult to talk about functions without talking about libraries, which is the subject of the next section.

Function Libraries

You might find that you have a bunch of functions that you use quite often. Having to place them into every script you write could become quite tedious after a while. This is where function libraries come in handy.

One of the easiest things to do is place whatever functions you need into a file and then include that file at the start of your script. That makes whatever functions are contained in the file available for use as if you had written them in. To do this, simply use the period notation. Say that you had a modified version of the `scope` file (it doesn't need to be executable, a simple text file will do) like this:

```
scope ()
{
  local lclVariable=1
  gblVariable=2
  echo "lclVariable in function = $lclVariable"
  echo "gblVariable in function = $gblVariable"
}

another_scope_function()
{
  echo "This is another_scope_function..."
}

yet_another_function()
{
  echo "This is yet_another_function..."
}
```

You could gain access to all these functions by doing the following:

```
#!/bin/bash

. ~/lib/scope    # Define the path you need to access the function library file

scope
another_scope_function
yet_another_function

exit 0
```

This would output the two echo lines to your screen:

```
This is another_scope_function...
This is yet_another_function...
```

As you can see, it is pretty easy to include a library of functions like this. It is advisable to put them all into a `~/lib/` directory to avoid clutter in your home directory.

getopts

One other item of interest is `getopts`, a shell built-in (which means it is implemented by the shell internally) that is used to check whether command-line options passed to the script are valid. You could think of it as a command-line parser. The syntax for `getopts` is as follows:

```
getopts opstring name
```

In this case, `opstring` contains the list of characters that are to be recognized as valid options. If one of the characters is followed by a colon, it means that that option should have an argument, separated by a space. `name` is a shell variable, which is used to store the next option in the list.

`getopts` uses two variables to help it keep track of everything:

- `OPTIND`—Stores the index of the next argument to be processed.
- `OPTARG`—If an argument is required, it is placed in here by `getopts`.

Most often, `getopts` is used in some sort of loop to go over the options and arguments supplied to the script. This "Try It Out" section walks you through a very brief example to see this in action.

Try It Out Use getopts

1. Create the following script and save it as `~/bin/get.sh`:

```
#!/bin/bash

# get
# A script for demonstrating getopts

while getopts "xy:z:" name
do
  echo "$name" $OPTIND $OPTARG
done
```

2. Make the script executable.

```
chmod 755 ~/bin/get.sh
```

3. Call the script from the command line, passing it a variety of parameters, like so:

```
$ ~/bin/get.sh -xy "one" -z "two"
```

You should get the following results:

```
x 1
y 3 one
z 5 two
```

How It Works

There are really only two important lines in this example. The first deals with the arguments that have been given to `getopts`:

```
while getopts "xy:z:" name
```

From this line you can see that parameters `y` and `z` should have arguments and that `name` is the variable that is going to store the next option for you.

The second important line simply prints out the various variables pertinent to `getopts`:

```
echo "$name" $OPTIND $OPTARG
```

Finally, you execute `~/bin/get.sh` from the command line, passing it a few parameters to deal with:

```
$ ./get -xy "one" -z "two"
```

As expected, you received a list of name variables, printed out with the corresponding values of `OPTIND` and `OPTARG`. In this instance, you passed arguments to both `y` and `z` and they showed up in the `OPTARG` variable on the second and third lines when `name` contained the parameter that required an argument.

Signals and Traps

Certain process level events throw up signals, which can be useful for determining an action to take based on what has happened to that process. For example, a user might issue a **Ctrl + C** command to a process that is trying to write to a temporary file. This type of situation should be dealt with appropriately lest you lose important information when your temporary files are deleted on the next reboot.

Pressing **Ctrl + C** sends a signal to your shell process; how you react to this is up to you. You can use the `trap` command to take an action based on the type of signal you receive. To get a list of all the signals that can be sent to your processes, type the following:

```
$ trap -l
```

The following are some of the more common signals you might encounter and want to use in your programs:

Signal Name	Signal Number	Description
`SIGHUP`	1	Issued if a process is left hanging—the terminal is disconnected.
`SIGINT`	2	Issued if the user sends an interrupt signal (**Ctrl + C**).
`SIGQUIT`	3	Issued if the user sends a quit signal (**Ctrl + D**).
`SIGFPE`	8	Issued if an illegal mathematical operation is attempted.
`SIGKILL`	9	If a process gets this signal it *must* quit immediately and will not perform any clean-up operations (such as closing files or removing temporary files).

Trapping these signals is quite easy, and the `trap` command has the following syntax:

```
trap command signal
```

`command` can be any valid Unix command, or even a user-defined function, and *`signal`* can be a list of any number of signals you want to trap. Generally speaking, there are three common uses for traps:

removing temporary files, ignoring signals, and ignoring signals during special operations. An example of how to use signals and traps is examined shortly. However, signals and traps can play a part in file handling, so you should take a look at that first.

File Handling

A big necessity when it comes to dealing with scripts is the capability to work with files. Whether your script is creating files for storing or retrieving data, working as part of a CVS application, or simply using a temporary file to help with processing, you must be aware of how to deal with files securely and neatly.

This section discusses how shell scripts can be used to perform file-related tasks efficiently. To begin with, you will look at how to determine whether a given file exists. This is obviously important for a healthy, robust file-handling script. Taking things a step further, you learn how to clean up files in the event something unforeseen happens to your scripts.

File Detection

As you may have surmised, it is quite important to be able to tell whether a file exists. Things can go horribly wrong if you try to overwrite files that already exist, or write to files that don't exist. Luckily, there is a quick solution to this. You can also quite easily decide whether a file is readable or writable. Actually, there is no need to stop there—you can test to determine pretty much anything about a file.

For example, if you want to determine whether to write to a file, you need to check whether the file exists and is writable. To do that, use the following `if` statement:

```
if [ -w writeFile ]
then
  echo "writeFile exists and is writable!"
fi
```

The test in this case is given in generic form by:

```
[ option file ]
```

Where *`option`* and *`file`* are determined by what you need to test for and the file you want to test. The following table lists the most common options used.

Expression	Meaning
`-d file`	True if: `file` exists and is a directory.
`-e file`	True if: `file` exists.
`-r file`	True if: `file` exists and is readable.
`-s file`	True if: `file` exists and size is greater than zero.
`-w file`	True if: `file` exists and is writable.
`-x file`	True if: `file` exists and is executable.

You can combine these tests using `&&` (logical *and*) or `||` (logical *or*) to fine-tune your test even more:

```
if [ -r writeFile && -x writeFile ]
then
  echo "writeFile exists, is readable, and executable!"
fi
```

and

```
if [ -r writeFile || -w writeFile ]
then
  echo "writeFile exists and is readable or writable!"
fi
```

Cleaning Up Files

It is not very good practice to allow scripts to create a whole bunch of temporary files and then leave them lying around. All sorts of information could be lost or left hanging around. For example, you may decide that a script is taking too long to execute and it's time to go home. What do you do?

Most often, people will hit **Ctrl + C** to terminate their script's execution. If there's no proper file handling in place, it could lead to some sticky problems. This is where signals and traps come into the equation. By capturing signals sent to your processes, you can call functions that will act appropriately. The following "Try It Out" section captures an interrupt sent by a user and uses `trap` to clean up a temporary file created during the course of the script.

Try It Out   Clean Up a Temporary File with trap

This example simply shows you how to remove a temporary file if a given signal is encountered.

1. Type the following code and save into a script. Name the script `~/bin/sigtrap.sh`:

```
#!/bin/bash

# sigtrap
# A small script to demonstrate signal trapping

tmpFile=/tmp/sigtrap$$
cat > $tmpFile

function removeTemp() {
    if [ -f "$tmpFile" ]
    then
        echo "Sorting out the temp file... "
        rm -f "$tmpFile"
    fi
}

trap removeTemp 1 2

exit 0
```

2. Make the script executable:

```
chmod 755 ~/bin/sigtrap.sh
```

3. Run the script at the command line with:

```
$ ~/bin/sigtrap.sh
```

   You should find that the script waits for you to enter text up until you press **Ctrl + D**.

4. Type in some text at the command line and press **Ctrl + D**. Once this is done, check that the file you created is in the `tmp` directory (it will be named something similar to `sigtrap(procid)`).

5. Now run the script again, but before you press **Ctrl + D**, press **Ctrl + C**. This time you should receive the message "Sorting out the temp file...." If you go and check for another file with the name similar to `sigtrap(procid)`, you will find that it is no longer there.

How It Works

The first line creates a temporary file using the shell's process ID, suffixed by the word sigtrap:

```
tmpFile=/tmp/sigtrap$$
```

The next line uses the `cat` command without any parameters. This causes the script to wait for input from the user. You need the program to wait for a little while to give you time to send the appropriate signal:

```
cat > $tmpFile
```

Next, a function was created to remove any temporary files the script had created before exiting:

```
function removeTemp() {
    if [ -f "$tmpFile" ]
    then
        echo "Sorting out the temp file... "
        rm -f "$tmpFile"
    fi
}
```

This is the main use of trapping. You will often want to call a specific function based on the type of signal you receive and the type of task your script is completing.

Finally, the `trap` command was set to call the `removeTemp()` function in the event that the process received signals 1 or 2 (the signals for the process being hung, or the user sending an interrupt, **Ctrl + C**):

```
trap removeTemp 1 2
```

You might find that you want to perform different operations depending on which signal is received. In that instance, simply create several `trap` statements with their corresponding functions to handle execution.

Arrays

It's often necessary, and useful, to be able to work with arrays. Shell scripts are no different from any other scripting or programming language in that respect. Naturally, it is possible to declare and use arrays using your shell's notation. This section concentrates on the bash shell's array notation, but whatever lessons you learn here apply to any shell you care to use.

Now, there are several things that you need to be able to do with arrays: declare them, populate them with information, and manipulate the information held within them as needed. You can do all of this from within the shell, and, as you might expect, there is generally more than one way to do things.

Declaring an Array

There are several ways to declare an array, and how you decide to do this really depends on what is the most expedient for you at the time. It is even possible to initialize arrays using values stored in text files. The first, and simplest, method of declaring an array looks like this:

```
array1[index]=value
```

This snippet creates and array called `array1`, which has a value referenced by the index number given between the square brackets. Another way to create and populate an array is like this:

```
array2=(value1 value2 value3 value4)
```

`array2` has been populated with the values `value1`, `value2`, and so on. The index numbers are automatically assigned, beginning with 0. The third method of initializing an array is more or less a combination of the first two:

```
array3=([0]=value1 [13]=value2 [7]=value3)
```

Notice that when declaring values, your index numbers need not be in any particular order, nor do they need to be in sequence—you can place them wherever you like.

How do you find out what values are in an array? You need to perform an operation called dereferencing.

Dereferencing an Array

To find out what value is held at a certain index within in array, use the curly bracket notation, like this:

```
${array[index]}
```

Pretty simple stuff! So to find out the value of `array3` where the index value is 13, you would write the following:

```
value=${array3[13]}
Echo "$value"
```

This, as you may have guessed, would print out:

```
value2
```

There is special notation that you can use to determine all the values within an array. You also can find out how many elements an array contains. The following two lines perform these actions, respectively:

```
arrayelements=${array2[@]}
arraylength=${#array2[@]}
```

Using `array2`, which was declared in the last section, the `arrayelements` variable would contain the values `value1 value2 value3 value4`, and the `arraylength` variable would contain the value 4.

Finally, you may not want to return all the elements of an array but rather a range of them. If this is the case, use the following notation:

```
${array[@]:3}
${array[@]:3:2}
```

The first line goes to the fourth value in the array (because array indexes start from 0) and then returns every remaining value in the array, while the second line returns only the next two values after the fourth element.

While not strictly part of dereferencing, bash version 3 has a new notation that allows for the expansion of indices. To find out what index values your array holds, use the following notation:

```
${!array[@]}
```

For `array2`, which was presented earlier, this would return: 0 1 2 3.

Removing Values from an Array

You might want to get rid of some values in your array, or even drop all the values from an array entirely. If this is the case, you can use the `unset` command like this:

```
unset array[1]
unset array[@]
```

The first command removes the value at index position 1, and the second removes all values from the array. Here's a little exercise that shows you how to use the values of a text file to populate an array.

Try It Out — Use Text File Values in Arrays

1. Type the following text and save the file as `~/tmp/sports.txt`:

```
rugby hockey swimming
polo cricket squash
basketball baseball football
```

2. Now create the following script file and call it `~/bin/array.sh`:

```
#!/bin/bash

# array
# A script for populating an array from a file

populated=( 'cat ~/tmp/sports.txt | tr '\n' ' '')
echo ${populated[@]}

exit 0
```

3. Make the script executable:

```
chmod 755 ~/bin/array.sh
```

4. Execute the script by typing the following at the command line:

```
$ ~/bin/array.sh
```

Your output should simply be the contents of the `sports` file minus the new lines:

```
rugby hockey swimming polo cricket squash basketball baseball football
```

How It Works

The money line here is:

```
populated=( `cat ~/tmp/sports.txt | tr '\n' ' '`)
```

This line uses one of the array declaration notations presented earlier to declare and populate an array called `populated`. The command within the parentheses pipes the results of the `cat ~/tmp/sports.txt` command (which simply writes the contents of the file `sports.txt` to the standard output) to the `tr '\n' ' '` command.

`tr` converts the character in the first string to those in the second string. In this case, you are removing newline (`\n`) characters and replacing them with white space so that the array can be populated properly. If you only have one line in your file, you would simply use the `cat sports` command enclosed in back ticks.

Obviously, you need to ensure that the results of the command enclosed by the parentheses are correctly formatted. Otherwise, you will get some strange results.

Now that we understand some advanced scripting techniques, you will probably want to keep the scripts away from the prying eyes of malicious crackers. Security is a very hot topic in most information technology departments these days and should be taken seriously. The next section will help you keep your scripts, and subsequently your systems, secure.

Shell Security

Talking about secure shell scripting is opening a big of a can of worms. The problem with shell scripts is that they are used to run commands that use other programs, files, or utilities. Often these other programs can cause a security leak. Even if you have been exceptionally security conscious, it is still possible for malicious users to thwart your intent. Having your own scripts used against you is never particularly soothing to the ego, either.

If you are extremely concerned about security, it is probably best not to use shell scripts for anything but the simplest tasks. Shells weren't really designed with security in mind—they were designed to make life easy for you. Part of making life easier is handling a lot of things behind the scenes. It is these hidden aspects of most scripts that can harbor danger.

Where Can Attacks Come From?

A good example of how shell input can be used to modify the behavior of a script comes from changing filenames. Your script may be dutifully searching through a list of filenames and piping them off to another utility when it comes across one that has a special character such as a semicolon followed by a shell command — perhaps the `useradd` command. The script may assume that you want to run the `useradd` command, which creates an unwanted user account on your system. Well, it may well be that this shell command cannot be run without increased system privileges, or cannot do anything more malevolent than break your script, but there is the possibility that there is malicious intent.

Another point of concern is the temporary files that are often used by shell scripts. These are often held in the `/tmp` directory, which is visible and useable by anyone on the system. It's quite hard to see how someone could do something malicious without knowing the intimate workings of your script, but it is possible that a malicious user could remove temporary files or modify them in such a way as to produce unwanted or unexpected results.

You also should always keep in mind the environment your script is running in (or is intended to run in), both in terms of where you actually keep your script and in what environment it executes to ensure that if an unauthorized user runs your script, he will not have more access than the script needs.

Taking Precautions

There are several steps you can take to help control attacks such as those mentioned in the previous section. By adhering to some general security-related principles, you can make it a lot harder for someone to mess around with your scripts.

You can create a secure subdirectory in the `/tmp` folder for use by your scripts, so that any temporary files generated by your scripts are not modifiable by anyone else. This is not a promise of security at all, but it does put up an extra obstacle for would-be hackers. Hackers could still replace your directory with their own, but it would be hard to do anything more than that.

Keep your scripts in a place where they are not modifiable by all and sundry. This means that you need to contain them in secure directory structures with the proper permissions set — in other words, don't let everyone have write permission on them, among other things. Further, you need to ensure that hidden environment variables are set or are what you expect. Having modified environment variables can alter the execution of your script before it has even begun, so set your `PATH` and `IFS` variables at the start of your script.

Finally, you also don't want to let scripts with elevated privileges run amok. Give scripts enough privileges to perform the required task, and no more.

Next, take a look at a special type of shell that can aid you in your bid to become a secure shell scripter.

Restricted Shells

A restricted shell is exactly what its name implies — restricted. It only has enough functionality to perform a limited set of tasks. Obviously, this makes it a better candidate for secure programming, but you shouldn't assume that it is totally safe. As mentioned earlier, sometimes the security problem can come from the programs that the shell is interacting with and not directly from the shell itself.

The following table takes a look at some of the features of restricted shells and why they have been enforced.

Feature	Reason
Unable to change directory with `cd`.	Prevents users from running code from an unsecured directory.
Unable to set some environment variables like `SHELL`, `PATH`, and `ENV`.	Changing environment variables can lead to unexpected results.
Unable to use IO redirection with operators such as `>`, `>&`, `<>`, and so on.	Prevents users from creating unwanted files.
Unable to use `exec` built-in to substitute processes.	Any spawned processes or shells need not run with the same level of restriction as the parent shell.
Unable to use commands that contain slashes.	Prevents possibility of using commands to change into unauthorized directories.
Unable to disable restricted mode.	This one is quite obvious—you wouldn't want a hacker to simply turn off restrictions!

To run a restricted shell, simply invoke it with the `-r` option. Alternatively, if you want to run only certain commands in a restricted manner, you can use the `set -r` and `set +r` options. The following snippets show this in action:

```
#!/bin/bash -r
# This script won't work

cd /some/other/directory
set +r

exit 0
```

Alternatively, you could do something like this:

```
#!/bin/bash
# This script won't work

cd /some/other/directory
echo "`pwd`"

set -r
cd
echo "`pwd`"
set +r

exit 0
```

If you run this script, notice that the `cd` command between the two `set` commands will not work because you cannot change directory in restricted mode.

Another aspect of security that is of great importance is ensuring that you clean up your temporary files — also known as *wiping*. You saw a basic example of this in action in the section on file handling, where you trapped a signal from an interrupt and used it to remove a temporary file from the `/tmp` directory before stopping execution.

This section covered the basics of keeping your scripts secure. While this is important to do as a normal user, it is doubly important for system administrators to keep their scripts secure. Most system administration scripts, as you will see in the next section, are run as the root user.

System Administration

If you ever want to be a Unix system administrator, you will need to know something about scripting. Administrators have a wide variety of tasks that they need to perform to keep the systems and platforms in their care in proper working order. Invariably, this involves, among other things, having to find out information from and about the system, moderating how the system uses its resources, and setting up and installing software and hardware.

Scripting plays an important role in this. As you have already learned in this chapter and many of the ones before, shells provide you with all the commands and utilities you need to perform pretty much any type of administration task. From backing up files to adding new users, anything remotely related to the platform on which users can go about their daily lives falls under the system administrator's purview.

One of the neat things about scripts is that they can perform any repetitive task quite well. For example, if you work at a university as the computer lab's administrator, you might soon become pretty sick of adding new users each year. Writing a little script to do this for you would certainly make life a lot easier, wouldn't it? In fact, because most students would probably have exactly the same rights, you could probably write a script that reads in all the names from a text file and creates them as new users, all with standard permission (or whatever you wanted).

Pretty much everything you have been doing until now falls on the list of administrator tasks. All the commands you have looked at, all the various types of variables, utilities, and so on, all form part of the toolkit system administrators use to fulfill their role. Most of the time you will want to access information or perform operations on the following:

- The file system
- Logs
- Users
- Processes
- Resources

The information you need is often the same type of thing again and again. Many administrators use `cron` (see Chapter 11, "Running Programs at Specified Times") to run scripts each hour, day, or week to print out whatever system information it is that they need. Because you have already seen `cron` in action, it isn't discussed in-depth here. Just know that whatever scripts you want run on a regular basis can be sent to `cron` to run.

Please be aware that many system administrator tasks need superuser privileges. As a result, you need to be very careful about what you decide to automate with scripts.

Gathering Information

Naturally, you want to be able to find out information from your system about how it is operating and what is happening with users, processes, and files. You also need to keep records, or logs, of what your system has been doing. One of the first things to do is take a look at the commands and utilities available for retrieving information about your system.

There are, of course, a host of commands related specifically to system administration. The following table lists some of the more common ones, and their use.

Command	Use
`df`	Provides information on the file system of a given file. If you don't supply `df` with a filename, it displays file system information for all mounted file systems.
`du`	Gives the file system's block usage for each file supplied as an argument. If nothing is supplied, the block usage of the files in the current directory is given.
`lastlog`	Accesses log information to print out the details of the last login. You can specify a user to retrieve only that user's log information.
`lsdev`	Retrieves information about installed hardware from the `/proc` directory. Use it to obtain an overview of what hardware a system is running.
`lsof`	Displays a list of all files that are currently open. By default it displays all files open by all processes.
`ps`	Provides information on processes, sorted by owner and process ID.
`stat`	Provides more detailed information on files and directories.
`top`	Returns a list of the most /CPU-intensive processes.
`vmstat`	Provides information on the state of your system's virtual memory—processes, memory, paging, block IO, traps, and CPU activity.
`w`	Shows information, including information on processes, on all current users unless a specific user is specified.

There are other utilities you can use to gather information, but these commands give you a good base from which to work. Use them from within scripts to display information on a regular basis (using cron), or on startup, enabling you to keep abreast of what is happening without having to search repetitively.

Many of these utilities have quite a few options available to customize exactly the type of information you can gather with them. Play around with them and consult the man pages for more information. The next section examines some of the more common system administration jobs.

Performing Tasks

Gathering information is only one side of the coin. You also need to maintain a system in good working order. Unix comes with utilities to help with precisely this. The following table lists some of the more common commands used by system administrators.

Command	Use
`chown,`	The superuser can use `chown` to change the ownership of a file. Otherwise, the owner of the file can use `chown` to change the group ownership of a file.
`chgrp`	Change group ownership of a file.
`dump`	Back up files in binary format. `restore` can then be used to retrieve files backed up with `dump`.
`mke2fs`	Create new ext2 file systems.
`mkswap`	Create a swap partition, which must then be enabled using `swapon`.
`mount, umount`	Mount and unmount file systems on devices.
`ulimit`	Set limits on the resources processes can consume.
`useradd, userdel`	Add and delete users from a system.
`wall`	Write to all terminals logged on. Administrators can use it to send system-wide messages.
`watch`	Execute commands repeatedly at a specified interval.

The work of a system administrator is never done. Having played around with the commands in this table and the one before, you should be able to do quite a bit of useful system-related programming. However, there is one topic that hasn't been touched yet that is of vital importance to tracking and recording information—the logs! System logging is discussed in the following chapter, so all that's said here is that making good use of system logs is an essential component of any system administrator's job description.

Debugging Scripts

Like any programming or scripting language, shell scripts require some form of debugging. There are quite a few things that can go wrong with a shell script, ranging from a simple syntax error to more complex and subtle errors in logic. Unlike many fully featured languages, however, shells don't come with a built-in debugger, so you have to use a bit of cunning and guile to ensure that scripts behave as expected.

How you go about checking for errors really depends on the type of errors you are trying to capture. For example, running this script will kick up an error:

```
#!/bin/bash

# echobug
# Faulty echo shell

ech "Guess the secret color" \n"
```

You should be able to see why pretty much immediately: a simple typo (ech instead of echo in that last code line) prevents the script from running properly because there is no ech command. This type of error is known as a syntax error, and one of the ways to search for and correct them is by using the -n option with sh command interpreter, like this:

```
sh -n scriptname
```

This does not execute your script; it simply reads each command. Even better, use the -v option of sh with -n to give a verbose output. Basically, this forces sh to echo out each command as it executes. This helps you locate any errors a lot faster.

What if the error is not a syntax error but something that is just not behaving as you expect? There are a couple of things you can try to find out what is going on in the script.

First, the -x option of sh can help. This flag echoes the result of each command run by the script to the screen so that you can ensure that you get what you expect. Of course, for larger scripts, you may not want to debug the entire thing at once. If this is the case, insert set -x into your script at the place where you want to begin debugging and set +x where you want to stop debugging. To debug only the one line of the echobug script, you would do the following:

```
#!/bin/bash

# echobug1
# Faulty echo shell

set -x
ech "Guess the secret color"
set +x
```

When you run this shell from the command line with the $ ~/bin/echobug1.sh command, you get output with a preceding (+) sign. Any line prefixed with a preceding sign is a command that is run by the shell. Everything else is a result of the shell's processing.

```
$ ~/bin/echobug1.sh
+ ech Guess the secret color
~/bin/echobug1.sh: line 6: ech: command not found
+ set +x
```

As well as this, you could insert echo statements into your code to print out values of variables to determine whether they contain the expected values. This tactic is especially handy for determining whether the results of commands using regular expressions are what you wanted.

Further, inserting an echo statement into flow-control structures such as if and while statements can help determine whether your conditions are working properly. If, for example, you expect an if statement's condition to evaluate to true at least once in a script's lifetime, and you insert this statement into the if loop's body:

```
echo "You have reached the body of the if statement ok!"
```

You can quite easily tell whether your script ever gets to that section of the code. If it doesn't, you know that the problem is either with your condition, or that the script is terminating before it gets to the if loop.

Summary

This chapter introduced you to more-advanced scripting concepts, including input-output redirection. You learned quite a bit about shell functions, including:

- How to pass parameters to a function
- How to return a value from a function to the script
- How nested functions can help in complex situations
- How to use function libraries to save yourself time and effort

Additionally, you explored the concept of scope, both global and local, and learned how to use the `trap` command to respond to signals from processes and to clean up temporary files. You learned the importance of safeguarding your scripts by keeping them in secure directory structures and using restricted shells, and you explored some other administrative tasks, such as information-gathering, utilities for system maintenance and debugging scripts.

Exercises

1. Create a function that determines the sum of two values passed to it, and make it available to all shells.
2. Write a script that reads information from the end of one file and appends it to another. To make this more useful, make it read from a system log file.
3. Write a script that attempts to divide by zero. It should send an error message to the screen before ceasing execution.
4. Write a script for a system administrator. The script should tell the administrator what day it is, who is logged on, and what files are being used. Before exiting, the script should send a message to all users saying that the administrator is now in the office.

System Logging

As you know by now, system administration is quite an expansive concept, basically covering all aspects of keeping things running. It involves responsibilities such as installing software, keeping software up-to-date, managing disk space, controlling access to the system, and managing user accounts. One of the most important (and oftentimes tedious) administrative jobs is managing log files. Because your system is involved in a multitude of tasks that are noninteractive and invisible to the user, logs are your eyes and ears to what's going on within the system. You need to monitor the log files to have any sense of what the computer is doing at any given time, and it is the log files that you consult whenever things are not going the way they should be.

Unix systems have a very flexible and powerful logging system, which enables you to record almost anything you can imagine and then manipulate the logs to retrieve the information you require. This chapter provides a thorough explanation of how logging works in Unix, how to make it keep track of the things you need to know, and how to automate a good bit of the process so you do not have to spend all of your time reading log files.

Log Files

Log files are extremely important to system administration because they are the voice of the system—the mechanism by which the system communicates with the administrator. The administrator is aware of what's happening on the system by reading log files and can use those files to create a snapshot of what's occurring on the system at any given time.

The following sections examine the logging process in detail. You'll find that logging on Unix is an extremely flexible process that gives you a great amount of control over exactly what gets logged and where those logs get stored. Unix gives you the power to specify exactly what messages are written to which file on your system.

Each vendor differs slightly in where it chooses to place log files. Generally, the SYSV-derived systems (such as HP-UX, IRIX, and Solaris) place their log files in the `/var/adm` hierarchy, while the BSD and Linux distributions (including MacOS X) use the `/var/log` directory for log files. The `/etc/syslog.conf` file, which is discussed in the following section, can tell where log files will be written.

The log files contain a wealth of information. The most important kinds of messages written to log files include:

- System boot messages and boot-related failures
- User logins and locations
- Security information such as failed logins
- E-mail activity (successes and failures)
- Cron job status

Introducing Syslogd

System logs are the method by which programs running on your system can communicate with you. In situations where things are working correctly and as expected, the logs serve as a manifest of activity on your system. When things are not working properly, the logs are invaluable in showing you exactly what's happening on your system. Keep in mind the basic Unix philosophy of having many small programs or utilities, each performing a dedicated task. With many specialized programs running at once, it is critical to be able to know at any moment what any of these programs are doing. This is where syslog fits in.

Syslog is a specialized application that focuses on system logs. It's one of the great and unsung parts of a Unix operating system. Syslog, which stands for system logger, is a utility that provides central and unified logging capability to the entire system. Rather than having each application manage its own log files in a unique fashion, the syslog daemon (syslogd) manages all logs throughout the system. Syslogd does not generate the messages that appear in log files on your system. It acts as a crossing guard on your computer, showing the log messages generated by various programs which way to go. The operation of the system logger is quite straightforward. Programs send their log entries to syslogd, which consults the configuration file `/etc/syslogd.conf` and, when a match is found, writes the log message to the desired log file.

There are four basic syslog terms that you should understand:

- Facility — The identifier used to describe the application or process that submitted the log message. Examples are mail, kernel, and ftp.
- Level — An indicator of the importance of the message. Levels are defined within syslog as guidelines, from debugging information to critical events. These serve as labels. How these levels are processed is entirely up to you.
- Selector — A combination of one or more facilities and levels. Log messages coming into syslog are matched against the selectors in the configuration file. When an incoming event matches a selector, an action is performed.
- Action — What happens to an incoming message that matches a selector. Actions can write the message to a log file, echo the message to a console or other device, write the message to a logged in user, or send the message along to another syslog server.

Understanding the syslog.conf File

Here's an example of a system logger configuration file, `/etc/ syslog.conf`:

```
*.err;kern.*;auth.notice;authpriv,remoteauth,install.none;mail.crit
                                                        /dev/console
*.notice;*.info;authpriv,remoteauth,ftp,install.none;kern.debug;mail.crit
                                                        /var/log/system.log

# Send messages normally sent to the console also to the serial port.
# To stop messages from being sent out the serial port, comment out this line.
#*.err;kern.*;auth.notice;authpriv,remoteauth.none;mail.crit
                                                        /dev/tty.serial

# The authpriv log file should be restricted access; these
# messages shouldn't go to terminals or publically-readable
# files.
authpriv.*;remoteauth.crit                              /var/log/secure.log

lpr.info                                                /var/log/lpr.log
mail.*                                                  /var/log/mail.log
ftp.*                                                   /var/log/ftp.log
netinfo.err                                             /var/log/netinfo.log
install.*                                               /var/log/install.log
install.*                                               @192.168.1.50:32376

*.emerg
```

As you can see, `/etc/syslog.conf` is a plain text file, and its body looks like two columns. The first column — actually the first part of each line — is the source of the logging information, that is, the system or program that's providing the information. The source is generally defined in two parts, a facility and a level separated by a period — *`facility.level`* — and is commonly called the *selector*.

The second column (the end of each line) is the information's destination, which can be many things, including a text file, a console, a serial port, even a system logger running on another system. Toward the end of the example file you'll notice that an `install.*` selector shows up twice. It's completely legal to send the same result to multiple places; in this case, log entries belonging to the facility install are being appended to the text file `/var/log/install.log` as well as being sent to a network syslog server located at the IP address 192.168.1.50 (on port 32376).

Here are the available facilities for the selector.

Facility	Description
auth	Activity related to requesting name and password (getty, su, login)
authpriv	Same as auth but logged to a file that can only be read by selected users
console	Used to capture messages that would generally be directed to the system console
cron	Messages from the cron system scheduler
daemon	System daemon catch-all
ftp	Messages relating to the ftp daemon
kern	Kernel messages
lpr	Messages from the line printing system
mail	Messages relating to the mail system
mark	Pseudo event used to generate timestamps in log files
news	Messages relating to network news protocol (nntp)
ntp	Messages relating to network time protocol
local0–local7	Local facilities defined per site

The following table explains the available `syslog.conf` levels.

Level	Description
emerg	System is unusable. Messages go to all logged in users on all terminals.
alert	Action must be taken immediately.
crit	Critical conditions.
err	Error conditions.
warning	Warning conditions.
notice	Normal but significant condition.
info	Informational messages.
debug	Debug-level messages. Should be off in general use, as the verbose nature of these messages will quickly fill disks.
none	Pseudo level used to specify not to log messages.

The combination of facilities and levels enables you to be discerning about what is logged and where that information goes. As each program sends its messages dutifully to the system logger, the logger makes decisions on what to keep track of and what to discard based on the levels defined in the selector.

When you specify a level, the system will keep track of everything at that level and higher. The level acts as a low-water marker. For example, it stands to reason that if you are interested in being notified of a warning in your mail system, you would also want to be notified of any err, crit, alert, and emerg messages.

Let's take a look at a few example lines from /etc/syslog.conf:

```
lpr.info                                          /var/log/lpr.log
mail.*                                            /var/log/mail.log
ftp.*                                             /var/log/ftp.log
```

Messages from the printing system (lpr) with a logging level that is equal to or greater than info will be logged to the text file /var/log/lpr.log. The last two examples show the use of wildcards in selectors. By using a wildcard for a level, you tell the system to log absolutely every message from that facility to the location specified. In this case, any and all messages from the mail facility are going to the text file /var/log/mail.log, and the ftp server is logging to the file /var/log/ftp.log.

The following "Try It Out" creates an entry to log ssh activity to a new logfile, ssh.log. The example was done on a system running Mac OS X, so you may need to consult your system documentation for the location of sshd_config, if it is not located in the /etc directory. Common locations for sshd_config are /etc/ssh and /usr/local/etc/ssh. Additionally, while Mac OS X sets SyslogFacility to AUTHPRIV, you may find another default SyslogFacility. Whichever one you use, you'll change it to LOCAL7 for this exercise.

Try It Out Configure a Log File

Configure syslog to log all ssh-related activity to a log file, called ssh.log.

1. Edit /etc/sshd_config. Change the line reading SyslogFacility AUTH to:

   ```
   SyslogFacility LOCAL7
   ```

2. Edit /etc/syslog.conf. Add the following line to the end of the file:

   ```
   local7.*                    /var/log/sshd.log
   ```

3. Enter the command:

   ```
   sudo touch /var/log/ssh.log
   ```

4. Restart syslog, by entering the appropriate command for your system (for example, sudo kill -HUP `cat /var/run/syslogd.pid`).
5. Test it out by making a connection to localhost.

   Open a terminal window, type **ssh localhost**, and proceed to log in to your system as yourself.

   When you receive a prompt, type **exit** to log out.

   Then type this command:

   ```
   sudo tail -f /var/log/ssh.log.
   ```

You will see an entry with details of your connection.

If you do not see your connection logged, you need to restart your ssh daemon by issuing the command:

```
sudo /etc/init.d/sshd restart.
```

How It Works

Here's what happens:

1. Editing the `sshd` configuration file enables you to make changes to the way the ssh daemon logs its activity, among other options. The `sshd` file logs its activity using the AUTH facility by default. For this exercise, this is changed to a custom facility, `LOCAL7`, which is intended for local use and will not be in use by existing programs on your system. Now you can easily direct all `sshd` messages into a specified text file.
2. The syslog daemon is instructed to match local7 events and append them to a text file `/var/log/sshd.log`.
3. The text file needs to exist on your system before being written to. Syslog does not create a file for you, so you create the file `/var/log/ssh.log`, using the `touch` command.
4. Changes to `/etc/syslog.conf` do not take effect until you restart the syslog daemon. Issue the vendor-appropriate command to do so on your system. (Entering the command `man syslog` should tell you how it is done on your system.)

What's the Message?

Now let's take a look at the content of the messages that will be managed by syslog. The messages that it outputs are structured in a very specific fashion, which is the very aspect that makes parsing system log files a trivial matter for perl, sed, and other utilities that work with text, and especially with regular expressions.

Not all messages are logged in the same way or contain the same type of information. For this reason, you should become familiar with the specific format of the type of log you want to parse before writing scripts or regular expressions to extract the information.

Here's an example message from `ssh.log`:

```
Jan  7 15:31:37 pandora2 sshd[16367]: Accepted password for craigz from
192.168.1.222 port 5242 ssh2
```

The message has the following format:

```
Date time hostname process[pid]:action:version
```

So the log message can be translated to the following:

On Jan. 7 at 3:31 p.m. `sshd` running on the host pandora2 with the PID of 16367 performed the following: accepted a connection from the user craigz coming from the host 192.168.1.222 on port 5242; and the client version was ssh2.

All of the `sshd` log messages on your system will follow the same format, whatever that format is. That means you can use any of the utilities you have already seen (perhaps in a shell script) to extract information when you need it. You just need to familiarize yourself with the format used by the programs and utilities on your system.

The Logger Utility

Most Unix systems provide the logger system utility, which can be used to send messages to syslogd. The program can send messages to a user-specified log file, and the facility and level can be assigned. Here's an example of the `logger` command:

```
darwin$ logger -p local7.info -t test_logger_message "test message"
```

The `-p` flag stands for priority, in this case `local7.info`, and the `-t` flag stands for `-tag`, which is a label that will accompany your message.

In the "Configure a Log File" exercise, if syslog was configured to log messages of the local7 facility to the file `/var/log/sshd.log`, this logger command would append the following line to that text file:

```
Nov 8 19:13:09 localhost test_logger_message: test message
```

It is useful to include the logger command in shell scripts that you create for system administration. By utilizing the logger command, you get access to standard logging without having to write that code from scratch. This makes it much easier to keep track of what your scripts are doing and to ensure that you do not introduce errors involving logging in your scripts.

Shell scripting was discussed in Chapters 13 and 14.

Rotating Logs

As syslog evaluates events in real time and sends messages to the various log files as configured in `/etc/syslog.conf`, it appends messages to existing text files. As more and more messages are appended, the text files get quite large, and you soon realize that it's simply not practical to retain every message ever issued by the system.

As a system administrator, you need to review recent system messages in a timely fashion, but you also must not allow log files to fill up all of the free disk space. Establishing a log retention policy is a good solution. As with all aspects of logging, there are many options when it comes to managing log file retention. Each site has different needs, and you need to devise a policy that is sensible for you and your situation.

Following is an example of a basic policy; of course, you can use any policy or variation you want:

Maintain each log file for a week. That is, each log file contains entries for 7 consecutive days. Then, archive log entries dated earlier than 1 week ago into a separate file. There are seven archive files, used one per week in order, each containing 1 week of logs. These older files kept on the system along with the current log file provide 2 months of system log data. The older log files should be kept in the same directory as the current logs and should be compressed, in order to take up the least amount of disk space possible.

Most Unix systems come with a facility to manage log rotation already installed. It can be configured to implement any desired log retention policy. These programs usually run from the cron facility, or the periodic daemon, and will parse the log files for you, creating and archiving previous dates log files automatically. A successful implementation of the example policy just described would result in a directory listing that resembles the following:

```
system.log
system.log.0.gz
system.log.1.gz
system.log.2.gz
system.log.3.gz
system.log.4.gz
system.log.5.gz
system.log.6.gz
system.log.7.gz
```

The way logging policies are implemented differs between Unix releases, and so do the programs used to implement them. For example, FreeBSD provides newsyslog, while Red Hat offers the excellent and flexible logrotate. Either of these makes your job quite a lot easier.

Monitoring System Logs

The system logging configuration's flexibility is of tremendous benefit to the system administrator. Knowing exactly what kind of messages are retained and where those messages are kept on the system makes the task of investigating abnormal or erratic behavior that much easier.

However, the central task of systems administration is to keep things running, so while it's helpful and necessary to take a look back to figure out what went wrong in the event of a system failure, it is more important to have an accurate sense of what is going on with the system right now.

Given an infinite amount of free time and a considerable degree of patience, you could open up terminal windows for each log file on your system, issue the `tail -f` command in each of those windows, and read each log file in real time. Reading each message as it comes through syslog certainly will give you an up-to-date and accurate sense of exactly what's happening, so you can take any corrective measures necessary to ensure that system continues to behaves correctly.

In practice, though, this is far from practical. Even if you would not mind reading all of your log files in real time, you would not be able to accomplish the task because you'd have to take breaks for sleep and other necessary maintenance of your own system. However, it's vital that those files be monitored with the same vigilance as if you were reading them yourself.

This is where automation is critical. There are several excellent packages available that can automate watching the logs for you. Two such tools are logwatch and swatch, which are explored in the following sections. These two programs provide complimentary actions. Logwatch gives you convenient summaries of your log files, while swatch (Simple WATCHer) actively monitors your log files for predefined triggers and sends alerts based on those events.

Logwatch

Logwatch is available from `http://www2.logwatch.org:81/`. It's included with most Red Hat–based distributions, and may already exist on your system. If you need to download and install the software, both RPM (Red-hat Package Manager) and source-based downloads are available. (As of this writing, the most recent version of logwatch is 5.2.2.) This section takes you through the source-based installation.

The software runs as a script, so there's no need for compilation. Simply download the source and run the following commands:

```
$ tar -zxvf logwatch-5.2.2.tar.gz
$ cd logwatch-5.2.2
$ sudo mkdir /etc/log.d
$ sudo cp -R scripts conf lib /etc/log.d
```

For more information on installation, consult the `README` file included in the logwatch distribution.

The distribution also comes with documentation in man page format. To install the man page, issue the following command:

```
$ sudo cp logwatch.8 /usr/share/man/man8
```

You will also want to copy the logwatch Perl script to a central location; `/usr/sbin` is generally a good place for such scripts.

```
$ sudo cp scripts/logwatch.pl /usr/sbin
```

Logwatch handles most standard log files without any additional configuration, but it is extremely flexible and you can create custom log file definitions easily. All you need to do is generate a configuration file in the `/etc/log.d/conf/logfiles` directory, define a service filter in the `/etc/log.d/conf/services` directory, and then create that filter in `/etc/log.d/scripts/services`. The filter basically reads log entries and outputs report information. For more information on the process of configuring custom log filters, refer to the document included with the logwatch software, HOWTO-Make-Filter.

Logwatch's configuration file, `/etc/log.d/conf/logwatch.conf`, is quite well commented and easy to read. Consult that file to customize your installation of logwatch.

An entry in the crontab like the following will run logwatch nightly at 11:00 p.m.:

```
0 23 * * *      /usr/sbin/logwatch.pl
```

Following is an example of logwatch output from a live server (all IP addresses have been replaced with 192.168.x.x addresses for the sake of privacy). The report is tracking the logs from an ftp server and an Apache server, and is reporting on disk space remaining on a Mac OS X system. This is fairly representative of the kinds of reports that logwatch generates. This report is sent via e-mail to an address that is added to the logwatch configuration file.

```
################### LogWatch 5.2.2 (06/23/04) ######################
      Processing Initiated: Sat Nov 13 23:00:05 2004
      Date Range Processed: yesterday
```

```
     Detail Level of Output: 5
          Logfiles for Host: xxx.local
 ################################################################

 --------------------- ftpd-xferlog Begin ------------------------

TOTAL KB OUT: 121287KB (121MB)
TOTAL KB IN: 718967KB (718MB)

Incoming Anonymous FTP Transfers:
   192.168.1.1-> /Library/WebServer/Documents/file_depot/work/a_and/AE_1.mov b

 ---------------------- ftpd-xferlog End -------------------------

--------------------- httpd Begin ------------------------

1798.89 MB transfered in 550 responses  (1xx 0, 2xx 373, 3xx 141, 4xx 35, 5xx 1)
 74 Images (0.76 MB),
 140 Movies files (1785.90 MB),
 327 Content pages (0.17 MB),
 2 Redirects (0.00 MB),
 1 mod_proxy connection attempts (0.00 MB),
 6 Other (12.06 MB)
Connection attempts using mod_proxy:
   192.168.1.10 -> 192.168.1.12 : 1 Time(s)

A total of 3 unidentified 'other' records logged
  \x05\x01 with response code(s) 1 501 responses
  GET /work/client_logo_hi_res.psd HTTP/1.1 with response code(s) 4 200 responses
  GET /editors/ediitor HTTP/1.1 with response code(s) 1 401 responses
A total of 1 ROBOTS were logged
 ---------------------- httpd End -------------------------
------------------ Disk Space --------------------

Filesystem              1K-blocks     Used   Avail Capacity  Mounted on
/dev/disk0s9             30005340 21754248 7995092    73%    /
devfs                          92       92       0   100%    /dev
fdesc                           1        1       0   100%    /dev
<volfs>                       512      512       0   100%    /.vol
automount -nsl [291]            0        0       0   100%    /Network
automount -fstab [301]          0        0       0   100%    /automount/Servers
automount -static [301]         0        0       0   100%    /automount/static
------------------ Fortune --------------------
All science is either physics or stamp collecting.
        -- Ernest Rutherford
 ###################### LogWatch End #########################
```

As you can see, the output is verbose, well organized, and clear. This type of information is obviously quite useful for any system administrator.

Swatch

Reading log file summaries nightly can keep you well apprised of the events of the day. However, there are certain kinds of events that you should know about as they happen or as quickly afterward as possible. These events include a disk or volumes coming close to filling up, failed root login attempts, other login failures, and similar events of a critical nature.

Swatch is a utility that can perform many actions upon recognizing a trigger event. For example, a failed root user login attempt that's written to a log can be set as a trigger event, and the corresponding action would be to notify the system administrator.

You can download swatch from `http://swatch.sourceforge.net`. (The current version as of this writing is 3.1.1.) To install swatch, download the archive and execute the following commands.

```
$ tar -zxvf swatch-3.1.1.tar.gz
$ cd swatch-3.1.1
$ perl Makefile.PL
$ make
$ make test
$ make install
$ make realclean
```

If you run into errors during the install process that resemble the following, you need to install the required CPAN (Comprehensive Perl Archive Network) modules listed in the errors.

```
Warning: prerequisite Date::Calc 0 not found at (eval 1) line 219.
Warning: prerequisite Date::Parse 0 not found at (eval 1) line 219.
Warning: prerequisite File::Tail 0 not found at (eval 1) line 219.
Warning: prerequisite Time::HiRes 1.12 not found at (eval 1) line 219.
```

Do this with commands like these:

```
$ sudo perl -MCPAN -e "install Date:Calc"
$ sudo perl -MCPAN -e "install Date::Parse"
$ sudo perl -MCPAN -e "install File::Tail"
$ sudo perl -MCPAN -e "install Time::HiRes"
```

Swatch expects a configuration file called `.swatchrc` to be located in the home directory of the user who is executing the program. An alternate configuration file can be specified on the command line with the `-config-file` directive.

The configuration file consists of tab-separated fields (an example config file entry follows after the table). Two fields are mandatory and the others are optional. The mandatory two fields are pattern and actions; throttle is an optional field. The pattern is what will be matched, and the action is what is to happen when a match is found. The following table lists possible actions.

Action	Description
`Bell`	Sounds the system bell.
`Echo`	Sends the matching line to STDOUT. Formatting options such as red and blink are available.
`Mail`	Sends the matched line to the user running the command. Alternate user or subject can be specified.
`Pipe`	Takes a command as an argument, and pipes the matched line into that command.
`Exec`	Similar to pipe; takes a command as an argument. Using special variables ($* and $0), the matched line can be sent to the command. Portions of the matched line can be specified using $1, $2, and so on.
`Write`	Takes a username or a colon-separated list of usernames as an argument and uses the system write command to send the matched line to the specified user(s).
`Throttle`	Sets the number of hours, minutes, and seconds that must pass before an action is taken on the match. For example, throttle 2:00:00 would limit the actions for the specific pattern being watched to only occur once every 2 hours. This is useful in preventing a deluge of actions being taken in the event the same trigger occurs over and over.
`Ignore`	The matching line is ignored, and no action occurs.

Here is a simple example swatch configuration file:

```
ignore /worthless_message/
watchfor /[dD]enied|/
echo=red
mail address=admin@my.organization.com, subject="Important Event"
throttle 1:00:00
```

This configuration would discard any lines with the text "worthless_message" in them. However, upon finding the text "Denied" (or "denied") in a line, it would take several actions:

- Send the line in red text to the terminal of the user running the command
- Send an e-mail to the user `admin@my.organization.com` with the subject of "Important Event"
- Ensure that this e-mail goes out only once per hour (`throttle` command)

Swatch allows for very fine selection of text from your log files, and you should check the examples folder that comes with the software, as well as read the documentation for swatch, to get some ideas of how to configure the software to best serve your needs.

Summary

In this chapter, you learned what logs are and what they are needed for. You examined the system logging daemon (syslogd) and learned how syslog works as well as how you can use it to customize your logging.

You saw how to create a file for logging and how to set up syslogd to log to it using the `syslog.conf` configuration file, and you explored log rotation. Deciding which messages to log and how to store them is only part of the job; you took a look at a couple of utility programs for monitoring system logs: Logwatch and Swatch.

By now, you realize the power and flexibility that Unix systems provide for maintaining an accurate picture of how your system is faring as well as providing a platform for reacting to incoming information. Building a picture of what is happening on your Unix box or on an entire system is a task with which you probably feel comfortable now.

Exercises

1. You want kernel alerts printed to the screen. How do you go about it?
2. Modify the `syslog.conf` file so that mail debug messages are sent to another host (you can assume the host's name is Horatio and that it has a system logging daemon).
3. How do you make swatch e-mail the root user if there has been any failed login attempts using invalid passwords? The action should also sound the system bell and provide a meaningful subject line for the e-mail. (Assume that the string `INVALID` will be present in one of your logs as a result of the failed login.)

Unix Networking

Access to computer networks for computer applications to communicate important data has changed from an expensive luxury to an absolute requirement of continuous necessity virtually overnight. While there have been numerous implementations of computer networks, the heart of the network revolution, the Internet, has but one protocol, TCP/IP. The protocol is in use all over the world and is used by nearly every computer system from Mac OS X and Novell Linux Desktop to Sun Solaris and IBM's AIX, even Microsoft's non-Unix Windows systems. And it's based on the implementation of TCP/IP originally developed for the Unix-based BSD operating system.

With the use of the Internet and all other networks growing at an incredible rate, it's necessary to provide networking tools and services to take advantage of today's quick computing bandwidth and computational power. This chapter examines these important tools and explores how the underlying TCP/IP protocols work while bringing together lessons from previous chapters on system automation and shell scripting to show how to manage or administrate network resources on a Unix system.

Mac OS X systems utilize TCP/IP for networking, and while TCP/IP is traditionally configured using GUI-based preference panes, all of the command-line utilities mentioned in this chapter work the well with Mac OS X as they do with other Unix systems.

TCP/IP

TCP/IP actually refers to many different aspects of the protocol suite that provides methods for various communication methods over networks driven by or interconnected by two specific protocols at specific protocol layers: Transmission Control Protocol (TCP) and Internet Protocol (IP).

Introducing TCP

TCP is the reliable, connection-oriented transport layer protocol of the TCP/IP protocol suite. It provides a method for guaranteeing that data arrives at its destination, in order. The *in order* part of that statement is important because the protocol breaks the data into packets, properly referred to as *segments*. The guarantee comes from the fact that TCP contains a retransmission scheme in case the receiving host does not send an acknowledgment of a segment back to the sender.

The TCP header consists of the following things:

- **Destination and source port** — The beginning and end points to a connection for protocols layered on top of TCP.
- **Sequence number** — Where in the sequence of packets any given packet is.
- **Acknowledgement number** — When an acknowledgment packet is sent, the highest packet number of all the packets that have been collected is put as the acknowledgment number.
- **Window** — Restricts the number of packets sent depending on how much time a slow link in the networks takes to process packets.
- **Checksum** — Ensures data sent is correct.

Most application-layer protocols used on the Internet use TCP as their transport layer protocols, including HTTP, FTP, SMTP, TELNET, and POP. There'll be more about these protocols later in the chapter.

Introducing IP

IP is the method or protocol by which data is actually sent from one computer to another on the Internet. Each computer, or host, is assigned at least one address that uniquely identifies it from all others. When TCP divides the data into various packets for transmission, IP provides each packet with both the sender's Internet address and the receiver's address and then sends the packet to a network gateway that knows its position within the interconnection networks that form the Internet. The gateway computer reads the destination address and forwards the packets to an adjacent gateway that, in turn, reads the destination address and so forth across the Internet until one gateway recognizes the packet as belonging to a system within its immediate neighborhood or domain. That gateway then forwards the packet directly to the computer whose address is specified.

Because a message is divided into a number of packets, each packet can, if necessary, be sent by a different route across the Internet. Packets can arrive in a different order than how they were sent, and just as it was TCP that divided the packets up, TCP is the protocol that puts them back in the right order. Unlike TCP, IP is a connectionless protocol, which means that there is no continuing connection between the end points that are communicating. Each packet that travels through the Internet is treated as an independent unit of data without any relation to any other unit of data.

Other Protocols Used with TCP/IP

As previously mentioned, TCP/IP contains many different protocols that all work together to make TCP/IP networks function. Other protocols within the suite often referred to as TCP/IP include the following examples of protocols that work at various layers of the overall connection to ensure the correct transmission of data.

ICMP (Internet Control Message Protocol)

Internet Control Message Protocol (ICMP) is used to send traffic control information between IP-connected hosts and gateways. ICMP datagrams are created and transmitted in response to IP packets that require some form of status response to the original sender, usually indicating a connectivity failure between hosts.

Consequently, Unix tools such as `traceroute`, discussed later in this chapter, are used to determine status information about the network. Many tools common to Unix systems, such as `traceroute`, use ICMP, despite the fact that ICMP is not a connection-oriented protocol and many gateways set ICMP to a low priority such that ICMP data may be lost in event of congestion.

UDP (User Datagram Protocol)

UDP, the User Datagram Protocol, is a transport-layer protocol akin to TCP and ICMP. However, unlike TCP, it is unreliable in the sense that a packet is not guaranteed to arrive at its destination. This in turn allows greater flexibility to an application that wants to do its own flow control, and can be used in places where a connection-oriented approach is not appropriate, such as for multicast data. That is, UDP provides a method for other protocol layers that are broadcasting data to one or more computers at any given time—protocols such as NFS, DNS, and RTP—to allow the given protocol greater control over how the data flows or is broadcast simultaneously to various clients.

ARP (Address Resolution Protocol)

ARP is a network-layer protocol used to convert an IP address into a physical address of the network interface hardware, such as an Ethernet address for an Ethernet card. A host wishing to obtain a physical address sends a TCP/IP-based request using the ARP protocol. The host on the network that has the IP address in the request then replies with its physical hardware address.

RARP (Reverse Address Resolution Protocol)

If ARP maps an IP address to a network card, then it follows that RAPR is used to map a known hardware address of a network interface card to an IP address. This occurs at startup; the software built into the hardware uses RARP to request its IP address from a server or router. Most computers use Dynamic Host Configuration Protocol, discussed later in this chapter, instead of RARP.

IGMP (Internet Group Management Protocol)

Internet Group Management Protocol (IGMP) is standard for IP multicasting in the Internet used to establish host memberships in particular multicast groups on a single network. The mechanisms of the protocol allow a host to inform its local router that it wants to receive messages addressed to a specific multicast group. *Multicasting* is a method of sending data to a specific list of machines on a network, rather than to all machines, which would be *broadcasting*, or to a single, specific machine. IGMP is the protocol that allows multicasting to happen on a TCP/IP network.

HTTP (Hypertext Transfer Protocol)

Hypertext Transfer Protocol (HTTP) is the underlying protocol used by the World Wide Web. HTTP defines how messages are formatted and transmitted, and what actions Web servers and browsers should take in response to various commands.

HTTP is called a stateless protocol because each command is executed independently, without any knowledge of the commands that came before it. This is the main reason that it is difficult to implement Web sites that react intelligently to user input.

Unlike protocols such as UDP and TCP, HTTP, as well as other protocols such as File Transfer Protocol (FTP), Simple Mail Transfer Protocol (SMTP), and Simple Network Management Protocol (SNMP), is an application protocol that resides on top of the protocol stack that TCP and IP create for network connectivity.

FTP (File Transfer Protocol)

FTP is another application-layer protocol and is used to exchange files over the Internet. It works in the same way as HTTP for transferring Web pages from a server to a user's browser and SMTP for transferring electronic mail across the Internet in that FTP uses the Internet's TCP/IP protocols to enable data transfer.

SMTP (Simple Mail Transfer Protocol)

As mentioned, SMTP is the protocol for sending e-mail messages between servers. However, unlike HTTP or FTP, another protocol, such as Post Office Protocol (POP) or Internet Message Access Protocol (IMAP), is usually employed for retrieving the messages from the last point, the mail server queuing the messages, and the client requesting the collection of messages waiting in the mail queue. In addition, SMTP is generally used to send messages from a mail client to a mail server.

Network Address, Subnetworks, Netmasks, and Routing with TCP/IP

The IP addressing scheme as described within the protocol is integral to the process of routing IP packets through a network or interconnected network of computers. Each IP address has specific components and follows a basic format that can be subdivided and used to create addresses from subnetworks to specific machine.

Each host on a TCP/IP network is assigned a unique 32-bit logical address that is divided into two main parts: the network number and the host number. The network number identifies a network and must be assigned by a service provider. The host number identifies a host on a network and is assigned by the local network administrator. The 32-bit IP address is divided into four 8-bit groups, separated by dots, and represented in decimal format. Each bit in a group has a value ranging from 0 to 255.

However, which part of an IP address identifies the network and which part is associated with the host depends on which class network the IP address is a part of—that is, the class of the address determines which part of the address belongs to the network address and which part belongs to the host address. All hosts on a given network share the same network prefix but must have a unique host number. There are five different network classes, but the most common three are as follows:

- **Class A Network**—In a Class A Network the first group of four numbers ranges anywhere from 1 to 126 and identifies the network while the remaining three groups indicate the host within the network. Thus a Class A Network can have 16 million unique hosts on each of 126 networks. An example of a Class A IP address is 16.42.226.10, where 16 identifies the network and 42.226.10 identifies the host on that network.
- **Class B Network**—In a Class B Network the first group of four numbers represents an IP address range anywhere from 128 to 191. In this setup the first two groups of digits identify the network, and the remaining two indicate the host within the network. Thus a Class B Network can have 65,000 hosts on each of 16,000 networks. An example of a Class B IP address is 128.204.113.42, where 128.204 identifies the network and 113.42 identifies the host on that network.
- **Class C Network**—In a Class C Network the first group of four numbers ranges anywhere from 192 to 223, and the first three groups of digits identify the network and the remaining group indicates the host within the network. Thus, a Class C Network can have 254 hosts on each of 2 million networks. An example of a Class C IP address is 192.168.42.1, where 192.168.42 identifies the network and 1 identifies the host on that network.

In any case, no matter what class of network is in use on a given subnetwork, a number of IP numbers are reserved for special use. For example, one address for any give subnetwork will represent the router or gateway from which any computer within the network will use to reach computers on another network. Other reserved IP address might include a broadcast address — a packet addressed to the broadcast IP will be sent to every host computer on the subnetwork — or an address that represents the entire subnetwork. Moreover, the address 127.0.0.1 is assigned to the loopback interface on any given system. That is, besides any given unique address, 127.0.0.1 will represent to a Unix system a software connection to the machine itself. In addition, the address 0.0.0.0 represents the entire network for any given Unix system. In other words, on a Class C Network, only 253 (out of 256) IP numbers are actually available for use as host names on a given subnetwork.

What Is a Subnetwork?

IP networks can be divided into smaller networks called subnetworks, or subnets, that provide the network administrator with several benefits, including extra flexibility, more efficient use of network addresses, and the capability to contain broadcast traffic because a broadcast will not cross a router.

Whereas the network part of an IP address must be assigned by a service provider, the subnet and host address are under local administration. As such, the outside world sees an organization as a single network, from the network address, and has no detailed knowledge of the network's internal structure.

Thus a given network address can be broken up into one or many subnetworks. For example, 192.168.1.0, 192.168.42.0, and 192.168.72.0 are all subnets within network 192.168.0.0, with all the zeros in the host portion of an address specifying the entire network should the netmask be set to denote that the first three numbers of the IP address have to be the same for a machine to be on the same subnet.

If a network is implemented as a collection of subnets, there has to be some way to tell it apart from a nonsubnetted network. As previously noted, an IP address defines the network and the host. If a network is to have a subnet, there needs to be a representation of it in the IP address. This is identification is called the submask or netmask.

A subnetted IP address is represented by assigning a bit mask for each bit in the IP address. If the bit mask is on, that part of IP address is considered part of the network address; if off, it is considered part of the host address.

Should the mask be set to *on* for a section of the IP address, the value in the netmask is 255. If *off*, the value is 0. For example, if the netmask is set to 255.255.255.0 the first three sets of IP addresses have to be the same for an address to be on the same subnet.

Thus if our group of example IP addresses, 192.168.1.0, 192.168.42.0, and 192.168.72.0, had a netmask of 255.255.255.0, should any of these computer systems want to communicate with each other, they would have to first route the traffic via a network gateway to communicate between subnets.

The same would be true for two systems with IP addresses 192.168.0.42 and 16.42.226.10 if the netmask was set to 255.0.0.0, 255.255.0.0, or 255.255.255.0.

However, if the netmask were 255.255.0.0 for the IP addresses of 192.168.1.0, 192.168.42.0, and 192.168.72.0, there would be no need to pass any packets via a network gateway because all of three addresses would present machine on the same subnet.

Thus, if the IP address is similar, it must be on the same subnet. Otherwise, network packets need to go through the gateway.

IP Routing

IP routing protocols are dynamic, which calls for routes to be calculated automatically at regular intervals by software in routing devices. This contrasts with static routing, where routes are established by the network administrator and do not change until the administrator changes them.

Both methods can be configured on a Unix box. Static routes are set using the route command by the initialization scripts during system boot. The most common configuration uses a default gateway to which all traffic not destined for hosts on the local subnet is directed. It is the function of the default gateway to figure out how to route the packets to their destination.

Dynamic routing under Unix means that the routed daemon is running on the system. The routed daemon uses the Routing Information Protocol to do dynamic route discovery.

Routing Information Protocol

A number of networks use TCP/IP routing inside a network domain. Routing a network using TCP/IP is handled by what is known as the Routing Information Protocol, or RIP. RIP works by using the IP broadcast mechanism on the local subnet to get information on how best to route the traffic to its destination.

On a TCP/IP-based network each host is configured with a static default route or gateway system to mange the network. Each time a host sends a TCP/IP packet to a destination outside of the subnet the packet is sent to the gateway from which a dynamic route is discovered for the packet to take. That is, RIP generates queries using the IP broadcast addresses on the attached subnets.

A router or gateway host on the attached subnet answers these RIP broadcasts with its own routing table, which contains information on how to get to other subnets along the way.

Using this method, soon all routers on the network know the possible routing paths to any remote destination within the overall network. The path that RIP chooses for the packets is based on the least number of network hops, or connections from the origin to the destination.

An IP routing table consists of destination address or addresses for possible hops pairings to enable dynamic routing. This means that the entire route is not known at the onset of the journey for the data packet and is calculated by matching the destination address within the packet with an entry in the current network router's routing table.

Because the entire network is not known, each node does not care whether the packets get to their final destination, nor does IP provide for error reporting back to the source when routing anomalies occur. This task is left to another Internet protocol, the ICMP, which is discussed elsewhere in this chapter.

Domain and Host Names

Before a path to a network resource can be determined, the network location of a host needs to be found. On a small network this might simply mean a user entered in the IP address into an application, or the application may already know the IP address in question. This method is impractical on a network divided into multiple subnetworks or on the Internet as a whole.

To solve this issue Domain Name System (DNS) network service has been developed to translate alphanumeric domain names into IP addresses. A domain name is a mnemonic, a placeholder for an actual IP address and, because domain names are alphanumeric, can be made up of words or numbers that are easier to remember. The network, however, is still based on IP addresses, so every time a domain name is used, a DNS service located on the network must translate the name into the corresponding IP address for the routing process to begin. For example, the domain name `www.wrox.com` might translate to 208.215.179.178 whereas the domain name for `www.weinstein.org` translates into the IP address 69.36.240.162. Better yet, because a DNS entry can be updated and associations can be changed a host can change networks or subnets without requiring every user or application to know the new IP address.

The DNS system is, in fact, its own network. If one DNS server cannot translate a particular domain name to a specific IP address, the DNS server will ask another DNS server, and so on, until the correct IP address is returned.

DNS

Depending on system and configuration, when a domain or host name is entered the system will check local files to see if it already has a name to an IP-address mapping for that host name. If found, the local entry is treated as authoritative, and the routing process begins. This mapping is kept in the `/etc/hosts` file. In the absence of a nameserver, any network program on the system consults this file to determine the IP address that corresponds to a host name.

Otherwise, a request to a DNS service is generated, and in most cases a network request is sent out to a nameserver for a resolution. A *nameserver* is simply a server on the network that translates names from one form into another, from domain name to IP address or, in some cases, from IP address to domain name. Note that this means that for a system to properly function the IP address of the DNS service (the nameserver)—if it is not located on the system in question—must be known for the DNS process and all other network requests dependent on it to be successful. Thus, in most cases the system looking for resolution to a request will have a list of at least one, if not more name servers, listed by IP address.

A list of IP addresses where DNS services are located can be found in the `/etc/resolv.conf` file:

```
nameserver      192.168.0.2
nameserver      216.231.41.2
```

If the server being queried has authoritative data for that hostname, it returns the IP address. If the server being queried does not hold the definitive result, and it is configured to forward queries to other nameservers, it will consult the list of root nameservers.

Starting from the right, the query will be broken down by finding the definitive system that holds data for that domain. For example, to resolve `www.wrox.com`, the root nameserver that holds authoritative data for the top-level domain (TLD), `.com`, will answer the DNS request. If the request is for `www.weinstein.org`, another set of root nameservers, those that know of the domains within the `.org` TLD, will be queried. The next right host element of the domain or host name is then evaluated, the query for a nameserver that holds the authoritative data for `wrox` or `weinstein`, respectively, is then asked, and requests for a specific host or subdomain will then be forwarded to that DNS system. This whole process repeats until the system holding the definitive information for the destination in question is reached. Once this happens, the IP address of the system that will respond to the domain name in question is known, and the TCP/IP routing of packets between the two systems can begin.

Setting Up a Unix System for a TCP/IP Network

As you might expect, you can find a number of software tools for adding a Unix-based system to a TCP/IP network as well as software for managing a TCP/IP network, subnet, or host.

As mentioned in the discussion on the TCP protocol, a TCP packet includes information about a port. TCP can make network connections between a port on the source and a port on the destination hosts; the data packets are transmitted between actual systems through these ports. Moreover, with TCP a certain range of ports are assigned specific duties; for example, ports less than 1024 on all Unix systems tend to be accessible only by an application with root privileges because these ports are assigned to established protocols such as HTTP or FTP. Port 80, for example, is the port that any daemon assigned to providing Web services, responding to HTTP requests, will bind itself to so that it can listen for requests from remote clients on the network. Because the remote client knows that port 80 is the HTTP port, it will, unless directed otherwise, send all HTTP requests to port 80. TCP supports multiple ports, meaning that one host can answer requests for multiple protocols. Moreover, this means that multiple outgoing requests can also be made because both systems, the client and the server, will have to respond as well as answer to these requests multiple times to complete a network session.

Configuring for a TCP/IP Network Request

There are two ways to configure a Unix system for a TCP/IP network, either with a static IP address that never changes, or with a dynamic IP address that is pulled from a pool of IP addresses that, for the time being, the host can use to access the network. Either method has its own set of advantages and disadvantages.

On various Unix systems, you will find two very useful command-line tools for checking the configuration of a network interface card as well as setting static IP address for a network interface card—ifconfig and route.

Try It Out Use Ifconfig and Route

1. From the network administrator or service provider, get a static IP address to assign to a Unix system (for example the IP address of 192.168.0.42).
2. Use the following command:

```
% sudo ifconfig eth0 192.168.0.42 netmask 255.255.255.0
```

3. To test the settings have been assigned properly, type `ifconfig` again at the command line, this time omitting any arguments:

```
% ifconfig
```

The output should look something like this:

```
eth0      Link encap:Ethernet  HWaddr 00:E0:18:90:1B:56
inet addr:192.168.0.42  Bcast:192.168.0.255  Mask:255.255.255.0
UP BROADCAST RUNNING MULTICAST  MTU:1500  Metric:1
RX packets:1295 errors:0 dropped:0 overruns:0 frame:0
TX packets:1163 errors:0 dropped:0 overruns:0 carrier:0
collisions:0 txqueuelen:100
```

```
Interrupt:11 Base address:0xa800

lo        Link encap:Local Loopback
inet addr:127.0.0.1  Mask:255.0.0.0
UP LOOPBACK RUNNING  MTU:3924  Metric:1
RX packets:139 errors:0 dropped:0 overruns:0 frame:0
TX packets:139 errors:0 dropped:0 overruns:0 carrier:0
collisions:0 txqueuelen:0
```

4. To assign the default gateway for 208.164.186.12, use the following:

```
% sudo route add default gw 208.164.186.12
```

How It Works

The ifconfig utility is the tool used to set up and configure the network card. No matter how the network information is saved, at startup and at any time while the system is running, ifconfig is the tool for configuring the network card. The network information does need to be saved if the configuration is to be kept, because the settings will not survive a reboot.

Usually, the need for using ifconfig directly at the command line is for testing, to see the current settings or to change the TCP/IP networking settings manually. To make the changes permanent, the user has to set them in the files related to networking functionality; for example, on a FreeBSD machine the information for ifconfig is kept in the `rc.conf` file:

```
defaultrouter="192.168.0.1"
hostname="chaffee.weinstein.org"
ifconfig_xl0="inet 192.168.0.15  netmask 255.255.255.0"
```

For a Linux system the information for network configuration is stored in the location `/etc/sysconfig/`network.

In any case, in the previous example, the default route is set up to go to 192.168.0.1 using the route command tool.

A Dynamic Setup

One problem with assigning static IP addresses and routing information, such as in the previous examples, is the issue of changing networks and configurations when traveling with a portable system such as a laptop, or notebook, computer. It can also be tedious for a network administrator to keep track of which IP addresses have been assigned and which are free for a collection of desktop systems on any given network. One solution that has popped up over the years is for network administrators to assign a pool of IP addresses that can be temporarily assigned to mobile systems through a service known as Dynamic Host Configuration Protocol (DHCP). DHCP gives a user the ability to receive the needed IP address, network mask, routing information and DNS server addresses in a dynamic manner.

Try It Out Use DHCP

1. From the network administrator or service provider, find out if a DHCP service is up and running on the network

2. Configure the system to use the DHCP client to assign the dynamic information to the network interface. On FreeBSD, for example, enter the following line in the file /etc/rc.conf:

```
ifconfig_ed0="DHCP"
```

For a Linux system, edit the file /etc/sysconfig/network-scripts/ifcfg-eth0 such that it contains the following:

```
DEVICE=eth0
BOOTPROTO=dhcp
ONBOOT=yes
```

3. Reboot the system.

4. To test the settings have been assigned properly, type ifconfig again at the command line, this time omitting any arguments for the command, as follows:

```
% ifconfig
```

The output should look something like this, only instead of a static IP address assigned by what is contained on one of the system files, the IP address should have been assigned by the DHCP server:

```
eth0      Link encap:Ethernet  HWaddr 00:E0:18:90:1B:56
inet addr:192.168.0.72  Bcast:192.168.0.255  Mask:255.255.255.0
UP BROADCAST RUNNING MULTICAST  MTU:1500  Metric:1
RX packets:1295 errors:0 dropped:0 overruns:0 frame:0
TX packets:1163 errors:0 dropped:0 overruns:0 carrier:0
collisions:0 txqueuelen:100
Interrupt:11 Base address:0xa800

lo        Link encap:Local Loopback
inet addr:127.0.0.1  Mask:255.0.0.0
UP LOOPBACK RUNNING  MTU:3924  Metric:1
RX packets:139 errors:0 dropped:0 overruns:0 frame:0
TX packets:139 errors:0 dropped:0 overruns:0 carrier:0
collisions:0 txqueuelen:0
```

How It Works

When a Unix system is started, it wants to assign an IP address to the network card. If the IP address is static, this information is located on the system and assigned by ifconfig, as noted in the previous example. If the information is to be assigned dynamically, the system broadcasts a message requesting a DHCP server. This request includes the hardware address of the requesting client, and any DHCP server receiving the broadcast will send out its own broadcast message to the client offering an IP address for a set period of time, known as the lease period.

The client selects one of the offers received. Normally, it looks for the longest lease period. Once an address is selected, the client lets the DHCP server know it has selected an offered, leased IP address and identifies the selected server.

The selected DHCP server then gives an acknowledgment that includes the IP address, subnet mask, default gateway, DNS server, and the lease period. Then the client, using ifconfig, assigns the proper information to the network interface.

Sending a TCP/IP Network Request

There are a number of clients, depending on what service is to be requested, for a Unix system. In addition, there are a number of command-line tools on various Unix systems that can be used to verify that a network is properly configured and working.

To test a network connection or to verify whether a network connection to one or more hosts is faulty or slow, the `ping` command, from the submariners' term for a sonar pulse, sends an ICMP Echo Request message that requests the remote host to send an echo reply that includes the sent message data. If all is well, the remote host will send a reply, and the amount of time passing between request and reply can be calculated.

Try It Out Test with ping

At the command line enter the following:

```
% ping www.wrox.com
```

The output should look something like this:

```
% ping www.wrox.com
PING www.wrox.com (204.178.64.166) from 192.168.0.15 : 56 data bytes
64 bytes from 208.164.186.2: icmp_seq=0 ttl=128 time=1.0 ms
64 bytes from 208.164.186.2: icmp_seq=1 ttl=128 time=1.0 ms
64 bytes from 208.164.186.2: icmp_seq=2 ttl=128 time=1.0 ms
64 bytes from 208.164.186.2: icmp_seq=3 ttl=128 time=1.0 ms

--- 208.164.186.1 ping statistics ---
4 packets transmitted, 4 packets received, 0% packet loss
round-trip min/avg/max = 1.0/1.0/1.0 ms
```

How It Works

As noted, the `ping` command sends an ICMP Echo Request message to the remote machine to send an echo reply that includes the sent message data. When the reply message returns, the round-trip for the `ping` request can be calculated and information about the network status to a host can be determined.

When connection attempts to a remote machine fail with time-outs, `"host unreachable"`, and `"network unreachable"` errors, or if the packet loss is high, the connection is not getting through somewhere along the path. One issue may be that a network firewall, a network device designed to block or filter network traffic between machines on a private network and the outside network at large, might not allow ICMP traffic to pass.

Another issue may be a temperamental network connection. Try waiting a few moments to see whether the network connection will re-establish itself, and then make sure the DNS system is responding properly and the network interface of the computer is configured and running properly.

Try It Out nslookup, dig, and host

To check the responsiveness of a DNS server or to look up the IP address of a domain/host name manually, try the following with the `nslookup`, `dig`, or `host` commands:

```
% nslookup www.weinstein.org
```

The results, depending on which command is used, will look something similar to:

```
% nslookup www.weinstein.org

*** Can't find server name for address 192.168.0.4: Timed out
Server:  dns.chi1.speakeasy.net
Address:  64.81.159.2

Non-authoritative answer:
Name:    www.weinstein.org
Address:  69.36.240.162
```

Notice that in this example the first DNS server, at 192.168.0.4, did not respond and the system had to check a second DNS server that was listed in `resolv.conf` file to resolve the domain name provided to nslookup.

How It Works

Tools such as nslookup, dig, and host query the configured nameserver of a system to determine the IP address of a given domain name.

In the previous example, the Unix system sent a query to two nameservers that it had been configured to retrieve information from. The first nameserver, at IP address 192.168.0.4, did not answer the query, so the system checked with a secondary nameserver that it had been configured to know about, at 64.81.159.2. This server not only provided information about itself but also was able to provide information about the possible IP address of the requested domain name.

Try It Out Use Netstat

Another possible cause of a failed attempt to connect to a remote host might be the configuration of the network interface, which can be checked using ifconfig, as previously covered, or another tool, netstat.

To check the status of the interfaces quickly, use the `netstat -i` command, as follows:

```
% netstat -i
```

The output for netstat is as follows:

```
Kernel Interface table
Iface  MTU  Met RX-OK  X-ERR RX-DRP RX-OVR TX-OK  TX-ERR TX-DRP  TX-OVR Flg
eth0  1500   0  4236     0      0       0   3700     0      0     0       BRU
lo    3924   0 13300     0      0       0  13300     0      0     0       LRU
ppp0  1500   0    14     1      0       0     16     0      0     0       PRU
```

How It Works

The `netstat` command symbolically displays the contents of various network-related data structures. There are a number of output formats, depending on the options for the information presented; for the example, in the previous section, netstat is supplying information about the network interfaces that have been automatically configured.

```
eth0  1500   0  4236     0      0       0   3700     0      0     0       BRU
```

That is, each line on the table is a list of cumulative statistics regarding packets transferred, errors, and collisions for a specific network interface. The network addresses of the interface and the maximum transmission unit are also displayed.

Another option for netstat is to prove information about all current network connections:

```
% netstat
Active Internet connections (w/o servers)
Proto Recv-Q Send-Q Local Address          Foreign Address        State
tcp        0      0 www.weinstein.org:ssh  dsl.chi.speakeasy.net:60371 ESTABLISHED

tcp        0    256 www.weinstein.org:ssh  dslchi.speakeasy.net:1830 ESTABLISHED

Active UNIX domain sockets (w/o servers)
Proto RefCnt Flags       Type       State         I-Node Path
unix  10     [ ]         DGRAM                    754    /dev/log
unix  2      [ ]         DGRAM                    4939915
unix  2      [ ]         DGRAM                    372659
unix  2      [ ]         DGRAM                    271499
unix  2      [ ]         DGRAM                    1784
unix  2      [ ]         DGRAM                    1606
unix  2      [ ]         DGRAM                    1535
unix  2      [ ]         DGRAM                    884
unix  2      [ ]         DGRAM                    766
```

In this example default display information about active networks sockets shows the protocol, receive, and send queue sizes (in bytes); local and remote addresses; and the internal state of the protocol.

Note that on any given system at any given time there might be a few or many network connections; as such, the output from the `netstat` *command maybe longer or shorter then the example provided here.*

As will be discussed later in the scripting section of this chapter, the data from these tools can be collected and processed automatically. A set of scripts can collect the data from one or more tests and compare it to that of previous tests that have been run and processed. The information can then be compiled such that a picture of the health and status of the network and the network connection at any given time can be put together to aid troubleshooting issues.

Answering a TCP/IP Network Request

The `/etc/services` file provides the mapping from port numbers to service names. A typical services file for a Unix system will look similar to the following:

```
# /etc/services:
# $Id: services,v 1.22 2001/07/19 20:13:27 notting Exp $
#
# Network services, Internet style
#
# Note that it is presently the policy of IANA to assign a single well-known
# port number for both TCP and UDP; hence, most entries here have two entries
# even if the protocol doesn't support UDP operations.
# Updated from RFC 1700, ``Assigned Numbers'' (October 1994).  Not all ports
```

```
# are included, only the more common ones.
#
# The latest IANA port assignments can be gotten from
#       http://www.iana.org/assignments/port-numbers
# The Well Known Ports are those from 0 through 1023.
# The Registered Ports are those from 1024 through 49151
# The Dynamic and/or Private Ports are those from 49152 through 65535
#
# Each line describes one service, and is of the form:
#
# service-name  port/protocol  [aliases ...]   [# comment].

tcpmux          1/tcp                           # TCP port service multiplexer
tcpmux          1/udp                           # TCP port service multiplexer
echo            7/tcp
echo            7/udp
ftp             21/tcp
ftp             21/udp
ssh             22/tcp                          # SSH Remote Login Protocol
ssh             22/udp                          # SSH Remote Login Protocol
telnet          23/tcp
telnet          23/udp
smtp            25/tcp          mail
smtp            25/udp          mail
nameserver      42/tcp          name            # IEN 116
nameserver      42/udp          name            # IEN 116
http            80/tcp          www www-http    # WorldWideWeb HTTP
http            80/udp          www www-http    # HyperText Transfer Protocol
kerberos        88/tcp          kerberos5 krb5  # Kerberos v5
kerberos        88/udp          kerberos5 krb5  # Kerberos v5
pop3            110/tcp         pop-3           # POP version 3
pop3            110/udp         pop-3
nntp            119/tcp         readnews untp   # USENET News Transfer Protocol
nntp            119/udp         readnews untp   # USENET News Transfer Protocol
ntp             123/tcp
ntp             123/udp                         # Network Time Protocol
```

As you can see, port 80 in `/etc/services` points to the service name called `http`, which refers to the protocol that a daemon listing to port 80 will need to handle.

In many cases, on a Unix system, a daemon called inetd is designated to manage the various application that will handle inbound requests for a network service. The inetd configuration file, `/etc/inetd.conf`, lays out precisely what action needs to be taken for a given service in `/etc/services`.

inetd

One of the many processes started at boot time by init is inetd, a long-running daemon that keeps a close watch for incoming network connections. When it senses incoming network traffic, it checks the incoming port, consults `/etc/services` to get the service name, and then reads its own configuration file, `/etc/inetd.conf`, to determine what process to start to handle the incoming connection:

```
# $FreeBSD: src/etc/inetd.conf,v 1.69 2004/06/06 11:46:27 schweikh Exp $
#
# Internet server configuration database
```

```
#
# Define *both* IPv4 and IPv6 entries for dual-stack support.
# To disable a service, comment it out by prefixing the line with '#'.
# To enable a service, remove the '#' at the beginning of the line.
#
ftp     stream  tcp     nowait  root    /usr/libexec/ftpd       ftpd -l
#ftp    stream  tcp6    nowait  root    /usr/libexec/ftpd       ftpd -l
#ssh    stream  tcp     nowait  root    /usr/sbin/sshd          sshd -i -4
#ssh    stream  tcp6    nowait  root    /usr/sbin/sshd          sshd -i -6
telnet stream  tcp     nowait  root    /usr/libexec/telnetd    telnetd
#telnet stream  tcp6    nowait  root    /usr/libexec/telnetd    telnetd
#shell  stream  tcp     nowait  root    /usr/libexec/rshd       rshd
#shell  stream  tcp6    nowait  root    /usr/libexec/rshd       rshd
#login  stream  tcp     nowait  root    /usr/libexec/rlogind    rlogind
#login  stream  tcp6    nowait  root    /usr/libexec/rlogind    rlogind
finger stream  tcp     nowait/3/10 nobody /usr/libexec/fingerd fingerd -s
#finger stream  tcp6    nowait/3/10 nobody /usr/libexec/fingerd fingerd -s
#exec   stream  tcp     nowait  root    /usr/libexec/rexecd     rexecd
```

In this new example, one can see that three entries are active and the rest have been disabled with a preceding comment (#). The three active ports are an application at `/usr/libexec/ftpd`, which will be invoked by root to answer any TCP requests on the `ftp` port, defined in the `/etc/services` file in the previous example as port 21. The same can also be said about the entry for `telnet` and `finger`.

The advantage to inetd managing these ports and applications is that only one dedicated program needs to manage a single network connection at a time. The advantage is clear: The daemons themselves are simpler to code, and the general Unix toolbox philosophy of tying small programs together using input-output pipes is usefully applied.

Notice, however, that unlike the previous example, this example has no entry for an application to handle HTTP requests on port 80. That is because, unlike FTP or TELNET, the Apache Web Server — the most common application on Unix for handling HTTP requests — runs in a standalone mode outside of inetd, in which it handles the traffic for the HTTP port on its own.

HTTP traffic is handled outside of inetd because there is a trade-off with using a generic Internet daemon such as inetd. Starting up an executable on Unix is typically an resource-expensive operation, using CPU, memory, and disk access that could be used by other applications at the same time; often, it is more expensive than actually running the program once it has been invoked. Therefore, it is important to consider the type of traffic the network service will incur. If connections are relatively infrequent but take much effort to process, then an inetd-based implementation is appropriate because it relegates the network code to inetd and allows the application to worry about the proper procedure and resources for handling the request. If, however, the frequency is high, such as the frequency of requests for a popular Web site, a standalone implementation is better.

Network Management Tools

As wonderful as the thought may be, computers are not completely independent systems that have enough knowledge to look after themselves and fix any problems that may creep into the system from time to time. Computer systems are, however, complex systems with interlocking components that interact in expected and unexpected ways. Not matter what kind of computer system is in use, be it a personal desktop system or a cluster of servers handling complex calculations, the job of making sure that computer systems are up and running will fall into the hands of a system administrator.

Additionally, many programs and services these days require network access of some sort. In many cases a network administrator holds court on making sure the network is operational and the computer systems in need have the proper access. In some cases the duties of these positions fall solely on one person, who may or may not be formally trained in dealing with the issues at hand.

No matter what the background or skills of the administrator in question, the fundamental goal is to keep the system running as smoothly as possible with the minimum amount of inconvenience to the users who are dependent on the system. Luckily, there are several Unix tools that make network management easier for everyone.

Tracking the Performance of a Network with Traceroute

There are a number of tools that system and network administrators depend on; this section will take a look at one called traceroute and show how, in combination with other tools such as AWK, shell scripting, and cron, a administrator can keep routine performance of the network connection on a Unix-based system.

Try It Out Use Traceroute

At the command line, enter the following:

```
% traceroute www.yahoo.com
```

The results will look something like this:

```
traceroute to www.yahoo.akadns.net (66.94.230.38), 30 hops max, 40 byte packets
1  192.168.0.1 (192.168.0.1)  0.8 ms  0.517 ms  0.383 ms
2  er1.localisp.net (66.42.138.1)  13.613 ms  12.664 ms  12.954 ms
3  220.ge-0-1-0.cr2.localisp.net (69.17.83.153)  12.741 ms  10.753 ms  12.042 ms
4  exchange-cust1.chi.equinix.net (206.223.119.16)  35.405 ms  28.537 ms  27.729 ms
5  ae0-p803.pat1.pao.yahoo.com (216.115.98.13)  69.158 ms  68.504 ms  68.886 ms
6  ge-0-0-2.msr1.scd.yahoo.com (66.218.64.134)  68.871 ms ge-1-0-
2.msr1.scd.yahoo.com (66.218.82.193)  76.226 ms ge-0-0-2.msr1.scd.yahoo.com
(66.218.64.134)  69.488 ms
7  v142.bas1-m.scd.yahoo.com (66.218.82.226)  70.22 ms unknown-
66-218-82-230.yahoo.com (66.218.82.230)  69.481 ms v142.bas1-m.scd.yahoo.com
(66.218.82.226)  70.71 ms
8  p7.www.scd.yahoo.com (66.94.230.38)  69.576 ms  70.754 ms  70.517 ms
%
```

How It Works

The Internet and other computer networks work by routing packets of information between computers from the origin to the destination. Think of looking up package information from the tracking system of a large shipping company. Depending on the type of shipping method (overnight, two-day, etc.) the package will move from one shipping point, or hub, to the next in time to arrive at the destination point on schedule. In theory, one can track the time it took the package to move from one hub to the next, as well as the over all shipping time.

This is how traceroute works, tracking the time and route it takes information to pass between the large and complex aggregation of network gateways or hubs. The only necessary parameter is the destination host name or IP number.

Of course, use of traceroute and other networking tools such as ping and nmap is not to be taken lightly. Administrators and users should limit their use of these tools to networks they look after. Using these tools on networks maintained by others, especially heavy use, is considered antagonistic because these tools can be used in a malicious manner as well as a helpful one.

In any case traceroute attempts to trace the route a networking packet would follow to some host computer and then listen for a reply from the various hubs on the route.

The results from traceroute provide data as to what route was taken and how long, in milliseconds, it took to reach each point on three different tries. The first line of output is information about the trace: the target system, the system's IP address, the maximum number of hops (connections) that will be allowed, and the size of the packets being sent.

```
traceroute to www.yahoo.akadns.net (66.94.230.38), 30 hops max, 40 byte packets
```

The following lines denote each hub, system, or router, in the path between the two points. Each line shows the name of the system, as determined from DNS records, the system's IP address, and three round-trip times in milliseconds.

```
exchange-cust1.chi.equinix.net (206.223.119.16)  35.405 ms  28.537 ms  27.729 ms
```

The round-trip times provide information about how long it took a packet to get from the beginning point to that specific location and back again. This time is known as the latency between the two systems. By default, three packets are sent to each system along the route, so we get three times.

Sometimes, a line in the output may have one or more times missing, with an asterisk where it should be:

```
exchange-cust1.chi.equinix.net (206.223.119.16)  35.405 ms  *  27.729 ms
```

In this case, the machine is up and responding but was unresponsive for one of the test packets. This does not necessarily indicate a problem; in fact, it is usually normal, and just means that the system discarded the packet for some reason.

However, a trace may end in all timeouts, like this:

```
4  exchange-cust1.chi.equinix.net (206.223.119.16)  35.405 ms  28.537 ms  27.729 ms
5  ae0-p803.pat1.pao.yahoo.com (216.115.98.13)  69.158 ms  68.504 ms  68.886 ms
6  * * *
7  * * *
8 * * *
```

In this case, a little more concern is justified because it means that the target system could not be reached. More accurately, it means that the packets could not make it there and back; they may actually be reaching the target system but encountering problems on the return trip. The concern here is that this is possibly due to some kind of problem. However, it may also be perfectly normal, depending on the target system; many administrators intentionally block tools such as traceroute from further access as a security measure.

Firewalls

As briefly mentioned earlier in the chapter, a *firewall* is a network device designed to block or filter network traffic between machines on a private network and the outside network at large, and it might not allow ICMP traffic to pass. Simply put, a firewall intercepts any network traffic going to and from the machines behind the firewall and, depending on a set of predefined rules, decides whether or not to permit that traffic.

Rules for a network, which are determined and configured by a network administrator, can be very broad, very specific, or somewhere in between. For example, a network administrator can decide to block all FTP requests from outside machines to any possible FTP servers on the internal, private network. FTP can be a security risk because it transmits username and password in clear text for any network device to read. Or the network administrator might be concerned that a known weakness in FTP server software could be used to compromise an internal system. In any case, the administrator has decided to keep outside system from locating the internal FTP server and can create a rule to block all incoming traffic for FTP.

However the administrator might want to allow a limited number of machines from a remote network to have access to FTP servers in the private network. If the administrator knows the IP subnet for the remote office, he or she can set the firewall to allow connections only from that subnet. The administrator can also limit things even further, allowing access from only a specific list of machines based on their IP address.

But that's not all a firewall can do. Systems behind the firewall can, at any given time initiate outbound network traffic. That traffic again must pass through the firewall before it can be seen by the outside world. Thus the firewall can be also be configured to allow or deny traffic to a set of destination IP addresses as well.

In this way a network administrator can control what information is provided about a private network, control what critical business or personal information is shared, and limit the potential risk an internal system or user might encounter by accessing a remote host that as been determined to be off-limits by business, security, or personal policy.

Routinely Checking Network Latency

The time it takes for data to complete a round-trip on the network is an important number to many network administrators. The latency on a network can affect the speed of important network services such as DNS or higher level applications such as a corporate Web site. Knowing the normal performance of the network allows the administrator a working base for troubleshooting any issues that may occur. Moreover, the collected data can provide information on network traffic patterns and can help in providing benchmarks for improving performance.

Try It Out Process Traceroute Data with AWK

1. In vi, create a file called `mean.awk` with the following contents and save the file:

```
/^ *[0-9]/      {
trottime = 0; attempts = 0;
for (field = 5; field <= NF; ++field) {
if ($field == "ms") {
trottime = $(field - 1) + trottime
attempts = attempts + 1
}
}
if (attempts > 0) {
average = trottime/attempts
```

```
printf "Point: " $2 ", Average Latency: " average "\n"
}
}
```

2. Next, create a shell script called `mean.sh` and enter the following:

```
#! /bin/bash
# run traceroute and parse the data with mean.awk
traceroute www.yahoo.com > trace_results.data
awk -f mean.awk trace_results.data
```

3. Finally, with the command `crontab -e`, put the following entry in a local `crontab` file to enter the automation for the shell script:

```
# run our shell script for testing the network
* */12 * * userid cd ~/bin; ./mean.sh | mail -s "Network Data" userid
```

How It Works

First, the AWK script will evaluate each line of the `trace_results.data` file that contains any numeral. This is defined in the regular expression in the first line of the file.

```
/^ *[0-9]/
```

Next, two variables, `trottime` and `attempts`, are set to zero, after which a control loop using the `for` statement is defined.

```
for (field = 5; field <= NF; ++field) {
```

The loop conditions first define a variable named `field` and a value of 5. Why 5? Take a look at the output of traceroute:

```
ae0-p803.pat1.pao.yahoo.com (216.115.98.13)  69.158 ms  68.504 ms  68.886 ms
```

The fifth field is where the data that the script is interested in, the time results, begins. (Well, not really, the fifth field is actually one field past the first time result, but not to worry!) Remember, the default delimiter is a blank space.

The next condition is the test condition. Is the value of field on the current iteration of the loop less than or equal to the total number of fields for the current line that is being evaluated? The final condition is that, at the end of each loop iteration, the value of field is incremented by one.

Within the loop, the first line is another conditional statement: If the value of the variable field is equal to "ms", continue on to the next set of commands (remember, in the first iteration of the loop this will be true because the fifth field of the line will contain the value "ms" that tails the first-time value. Note that to test a variable to see if it equates to the test condition, two equal signs are run together (==). If only one equal sign is used, value is assigned to the variable and this `if` statement will always test true.

If the test condition is true, we step back one field, `$(field -1)`, and add that value to the current value of `trottime` and increment the value of the `attempts` variable. When all the data within the line is collected, and the limiting conditions for the loop have been reached, the script moves on the next part—calculating an average and printing the data.

Again an `if` condition is put into place; why print data if there are no results to print? If there is data, then the average is calculated and the summary of data for that line is printed.

```
if (attempts > 0) {
average = trottime/attempts
printf "Point: " $2 ", Average Latency: " average "\n"
}
```

The rest of the items, the way the shell script works, and the `crontab` entries are covered in previous chapters.

There is one problem with automating this or other similar tasks. Running a tool such as traceroute sends out packets that will affect the time of other packets of data on the network. Because of this impact on the network, it is unwise to use traceroute during normal operations or from automated script if it is truly unnecessary. Even if it is necessary, it should be used sparingly; the preceding example invokes the shell script only twice a day.

Summary

The key to all of these operations is that the data has some kind of structure. Consider a filing cabinet that consists of multiple drawers, with each drawer holding a certain set of contents: project-related documents in one drawer, employment records in another. Sometimes drawers have compartments that allow different kinds of things to be stored together. These are all structures that determine where things go, that are used when it comes to sorting the papers that will be placed within, and that determine where things can be found.

- TCP is the transport-layer part of the TCP/IP protocol.
- IP is the network protocol actually charged with transmitting data between hosts.
- TCP/IP networks have a topology that allows them to be subdivided into subnetworks and provides proper methods for routing information within and between networks and subnetworks.
- Domain names provide an alphanumeric mnemonic for locating networks and hosts.
- DNS is a network service that provides for translating domain names into IP addresses.
- Ifconfig is the tool for configuring network cards and can be fed static or dynamic information.
- Tools such as netstat, ping, and nslookup can provide information about the performance of the network.
- Data from system tools such as traceroute, which provide information about the performance of a network between two points, can be processed by AWK to provide information and help administrate a system or network.
- AWK can be combined with other tools, such as a shell script, to complete and manage a complex task.

Exercise

Create a shell script that is executed every 2 hours and use the `ps` command generates a report detailing what processes are active and how many CPU resources they are using.

Perl Programming for Unix Automation

Perl is a high-level, object-oriented programming language that supports many programming concepts found in languages such as C and C++. Moreover, for many Unix system administrators, Perl is the tool they depend the most on when it comes to getting the job done.

This chapter introduces the Perl language, the benefits of the language, how it fits into the Unix system administrator's tool chest and, most importantly, how to put Perl to use by writing and troubleshooting Perl scripts.

The original development goals for Perl, an acronym for Practical Extraction and Report Language, focused on developing an interpretive scripting language for file and text manipulation facilities. From this it has found a wide base of users who find it particularly well-suited for tasks involving quick prototyping and system management. Perl is also used in many cases as a bridge between systems by providing programming tools for bringing together a wide variety of applications, making Perl especially popular with programmers, system administrators, mathematicians, journalists, and even business managers.

Perl's open distribution policy and large support base of fellow users has also helped the popular rise of the language and its interpreters designed to process Perl syntax on various platforms. But it is various Unix systems, such as FreeBSD, Linux, and Solaris, that have really taken in the standard Perl library modules and documentation.

The following exercise lets you try out a little Perl to get started.

Try It Out "Hello World" in Perl

1. Use a text editor to create a file called `hello.pl` with the following contents:

```
#!/usr/bin/perl -w
# Classic "Hello World" as done with Perl

print "Hello World!\n";
```

2. After saving the file and quitting the editor, change the permissions on the file and run the following script:

```
% chmod 755 hello.pl
% ./hello.pl
Hello World!
```

How It Works

Like a shell script, the first line in this example tells the Unix system how to run this script, using the Perl interpreter. In most Unix systems, such as the Mac OS X system the scripts in this chapter were written and tested on, the Perl interpreter can be found at `/usr/bin/perl`; however, this is not always the case. If, when executing this example script, an error such as "command not found" or "bad interpreter: No such file or directory" was displayed instead of the expected "Hello World!" chances are the Perl interpreter is located elsewhere on the system.

To quickly locate or verify where the Perl interpreter is, use the `which` command as follows:

```
which perl
/usr/bin/perl
 /usr/bin/perl:
```

In any case, besides providing a location for where the Perl interpreter can be found, this line allows options for how to invoke Perl:

```
#!/usr/bin/perl -w
```

In the case of the "Hello World" example, the `-w` switch communicates to the Perl interpreter that it would provide an additional level of reporting of warnings along with critical warnings or fatal syntax errors that are encountered while processing the script into machine code.

Another method for making sure Perl provides a robust collection of warning messages, and one recommended for the latest version of the language, is to use the following method, instead of the `-w` switch:

```
#!/usr/bin/perl
use warnings;
```

As with other scripting examples that have been discussed, Perl provides a method for entering comments that document what and how the script works. Any line prefaced with a pound (`#`) symbol denotes the line as a comment line within the file. Each comment line must be preceded by a `#`, and must be on a line by itself, as in the second line of code:

```
# Classic "Hello World" as done with Perl
```

As discussed in Chapters 11 and 13, comments are a useful feature for any configuration or script file and need to be used to the fullest extent possible. Comments must at least communicate information about who created or modified an entry in the file, when the entry was added or modified, what commands are used, what files the commands require for proper execution, who to contact if something goes wrong, and why and how the entry was added or modified.

Also remember that documentation is only effective if it remains current. The final line in the example is the main body of the script, the print function that outputs the text within the double quotation marks.

```
print "Hello World!\n";
```

As with other scripting environments, this script uses the `\n` escape sequence to communicate that at the end of this text string a new line is to be provided at standard out.

Perl's Advantages

As noted, Perl is an interpreted language optimized for string manipulation, system integration, and prototyping complex applications. Perl is helpful with system administration and system integration because it has built-in functions that are the same as or equivalent to many Unix commands. Moreover, Perl has a syntax that is easy to pick up on the fly, because it incorporates syntax elements from the Bourne shell, csh, AWK, sed, grep, and C.

Perl is regarded by many as something of a grab bag of features and syntax. As with other Unix tools, Perl has a powerful regular expression engine built directly into its syntax. For those who find regular expressions difficult to understand and use, this can be a detriment.

Another example pro (or con) can be found in Perl's versatility in permitting the use of different programming styles (procedural, functional, and object-oriented) all within in the same script. Again, the difference as to whether you feel Perl is helpful or not lies in whether the organic evolution of the language, and its "There's more than one way to do it" approach is considered a virtue or a vice.

A final pro (or, again, con) can be seen in the fact that Perl is an interpretive language. For Perl this means that the interpreter translates the high-level syntax of the language into an intermediate form, line-by-line, on-the-fly, right before execution. In contrast, a compiler translates high-level instructions directly into machine language before the application is ever executed.

The advantage of an interpreter, however, is that it does not need to go through the compilation stage during which machine instructions are generated. Thus Perl is a strong candidate for prototyping proposed applications before undertaking the task in a common compiled language such as C or C++. This means the processes and logic of the application can be understood and fine-tuned before formal coding.

However, the Perl interpreter process is a resource-consuming process because the interpreter is processing high-level code on-the-fly. That is, unlike a C or C++ compiler, the Perl interpreter has no time to optimize the low-level code before execution, resulting in a performance hit for intense scripts.

In any case, compared to other interpretive programming environments discussed in this book, such as a shell script, Perl has a definite advantage.

Useful Perl Commands

It can take years to master all of the features of Perl, if in fact they can all be mastered. Thus a single chapter is not going to turn you into a Perl guru. A few fundamentals, however, can go a long way, so the following sections detail some of the basics of Perl.

Variables

You'll recall from Chapter 9 that the AWK programming language is a typeless language. That is, with AWK you do not declare what type of content the variable will contain. Perl is the same; you do not declare a variable's type before putting the variable to use. Variables can be created arbitrarily and are defined at creation. All scalar variables—that is, all variables that contain one element—are preceded by the dollar sign (`$`). The following are valid variables and declarations:

```
$name = "Paul";
$age = 29;
$Where_to_find_him = 'http://www.weinstein.org';
```

Perl also allows for variables with multiple elements, which are defined by the use of the at sign (`@`).

```
@authors = ("Paul","Joe","Jeremy","Paul");
@list = (1,2,3,4);
```

Array elements can also be dereferenced using `$` and the element number. That is, you can access the name "Paul" in `@authors` array in the following manner:

```
$authors[4];
```

Perl also allows associative arrays or hashes. A hash is similar to an array, except instead of a numeric index, a hash uses alphanumeric indexes. The index is usually referred to as a key, and hashes are specified with a percent sign (`%`), as in the following:

```
%person = (
name => 'Paul',
age => '29',
url => 'http://www.weinstein.org',
);
```

Here the hash called person has three alphanumeric indexes or keys: name, age, and url. The values for these three indexes are `'Paul'`, `'29'`, and `'http://www.weinstein.org'`, respectively.

Operators

Perl allows for the same basic mathematical operators that all other languages have:

```
# Addition
$result = 5 + 5;
$a = 5;
$b = 6;
$result = $a + $b;

# Subtraction
$result = 5 - 5;
$a = 5;
$b = 6;
$result = $a - $b;

# Multiplication
$result = 5 * 5;
```

```
$a = 5;
$b = 6;
$result = $a * $b;

# Division
$result = 5 / 5;
$a = 5;
$b = 6;
$result = $a / $b;
```

In all of these examples, the results of the mathematical operations are assigned to the variable `result`, which can then be sent out using the `print` function or used later in the script as a test condition for controlling a branch of code. In the case of the first addition example, the value that would be found in `$result` is 10, the value of 5 plus 5. In the second addition example, the value of `$a` is added to the value of `$b`, with the sum being assigned to the variable result. Since `$a` is set to 5 and `$b` is 6, the value in `$result` will obviously be 11.

Basic Functions

Functions are a fundamental part of most programming languages, often used as an operator to produce a change in a variable or return a value that can be assigned to a variable. Perl provides a number of useful functions for the manipulation of text, and while the following list is by no means comprehensive, it does cover the functions that can usually be found in just about any Perl script.

print

The `print` function outputs a string to standard out or to some other stream such as a pipe or a file. It has the same control characters as you find in many other languages, such as the print functions covered in the discussion on AWK in Chapter 9.

```
print "Hello Again\n";
```

As the preceding example (taken from the simple Hello World script) shows, the format to print to standard out is straightforward. To print to a file that has a file handler called FILE, see the discussion on writing and appending to a file a bit later. The `print` statement looks similar to this example:

```
print FILE "Hello Again\n";
```

If you want to print out a variable in a string of text, you can join the variable's contents to a string statement with the dot (`.`) character, as shown in the following:

```
print "How are on this day, the " . $date . "?\n";
```

chomp, join, and split

The functions `chomp`, `join`, and `split` are three key functions for manipulating data in variables in Perl. For example, given a variable, be it a scalar or an array, `chomp` eliminates the newline character(s) at the end of the variable. `chomp` also returns the number of newline characters deleted.

```
# chomp in action for a scalar and an array
chomp $name;
chomp @authors;
```

The `join` function joins two separate strings in a single string, just as the dot operator does. Unlike the dot operator, however, an argument to the `join` function can include a value for a field separator to delimit the combined strings.

```
# joining a number of strings together with a colon delimiter
$fields = join ':', $data_field1, $data_field2, $data_field3;
```

Thus, in this example of the `join` function, the values in `$data_field1`, `$data_field2`, and `$data_field` will be combined; only the colon between each string will separate each string. If, for example, the variables contained Paul, Joe, and Craig, the `$fields` variable would contain the string Paul:Joe:Craig.

The opposite of the `join` function is the `split` function. `split` scans a string and splits it based upon a delimiter given as an argument, breaking the string into a group of strings, as the following code illustrates:

```
# splitting a string into substrings
($field1, $field2) = split /:/, 'Hello:World', 2;

# splitting a scalar and creating an array
(@fields) = split /:/, $raw_data;
```

In the first split example, the function will split the string `Hello:World` at the colon. That is, the text before the colon, `Hello`, will go into the first variable and `World`, the text after the colon, will go into the second. Notice the trailing number 2 in the function arguments. That is a limit, specifying that split is to divide the string into no more than 2 fields. A limit is not necessary, because it may not always be known ahead of time.

The real power of the split function is its capability for pattern matching with regular expressions:

```
# split raw_data at any point in which a number is located and put into fields
(@fields) = split /[^0-9]/, $raw_data;
```

Compare this new example of the `split` function to that of the previous two. In the first two examples, the `split` function is analyzing a string. In the first example the string is the bare "Hello:World"; the second is the value of the variable `$raw_data`. In both examples the `split` function is dividing the string whenever the colon is detected.

However, in this third example the `split` function is dividing up the value in `$raw_data` whenever a numeric, within the range of 0 to 9, is found and adding each group into the array fields. The power here of the regular expression is that even if the programmer has no idea what the format is of `$raw_data`, say the input from a file with no set field separator read into the variable, the programmer can strip out meaningful data.

open, close, opendir , readdir, and closedir

The functions `open`, `close`, `opendir`, `readdir`, and `closedir` are all used by Perl to access the underlying file system on Unix.

The `open` function, for example, opens a file given to it as an argument. The resulting file handler is then used to handle the contents of the file, be it for reading, appending, or writing.

```
# open the file and slurp its contents into an array and then close the file.
open(FILE, "/etc/passwd");
@filedata = <FILE>;
close(FILE);
```

In this example, the file handler for the file `/etc/passwd` is `FILE`. After the file has been opened, the file handler dumps the contents, or *slurps* the file, into an array. Then the file is closed using the `close` function. The following "Try It Out" section shows you how to use some of the functions described here.

Try It Out Opening Files and Directories in Perl

1. Use a text editor to create a file called `file.pl` in your home directory with the following contents:

```
#!/usr/bin/perl -w
# Create a file that will have a directory listing of user's home dir

print "About to read user's home directory\n";
# open the home directory and read it
opendir(HOMEDIR, ".");
@ls = readdir HOMEDIR;
closedir(HOMEDIR);

print "About to create file dirlist.txt with a directory listing of user's
home dir\n";
# open a file and write the directory listing to the file
open(FILE, ">dirlist.txt");
foreach $item (@ls) {
     print FILE $item ."\n";
}
close(FILE);
print "All done\n\n";
```

2. After saving the file and quitting the editor, change the permissions on the file and run the following script:

```
% chmod 755 file.pl
% ./file.pl
```

3. Once the script prints "All Done" locate the file `dirlist.txt` and display the contents of the file using `cat`. The output will look something akin to the following:

```
% cat dirlist.txt
.
..
.bash_history
.bash_profile
.bashrc
 Applications
 Desktop
 Documents
 Downloads
 file.pl
 Library
 Movies
 Music
 Pictures
 Public
```

How It Works

The opendir function opens the directory named in the function argument and creates a file handler for the opened directory, which is also given in the function's argument.

```
opendir(HOMEDIR, ".");
```

In the "Try It Out" example, the opendir function is opening the current directory, as denoted by the dot (.) with double quotes ("). The dot represents the current directory in UNIX file systems, with two dots (..) denoting the directory one level up. The opendir function can also take absolute directory paths as an argument, besides this example of a relative directory path. But be careful with relative paths, since these paths are relative to where the script file is located on the file system, not where the user or application invoking the script is working in.

```
@ls = readdir HOMEDIR;
closedir(HOMEDIR);
```

Once the directory is opened and a file handler has been assigned to it, the readdir function can be used. This function takes the argument of a handler that represents the directory to be read and sends entries of the directory, in the case of this example, to @ls.

As covered in discussing the open and close functions for files, the closedir function closes the directory noted in the file handler, in the example called HOMEDIR, which was originally created using the opendir function.

In other words, the opendir, readdir, and closedir functions are similar to the open and close functions for files:

```
# open a file and write the directory listing to the file
open(FILE, ">dirlist.txt");
foreach $item (@ls) {
     print FILE $item ."\n";
}
close(FILE);
```

The difference is that with files, there is no read, write, or append function. To write to a file, one right angle bracket, (>) is used to denote that a new file is to be created and written to. To append to an existing file, two right angle brackets (>>) are used. To simply read a file, no right angle brackets are used.

Because this example takes multiple entries that have been read from the directory and assigned to an array, a controlled loop, foreach, is used to process each element in the array, @ls assigns it to a variable, $item, and then prints to the file. The foreach loop and other controlled branches of code are covered in the section called "Loops and Conditionals."

Note that, as mentioned about the print function, the file handler needs to be provided such that it knows to print to the file stream and not to standard out.

my and local

The my and local operators declare a variable to be of limited scope, such as a variable for a specific purpose within a subroutine or loop. my declares a new variable to exist within a limited sphere such as a loop; local declares an existing global variable or variables to have values that are to be limited to an enclosed block of code, again such as a loop.

```
# Global variable $name is given a name
$name = Paul

# Enter our loop
foreach (@filedata) {
   # declare a new variable for just the loop
   my $current_file_file;
   # create a local version of name to temporarily assign values within the
   # loop to
   local $name
...
}
```

In the example code, there are two variables that have been defined three different times: `$name` and `$current_file_file`. The variable `$name` is first declared outside of any loop or subroutine and is assigned a value. This is known as a global declaration. In this case the value of the global variable can be used at any point within the blocks of code that follow, be it a loop, subroutine, or some other expression. The variable `$current_file_file`, however, is not a global variable. The `my` operator declares that this variable, `$current_file_file`, is limited in scope to the block of code that the variable was declared in, in this case the `foreach` loop, and once the block of code has been processed, the variable and its value will no longer exist. That is, once the loop is completed, the variable `$current_file_file` will no longer exist and the memory that was assigned to it will be freed and used for some other need.

The `local` operator is slightly different compared to `my`. As with `my`, `local` limits the scope of the variable to a specified block of code; in the case of the preceding example, the `foreach` loop. However, unlike `my`, the `local` operator changes the scope of an existing variable. That means in the working example going into the `foreach` loop the variable `$name` is global and has the value `Paul`. However, once the scope of the variable is changed using the `local` operator, the variable can be used within the loop to hold a different value. Once the block of code ends, the variable returns to its global nature and regains the value of `Paul`.

Using global- and limited-in-scope variables can help manage memory resources, and their use is highly recommended when coding scripts that may make heavy use of the system's hardware resources, such as processing large text files.

Loops and Conditionals

Speaking of loops, what good would Perl be without a strong set of commands for creating blocks of code that can be executed on one or more sets of conditions?

while

Before any Perl code within the loop, defined by the beginning and closing brackets, can be executed, the conditions for how the loop will run need to be defined. That is, before any loop can be defined and entered, any condition that returns a true or false response needs to be defined, otherwise the loop will run indefinitely and the program will never end.

```
while ( $counter < 10 ) {
   print $counter . "\n";
   $counter++;
}
```

For example, the previous code sets up a common method for controlling a loop by use of a counter. While the value of the variable `$counter` is less than 10, the loop will run. Note the last line within the block of code for the loop:

```
$counter++;
```

This line increments the value within `$counter` by one and is a common syntactical shortcut for programmers. That is, it has the same effect as writing the following:

```
$counter = $counter + 1;
```

do...while

The `do...while` loop is similar to the `while` loop, except the test condition is checked at the end of the loop, not before; thus, it runs through the block of code within the loop at least once.

```
do {
   print $counter . "\n";
   $counter++;
} while ( $counter < 10);
```

Thus, compare the `do...while` example to the previous example with the `while` loop. In the `while` loop the condition for the `$counter` variable is at the beginning of the loop, whereas here the condition is tested at the end. This means that, in the `while` loop example, if the `$counter` is greater than 10 before the loop is encountered, the loop will never be executed since it fails the test even before the loop starts. With the `do...while` loop, however, even if the `$counter` is greater than 10, the block of code within the loop will be executed at least once since the test condition does not come until after the block of code for the loop has been entered.

foreach

The best way to traverse an array is to use the `foreach` loop to run through its elements. For example, the following loop will print out the elements in the array called `authors` by passing each element into the scalar temp as each iteration is started, until each array element has been printed.

```
foreach $temp (@authors) {
print $temp . "\n";
}
```

if...else

The venerable `if...else` commands can be used to test conditions and optionally perform commands. The basic syntax can be seen in this example:

```
if ( $name eq 'Paul' ) {
print "Hi Paul\n";
} elsif ($name eq 'Joe') (
print "Hi Joe\n";
} elsif ($name eq 'Jeremy') {
print "Hi Jeremy\n";
} else {
   print "Sorry, have we meet before? ";
}
```

The example demonstrates a number of test conditions to be tested; if a condition is true, then the block of code following the test is executed. Thus if the value of the variable `$name` is equal to (`eq`) `Paul` the one-line `print` statement within the brackets is executed. If not, the next test condition—is the value of `$name` equal to `Joe`—is tested. If all the tests fail, the last line within the final `else` block is executed.

More Perl Code Examples

The best way to understand how Perl commands work is to take a working script apart. The following "Try It Out" example gives you an opportunity to do just that.

Try It Out Check Input from Standard In

1. With a text editor, enter the following script, save it as `check.pl`, and change the permissions to allow the script to be executed.

```
#!/usr/bin/perl -T
# check.pl
# A Perl script that checks the input to determine if
# it contains numeric information

# First set up your Perl environment and import some useful Perl packages
use warnings;
use diagnostics;
use strict;
my $result;

# Next check for any input and then call the proper subroutine
# based on the test
if (@ARGV) {
   # If the test condition for data from standard in is true run
   # the test subroutine on the input data
   $result = &test;
} else {
   # else the test condition is false and you should run an error routine.
   &error;
}

# Now print the results
print $ARGV[0]." has ".$result." elements\n\n";
exit (0);

sub test {
   # Get the first array element from the global array ARVG
   # assign it to a local scalar and then test the local variable
   # with a regular expression
   my $cmd_arg = $ARGV[0];
   if($cmd_arg =~ m/[0-9]/) {
      return ('numeric');
   } else {
      # There was a error in the input; generate an error message
      warn "Unknown input";
   }
}

sub error {
   # There was no input; generate an error message and quit
   die "Usage: check.pl, (<INPUT TO CHECK>)";
}
```

2. Run the script at the command line with various arguments or totally without arguments, such as what follows. Note the various lines of output from the script depending on what input argument is supplied:

```
% ./check.pl
Usage: check.pl, (<INPUT TO CHECK>) at ./check.pl line 41.
%

% ./check.pl 42
42 has numeric elements

%

% ./check.pl h2g242
h2g242 has numeric elements

%

% ./check.pl hg
Unknown input at ./check.pl line 35.
hg has 1 elements

%
```

How It Works

To invoke the Perl interpreter note, this example uses a `-T` switch, which runs Perl in a taint mode:

```
#!/usr/bin/perl -T
```

If any script written in Perl is to be used by a collection of users, or if the script originated from an outside source, taint mode makes sure Perl doesn't implicitly trust any input supplied by a user running the script. That is, when used in taint mode, the Perl interpreter assumes that all user input is tainted, or potentially malicious, and places restrictions on the actions that the script may perform on that input.

Perl uses a special set of rules that limit the actions that may be performed on tainted data. For example, tainted data may not be used in Perl functions that interact directly with the underlying system. When the interpreter encounters an action that uses tainted data in a manner it considers unsafe, it simply halts execution with an error. It's then up to the system administrator to troubleshoot the code (if the script came from an unknown source) and determine what changes are necessary to make the code safe, or double check what input the user provided to create such a issue.

Most important of all, you must not view taint mode as a catchall for security issues with Perl scripts. While taint mode will help prevent buffer-overflow vulnerabilities, it cannot detect all possible forms of malicious input, such as an SQL command to drop a database table if the script in question interacts with a backend database.

The next section of code sets up a few other environmental conditions for the Perl interpreter to provide while executing the example script:

```
# First set up your Perl environment and import some useful Perl packages
use warnings;
use diagnostics;
use strict;
my $result;
```

First, the use function imports some Perl code into the current script. The source of this code is the Perl module named for the use function—use warnings imports conditions defined in a standard Perl module called warnings, for example. Some of the warnings from the module can appear quite cryptic. This is where use diagnostics can help. When this module is activated, the warnings generated by use warnings and -w are expanded greatly. Of course, both of these functions are designed for use during the development cycle and probably should be turned off after the troubleshooting has been completed since they are big modules that you shouldn't load for just any reason.

The use strict module enforces that all variables must be declared by my to keep track of their scope and limit the memory usage to those sections of the code that only request a specific variable(s) to use. The strict module also requires that most strings be quoted and that there are no bare words (or unquoted string text) in the middle of the code. Finally, strict also enforces a policy of no symbolic references within the script. In other words, strict enforces good coding practices. Yes, there is such thing as good coding practice, as showcased a bit later, even in a programming language that considers any and all programming styles as valid.

Finally, because the use of the strict module requires it, the one global variable for the script, $result, is declared.

The only new elements in this if-else condition that haven't been covered before are the @ARGV array and the subroutine calls:

```
# Next check for any input and then call the proper subroutine
# based on the test
if (@ARGV) {
   # If the test condition for data from standard in is true run
   # the test subroutine on the input data
   $result = &test;
} else {
   # else the test condition is false and you should run an error routine.
   &error;
}
```

The @ARGV array contains the command-line arguments given at the invocation of the Perl script. The script expects only one argument, so the first element in the array is the one that is of interest for testing.

Depending on the test, one of two subroutines will be entered, &test or &error. The subroutine test is expecting to return a value and is assigning that value to the variable $result. Of course, in this example $result is a global variable, and the assignment could be done within the subroutine test, but this method provides an example for returning results from a subroutine in Perl:

```
# Now print the results
print $ARGV[0]." has ".$result." elements\n\n";
exit (0);
```

The final segment of the example script's main body prints out the results and then terminates the script using the exit function in Perl. The exit function can return a value that can be evaluated by the Unix command line. In this example, it returns 0, denoting true, or successful execution.

```
sub test {
   # Get the first array element from the global array ARVG
   # assign it to a local scalar and then test the local variable
   # with a regular expression
   my $cmd_arg = $ARGV[0];
```

```
        if($cmd_arg =~ m/[0-9]/) {
           return ('numeric');
        } else {
           # There was a error in the input; generate an error message
           warn "Unknown input";
        }
  }
```

When the `test` subroutine is entered, the first item of business is to delegate a local variable called `$cmd_arg` and assign the value of `$ARVG[0]`. The next is to test the variable for any numeric values within the string:

```
        if($cmd_arg =~ m/[0-9]/) {
```

The regular expression, number range between `[0-9]`, is to be matched (m//) and is then bound (=~) to the string in `$cmd_arg` for searching. If this match is true, the string `numeric` is returned to the point where the subroutine was called. If it is false, the `warn` function prints an error message (`Unknown input`) that includes the string provided to it in the standard error message along with the line number from which the warn message was triggered. For troubleshooting and debugging, which are discussed in the next section, this is valuable information.

The `warn` function does not terminate the execution of the script. Here's one of the example invocations of the script:

```
% ./check.pl hg
Unknown input at ./check.pl line 35.
hg has 1 elements

%
```

The warn message is printed, but the script still exits out of the subroutine and then executes the final `print` statement in the main body of the script. Note that the routine has terminated, returning a value of 1 to be passed to the value `$result`, which is then printed. An `if` condition could be placed around the `print` statement such that if `$result` is 1 (false in Perl, as with most Unix systems), the final `print` statement would not be executed:

```
print $ARGV[0]." has ".$result." elements\n\n" if $result;
```

That is the same as saying:

```
if ($result) {
   print $ARGV[0]." has ".$result." elements\n\n";
}
```

The last segment of code to examine is the error subroutine:

```
sub error {
   # There was no input; generate an error message and quit
   die "Usage: check.pl, (<INPUT TO CHECK>)";
}
```

The `die` function prints a message to standard out, just as `warn` does; however, `die` then terminates the execution of the script and goes no further. Hence the output for when the test fails to find any input looks like this:

```
% ./check.pl
Usage: check.pl, (<INPUT TO CHECK>) at ./check.pl line 41.
%
```

One final note about this script should be made: This chapter has noted that Perl is an anything-goes language. This example script can actually be executed in one line:

```
#!/usr/bin/perl -T

print $ARGV[0]." Has nummeric elements\n\n" if ($ARGV[0] =~ m/[0-9]/);
```

This one-line script will print the following output if a number is present, and nothing if no number is matched or no input is provided:

```
% ./check.pl h2g2
h2g2 has numeric elements

%
```

Moreover, even with the `strict` and `warnings` modules, this script is valid enough to pass without any issues, but as covered in the following section, such quick-release coding can be detrimental to many, including you, when it comes time to troubleshoot or modify the code in question.

Troubleshooting Perl Scripts

Before a Perl script can be debugged, let alone executed, you need to validate the script's syntax. This, of course, will happen automatically, every time you try to execute a script. For example, if the Unix system cannot locate the Perl interpreter in the first line of the script, the shell will return a `command not found` error. Other common syntax errors include leaving the semicolon off the end of a line and putting a semicolon on a line where it shouldn't be.

You can also check the syntax of any script, such as the `hello.pl` or `file.pl` without trying to execute the script, as follows:

```
% perl -c hello.pl
hello.pl syntax OK
%
```

The `-c` switch tells the Perl interpreter, which is being invoked at the command line instead of in the first line of the script, to check only the syntax of the file provided as an argument and skip executing the script.

At the command line you can also add the `-w` switch to turn on warnings.

Note, however, if you try this with the `check.pl` script, the following error will occur:

```
Too late for "-T" option at check.pl line 1.
```

This is because the `-T` switch, which tells the Perl interpreter to run in taint mode, needs to be provided when the Perl interpreter is first invoked and the script environment is established. Because Perl is invoked at the command line and not in the first line of the script in the preceding example, the interpreter prints the error that it is too late for the taint mode to be established because Perl is already running. To avoid this message, comment out the `-T` switch during testing and debugging, as noted in the following. Just don't forget to uncomment it when all the bugs have been found!

```
#!/usr/bin/perl #-T
```

If the `use strict` module is included within the script, the syntax check also tests for inappropriate scalar scoping, which goes a little beyond the normal syntactical problems that are identified.

Of course, a successful syntax check does not mean that the manner in which any given statement is expressed will return the result intended.

The Perl debugger, on the other hand, is the tool to use to track the execution of the script itself. The debugger is an interactive Perl environment initialized when Perl is called with the `-d` switch:

```
% perl -d check.pl
```

As with the previous example of the syntax check, a filename for the file containing the script to debug needs to be provided as an argument. Because it is interactive, the next step is to use the debugger's commands for controlling how to step though the script to catch any bugs in question. The following table explains these commands.

Command	Description
`s`	Executes only a single step, or line, in the script
`n`	Steps carefully to avoid falling into a subroutine
`c`	Continues processing until a break of some sort
`r`	Continues running until you do a return from the current sub
`w`	Shows a window of code around the current line
`b`	Sets a break point (uses line number or sub name)
`x`	Displays value of variables (including arrays and hashes)
`W`	Sets a watch expression
`T`	Displays a stack back trace
`L`	Lists all the breaks
`D`	Deletes all the breaks
`R`	Restarts the script to test again

The commands listed in the table are used in Perl's interactive debugging environment to control what Perl is executing, such that the behavior of the script can be examined to locate any errors in logic.

In any case, when you run the debugger on `check.pl`, the first section of output is as follows:

```
Default die handler restored.

Loading DB routines from perl5db.pl version 1.07
```

```
Editor support available.

Enter h or `h h' for help, or `man perldebug' for more help.

main::(check.pl:10):     my $result;
DB<1>
```

The debugger skips past the comments and such and stops on what looks like the first line of executable code, line 10. Use `w`—note this is lowercase w, uppercase W is a different command—to verify where the debugger is:

```
DB<1> w
7:       use warnings;
8:       use diagnostics;
9:       use strict;
10==>    my $result;
11
12       # Next check for any input and then call the proper subroutine
13       # based on the test
14:      if (@ARGV) {
15          # If the test condition for data from standard in is true run
16          # the test subroutine on the input data
```

The `w` command displays a window into the code that is about to be executed. That is, it shows the line about to be executed. The arrow symbol (==>) indicates the line that is about to be executed, as well as the code surrounding that current line of code, thus providing perspective. To single-step through each command line, enter:

```
  DB<1> s
main::(check.pl:14):     if (@ARGV) {
  DB<1> s
main::(check.pl:20):        &error;
  DB<1> s
main::error(check.pl:42):          die "Usage: check.pl, (<INPUT TO CHECK>)";
  DB<1>
```

The debugger executes the first `if` statement and executes the error subroutine. You can check the value of the array to ensure that the `if` statement was executed correctly:

```
DB<1> x @ARGV
empty array
DB<1>
```

Sure enough, the array is empty, and the error subroutine is the correct path for the script. To test the other branch of code within this script, you need to provide a text argument when the debugger is invoked. Remember what this script does: It checks the input of a string of text and prints out a message based on whether the input string contains a number or not. Because you invoked this script with no argument to the script (only an argument—the `-d` switch—to Perl itself), the script branched off to the error message. Thus if you wanted to test other branches of the script, you need to provide an input string to test these braches.

More information and one-on-one help with the Perl debugger can be found online at `http://debugger.perl.org`.

You should now understand the basic idea of the Perl debugger. Of course, the most important piece of information to remember when debugging or troubleshooting a script is to make sure you have a clear mental image of the program's actions at every major branch, with every module, throughout the debugging process. When debugging a script or program, you will find that most of the logic errors that occur do so because the program code is executing in a manner different from what you had envisioned.

Summary

Perl is a powerful Unix tool that has grown beyond its initial designs of a language for text manipulation. The key to Perl is to understand that it can be and is many things to many people. The usefulness of Perl has made a few people refer to it as a Swiss Army Knife or the glue and duct tape that holds the Internet together.

Because of its roots, Perl is an easy-to-learn language, and most tasks require only a small subset of the Perl language. Moreover, understanding how Unix-based systems operate makes Perl that much easier to learn since, while Perl can be found on many systems, Unix and non-Unix alike, Perl was originally developed and is most closely associated with Unix. Perl is very much a part of any Unix-based system with open code, file manipulation, and regular expressions. In addition to these topics, this chapter covered the following subjects:

- The nature of Perl as a powerful programming language that can step beyond the limitations of other Unix tools such as shell scripts and AWK
- The pros and cons to selecting Perl as the tool to use to solve a problem
- Basic Perl commands and functions, such as `split` and `join`, for text manipulation
- An understanding of how to write and execute a Perl script
- Basic steps to troubleshooting a Perl script

There are a number of resources for learning more about Perl; this chapter just scratches the surface. Good next steps include the Online Documentation of Perl at `www.perl.org/docs.html` and the classic tutorial on Perl published by O'Reilly and Associates, *Learning Perl*. You can also consult Wiley's *Perl for Dummies* or *Perl Database Programming*.

Exercises

1. Write and debug a Perl script that reads the contents of `/etc/passwd` and outputs the contents of the username and ID fields only.
2. Use the following examples to invoke the Perl debugger for the `check.pl` script example from this chapter. Step through each line of code. What is different about each invocation?

```
perl -d check.pl h2g2
perl -d check.pl h2
perl -d check.pl
perl -d check.pl 42
```

3. Correct the `check.pl` script such that if a string to be tested contains no numeric elements, the message printed by the script communicates this to the user. If "hg" is the given test string, instead of a message that reads, "Unknown input at ./check.pl line 35. hg has 1 elements," the output should read "hg has no numeric elements."

Backup Tools

Backups — the word is discussed many times in almost any technical book you have ever read, and with good reason. The concept is simple: Store a copy (backup) of irreplaceable or critical files and data in a safe place in case of a problem with the primary system. Backups are by far the best insurance policy against loss of crucial information in times of system disruptions, accidents, misconfigurations, or malicious activities. Despite that fact, most home users and some corporate users do not give backups the attention they deserve, often putting them second to everything else. If there's vital information stored in your system, however, there's no substitute for backing up that information. Backups are as necessary as any production issue. This chapter discusses basic backup concepts and methods, as well as the recovery of the backup data.

Backup Basics

Effective backups require considerable planning, including deciding the how, when, and where of your backups. The planning is all worth it the first time you have to call on your backup to restore lost data.

Everyone makes mistakes. If you have used computers in any capacity, you surely have accidentally deleted a file that was extremely important or lost a vital document when the power went off suddenly or the system rebooted with no warning. These things happen, and a backup is the insurance policy that can make one of these occurrences go from being a devastating event to a minor inconvenience. Most users, especially home users, store their data on their local hard drive, which allows for extremely easy retrieval and modification of data. What happens when the hard drive fails? All hard drives are rated to fail eventually — mean time before failure (MTBF) — and you risk losing your important information by not regularly backing up your data to separate media.

If you are a home user, consider what it would cost you in time and money if you lost all the data you accumulated over a 1-year period. What if you lost even 30 days of data at work? What if everyone in your company lost their data for a 3-day period? Any of these situations could represent a serious loss of money, time, and productivity if you had no regular backups and had to recreate all the lost data.

You back up your data to protect not only against hardware failure but also against other external and internal events such as natural disasters, malicious entities destroying data, and disgruntled employees removing information from your system — or any other incidents that could destroy that data.

Determining What to Back Up

Deciding what to back up is a time-consuming process, but well worth the effort, especially if you have to recover information. You do not want to be the person to tell your manager that a crucial business file can't be restored because it wasn't backed up. Even if you don't manage a corporate backup system, you don't want to go through the trouble of backing up your files only to discover that you overlooked a critical directory or file.

You generally want to back up the entire file system. If that isn't possible because of resource constraints (money and/or time), you have to select the individual file systems or files that you need to back up. At a minimum, you want to back up home directories, custom configuration files, special applications installed and their configuration files (including license files), and any other data that, if lost, would cause significant financial loss or cause personal or business interruptions.

User home directories are very important to back up because this is where common users do their work, which is usually the most important work occurring on the system. Users tend to accidentally delete or lose their data, sometimes representing weeks or months worth of work. By backing up users' home directories, you are ensuring that there is minimum loss of productivity when a file is lost.

When you modify configuration files, you will want to save the changes so that, in the event of a disaster, you can recover that work without having to go through the process of reinitiating the configurations. That will save a significant amount of time between when a system is down and when it's brought back up. This includes many of the files in `/etc`, but there are many others throughout the system that you probably want to back up; these will vary depending on your system configuration.

Another segment of files you will want to back up are special, custom, or in-house-developed applications that are installed, including their associated configuration and license files. For instance, you will want to back up your Oracle database because your company's most important information could be stored in there. These files are typically the backbone of your company's information program, so they should be studied carefully for backup validity and backed up on a regular basis.

You may be running a small shop or home system and determine that you don't need to back up entire file systems; you only need to back up your home directory that contains your important files. If this is the case, you should still have a backup strategy — even if it's only a small backup to a CD-ROM once a week — so that you do not lose the work you have stored on your system.

If you can't back up the entire system, spend time determining which files and directories should be backed up. The time invested in investigating which files are critical to you and your system and interviewing those who are knowledgeable of the system can save you many hours when restoring a machine to production, or when recovering files for your personal use.

Backup Media Types

The types of media to which you back up your data are extremely important. If your medium does not have the capacity to store all your critical data or cannot endure the time period you need your backups for, the backups lose their effectiveness. There are many different media types to back up data, including:

- **Magnetic tape** — One of the oldest ways to back up data. It has stood the test of time and proven to be very durable. The newest versions of magnetic tape are very fast and can store a significant amount of data. The media and hardware required to use magnetic tape for backups can be very expensive and difficult to set up initially. This media is well suited to long-term storage (20 or more years). Most corporate backup systems rely on magnetic tapes.
- **CD/DVD-ROM** — A newer method (relatively speaking) of backing up data that has grown in popularity because of the extensive availability of the hardware for multiple platforms. The technology is growing and is generally fast while being able to store a sizeable amount of data. The media and hardware required to use this type of backup are readily available. The long-term durability of this type of storage has not been confirmed, but is generally thought to be 10–20 years, depending on the quality of media chosen. This is the most common backup hardware for home computers today.
- **Zip drives** — An older technology losing market share because of its low capacity and slow speed. The hardware and media is still readily available but is waning. This type of storage can maintain data for a significant amount of time (more than 10 years).
- **Hard drive/network backup** — This type of backup is more and more common with the price of hard drive space at a low point. This is not a preferred method because of the dependence on hardware and the capability to tamper with or accidentally remove data. This is not suitable for long-term storage and is not recommended for backups.

There are other media types, including USB drives, which are generally not yet large enough to hold a significant amount of backup data. Floppy diskettes are discounted as well because of their extremely limited storage space.

In deciding the type of media to use for your backups, you need to consider what you are backing up, the importance of the data (its value to you or to your business), the amount of data to back up, and the time frame in which you will need the backup to run (to find out if you need faster hardware, and so on), and how long you plan to save the data for restoration purposes. All of these issues play a role in determining which backup hardware and media are best suited to your situation. If you need to save your data for 30 years, for example, you will probably choose magnetic tape over online disk drive storage because tape backup has proven it viability over long periods of proper storage.

Backup Types

You back up your data so that you can restore it if you ever need to. For this reason, you must determine the best schema for backing up your data. Here are the three major types of backups:

- **Full:** Backs up all data within the scope of the backup definition. For instance, if you set your backup command to back up the `/etc` and `/home` directories, a full backup would copy the entire `/etc` and `/home` directories and files regardless if they changed since the last backup.

- **Differential:** Backs up all data that has changed since the last full backup. For instance, if you did a full backup of the `/etc` and `/home` directories on Friday and then ran a differential backup on those directories on Monday, only the files that had changed since Friday and would be backed up on Monday. For a complete restoration, you would need the full backup and the latest differential backup.
- **Incremental:** Backs up all data that has changed since the completion of any other type of backup. If you did a differential backup of the `/etc` and `/home` directories on Friday and then an incremental backup on Monday, all the files in those directories that had changed since Friday would be backed up. For a restoration, you would need the last full and differential backups, then all incremental backups for the time period you want restored.

There are pros and cons for each of these backups, as the following table shows.

Type	Advantages	Disadvantages
Full	Faster data restoration than a differential or incremental backup.	Backups take significantly longer than the other types. Requires the most media space.
Differential	Faster data restoration than an incremental backup. Backs up faster than a full type. Requires less backup media space than for a full backup.	Backup slower than an incremental. Requires more media space than by an incremental type.
Incremental	Much faster backup than full or differential. Significantly smaller backup media space required than for full or differential type.	Requires more time to restore than a differential or full backup does.

These types of backups will be discussed throughout the chapter, so you should be cognizant of the advantages and disadvantages with each type of backup.

When to Run Backups

You will want to run your backups when there is the least amount of activity on the system, so you capture all changes. This usually means backups in the middle of the night, which can be easily scheduled with crons (discussed in Chapter 11). Backups also typically take up a significant amount of resources on the system, slowing the system down if there are other resource-intensive processes running. The first time you run the backups, you should run them manually to ensure that they run properly and do not cause system slowdowns for other processes.

Another thing to consider is the frequency with which you run your backups. You will want to back up data when the loss of the data would be significant, such as potential financial impact or loss of productivity. If you cannot afford to incur the loss of even 1 day's worth of data, you do not want to have a backup schedule that backs up data every week. Generally, this is a full backup weekly at a minimum, with differential or incremental backups throughout the week to capture any changes made through the week. The frequency and type you use is dependant on your requirements for backup time frame and restoration time.

Verify Backups

After you have made your backups, verify them by restoring the data you backed up. For maximum assurance, you will want to restore the data and then work from it for a period of time to ensure that you are not missing critical data. You do not want to find out your backups weren't complete or were corrupted after you need them. Verify your backups frequently by using multiple methods, from restoring the entire backup to restoring individual files for error checking. As appropriate, you will want to restore your data on a test system and have users determine whether there is any data missing. During the restoration exercise, you will want to restore your system and then run off that system for a few days to make sure you have everything you need backed up. It is far better to find out that you are missing files or data in your backup design during a scheduled test, than to find out when you have a disaster scenario. A test of your backup is recommended every month or quarter as needs dictate and depending on the value of the data involved.

Storing Backups

Backup storage is a critical component that is often overlooked when planning a backup strategy. Storing your backups on-site may seem like a good idea, because you will have instant access to them, but what happens if you cannot access the building that houses your servers and backups for a long period of time, or perhaps never? If you store your backups on-site, for example, and the building burns down, you will have lost your backups as well as your system.

Losing access to your site means that you will need to restore your production systems to completely new hardware, so you must have access to your backup media. This is why you should store at least some of your backups off-site or at a minimum in a fireproof safe. If you do store backup media on-site, make sure they are properly protected in accordance with the sensitivity of the data stored on the media and not available to anyone who does not need access, because these could hold all your company's trade secrets.

If you do choose an off-site solution, you should ensure that the company storing your backup media is available by phone 24 hours a day; determine whether the company's response time is suitable for your needs; check out the storage facility's security; and take a look at any complaints that company has received from customers. The company storing your backup media is, in essence, holding the trade secrets of your company, so a thorough knowledge of the vendor's practices and procedures for storing backup media is essential. At frequent intervals, you should request a return of backup media to check the vendor's response times and capability to provide the media you request in a timely and proficient manner.

One common method for storing backup media is to hold the most recent week's backup on-site in a fireproof safe, so that any accidental deletions or other data loss can be restored very quickly. After that week is up, the backup media is moved off-site for a designated period of time (from 1 year to forever) to be available in case of emergency. You should store some of your backup media for an extended period of time in case of archival needs, but you should contact your legal department for guidance if you are doing this for a company because there are laws regulating how long data must be saved depending on the industry you are in.

Backup Commands

By default, Unix includes many utilities for backing up data to many different types of media, enabling you to use the tool that best fits your backup needs, and providing a great deal of flexibility especially in scripting of the tools as discussed elsewhere in this book.

Most backup commands require that you run them as a privileged user such as root, because the backup may need to access files readable by only special users based on restricted permissions, such as `/etc/shadow` for instance. You will also want to make that sure no users are using the files or file systems while you are backing up, because you can run into problems such as corrupt backups that may not be evident until you try to restore.

Using tar

The `tar` (tape archive) command enables you to create tape archives and, if needed, send them directly to a tape device. This command is very useful even if you do not have a tape drive, because you can use it to merge a large group of files into a single file called a *tarfile*. A directory that contains 100 files and 20 directories can be consolidated into a single tarfile, for example. This is not compression as WinZip, gzip, or bzip does, but you can combine `tar` with the `gzip` or `bzip2` command to create a compressed tarfile. Before the tarfile is compressed it will consume the same disk space as the directories it includes. If you use the `tar` command and do not have a tape drive to write the tarfile to, you can simply back it up to a CD-ROM or other means at a later time.

The `tar` command has many functions, including:

- `t`—Shows the table of contents for the tarfile
- `x`—Extracts or restores the contents of the tarfile
- `u`—Updates the contents of a tarfile

There are some directories that you cannot tar, such as `/proc`, so using `/` as the directory name can result in permission errors. There are also many directories you don't want to tar, such as `/tmp`.

The syntax for creating a tarfile is:

`tar -cvf` *tarfile_name_or_tape_device directory_name*

The `c` argument means to begin writing at the beginning of the tarfile, the `v` represents verbose, which provides a lot of output showing what the command is doing. The `f` option notifies the tar command that the user will be providing a tarfile name instead of using the default identified in `/etc/default/tar`.

To create a tarfile with the contents of the entire `/etc` directory to a properly configured tape device named `/dev/rmt0`, for example, you'd use the following command:

```
tar -cvf /dev/rmt0 /etc
```

This writes a copy of the contents of the `/etc` directory to the specified tape device.

If you did not have a tape device and wanted to save the tarfile to a directory called `/backups/etc-backup-122004.tar`, you would run the following command:

```
tar -cvf /backups/etc-backup-122004.tar /etc
```

It is customary to add the .tar extension to tarfiles so they are easier to recognize. If you use compression (as discussed later in this section), you can add `.tar`, `.gz` or `.tgz` to represent a compressed tarfile. This command creates the specified file that will contain a copy of all the files and directories in `/etc` in a single file (which will probably be quite large).

After creating a tarfile, you may want to view its contents. To do this, you can use the following command for a tar:

```
tar -tvf tarfile_name_or_tape_device directory_name
```

So to view the contents of the `/etc` backup you just created on the tape device, you would run the following:

```
tar -tvf /dev/rmt0
```

To view the contents of the `/etc` backup you created to `/backups/etc-backup-122004.tar`, you would use:

```
tar -tvf /backups/etc-backup-122004.tar
```

If you want only a simple listing, you can omit the `v` option, reducing output; your command would be

```
tar -tf /dev/rmt0
```

or

```
tar -tf /backups/etc-backup-122004.tar
```

which would show output similar to the following:

```
#tar -tf /backups/etc-backup-122004.tar
etc/
etc/profile.d/
etc/profile.d/ssh-client.sh
etc/profile.d/alias.sh
etc/profile.d/xhost.csh
etc/profile.d/xhost.sh
(...The rest omitted for brevity)
```

To restore the contents of a tarfile, use the `-xvf` options to `tar`. Here's the syntax for the extraction of a tarfile:

`tar -xvf` *tarfile_name_or_tape_device directory_name*

To obtain a copy of `/etc/passwd` from the tarfile you sent to the tape device earlier, you would type the following:

```
tar -xvf /dev/rmt0 etc/passwd
```

To extract the same file from the tarfile `/backups/etc-backup-122004.tar` that was created earlier, you would use the command:

```
tar -xvf /backups/etc-backup-122004.tar etc/passwd
```

To extract the entire contents of `/backups/etc-backup-122004.tar` to your current directory, you would use:

```
tar -xvf /backups/etc-backup-122004.tar
```

This command creates a directory called `etc` in your current directory and then extracts a copy of all the files that were archived in `/backups/etc-backup-122004.tar` to that `etc` directory (it won't go to the `/` directory unless that is your current directory).

Be careful where you are extracting files, because they will be extracted to the directory in which you are currently located. So if you extracted the `/etc/passwd` file from `/backups/etc-backup-122004.tar` while you were located in the `/` directory, the systems current `/etc/passwd` file would be overwritten (if you have the proper permissions) by the one you extracted from the tarfile. It is usually safe to extract the files in a temporary directory to prevent any accidental overwriting of files.

The `-u` option enables you to update your tarfile with extra files that will be appended to the end of the tarfile. If a file with the same name exists in the tarfile, it will be updated. This can be a slow process, so remain patient. The syntax for update is:

```
tar -uf tarfile_name_or_tape_device directory_name
```

To update the `/etc/passwd` file in `/backups/etc-backup-122004.tar` tarfile with a new copy of `passwd`, for example, you would run the following command:

```
tar -uf /backups/etc-backup-122004.tar /etc/passwd
```

This command does not work on tape archives because magnetic media is not necessarily designed to write in intermittent parts of the tape. This command will not erase the previous version. It will, however, append a new copy at the end of the tarfile if it has changed since the previous time the file was added to the tarfile.

GNU tar (available on some versions of Unix or for download) also has some scripts for simple backups and restores of files.

There are versions of tar that enable you to make complete backups of files using built-in scripts as well as many other functions not provided in other versions of tar. To review the comprehensive feature set available on one of the more popular versions, GNU tar, check out the online manual for GNU at `http://gnu.org/software/tar/manual/html_node/tar_toc.html`.

Compressing with gzip and bzip2

Compression of data is when you take a regular size of file and reduce the amount of disk space it consumes. It requires a special application called a compression program. When storing backups on any type of media, you generally want to conserve space to allow maximum utilization of the media. A compressed file generally cannot be read by the standard applications that it normally operates with because the file has been optimized for compression, which makes it unreadable. So if you compressed a text file, you would not be able to read it in a text editor such as vi. The file is also usually significantly reduced from its original size because of the compression, meaning it takes up less space than it did in its uncompressed form, depending on the file type.

Unix has some free alternatives for compressing data in the forms of gzip and bzip2, as discussed in this section.

gzip

GNU zip (gzip) is the most popular compression program available for Unix operating systems, and rightfully so because of its portability among different system architectures and its full feature set.

The command syntax for a simple compression of a file using gzip is:

```
gzip filename
```

To make a standard text file called `mytextfile` take up less space by compressing it, you would run:

```
gzip mytextfile
```

If you used the `ls` command to show the directory contents after running the preceding command, the output would include a new file called `mytextfile.gz`. The .gz extension is the standard extension gzip adds to any file that has been compressed with this tool. When the command completes, it removes the old uncompressed file and leaves only the compressed version in place. If you are compressing a large file and are concerned with speed, you can add `-1` to have gzip compress the file faster:

```
gzip -1 mytextfile
```

If you are more concerned with conserving space, you can use `-9` for best compression:

```
gzip -9 mytextfile
```

You can use any number between 1 and 9 to indicate your preference for speed or for better compression. The default compression state is 6, edging toward better compression at the cost of speed.

To view information on the gzipped file, you can use the `-l` option, which shows output similar to the following:

```
#gzip -l mytextfile.gz
compressed  uncompr. ratio uncompressed_name
       614      1660  64.8% mytextfile
```

The output shows the compressed file size, the uncompressed file size, the ratio of compression applied to the file, and the uncompressed filename of each file in the gzip archive.

To restore the file to its original uncompressed state, use either `gunzip` or `gzip -d`:

```
gunzip mytextfile.gz
```

or

```
gzip -d mytextfile.gz
```

This creates a new file called `mytextfile` that would be the uncompressed version of the regular file you had just created. The `gzip` command prompts you to overwrite a file if the file you are decompressing already exists. To override this behavior and have `gzip` decompression overwrite existing files, use the `-f` option when decompressing with `gzip -d` or `gunzip`. When the command has completed, it removes the compressed file and leaves only the uncompressed file in place. In Unix, compressed files and uncompressed files are all referred to as regular files.

There are other options for more advanced compression described in the `gzip` man page.

The following exercise provides you with an opportunity to try out `gzip` for yourself.

Try It Out Use gzip

1. Create a file called `test-file` in your `/tmp` directory using:

```
cd /tmp
touch test-file
```

2. Using vi, enter some text into the file — about 10 lines of random sentences — and then save the file.
3. Use the `ls -l` command to show the size of the file:

```
ls -l test-file
```

4. To show that you can view the file, because it is a regular text file, use the `cat` command:

```
cat test-file
```

   You should see the 10 lines of random sentences you created previously.

5. Use the `gzip` command to compress the file you just created:

```
gzip test-file
```

6. You now have a file called `test-file.gz` in your `/tmp` directory. Use the `-l` command to show statistics of the compressed file:

```
gzip -l test-file.gz
```

   You can see how much compression `gzip` applied.

7. Use the `ls -l` command to show the compressed file's size:

```
ls -l test-file.gz
```

The file should take up less space than the uncompressed version did, because `gzip` reduced the file size. The file is now unreadable and would show a bunch of unusual characters if you were to use the `cat` command to view it (do not try this as it can create problems in the terminal window.)

8. Decompress your file using `gzip` or `gunzip`:

```
gzip -d test-file.gz
```

or

```
gunzip -d test-file.gz
```

9. The `/tmp` directory has a file called `test-file` in it (the `test-file.gz` file no longer shows). Use the `cat` command to view the contents of the file:

```
cat test-file
```

10. You should see the same output you did when you used `cat` prior to compressing the file. Use the `ls -l` command again, and you'll see that the file is the same size as it was originally.

How It Works

The `test-file` text file was compressed successfully by the `gzip` command. Using `gunzip` or `gzip`, you were able to successfully decompress the file so that it appeared as if it had never been modified or compressed before.

Files that have been gzipped typically end in the .gz, .z, or .Z extension, so if you come across a file with any of those extensions, it was most likely compressed using `gzip`.

bzip2

The `bzip2` command offers the same type of functionality as `gzip`, with some improvements on the compression capability. The bzip2 type of compressed file is not as widely used as the gzip, but you will run across it, or you may find you prefer it. Typically, bzip2-compressed files end with a .bz, .bz2, .bzip2, .tbz, or .tbz2 extension. If you encounter a file with one of these extensions, it most likely was compressed using bzip2.

Here's the syntax for a simple file compression using bzip2:

```
bzip2 filename
```

To make a standard text file called `mytextfile` take up less space by compressing it, you would run:

```
bzip2 mytextfile
```

The `ls` command would show a new file called `mytextfile.bz2` in the directory.

As with the `gzip` command, you can use any number between 1 and 9 to indicate your preference for speed or for better compression. If you are compressing a large file and are concerned with speed, you can add `-1` to `bzip2`:

```
bzip2 -1 mytextfile
```

If you are more concerned with conserving space, you can use `-9` for best compression:

```
bzip2 -9 mytextfile
```

The default compression state for `bzip2` is 9, for best results.

To restore a file to its original uncompressed state, you would use `bunzip2` or `bzip2 -d`:

```
bunzip2 mytextfile.bz2
```

or

```
bzip2 -d mytextfile.bz2
```

This creates a new file called `mytextfile` that would be the uncompressed version of the regular file you just created. One thing to remember with bzip2 is that by default it will not overwrite an existing file. If you did want bzip2 to overwrite a file when decompressing, you need to use the `-f` option.

The `bzip2` command has a related command called `bzip2recover` that will attempt to recover a damaged bzip2 archive. See the bzip2 man page for more information on this and other functionality.

Using gzip or bzip2 and tar Together

The `gzip` or `bzip2` and `tar` commands complement each other very well, and, in fact, these two commands typically work together through command integration. To create a tarfile and compress it in the same command, use the following to filter the tarfile through gzip:

```
tar -cvzf tarfile_name_or_tape_device directory_name_to_tar_and_compress
```

If you prefer to use bzip2, you can use the following:

```
tar -cvjf tarfile-name_or_tape_device directory-to-tar-and-compress
```

It is customary to add an extension of .tar.gz or .tgz to a gzipped and tarred file or to add a .bz or .tbz extension to a bzipped file, so if you use the same file created for the tar example earlier, you would use the following command to tar and gzip the file

```
tar -cvzf /backups/etc-backup-122004.tar.gz /etc
```

or

```
tar -cvf /backups/etc-backup-122004.tgz /etc
```

Use the following to create a tar and bzipped archive:

```
tar -cvjf /backups/etc-backup-122004.tar.bz /etc
```

You can uncompress and untar a file with the individual commands, using the decompress command first. For example, to untar and uncompress the `/backups/etc-backup-122004.tgz` file, you first use

```
gunzip /backups/etc-backup-122004.tgz
```

which would result in a file called `/backups/etc-backup-122004.tar`. Then you would untar the file:

```
tar -xvf /backups/etc-backup-122004.tar
```

And you would have the untarred archive of the `/etc` directory created earlier. You can also do this with one command:

```
tar -xvzf /backups/etc-backup-122004.tgz
```

The `-xvzf` option takes the two preceding steps and combines them into one command. The result would put the previously tarred contents of the `/etc` directory in new subdirectory (called `etc`) of your current directory. You can use the same steps for a bzipped file, using `j` instead of `z`.

cpio

The `cpio` (copy in/out) command is more difficult to use than the `tar` command but provides some special functionality, such as the capability to save special files. The `cpio` command receives all of its file inputs (what files to backup) from other commands, allowing for easy-to-create scripts for automation. This command is not available on all versions of Unix and has a steeper learning curve than other methods, so make sure you sure to read the man pages before using it for backups. There are three primary options for the `cpio` command, described in the following table.

Option	Description
`-i`	Extracts files from standard input.
`-o`	Reads standard input for a list of file path names to back up (allowing for redirection to standard out).
`-p`	Reads file path names from standard input, saving a copy to a directory named later.

Here's an example of how to create a simple backup of the current directory:

```
find . -print | cpio -ov >cpio_archive
```

The same results could have been produced by using (as well as many, many other combinations):

```
ls * | cpio -ov >cpio_archive
```

If you have the `ls` *command aliased to* `ls -l`*, this command will fail.*

This gathers a list of all the files in the current directory (`find .`) and prints them. The results of the `find` command are redirected by way of the pipe (|) to the `cpio` command. `cpio` then reads the output of the `find` command (`-o`) and lists the filenames (`-v`). The output of `cpio` is then redirected (>) to file called `cpio_archive`. `cpio_archive` could have been replaced with a device name such as `/dev/rmt0` or `/dev/fd0` for a magnetic tape drive or floppy drive, respectively. (These device names are examples; your device names may differ.)

For instance if you had a directory called `/tmp/cpio-directory` that contained `cpio1-test-file`, `cpio2-test-file`, and `cpio3-test-file` and you wanted to create a backup of the `/tmp/cpio-directory` to a file called `cpio-archive-file`, you could run the following commands to `cd` into the `/tmp/cpio` directory, create a `cpio` archive, and then run an `ls` command to see the contents of the directory:

```
#cd /tmp/cpio-directory
#find . -print | cpio -ov >cpio-archive-file
cpio: .: truncating inode number
.
cpio: cpio1-test-file: truncating inode number
./cpio1-test-file
cpio: cpio2-test-file: truncating inode number
./cpio2-test-file
cpio: cpio3-test-file: truncating inode number
./cpio3-test-file
3 blocks
#ls
cpio1-test-file  cpio2-test-file  cpio3-test-file  cpio-archive-file
```

This creates a new file called `cpio-archive-file`, as shown in the output of the `ls` command. You could have replaced the filename `cpio-archive-file` with the name of a device, and the file would have been written directly to the device.

To view the contents of a `cpio` archive, use the `-itv` option and redirect the archive into the `cpio` command. For instance:

```
#cpio -itv <cpio-archive-file
drwxr-xr-x  2 user user        0 Dec 20 22:44 .
-rw-r--r--  1 user user       37 Dec 20 22:38 cpio1-test-file
-rw-r--r--  1 user user       37 Dec 20 22:38 cpio2-test-file
-rw-r--r--  1 user user       37 Dec 20 22:38 cpio3-test-file
3 blocks
#
```

This command displays the contents of the `cpio-archive-file` just created, as shown in the output following the command. If the file was on a magnetic tape drive, you could have run

```
cpio -itv </dev/rmt0
```

and if you had saved the same `cpio-archive-file` to that tape drive, you would have seen the same results.

To retrieve files from a cpio archive, run the following in another directory, `/tmp/cpio-directory2` in this example:

```
#cd /tmp/cpio-directory2
#cpio -i </tmp/cpio-directory/cpio-archive-file

3 blocks
#
```

If you did an `ls` at this point, you'd see that the directory contains the three files archived in `cpio` earlier (`cpio1-test-file`, `cpio2-test-file`, and `cpio3-test-file`).

There are many more options and ways to use cpio for backing up files. Refer to the man pages for more information on this very versatile and flexible command.

dump, backup, and restore

The `dump` command is a true backup tool in the sense that it is built for backing up entire file systems in a methodical, consistent manner. The `dump` command has two components: the actual `backup` command that performs a backup per the user's specifications, and the `restore` command that recovers the backed-up files. On some systems these commands are called `ufsdump` and `ufsrestore`, such as on Sun's Solaris, but the differences between the two are minor between the implementations. The benefits of using `dump` over other command-line backup utilities is that dump can:

- Identify when a file was last backed up
- Mark a file as having had a backup
- Back up many file systems on a single tape device (or back up file systems across many tapes)
- Easily back up remote systems

In addition, `dump`'s restores are fairly intuitive and simple.

The first step to using `dump` is to understand its available command-line options, which are described in the following table.

Option	Description
`-0` through `-9`	Dump levels. A level 0 dump indicates that everything will be copied to the backup device. All other numbers indicate incremental backups, which copy all files that are new or modified since the last lower level.
`-a`	Disregards tape length calculations and writes until an end-of-tape message is received (useful for appending data to a tape).
`-A`	Creates a table of contents of the dump in a file named immediately after the `-A`. This option is for later use with the `restore` command.

Table continued on following page

Option	Description
-f *output_name*	Writes the backup to the *output_name* file (including a tape device such as /dev/rmt0, a plain file, or even a remote system, such as linux2:/dev/rmt0). For instance, you could run the dump command with -f /var/my_backup_050105 to write the backup to a file called /var/my_backup_050105. To see the backups on your local screen, put a - after the f option to indicate standard output (good for troubleshooting).
-F *script_name*	Runs the *script_name* script after the backup has completed. This is useful for database backups where the database should be brought back online.
-j *option*	Uses compression level indicated immediately after the option (1–9). This uses bzip2.
-L *label_name*	Uses *label_name* to label the backup for reading by restore.
-q	Quits immediately when operator intervention is required.
-w	Shows a listing of all file systems that need to be dumped.
-W	Shows a listing of all dumps for backed-up file systems (derived from the file /etc/dumpdates).
-z *options*	Similar to -j except that gzip is used for the compression.

The proper back up of data is crucial, so dump is very cautious when it runs into an error and typically requires user intervention when a problem arises.

Backups typically must be run as root or another user with backup permissions.

When using dump for the first time, make sure you back up everything initially by running the dump command with a 0 switch, such as:

```
/sbin/dump -0u -f /dev/st0 /home
```

This command backs up everything in the /home directory and sends the backup to the device /dev/st0 (typically a tape drive in Linux). To back up the /home directory to a file called /var/backup-122204, you could run:

```
/sbin/dump -0u -f /var/backup-122204 /home
```

After you begin the command, you'll see output similar to that shown in Figure 18-1.

```
root@linux: / - Shell - Konsole
Session Edit View Bookmarks Settings Help
[root@linux /]# /sbin/dump -0u -f /var/backup-122204 /home
  DUMP: Date of this level 0 dump: Wed Dec 22 18:06:04 2004
  DUMP: Dumping /dev/scsi/host0/bus0/target0/lun0/part6 (/home) to /var/backup-122204
  DUMP: Excluding inode 8 (journal inode) from dump
  DUMP: Excluding inode 7 (resize inode) from dump
  DUMP: Label: none
  DUMP: Writing 10 Kilobyte records
  DUMP: mapping (Pass I) [regular files]
  DUMP: mapping (Pass II) [directories]
  DUMP: estimated 3022 blocks.
  DUMP: Volume 1 started with block 1 at: Wed Dec 22 18:06:04 2004
  DUMP: dumping (Pass III) [directories]
  DUMP: dumping (Pass IV) [regular files]
  DUMP: Closing /var/backup-122204
  DUMP: Volume 1 completed at: Wed Dec 22 18:06:05 2004
  DUMP: Volume 1 3570 blocks (3.49MB)
  DUMP: Volume 1 took 0:00:01
  DUMP: Volume 1 transfer rate: 3570 kB/s
  DUMP: 3570 blocks (3.49MB) on 1 volume(s)
  DUMP: finished in 1 seconds, throughput 3570 kBytes/sec
  DUMP: Date of this level 0 dump: Wed Dec 22 18:06:04 2004
  DUMP: Date this dump completed:  Wed Dec 22 18:06:05 2004
  DUMP: Average transfer rate: 3570 kB/s
  DUMP: DUMP IS DONE
[root@linux /]#
```

Figure 18-1

You can now run the `dump -W` command to see the status of file system backups, as shown in Figure 18-2.

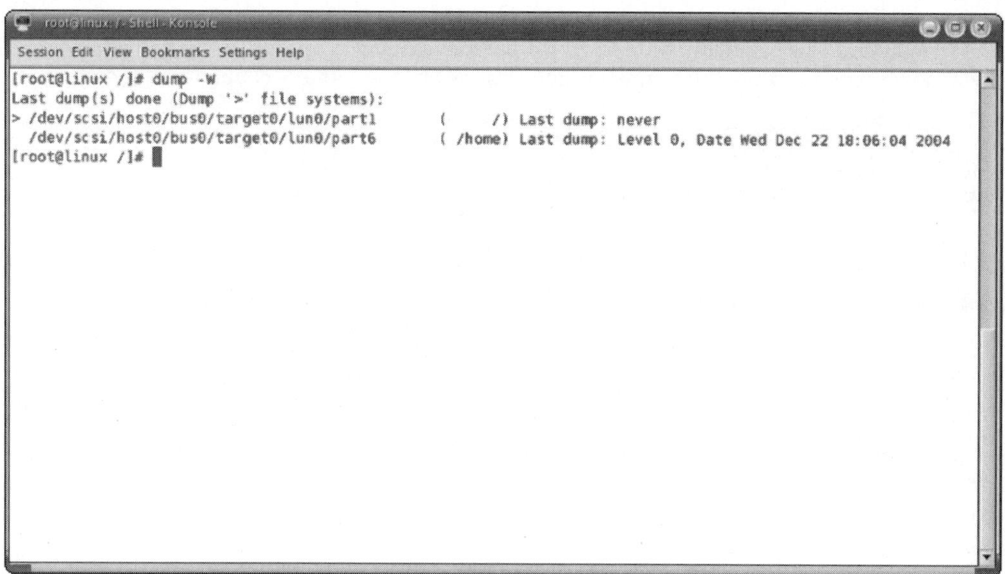
root@linux: / - Shell - Konsole
Session Edit View Bookmarks Settings Help
[root@linux /]# dump -W
Last dump(s) done (Dump '>' file systems):
> /dev/scsi/host0/bus0/target0/lun0/part1 (/) Last dump: never
/dev/scsi/host0/bus0/target0/lun0/part6 (/home) Last dump: Level 0, Date Wed Dec 22 18:06:04 2004
[root@linux /]#

Figure 18-2

If you prefer to see which file systems dump has determined need to be backed up (as shown in Figure 18-3), use dump -w (lowercase "w").

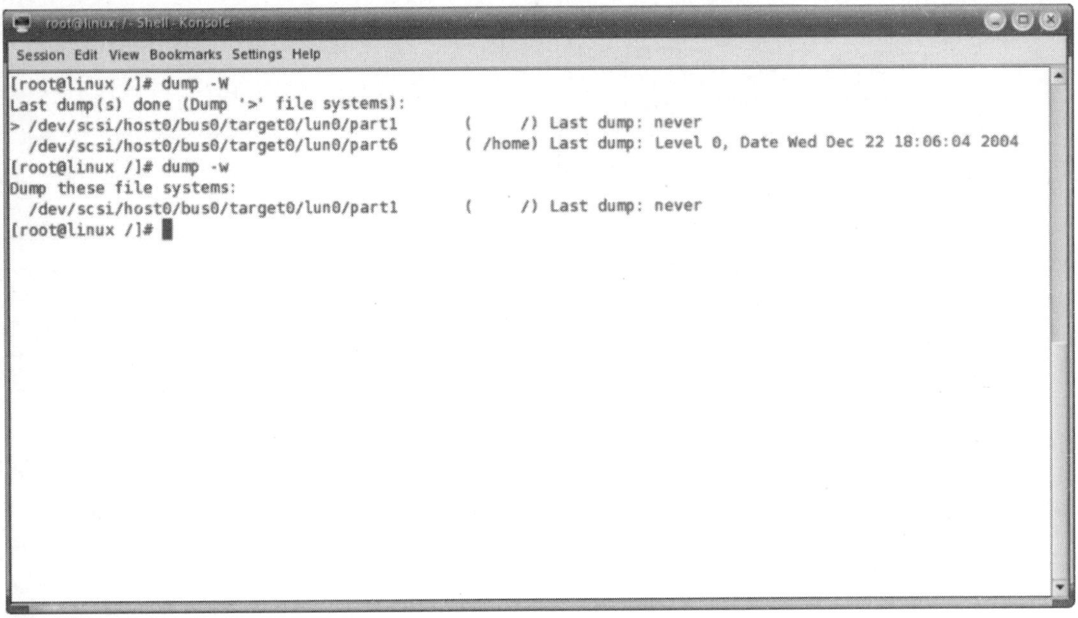

```
root@linux: / - Shell - Konsole
Session Edit View Bookmarks Settings Help
[root@linux /]# dump -W
Last dump(s) done (Dump '>' file systems):
> /dev/scsi/host0/bus0/target0/lun0/part1      (      /) Last dump: never
  /dev/scsi/host0/bus0/target0/lun0/part6      ( /home) Last dump: Level 0, Date Wed Dec 22 18:06:04 2004
[root@linux /]# dump -w
Dump these file systems:
  /dev/scsi/host0/bus0/target0/lun0/part1      (      /) Last dump: never
[root@linux /]#
```

Figure 18-3

Refer to the man pages for more information about scripting your backups to ensure that you get the options you need to efficiently and accurately back up your file systems.

After backing up, you need to restore to validate your backup or to recover from an accidental deletion or system failure. The command for restoring data from a dump is appropriately named restore. The following table shows some of the command-line options for the `restore` command.

Option	Description
`-f`	Indicates where to restore from (file or device).
`-F script`	Runs the named script at the beginning of the backup.
`-h`	Restores the actual directory, not the files referred to.
`-i`	Starts a restoration in interactive mode.
`-M`	Enables multivolume feature (when `-M` used for the dump). When used with `-f` option, it will use `filename001`, `filename002`, `filename003`, and so on.
`-N`	Only prints filenames; does not restore actual files.

Option	Description
`-r`	Restores an entire tape or file system (use this cautiously).
`-v`	Shows verbose output.
`-V`	Reads multivolume media other than tape (such as CD-ROMs).
`-x`	Restores specifically named files or directories.
`-X` *`filelisting`*	Extracts the files listed in *`filelisting`* from the restore.
`-y`	Does not abort if there is an error; continues restoring.

The interactive mode of `restore` (initiated with the `-i` option) has its own prompt (usually `RESTORE>`). While in the interactive mode, you can use the options described in the following table.

Option	Description
`add` *`directory_or_file`*	If used alone, it restores the current directory. If a directory or filename is added, it will be added to the restore.
`cd` *`directory`*	Changes to the named directory.
`delete` *`directory_or_file`*	Removes the current directory from the restore list if no arguments. If directory or file is specified, removes the named files from the restore.
`extract`	All files selected for extraction are extracted (restore is initiated).
`help`	Shows all available commands.
`ls` *`directory`*	Shows a listing of files in current directory if no files or directory named. If one is listed, then that is shown. Files to be restored have a * beside them.
`pwd`	Shows the current working directory.
`quit`	Exits the restore interactive session immediately.
`setmodes`	Sets the owner, modes, and times for files.
`verbose`	Shows extended information.

To initiate a restore, use the following command (using the backup file you created using the `dump` command):

```
restore -if /var/backup-122204
```

Figure 18-4 shows a sampling of some of the `restore` commands in interactive mode and the output they generate.

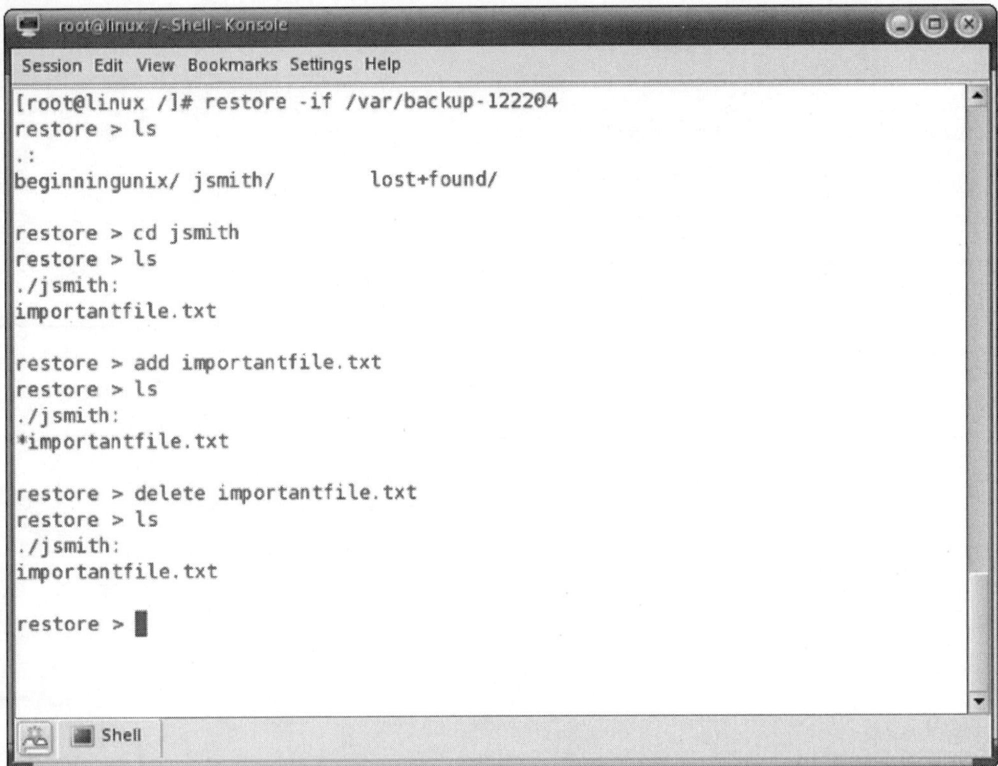

Figure 18-4

To do a restore in interactive mode, you can use the `cd` command to move around directories, use the `add` command to add directories or files, and then `extract` to actually restore the file.

The commands to restore are very straightforward and intuitive. `Dump` and `restore` can be used with the `mt` command for tape manipulation as well. Check the man pages for the `mt` command for more information on this specific sequence.

Other Backup Commands

In the tradition of multiple ways to do the same thing in Unix, there are other backup commands worth researching if the previously described commands do not work in your situation. Some of these commands are:

- `pax` (portable archive exchange) is very similar to `tar` and `cpio` but with some added functionality. More information is available at `http://directory.fsf.org/GNU/paxutils.html`.
- `rsync`—For fast, remote file synchronization. More information is available at `http://samba.anu.edu.au/rsync/`.
- `rdist`—For distributed copies of files and backup. More information is available at `http://www.magnicomp.com/rdist/`.

Backup Suites

For production or commercial environments, you may determine that you need some more functionality, ease of use, and support for your overall backup solution. There are many great software applications available for the Unix operating systems, including:

- ARCserver — `www3.ca.com/Solutions/ProductFamily.asp?ID=115`
- Arkia — `www.arkeia.com`
- IBM Tivoli Storage Manager — `www-306.ibm.com/software/tivoli/products/storage-mgr`
- LoneTar — `www.lone-tar.com`
- Veritas NetBackup — `www.veritas.com/Products/www?c=product&refId=2`

The following are some free backup suites that provide more ease-of-use than their command-line interface counterparts:

- Amanda — `www.amanda.org`
- Bacula — `www.bacula.org`
- Kbackup — `http://kbackup.sourceforge.net`

Summary

In this chapter, you learned the basics of backing up your data, including building your strategy for backups to the storage of your backup media. You also learned the major commands used for backing up your data, as well as the different media types available for backup.

Using the `backup` and `restore` commands, you can run simple backups. The `gzip` and `bzip2` commands enable you to compress your files to safe space on backup media as well. You also learned how to use the `cpio` and `tar` commands to create simple, portable files out of a larger group of files. Now that you have the tools to perform backups of your Unix system, you should start using these skills by backing up your system.

Exercise

Demonstrate how you would use the `tar` and then `gzip` commands to compress all your configuration files in `/etc` (the entire directory) and name the file `/tmp/etc_backup`.

Installing Software from Source Code

Although Unix systems come with a variety of software preinstalled or available through their packaging systems, one of the many benefits of Unix is that you can build and install other software from the original source code. In fact, most software for Unix systems is provided only in original source code form, so you definitely want to know what to do with it.

This chapter explores finding and retrieving software, using common build tools, building and installing software, and troubleshooting. It examines `make`, the GNU build system, GCC, and the basics of package management. To augment your grasp of these topics, you'll install several programs from source code.

> *To build software from source, Mac OS X users must have the Xcode Tools installed on their system. If the computer had Mac OS X 10.3 Panther installed at the factory, it will have an installer located at* `/Applications/Installers/Developer Tools/`. *If the installer is not present on your system, you can download the software from Apple. Information on the software, including downloading instructions, is available at* `http://developer.apple.com/tools/download/`. *To download Xcode Tools from Apple, you will need to register for a free account at Apple Developer Connection. Xcode Tools includes* `make`, *GCC, and other tools and utilities outlined in this chapter. The current version of Xcode Tools is 1.5.*

Understanding Source Code

Source code is the original data used to create software. It can be written in a programming language such as C or C++, which needs to be compiled before use, or in a language such as Perl or Python script, which is then ready to run as is. In most cases, the source code provides build instructions and/or build tools to help generate and install the final product: ready-to-use software for your system. Software that has been compiled and is in machine-executable format is not source code.

Because there are so many different Unix platforms available, and it takes a lot of time to provide ready-to-use binaries (executables) for each one, Unix developers commonly provide their software only in original source code downloads. Their software generally is portable enough for you to be able to build it on your choice of Unix systems. By acquiring the original source code, you can build the program for your personal system and, depending on your capability, customize it for your specific needs.

When you download source code, check for notes or README files that refer to your particular Unix version. You may need to download additional packages or documentation to get the program running properly on your machine.

The downloads usually provide the original code in C, C++, Perl, Python, or other programming languages along with documentation, instructions on how to build, scripts and utilities to help build and install the software, data files, example configurations, and various other files. Sometimes the downloads are simply ready-to-install (and maybe ready-to-run) scripts without any instructions.

Developers often provide security fixes or other needed improvements as source code patches before Unix distributors or vendors provide updated precompiled releases. Imagine an emergency virus situation where the only available software patch is provided solely as source code, rather than as a precompiled binary specifically intended for your Unix variant. To install this patch, you need to know how to work with code. Even if you work with precompiled software packages 99 percent of the time, it's a good idea to know how to build from source code so that you can keep your system up-to-date in times of crisis.

Of course, software provided directly from a developer (or software vendor) is often more current than the versions provided with your operating system or your distribution. Installing from source code is a good way to try newest features of the latest software, which may also include the least amount of testing and the newest bugs — downloaders beware!

Open Source Licensing

Software available in the original source code form is often called *open source*, but that's not the complete definition. Open source software is software that carries particular license terms. It's generally free to review, free to share, free to use, and (most importantly) free to modify. (*Free* is used here in the sense usually expressed as "free speech, not free beer.") You may choose to pay for some open source software or extra add-ons such as CDs or service.

Open source software licenses claim copyright on the source code and specify freedoms and limitations on the use and distribution of the code and its derivatives. Software authors often create their own license terms but they must honor any existing licenses if they reuse other developers' code.

Understanding the basics of open source licensing — especially in a commercial situation — is necessary so you can determine whether you can use and distribute the software. If you plan to work on an existing open source software project, or want to create your own software to be released under a typical open source license, you must be familiar with the terms of the licenses that apply to the code you're using. Let's take a look at two major kinds of open source licensing: BSD and GPL.

BSD Licenses

BSD-style licensed source code can be freely modified, and the modifications do not have to be redistributed. Some BSD-licensed code requires that advertising materials contain a notice that BSD code is used in the advertised program. BSD-licensed code is often used in proprietary or commercial software, such as in Microsoft Windows and Apple Mac OS X.

An example of a simple BSD license is found in Wietse Venema's popular TCP Wrappers code:

```
Copyright 1995 by Wietse Venema. All rights reserved. Some individual files may be
covered by other copyrights.

This material was originally written and compiled by Wietse Venema at Eindhoven
University of Technology, The Netherlands, in 1990, 1991, 1992, 1993, 1994 and 1995.

Redistribution and use in source and binary forms, with or without modification,
are permitted provided that this entire copyright notice is duplicated in all such
copies.

This software is provided "as is" and without any expressed or implied warranties,
including, without limitation, the implied warranties of merchantibility and
fitness for any particular purpose.
```

X11 and MIT licenses, which are used for a lot of open source X Window System software, are similar to BSD licenses, as is the original license used by the popular Apache Web server.

GNU Public License

The GNU General Public License (GPL) is also common. It's known as a *copyleft* license because it requires that any modified version of the distributed software be released under the same terms. The GNU Project and the Free Software Foundation, the proponents of the GPL, do not use the term open source for software released under the GPL, preferring to use the term free software.

If you work with code that carries a GPL, be aware that your own work on that code is likely controlled by GPL terms. That is, the GPL determines what can be done with derivatives of GPL-licensed code, and that almost always means that your work must be available under identical GPL terms. For those who believe that the best software is openly available for use and for development, the GPL is an excellent license. If you have any compunction about releasing your code for other developers to hack, the best choice is to start from scratch or, at the very least, avoid using any code that originates or derives from code with a GNU Public License.

More than 30 open-source licenses are commonly used. For more information and examples of a variety of licenses visit the Open Source Initiative Web site at `www.opensource.org` and the Free Software Foundation's comments at `www.gnu.org/licenses/license-list.html`.

If you use a portion of some code, be sure to clearly document that use and include a copy of the license with the new resulting code. In some cases, the use of some licensed code may affect your other code by insisting that its license takes precedence over all your code. (Yes, this does mean that, in some cases, the listed licenses can be longer than the actual code!)

Finding and Downloading Unix Software

There are several ways to find new software for your Unix machine. The easiest is to use the built-in features of your particular Unix variant. For example, many Linux variants offer tools that automatically search for updated versions or patches for software you already have installed. (The most frustrating way is to search the Web with your favorite search engine. While this may result in some jewels, even the best search engines usually come up with a lot of dead ends, such as insecure or outdated versions.)

Your best bets for fresh and exciting Unix software are Web software archives. These sites range from general archives that include Windows and Mac programs to archives so specific that they contain only programs released under particular software licenses. Here are some of the most popular and reliable archives containing a decent number of Unix programs:

- Freshmeat (`www.freshmeat.net`)—Cutting-edge releases
- Linuxberg (`www.linuxberg.com`)—Part of the Tucows archive
- Tucows (`www.tucows.com`)—A variety of Unix flavors, plus source code
- iBiblio (`www.ibiblio.org`)—A digital archive of all topics, including software
- Free Software Foundation (`www.fsf.org`)—Software licensed under the GPL
- Linux Software Map (`www.boutell.com/lsm`)—Software ported to Linux

Choosing Your Software

Developers frequently provide multiple downloads for the same program: the current official release, an older release stable on odd platforms, and several development versions used primarily for testing. How do you decide which one is for you?

Testing releases are often called alpha, beta, release candidates, or daily snapshots, and they are to be used with caution. By definition, testing software is potentially unstable.

Normally, you should download the official release, which is often labeled "LATEST." After you have installed the release and gotten it to work properly, you might find that there are good reasons—such as multiple bug patches or new features—to download a development version. It is important to realize that development releases often require development versions of prerequisite software. Other software that depends on the software being installed may be incompatible with the new testing code. Installing new software is often the first step in a domino effect that requires upgrades across the board.

In several cases, security patches or important bug fixes are available for open source projects, although the actual vendor or official developer of the project doesn't provide a fix (a patch) or an updated release. In fact, often the official Web site may not even mention that a security issue exists. It's a good rule of thumb to do a quick search for security issues for any software you install. A technology news site, such as Slashdot (`www.slashdot.org`), can point you in the right direction.

Downloading Files

After you've chosen the packages you want to work with, it's time to download the source code files. Downloads are usually compressed with the `tar`, `gzip`, or `bzip` command. The resulting file is called a *tarball* and typically has a `.tgz`, `.tar.gz`, or `.tar.bz2` filename extension. Some source code downloads are only available as shell archives, old-style compressed tar files (`.Z` extension), or ZIP files. Your Unix machine should be able to expand tarballs packed in any of these formats, so it doesn't matter which you choose.

Check File Size

The software archive often notes the size of the downloaded file. You can also see the file size once you start to download it, and you can abort the process if the file is too large for your disk. Remember, though, that this is a compressed file which may contain a large number of folders and individual files. Check the README file, the program's own Web site, or other documentation to see the actual size of the expanded and installed software. Installing a program for which you don't have enough disk space could lead to a nasty crash. You also need enough memory to handle all the expansion and installation processes.

Unfortunately, it's nearly impossible to give a blanket value for ample disk space. What you need to download and install a small command-line tool is very different from what you need to install a completely new shell or a powerful program such as Apache. In addition, the features you choose to enable will affect the disk space needed. For example, extracting the Apache 2 source (a 6 MB download) takes more than 22 MB, building it requires nearly 60 MB, and the installation needs an additional 20 MB of disk space. It all boils down to "it depends" and "do some research." Luckily, disk space is cheap these days. When in doubt, upgrade!

Download Tips

Download the file using your Web browser or an FTP client such as `nsftp` or `wget`. Be sure that your download client is set to download in binary mode, so that the tarball is executable when the download is finished. If you download in ASCII mode, the file downloads as text and is unusable. (Most browsers and FTP clients detect the file type automatically and set the mode accordingly.) Make note of where the downloaded file is being saved so that you don't have to search for it later.

Common locations for downloaded source tarballs include `/usr/src` for system source code, `/usr/local/src` for third-party software, and `~/src` for software that is only going to be used by you. Other options include `${HOME}/src` or `${HOME}/downloads`. Wherever you choose to store tarballs, try to use one consistent location so that you can control these files and delete them after you've installed the package.

Try It Out — Download Source Code Packages

Here's a file download in action. In this example, the curl program is used to retrieve a particular tarball from the MaraDNS project (`www.maradns.org`). This could have been made even easier by clicking the Download link on the project's Web page and selecting the Current Stable Release option, but using an FTP program better illustrates the process.

At the command prompt, invoke the curl program and specify both the target site where the package is to be stored and which package is desired:

```
 curl -o maradns-1.0.23.tar.bz2 -v http://www.maradns.org/download/maradns-
1.0.23.tar.bz2
* About to connect() to www.maradns.org:80
* Connected to www.maradns.org (66.33.48.187) port 80
> GET /download/maradns-1.0.23.tar.bz2 HTTP/1.1
```

```
User-Agent: curl/7.10/4 (i386--netbsdelf) libcurl/7.10.4 OpenSSL/0.9.6g ipv6
zlib/1.1.4
Host: www.maradns.org
Pragma: no-cache
Accept: image/gif, image/x-xbitmap, image/jpeg, image/pjpeg, */*

% Total    % Received  % Xferd  Average Speed          Time              Curr.
                                Dload  Upload  Total   Current  Left     Speed
100  423k  100 423k     0    0  70000  0       0:00:06 0:00:06  0:00:00  76326
* Connection #0 left intact
* Closing connection #0
```

How It Works

The `-o` (or `--output`) option chooses the filename under which curl will save the download, and the `-v` (or `--verbose`) option displays some debugging information. You can also use the `-O` (or `--remote-name`) option to save a few keystrokes. The file will be saved with the same filename it had on the originating site.

```
curl -O -v http://www.maradns.org/download/maradns-1.0.23.tar.bz2
```

The following is the same download but using `wget` instead:

```
wget http://www.maradns.org/download/maradns-1.0.23.tar.bz2
--16:07:10--  http://www.maradns.org/download/maradns-1.0.23.tar.bz2
           => `maradns-1.0.23.tar.bz2.1'
Resolving www.maradns.org... done.
Connecting to www.maradns.org[66.33.48.187]:80... connected.
HTTP request sent, awaiting response... 200 OK
Length: 433,164 [application/x-bzip2]

100%[====================================>] 433,164    77.43K/s    ETA 00:00

16:07:15 (77.43 KB/s) - `maradns-1.0.23.tar.bz2.1' saved [433164/433164]
```

Interestingly, `wget` *can resume aborted downloads for both FTP and HTTP. It has quite a few interesting and useful features that you can check out at* `www.gnu.org/software/wget/`.

Verify the Source Code

Code verification is an optional step in the download and installation process. Often, developers provide signatures, message digests, or checksums that can be used to verify the integrity of the software you downloaded. This process checks that the software downloaded correctly and also confirms that it is, in fact, the software you meant to download. Generally tools for downloading do an accurate job of downloading the file exactly as provided from the server and preventing any form of corruption. The main reason to verify a software package is that you are concerned that you might be downloading a maliciously altered package containing a Trojan horse or some other type of virus.

Does this happen? Yes. Some problem packages have been identified by using automated verification systems, such as that included with the Gentoo Linux variant. These examples include previously recorded checksums (using MD5) that are later used for checking the downloads in their build-from-source system. In October 2002, one of the download servers for Sendmail was serving a Trojan horse.

In November 2002, copies of `tcpdump` and `libpcap` that included Trojan horses were served from a popular download mirror. During the past decade, other compromised programs have been distributed by unknowing software archives.

NetBSD, OpenBSD, and FreeBSD also provide automated build-from-source systems that check the integrity of the downloaded source code against previously generated digests. They are briefly discussed later in this chapter.

Luckily, you can use verification tools to see whether you've got compromised software before you install it and endanger your system. The simplest test is with a checksum, a numerical tag that indicates how many bits should be in the downloaded package. Of course, the original, good checksum must be made against the real, original version of the download, and the checksum should be provided from an independent source. For example, if the checksum is hosted by the same server as the compromised download, then it also could have been compromised. An example of an independent source is an e-mail announcement that lists the MD5 digests for the downloads or using a different server than the downloads' server.

Getting an MD5 digest is as simple as running `digest`, `openssl`, `md5`, or the `md5sum` tool (depending on your Unix system) on the file. Here's an example that shows how to get a checksum under NetBSD:

```
$ md5 httpd-2.0.50.tar.gz
MD5 (httpd-2.0.50.tar.gz) = 8b251767212aebf41a13128bb70c0b41
```

This could be compared to the MD5 digest provided on the `www.apache.org` Web site.

For many years, MD5 was said to provide a unique digest for every unique file. But in 2004, a collision was found where two different files of the same size had the same MD5 digest. In response, many projects have started to use SHA1 digests as an alternative. You can use `digest`, `openssl`, `sha1`, or the `sha1sum` tool to output a SHA1 digest:

```
$ openssl sha1 Mail-SpamAssassin-2.64.tar.bz2
SHA1(Mail-SpamAssassin-2.64.tar.bz2)= ea4925c6967249a581c4966d1cefd1a3162eb639
```

This can be compared to the SHA1 digest provided on the SpamAssassin.org Web site.

For improved verification of the integrity of the downloaded source, many developers use digital signatures, providing a signed verification of the download. This signed verification will not match up if the download is later modified. This digital signature is created with a secret key owned by the developer. The public keys are usually available on the public key servers and are sometimes provided within the source tarball. Commonly, the signed verification is done using PGP or Gnu Privacy Guard (GPG).

Try It Out — Obtain a Digital Signature

You can use a digital signature to verify the MaraDNS package downloaded in the previous "Try It Out" example. This example will work only if the GPG software is already installed and set up. The MaraDNS download site also has a download for a GPG signature. The MaraDNS download included the public key (for this example it's at `maradns-1.0.23/maradns.pgp.key`).

1. First you need to extract the PGP key from the previously downloaded tar file:

```
bzcat maradns-1.0.23.tar.bz2 | tar xf - maradns-1.0.23/maradns.pgp.key
```

2. And retrieve the GPG signature for the bzip2 version of the downloaded source tar file:

```
wget http://www.maradns.org/download/maradns-1.0.23.tar.bz2.asc
```

3. To add that key to your own digital key ring, use the command:

```
gpg --import maradns-1.0.23/maradns.pgp.key
```

   Alternatively, you could use:

```
gpg --recv-keys 1E61FCA6
```

   where 1E61FCA6 is the key ID as identified with gpg.

4. Verify the downloaded file:

```
gpg --verify maradns-1.0.23.tar.bz2.asc maradns-1.0.23.tar.bz2
```

   The `.asc` file is the digital signature downloaded from the MaraDNS download page.

How It Works

The `gpg` tool checks your downloaded file against the public encryption key included in the original software package tarball download. If they are identical, the software is verified and is unlikely to be corrupted. If they're different, you could have a corrupted file, or worse, malicious code. Better to be safe than sorry, so do not open and install the software instead, contact the project developer immediately.

For detailed information, consult your GnuPG or PGP documentation.

Building and Installing

The normal steps for building and installing software are:

1. Extract the source code files to your build directory.
2. Go into the source code directory.
3. Configure the build for your system.
4. Run `make` to build the software.
5. Install software (as root if needed).

Assuming you have downloaded your software, you are ready for step 1, extracting the source code to your build directory.

Retrieving software downloads and building software from source should be done as a normal, nonroot user. Installing the software can be done as root, if needed. Of course, if you trust the software enough to install as root and later run it (or let other users run it), then you can probably trust the building steps too. Nevertheless, it is good advice to make a habit of using elevated privileges only for those tasks that truly need them. Also, if you are concerned about the build or later use of the software, you may want to consider creating and using a dedicated user for these steps.

Some common places to do builds are `/usr/src` for system software, `/usr/local/src` for extra software (sometimes referred to as third-party software or add-on software), or `${HOME}/src` for software installed for your own account. It's common to keep all source code under `~/src` and to extract the tarballs and do all the builds there. Keeping code in a central location makes for easier cleanup, and keeping files in your home directory is a nice reminder to do the extractions and builds as a normal, nonprivileged user.

If you have several administrators building and installing software, you may want to use a central place so they all can help, or use separate places so you don't conflict with each other's work. Some use dedicated user accounts for building software, which could help with organization, maintenance, and testing.

Extracting the Files

You can't use the tarball directly to install the software. First, you have to expand the compressed file to see the actual files it contains. The most common way to extract the source tar file is with this command:

```
tar xvzf source-download.tar.gz
```

The `tar` command works in a slightly different manner from other Unix commands. Specifically, tar's options do not use the hyphen. In this example, there are four options:

- `x`—Identifies a compressed file that needs to be extracted
- `v`—Invokes *verbose* mode, listing each file as it is expanded
- `z`—Decompresses the file in `gzip` format
- `f`—Defines the compressed file as `source-download.tar.gz`

If your Unix variant does not honor the `z` option, use this command to unzip files compressed with `gzip`:

```
gunzip -c source-download.tar.gz | tar xvf -
```

Some versions of tar support a `j` or `J` or `y` option that means to use `bzip2` compression. In addition, some versions of tar are smart enough to handle `bzip2` files when using the tar `z` option. (Have a look at your tar manual page for specific details.)

In most cases, the source tarball will be extracted in a subdirectory that uses the same name and version of the software as the directory name. For example, the `Mail-SpamAssassin-2.64.tar.bz2` tar file has all files within a `Mail-SpamAssassin-2.64` directory. Some ZIP or tar files will have all of the source at the top level of the file archive and may extract files to your current working directory (possibly overwriting files with same name). If you're concerned, you may want to view the filename list before extracting, or move the tarball into its own subdirectory before extracting it. You can view the files before extracting by using the tar `t` (table of contents) function.

Beginning the Build

After extracting the source code, go into the newly created directory (step 2). List its contents with the `ls` command. There are usually `README` and `INSTALL` files included. (Sometimes the names are slightly different, or they are located in a subdirectory, possibly called `docs` or `help`). Have a look at these files to find out about any prerequisite programs or libraries you may need, and also to get instructions on how to prepare your build, build the software, and install the results. These files can also be useful for doing simple configurations and getting started with the software.

Often the `INSTALL` *file is based on a premade template and is not specific for the particular software you want to install. If that's the case, you can use a standard build process like the one described in this chapter. If the* `INSTALL` *file describes a different process, use it because a standard process may not install such a program correctly.*

It's also a good idea to consult the Web site for the software. Unusual compilation or installation instructions can be found there, as well as answers to frequently asked questions about build problems.

Your goal is to configure the build process so that it properly detects your build environment and properly installs for your operating system. Sometimes, you may need to manually modify a makefile to define how you want the build and install done. The makefile is the file that dictates how the build is accomplished. Confusingly or not, a makefile is usually named `Makefile` with a capital M. You'll learn more about makefiles later in this chapter. Luckily, most modern software uses a script to help with this, rather than forcing you to configure the makefile by hand.

Using the Configure Script

To get the makefile in order, look for an executable called `configure` in the top-level directory of your expanded tarball. Run the `configure` script (step 3 in the build-and-install list) with this command:

```
./configure --help
```

Use the dot and slash at the beginning to identify the actual location of this script, because most likely your current working directory is not part of your `PATH` environment variable's value. (See Chapter 5 for more information about the `PATH` variable.) The `--help` option is self-explanatory. The output should list a variety of switches you can use when running `./configure` that will define how you want the code to be built and installed. For example, this is the output for a beta release of Blackbox window manager code:

```
$ ./configure --help
'configure' configures blackbox 0.70.0beta2 to adapt to many kinds of systems.

Usage: ./configure [OPTION]... [VAR=VALUE]...

To assign environment variables (e.g., CC, CFLAGS...), specify them as
VAR=VALUE.  See below for descriptions of some of the useful variables.

Defaults for the options are specified in brackets.

Configuration:
  -h, --help              display this help and exit
      --help=short        display options specific to this package
      --help=recursive    display the short help of all the included packages
```

```
  -V, --version           display version information and exit
  -q, --quiet, --silent   do not print `checking...' messages
      --cache-file=FILE   cache test results in FILE [disabled]
  -C, --config-cache      alias for `--cache-file=config.cache'
  -n, --no-create         do not create output files
      --srcdir=DIR        find the sources in DIR [configure dir or '..']

Installation directories:
  --prefix=PREFIX         install architecture-independent files in PREFIX
              [/usr/local]
  --exec-prefix=EPREFIX   install architecture-dependent files in EPREFIX
              [PREFIX]
By default, `make install' will install all the files in
'/usr/local/bin', '/usr/local/lib' etc.  You can specify
an installation prefix other than `/usr/local' using '--prefix',
for instance '--prefix=$HOME'.
...
```

The configure output also often lists other settings for selecting where specific files types will be installed, environment variables that can be defined, and different features that can be enabled or disabled.

If you prefer to use default values rather than figure out the appropriate options, just run `./configure` by itself. A configure script may help with many of the small details involved in building software, including:

- Finding an install tool
- Detecting AWK implementation
- Seeing how the `make` command works (the command used to perform the actual build)
- Checking for type of C compiler and C++ compiler
- Learning how to run the C preprocessor (`cpp`)
- Autodetecting your architecture and operating system
- Checking for various standard include files (headers)
- Determining whether to build shared or static libraries

The `configure` script may give you help with many more steps in detecting the building environment. See the "Tools to Help Create Makefiles" section in this chapter for more details.

A common option to set is `--prefix`, which defines where software should be installed. An install normally defaults to the `/usr/local` directory, and the software is configured during its build to reference files within that directory hierarchy. The files are installed in appropriate subdirectories, such as `/usr/local/bin/` for executables, `/usr/local/man/` for man pages, `/usr/local/share/` for text and data files, and `/usr/local/lib/` for installed libraries. Installing to `/usr/local` keeps the new program from overwriting your native system's files.

FreeBSD uses `/usr/local` *in its packaging system for installing third-party software, so under FreeBSD you may want to use a different* `--prefix`*. See Chapter 4 for more information about file system layout.*

Here's how you can use the `--prefix` option to install to your own home directory:

```
./configure --prefix=${HOME}
```

The build process could then make `bin`, `sbin`, `lib`, `man` and/or other subdirectories under your own home directory.

Many administrators install software to a directory named after the software, using an option such as `--prefix="/user/local/apache"` or `--prefix="/opt/gnome-2.6.2"`. In the first example, several subdirectories would be created: `/usr/local/apache/bin/`, `/usr/local/apache/conf`, `/usr/local/apache/modules`, and so on. The second example would install all the files under a `/opt/gnome-2.6.2` hierarchy. Some benefits of installing software to its own dedicated directory hierarchy are your capability to clean up easily, the ability to quickly see what's installed, and the option to install the same software multiple times (for simpler upgrades) by using different installation prefixes for each, such as using a version number.

Remember that if you install the executables to some arbitrary directory, they may not be available to run using your executable search path (discussed in Chapter 5). As a workaround, add the newly installed `/bin` directory to your `PATH` or use the full path to the command when running it. Ideas on how and where to install software are provided later in this chapter.

The normal successful completion of a configure script shows output that it created at least one `Makefile`. It may have other output, too, such as displaying how it was configured for your build.

It may take 20 seconds to several minutes to run a configure script.

Using make

After the `configure` script finishes successfully, you should have a new file called `Makefile`. Building and installing software is usually done with a command called `make`. (The next section in this chapter covers `make` in more detail.) In simple terms, `make` is used to create programs (as well as documentation, Web pages, and almost anything else) by making sure each component is up-to-date. It is useful for developers so they don't have to rebuild all the code when they only change one small file. (Other uses of `make` are covered later in this chapter.)

The two common `make` implementations are `GNU make` (also known as `gmake`), which is found on most Linux systems, and `pmake`. Several derivatives of `pmake` are maintained by the BSD operating system projects and are sometimes called `bmake`. Each of these `make` commands uses a standard syntax, but they also have various incompatibilities. In most cases, the `make` command provided with your system should work fine.

To continue with your build and installation, simply type **`make`** (step 4) at the command prompt. A variety of output will scroll by on the screen; most of it is `make` running the GCC compiler on each of the files.

The speed of your system and amount of code to compile can result in the build steps taking a few seconds to several hours. Some big projects such as GNU Libc, Koffice, and X.org may take more than a day to build on older computers. OpenOffice.org can take a week to build. Your best bet is to build a project on a Celeron 1000, AMD Mhz machine

When the `make` step completes successfully, it usually just exits without any obvious message. If there is a problem, `make` generally exits with the message `Error 1`. (Details about `make` and makefiles are discussed later in the chapter.)

Many software builds (such as GNU tar, PCRE, OpenLDAP, Ruby, and many more) also include a way to test the build before installing it, often by running the commands `make test` or `make check`. This can be useful in verifying that the software works correctly before actually installing and using it.

You might be able to run the new programs directly from the build directory to test before installing. In many cases, you can't do this because the programs have references to libraries, configurations, or other data that are not installed yet, and often the `make` step doesn't complete the build.

The normal final step (step 5) is to issue the command `make install`. This completes the build (if needed), creates installation directories, and copies over executables, configuration files, libraries, documentation, various data, and so on. Depending on where you chose to install the software, you may need to do this step with superuser privileges, such as:

```
su root -c "make install"
```

This command combines two elements. First, the `su root` component enables you to assume superuser powers, taking the option `-c` that informs the shell to run the command included at the command line. The second component is the command to be run as the superuser, `make install`. With this method, you have to provide the superuser password, but you don't have to log in and out in a separate action.

You may want to consider keeping a log of what you installed, sorted by software name, version, date, and purpose. You also may want to make a list of files installed.

Some installations will back up older, previously installed versions of the same filenames, but don't depend on that feature. Also, sometimes you have to run multiple installation targets to install extra components. See the installation directions to make sure. (The Lynx example installation later in this chapter shows an extra installation for documentation.)

When you are all done with the installation, you may want to remove your build directories to save disk space. Sometimes keeping them temporarily is useful for troubleshooting problems, but there's no reason to store tarballs for the long-term. You can always download them again.

Try It Out — Build a Program from Source Code

Now that you've seen the basic structure of a source code installation, it's time to give it a try. Follow these steps to install OpenSSL from the original source code on a Debian Linux system to your home directory.

OpenSSL provides tools and libraries for SSL and cryptographic support.

1. Under your home directory, create a directory (`src` in this example) in which you will build the software and then move into that directory:

    ```
    $ mkdir ~/src
    $ cd ~/src
    ```

2. Fetch the source code. Google and FreshMeat Web sites both lead to the `www.openssl.org` Web page. Use your Web browser to download the 2.7 MB `openssl-0.9.7e.tar.gz` version, unless a more recent version is available.

3. Extract the source code and go into the new directory:

```
$ tar xzf openssl-0.9.7e.tar.gz
$ cd openssl-0.9.7e
```

   The `tar v` (verbose) option is not needed; in this example it would list more than 1900 filenames as it extracts. The newly created directory is named `openssl-0.9.7e` and is 17 MB in size.

4. Use the `ls` command to find any files containing installation directions. (There are several `README*` and `INSTALL*` files.)

5. Use the `less` or `more` commands to read the files you found. The main `README` file says to read the `INSTALL` file to install `openssl` under a Unix derivative. The `INSTALL` file gives a quick guide for installation and also further details for the configuration. Available in the same directory is a FAQ (Frequently Asked Questions) that has ideas for troubleshooting various build problems.

You might have noticed that there are `config` *and* `Configure` *commands in the new directory, but no* `configure` *script (which is all lowercase). OpenSSL's build at this time doesn't use the standard* `autoconf` *configure system, but the method shown here behaves in a similar fashion.*

6. Following the `INSTALL` directions, run the `config` script with the `--prefix` switch:

```
$ ./config --prefix=${HOME}/openssl shared
```

   The build will be configured so the installation goes into an `openssl` subdirectory under your own home directory. The `shared` argument tells this specific script to build and install shared libraries. This `config` script detects your operating system, your hardware platform, and your environment's build tools; defines how the `openssl` libraries will be built; and makes sure that this local build is ready to go. The output may scroll by faster than you can read, but some status information is displayed when this step completes.

7. Start the build:

```
$ make
```

   Using the `Makefiles`' instructions, `make` jumps into various subdirectories and runs the compiler on various C files in order. On this particular AMD-K6 system with 256 MB of memory using `gcc 2.95.4`, this step took about 6 minutes.

8. To check the build before installing, run `make` with the `test` target:

```
$ make test
```

   This tests the SSL and TLS authentication, certification routines, hashing (like MD5 and SHA1) algorithms, private/public key generation, encryption and decryption ciphers, and more. (This may take a couple minutes to complete.)

9. Install the software. Remember that you chose to install it into your own home directory (as specified with the `--prefix=${HOME}/openssl` option during the config step), so you can continue with installation using your normal user account.

```
$ make install
```

How It Works

The installation step will create the necessary subdirectories and install more than 340 files totaling 7.6 MB. (This takes more than 2 minutes to complete.) Have a look at the new install:

```
$ ls -l ~/openssl
total 16
drwxr-sr-x    2 reed      reed          4096 Sep  7 11:00 bin
drwxr-sr-x    3 reed      reed          4096 Sep  7 11:00 include
drwxr-sr-x    3 reed      reed          4096 Sep  7 11:00 lib
drwxr-sr-x    7 reed      reed          4096 Sep  7 11:00 ssl
$ ls -l ~/openssl/bin
total 1264
-rwxr-xr-x    1 reed      reed          3656 Sep  7 11:00 c_rehash
-rwxr-xr-x    1 reed      reed       1283686 Sep  7 11:00 openssl
```

In this example, you built software without having the basic `configure` script available. Even though the regular `configure` options weren't available, OpenSSL provided an alternative configuration method that helped the software install properly.

Try It Out — Build Code That Requires a Prerequisite

In this example, you'll install Lynx, a popular Web browser and FTP client for text consoles. It uses the `autoconf` configuration system. Be sure to notice how this is configured to use OpenSSL, which you installed in the preceding example, for HTTPS support.

1. Move into your source building directory (`/src`, for this example):

```
$ cd ~/src
```

2. Find the source code for Lynx. The official Web site is `lynx.browser.org`. This example uses the latest development version downloaded with `wget`:

```
$ wget http://lynx.isc.org/current/lynx2.8.5rel.1.tar.bz2
```

3. Extract the source and go into the newly created directory:

```
$ tar xvjf lynx2.8.5rel.1.tar.bz2
$ cd lynx2-8-5
```

Notice the `tar j` option for using `bzip2` compression.

4. Look for any `README` or `INSTALL` files. In this case, Lynx provides a file called `INSTALLATION` that has the instructions. This version of Lynx has many build options.

5. Run `./configure --help` switch to see a list of the build options.

6. You must perform a special step to configure the Lynx build to install into your home directory and to use the previously installed SSL libraries:

```
$ LDFLAGS=-Wl,-R${HOME}/openssl/lib
$ ./configure --prefix=${HOME} --with-ssl=${HOME}/openssl -- \
libdir=${HOME}/share/lynx
```

   By default, the Lynx build does not know where to find the shared libraries because the installed location in your home directory is probably not in the default search path for shared libraries. Even when defining where it is located with `--with-ssl`, the `make` will error out.

7. Prepare for installation:

```
$ make
```

   This takes about 4.5 minutes on this build system.

8. To install the software, issue the command:

```
$ make install
```

   This installation routine backs up any existing Lynx binary by renaming it `lynx.old`.

9. You may want to install additional Lynx documentation, following the suggestions that print to the screen. Use these commands:

```
$ make install-help
$ make install-doc
```

The `install-doc` *is not needed; it provides samples and Web pages for testing Lynx and is used primarily by Lynx developers.*

How It Works

This is a pretty straightforward install, following the steps exactly. The only difference was the use of `LDFLAGS` (in step 6 of the preceding example) to tell `make` to compile in the location of the needed libraries. For example, the `--libdir` option tells Lynx where the configuration file and local documentation will be stored.

Use `ldd` to see that Lynx does, in fact, use your own `openssl` libraries:

```
$ ldd ~/bin/lynx
        libncurses.so.5 => /lib/libncurses.so.5 (0x40017000)
        libssl.so.0.9.7 => /home/reed/openssl/lib/libssl.so.0.9.7 (0x40055000)
        libcrypto.so.0.9.7 => /home/reed/openssl/lib/libcrypto.so.0.9.7
(0x40085000)
        libc.so.6 => /lib/libc.so.6 (0x40177000)
        libdl.so.2 => /lib/libdl.so.2 (0x40294000)
        /lib/ld-linux.so.2 => /lib/ld-linux.so.2 (0x40000000
```

The ldd tool is used to list the shared libraries needed to run a program. Notice that Lynx also detected `ncurses` (for console screen functions) in the native system and is using the shared library for it.

Run the newly installed Lynx by typing:

```
$ ~/bin/lynx
```

Introducing make, Makefiles, and make Targets

You don't need to know how `make` works to simply use it for compiling and installing software, but understanding `make` will help with troubleshooting and with porting software.

In addition to building software, `make` can also be used for managing Web sites and processing other documents. Its main purpose is to ensure that the individual components are up-to-date. For example, `make` is commonly used to compile many separate source code files and then to generate the final program. A developer would not want to compile each file in a project over and over again when working on just a single file. `make` helps solve this by only rebuilding the pieces that have been updated. The rules defining the steps needed are placed in a makefile (as noted previously, usually named `Makefile`).

As mentioned earlier in this chapter, there are several different types of `make`. They have some common syntax and usage but also offer their own incompatible custom features and configurations. On Linux systems, `make` is GNU Make. On BSD systems, `make` is a BSD Make usually called `pmake`, but also known as `bmake`. FreeBSD, NetBSD, and OpenBSD all maintain their own versions of the BSD Make, so they have slight incompatibilities. GNU Make (also known as `gmake`) can also be installed on BSD systems and is available via their package collections. You can also build and install GNU Make from source; get the files at `ftp.gnu.org/pub/gnu/make/`. On Mac OS X and Darwin systems, both `bsdmake` and `gnumake` are installed, and `make` is a symlink to `gnumake` by default.

Just to confuse you further, the `imake` *tool from XFree86 or X.org and* `qmake` *from QT are not* `make` *programs. They are used to generate makefiles, but perform no other tasks associated with regular* `make` *programs.*

Some projects require a specific version of `make`, but most makefiles are written in a portable, standard format. If you receive an error like this

```
Makefile:18: *** missing separator.  Stop.
```

when running `make`, it may mean that you are using a GNU Make and should use a BSD Make instead. However, if you see an error message like this

```
make: don't know how to make something. Stop
```

you should probably be running GNU Make instead of BSD Make.

It is a good rule of thumb to just use GNU Make because it is the most commonly used `make` *for open source projects.*

The Makefile

The syntax of a makefile can, at times, be very detailed and confusing. Basically, the makefile is made up of variable definitions and targets. A makefile can also have comments, which start with hashmarks (#).

As you learned in Chapter 5, variables are defined by assigning some value to the variable identifier. Commonly, variable names are all uppercase, but it is not required. There are several ways to define a value. Let's look at some of the common ones. Assigning a value with an equal sign, for example, means that the previous value is overridden:

```
SHELL = /bin/sh
```

You can append a value with plus-equal (+=) signs:

```
CFLAGS += -s
```

This also places a space before the new value. Spaces are ignored when assigning variables (but often make it more readable), so you could use `CFLAGS+=-s` to do the same thing.

If a variable is already defined, using question mark–equal (`?=`) ensures that it isn't redefined. In the following code line, for example, if `CRYPTO` is not already defined, this command sets its value to `yes` (otherwise it keeps its previous setting):

```
CRYPTO ?= yes
```

Variables are referenced by using `$(NAME)` or `${NAME}`. `make` uses a concept called expansion, where the value of variable is not figured out until it is referenced.

Define targets (also know as rules) by placing a keyword at the start of a line, followed by a colon. The following lines list shell commands to be used when processing that rule. Each of these commands must be indented with a tab (not spaces). For example:

```
showmetheday:
→@date +%A
```

The at sign (`@`) means to show the output but not print the command's name. (Chapter 11 has more details about the `date` command.) If you put this target in a makefile, and then ran `make` on a Friday, you'd get this output:

```
$ gmake
Friday
```

Usually, the main target is named `all` and is the first rule defined. The `install` target is also commonly used. You can choose to run a particular target and specify it at the command line, as in:

```
$ make showmetheday
Friday
```

Here's an example that uses BSD Make with a target that doesn't exist:

```
$ make whatever
make: don't know how to make whatever. Stop

make: stopped in /home/reed/tmp
```

Because the specified target doesn't exist, the `make` process exits with an error message.

A target can list other targets after the colon to have those dependencies done first. Take a look at the following makefile. It's a simple example of having rule dependencies and defining a variable on the same command line:

```
# This is an example Makefile
MYVARIABLE?=    alphabet soup

all: rule2
→@echo This is the "all" target.

rule1:
→@echo Hello from rule 1

rule2: rule1
→@echo $(MYVARIABLE)
```

Remember that those are tabs (indicated by right arrows) in the target bodies and not spaces.

Now run the process. Notice how it uses the top target as the default:

```
$ gnumake
Hello from rule 1
alphabet soup
This is the all target.
```

As you can see, it set the variable because the variable did not already have a defined value. Then `make` completed the first target, which had dependencies. You can also issue the `make` command choosing the target you want to run:

```
$ gnumake rule1
Hello from rule 1
$ gnumake rule2
Hello from rule 1
alphabet soup
```

The next example shows how to define a `make` variable by placing it on the command line as an argument to `make`:

```
$ gnumake MYVARIABLE="Unix is fun"
Hello from rule 1
Unix is fun
This is the all target.
```

You can also set the variable in this example in your Unix shell environment instead of using a make argument. (See Chapter 5 for more details on defining shell and environment variables.) For example:

```
$ MYVARIABLE=whatever
$ bsdmake rule2
Hello from rule 1
whatever
```

Here's another example of a target that doesn't exist:

```
$ gnumake help
gnumake: *** No rule to make target `help'.  Stop.
```

Although these examples are quite simple, make can be used to do a great deal. The make configuration syntax is basically a programming language. For example, it can do if/else conditionals, pattern matching and replacing, and a lot more. Normally, make is used to run GCC for compiling and linking software and then installing the software.

Tools to Help Create Makefiles

A popular suite of development tools is available to help create configure scripts and makefiles. These tools are often called auto tools, or the GNU Build System. Remember that the configure script is used to detect your build system environment to customize how the software is built and installed. The configure script generates a makefile or many makefiles from templates. The purpose of the configure script is so that you should never have to manually edit makefiles, simplifying the process and saving yourself a lot of time.

In most cases, as a software end-user, you do not need the auto tools. They are primarily used by the original developers. But sometimes you may have source code (such as prerelease software) that doesn't have the configure script or makefile templates. Auto tools can be of great help in getting such code to install properly. Here are some of the key auto tools:

- automake is the tool used to generate makefile templates, which are later used by configure to create the final makefiles. The original files are named Makefile.am. The templates generated by automake are then called Makefile.in.
- autoconf is the tool used to create the portable configure shell scripts. The input for autoconf is a configuration file called configure.ac or configure.in. The developer may also include add-on features for defining autoconf macros, usually named acsite.m4 and aclocal.m4. In many cases, a config.h.in file is used by configure to generate a config.h header file defining features or capabilities to be used during the build.

  In addition to makefiles, configure scripts also output config.status (a shell script that actually generates the makefiles and header files), config.cache (which records the results of the numerous configure tests), and config.log (which contains output and debugging information).

  Also related to autoconf and the configure scripts are the autom4te files config.guess (which figures out the exact hardware platform, operating system type and version) and config.sub.

- `libtool` is a tool to help create shared (and static) libraries in many different object formats using a variety of tools on various systems. It is useful for creating and installing portable and standardized libraries that can be utilized by unrelated projects.

  Files related to `libtool` include `ltconfig`, a script for generating the system-specific `libtool`; `ltmain.sh`, which provides the library building routines; and `ltcf-c.sh`, which is used by `ltconfig` to select the correct options and arguments for the the systems compiler when making libraries. Files ending in `.la` are `libtool` library files; they are plain text files that define many attributes of the related libraries.

Another software building tool that is getting more use is `pkg-config.`*, which provides meta-information about installed libraries. Learn more at* `www.freedesktop.org/Software/pkgconfig.`

Sometimes, you may find software that doesn't already include a `configure` script but does provide the `autoconf` files to generate one. Be sure to check the build instructions. The source may include an `autogen.sh` script that can be run to generate and then run the `configure` script. In other cases, you may need to run multiple `automake` and `autoconf` commands manually to create the `configure` script, as in this command sequence:

```
$ aclocal
$ autoheader
$ automake -a --foreign -i
$ autoconf
```

It is important to note that different versions of `automake` and `autoconf` are in use, so some features are not available or may be used but aren't supported. (For example, you may receive errors that indicate a given macro can't be found.) Again, be sure to read any build instructions (or ask the developers) to make sure you are using correct versions of `automake` and `autoconf`.

One of the problems with software using the auto tools system is that they include a lot of large pregenerated files that are sometimes difficult to modify. When new versions of `autoconf` and `automake` are released with improvements and fixes, already released software with pregenerated and old `configure` scripts cannot easily take advantage of these fixes. You may need to download newer versions of that software to take advantage of the new auto tools.

GNU Compilation Tools

When you install software from source code, part of the process involves compiling the code so that it's executable on your system. A wide range of compilers can be found to work with code written in almost any language. On Unix-based systems, however, you can get by with GCC and its associated compilation tools.

GCC is more than just the C compiler: It is the GNU Compiler Collection. The GCC suite includes support for C, C++, Objective C, Java, Fortran (F77), and the Ada language. GCC is highly portable and well used — nearly 100 percent of all open source projects using C or C++ use it. GCC can be used for cross-platform builds such as building software for different operating systems and/or hardware architectures using a different host platform.

GCC probably installed by default when you installed your operating system. If you don't have it or you want an updated version, see `www.gnu.org/software/gcc/gcc.html.`

The GCC tool is a front-end for controlling several other tools used in the compilation process, such as the cpp preprocessor, a compiler (like cc1 or cc1plus), an assembler, and a linker. Because gcc is a front-end to several tools, it has more than 500 command-line options that can be used with it.

The most commonly used assembler (the portable GNU assembler as) and linker (the GNU linker ld, which can be used to combine library archive files) are provided with the GNU Binutils suite. GNU Binutils also supplies tools for modifying libraries (ar), listing symbols (nm), displaying object file information (objdump), generating archive indexes (ranlib), and listing section sizes of object files (size). If you don't have Binutils, download it at www.gnu.org/directory/binutils.html.

The strip and strings tools are also provided with GNU Binutils. The strip command is used to strip out symbols such as debugging information from object files. It can be used to significantly reduce file sizes. The strings command is used by many Unix administrators for outputting the printable characters in files. For example, if you have some binary file or proprietary document format, you can filter it through strings to display just the human-readable content.

As mentioned in the previous section, automake, autoconf, *and* libtool *help set up the build environment for running* gcc *and* linker. *Building software and libraries can vary a lot between different Unix versions and, in most cases, a* configure *script and makefiles are available already so you don't have to figure it out.*

diff and patch

Some developers delay their official releases and only provide patches for recent security issues and bug fixes. Also, some projects provide updates in the form of patches to save bandwidth and time. Other developers provide patches for add-ons, new features, or other improvements for projects that they don't maintain themselves. Knowing how to use patch and diff can be very helpful in these situations. diff is the command used for comparing files; its output is called a patch. The patch command can use this diff output to modify a file (or several files).

The cmp *command can also tell you whether files are different, but* diff *is more useful because it tells you how they are different and provides information that can be used to recreate the differences.*

For example, to view the differences between two files, use the command diff old.file new.file, as in:

```
$ diff motd.orig motd
5,7c5,6
< Please note that the library will be closed on Saturday for
< construction. Any books can be put in the box outside. Videos
< due on Saturday will have their due dates extended for two days.
---
> Student Board Elections begin next week. Be sure
> to vote on Tuesday or Wednesday!
```

The less-than sign (<) means that the line is in the first file (motd.orig) but not in the second file (motd). The greater-than sign (>) means that a new line was added to the second file.

Commonly, patches are created using the diff -u switch for unified output. Many users consider unified output to be easier to read:

Unified output is another representation of the changes between two files. Perhaps the most significant difference between `diff` *and unified output is that unified output provides the context. Some developers prefer unified output for distributing patches because of some irregularities that can occur with* `diff`*. There is an excellent reference for gnu diff utilities at* `www.kcl.ac.uk/humanities/cch/ma/courses/acmtls/gnu/diff.html` *(nearly 80 printed pages).*

```
$ diff -u motd.orig motd
--- motd.orig   Mon Sep 27 10:21:14 2004
+++ motd        Mon Sep 27 10:21:07 2004
@@ -2,8 +2,7 @@

 Welcome to the University Shell System!

-Please note that the library will be closed on Saturday for
-construction. Any books can be put in the box outside. Videos
-due on Saturday will have their due dates extended for two days.
+Student Board Elections begin next week. Be sure
+to vote on Tuesday or Wednesday!

 To get help on using this system, type "help" and press Enter.
```

As you can see, the `-u` switch adds more context by including the lines that precede and follow the changed content. Lines beginning with a minus sign are only in the original file, and lines beginning with a plus sign were added to the new file.

If you need to view the differences between many files, some of which are contained within subdirectories, use the command `diff -ruN directory1 directory2`. The `-r` switch causes `diff` to recursively compare subdirectories. The `-u` switch causes output to print in the unified format. The `-N` option allows `diff` to compare files that don't exist in the other directory (by having it act as an empty file for the other directory).

There are many options for `diff` *output. Be sure to read the* `diff` *manual page for more details.*

The output of `diff` includes line numbers to indicate where the changes are located. The `patch` command can use the `diff` formats to update files, and even to create new files. The normal way to use `patch` is to go into the directory containing the files to be patched and then run `patch` with the `diff` file output (the patch) as its standard input. The `patch` tool also has other useful options, such as the capability to save the original files before patching them in case of a problem.

Installation Techniques for Better Maintenance

The main problems with installing software from source include cleaning up old files, upgrading to new versions, runtime configurations, remembering build steps and build configurations, and keeping track of dependencies. Dependencies occur when a program requires functionality provided by other software. For example, `psmerge` (a tool for merging Postscript files from the `psutils` project) is a Perl script. It has a dependency — a need — for Perl to be installed on the machine.

The more difficult situations occur when the dependencies are shared libraries. A lot of GNOME software uses GConf libraries, for example, but some versions of GConf are incompatible. If you upgrade GNOME-related software, the new packages could break because of a wrong version of a required library. Alternatively, if you upgrade GConf, you could break GNOME. You might think that it's only one dependency and would be easy enough to fix. However, depending on the GNOME software, you may have more than 60 different dependencies! Keeping track of software can get a lot more difficult.

One technique is to have all the software for a particular project installed to a directory that's named for the software and version number. For example, for `configure`-using builds, you can use the command `./configure --prefix=/opt/`*`name-version`* to have it install to `/opt/`*`name-version`*. Then you can upgrade different dependencies without overwriting anything, because the same software will be installed to different directories based on the version numbering. You can upgrade any programs that use the components by using `./configure` switches (and environment variables) to tell the builds where their dependencies are located.

This technique is very useful for software used constantly in production environments. You can have your Apache Web server running in `/usr/local/httpd-2.0.49/bin/httpd`, for example, and then configure a new build to install to `/usr/local/httpd-2.0.51`. Modify the configurations under `/usr/local/httpd-2.0.51/conf/` (based on the old configurations), and you can easily switch back and forth for testing and then for real production use. It is also very useful to install software packages to their own directories when you need to copy to other systems, so you don't have to build from source again. Just tar up the directory, transfer it to the other machine, and unpack the files into the same directory hierarchy.

You can also use symbolic links, or symlinks, to populate a `bin` directory (such as `/opt/bin` or `/usr/local/bin`) and man directories in your `PATH` so you (and your users) can easily run the commands and use the man pages:

Symbolic links were discussed in Chapter 4.

```
$ cd /opt/foo-1.2.3
$ for file in bin/* sbin/* man/*/* ; do ln -sf /opt/foo-1.2.3/$file /opt/$file;
done
```

In rare cases, you may have identically named files provided from different projects, so you may have to employ the full path names to use the correct versions.

If you want different versions of the same software to use the same configuration directory, you may be able to use the `configure` option `--sysconfdir` to point to the correct path. Be aware that, in some cases, a new installation may overwrite your configurations; in many cases, newly installed configurations may break your currently running software because of new features and incompatibilities.

Software using `configure` scripts and the GNU Build System can often be installed to a different location than the default destination by using the `DESTDIR` variable. For example:

```
# make install DESTDIR=/tmp/abc-3.4.5
# cd /tmp
# tar cvzf abc-3.4.5.tar.gz abc-3.4.5
```

(You would replace `abc-3.4.5` with the software name and version.)

In this example, the installation process places all the files into a separate directory, which is then tarred up to be reused on other systems or for reinstalling on the same system.

In many cases, paths are hard-coded into executables or documentation and other files, so the software should ultimately be installed to the same location as defined with the `configure --prefix` option.

Troubleshooting Build Problems

This book can't possibly list every single error or problem with building and installing software from source. You can have disk space errors, out-of-memory errors when building, wrong switches used with `gcc` for building libraries, incompatible libraries, missing headers, and numerous other problems. Here's an example of a failed configure step:

```
checking for iconv_open... no
checking for iconv_open in -liconv... no
configure: error: Blackbox requires iconv(3) support.
```

An error like that can mean several things: A library is actually missing, `configure` is looking in the wrong place for the library, `configure` detected it wrong, or the process failed elsewhere during its `iconv` detection. When you receive errors from a `configure` script, it is often useful to look at the new `config.log` file.

When you find error messages, it is a good idea to search your favorite search engines and Google Groups (`http://groups.google.com/advanced_group_search`). In most cases, someone else has already had the same or similar problem — and hopefully it's already solved.

Also, check the project's build FAQ, usually found on the project Web site, or consult the project's appropriate mailing list for assistance. When using a mailing list, be sure to explain clearly what your final goal is, what specific versions of related software you are using, what steps you followed, what the exact error messages or problems are, and what other steps you took to troubleshoot the problem. Including all this information makes it more likely that someone can help you.

Precompiled Software Packages

Often it is easier and less time-consuming to just install precompiled software packages as provided by your operating system vendor (or packages provided for your operating system). Packages are ready-to-use software bundles for individual projects or programs. A package usually contains the executables, sample or basic configurations, documentation, and supplementary data files. Packages also contain metadata that gives information such as a brief description of the package, who or where it was built, what it provides, and what packages it depends on (if any). Package systems usually provide tools for installing software, automatically installing prerequisite packages, displaying packages installed, listing available packages, displaying file lists, removing packages, retrieving packages, verifying installed files, providing package security notifiers, and a lot more.

Numerous packaging systems and techniques are available. Two of the most commonly used in the open source community are RPM and Debian's DPKG format. RPM previously stood for Red Hat Package

Manager, but now it is the recursive acronym, RPM Package Manager. The RPM tool and RPM-style packages are available for many operating systems, such as Mandrakelinux, SUSE, and Fedora Core. This system is also used by OpenPkg. The RPM tool is available for all Unix systems. DPKG format is primarily used with Debian GNU/Linux and Debian derivatives. Historically, the problem with RPM was that automatic updating of dependencies was weak. Debian provides a tool, `apt-get`, that has been very useful for installing and cleanly updating packages. It has been extended to work with RPMs also. (Red Hat and other systems using RPM also use Yum, Up2date, and other update systems.)

The Fink program on Mac OS X is a front-end to `apt-get` *as well as a collection of software organized into sections, much like the ports collections mentioned in the following paragraph. The Fink software collection includes patches to ease the installation process on Mac OS X, automating the application of diffs and correcting various paths to libraries, which differ on Mac OS X from the locations on other Unix systems. For more information about Fink, check the project's home page at* `http://fink.sourceforge.net/`.

The BSD operating systems provide build-from-source package systems. FreeBSD and OpenBSD call theirs ports, and NetBSD maintains `Pkgsrc` (package source). These are directories of specifications and descriptions of numerous software suites. (FreeBSD provides specifications for more than 10,000 different software suites, representing hundreds of thousands of files.) `pkgsrc` is a portable package building system for Linux, NetBSD, Darwin, Mac OS X, Irix, SunOS/Solaris, AIX, HPUX, BSD/OS, FreeBSD, Windows (with Unix add-ons), and other Unix-like operating systems. These build systems basically automate the entire build-from-source system with many functions:

- Fetch source code and any patches
- Verify source code against prerecorded digest checksum
- Recursively install any build or runtime dependencies
- Patch the source code as needed
- Configure the source code for the particular operating system
- Build the source
- Install the software and related files
- Create packages (tarballs plus metadata) to use elsewhere or for reinstallations

Some operating systems like Gentoo Linux use similar build-from-source systems. Build-from-source systems can be quite slow compared to using the prebuilt, ready-to-use packages, but still can save a lot of time over building from pure code. For example, to install KDE from FreeBSD ports without any prerequisites installed could take a few days on many systems.

It is often a bad idea to mix and match software built from source and from packages to solve dependencies, especially when you force a package to install (using RPM's `--nodeps`*, for example) when a packaged requirement is not installed. This is because some of the requirements or features provided with a package may not meet the other software's needs.*

Let's take a quick look at how to use the RPM tool to first check for the software you want and then install a package that's been downloaded.

Try It Out Use RPM

1. Type in the following at the command line:

```
$ rpm -qa | grep mysql
mysql-server-3.23.58-9.i386
```

   Depending on your individual setup, you will get either some output showing which version of MySQL you have on your machine or, if you don't have it at all, nothing.

2. To install a new version of MySQL, download the relevant RPM package from the MySQL site (via `http://dev.mysql.com/downloads/mysql/5.0.html`) and save it to a folder of your choice.

3. Issue the following command

```
$ rpm -Uvh MySQL-server-5.0.2-0.i386.rpm
Preparing...           ######################## [100%]
1:mysql-server    ######################## [100%]
```

That's pretty much it! It is installed!

How It Works

There's a lot you can do with RPM; consult the man page for more information. In this exercise, the `-qa` option got RPM to query all the installed package files, and then the output was piped to `grep` so that it could search for anything containing the string "mysql." This simply demonstrates a different method for using RPM.

Next, RPM was used to install a new version of MySQL from the RPM package. Notice the`-Uvh` options, which are most commonly used when installing with RPM. The `U` updates RPM to the latest version, `v` makes the output verbose, and `h` causes a row of hashes to be printed to track progress.

Be aware that RPM fails if there are dependency conditions that are not met during the installation. For example, if your new version of MySQL depends on another package that isn't already installed, the installation won't be successful. Having to keep track of everything's dependencies and versions can get pretty tedious, and it is recommended that you look for tools that can help with automating updates and so on. For example, Yum, which comes as a standard feature of the Fedora Core (`http://fedora.redhat.com/`), automatically figures out not only the RPM packages that need updating, but also all the supporting RPMs — and installs them all.

Summary

Building software from source is a common method for installing software on Unix-type systems. For many programs, it is the only way, because ready-to-use, already-built software may not be available. Also, many timely security updates or other software fixes are often available only in source code form. The most important things to learn how to do in building software from source:

- Finding and downloading source code files
- Extracting source code archives

- Locating and reading the build and installation instructions
- Configuring the build scripts and/or specifications
- Building the software
- Installing the software
- Cleaning up the build files

The skills used to build and install software from original source code can be used on a wide variety of Unix systems.

Exercises

1. On your Unix-based system, you need a program to fetch your IMAP-based e-mail. After searching using your favorite search engine, you decide on installing Fetchmail.
    a. Download the Fetchmail source.
    b. Extract the source tarball.
    c. Read the installation (from source) directions.
    d. Configure the build.
    e. Build the Fetchmail software from the source.
    f. Install Fetchmail to your system from this completed build.
    g. Extra credit: Configure Fetchmail to retrieve your e-mail.
2. You need to install a simple Web server that will be rarely used. You decide to use the `inetd`-based `micro_httpd`.
    a. Locate and download the source code for `micro_httpd`.
    b. Extract the source tarball for `micro_httpd`.
    c. Review the installation instructions.
    d. Build the software using `make`.
    e. Manually copy the man page and the new executable into place.
    f. Extra credit: Configure `inetd` or `xinetd` to run `micro_httpd`.

Conversion: Unix for Mac OS Users

Apple has provided a graphical user interface (GUI)-based operating system for its users since the introduction of the Macintosh computer in 1984. While much has changed under the hood between 1984 and today, the current version of the Macintosh operating system, Mac OS X, provides the user with a GUI interface that is quite elegant and powerful, while retaining a friendly almost childlike simplicity on the outside. Underneath the candy-coated interface, however, is a completely different engine. While a proprietary engine powered previous iterations of the Macintosh operating system, Mac OS X is powered by Unix.

This chapter aims to discuss the changes to the operating system with two different audiences: long-time Macintosh users who are getting started with Mac OS X/Unix as well as Mac OS X users who are interested in other Unix systems. This chapter uses Mac OS X as its reference Unix platform, as it is most likely that Macintosh users who are still using classic versions of the operating system will soon upgrade their systems to Mac OS X, either on their current computers or certainly when purchasing new equipment. Additionally, the information in this chapter will prove useful to long-time Unix users who are interested in working with Mac OS X.

A Very Brief History of Mac OS X

The Macintosh operating system was due for a serious overhaul by the end of the 1990s. Apple had attempted to create a new version of the Macintosh operating system that was to be called Copeland, which would bring desirable modern features to the long-in-the-tooth Mac OS 7. This effort proved to be more of a challenge than it had initially appeared to be, and eventually Apple made the decision to go outside the company and purchase the new OS. There was a brief flirtation with the BeOS, which was produced by Be Inc. — a now-defunct corporation founded in 1991 by Jean-Louis Gassée and Steve Sakoman, both former Apple executives. This plan ended up being scrapped in favor of NeXT Software, a company run by another former Apple executive, Steve Jobs. Apple purchased NeXT Software for approximately $400 million, around the end of 1996. NeXT was a company that manufactured computers from the late 1980s thru the early 1990s. NeXT went on to sell its operating system (NeXTStep, and later OPENSTEP) as well as WebObjects software for x86, HP, and Sun hardware for several years after getting out of the hardware business.

When the first NeXT computer was shipped in 1998, it was a technical marvel. It ran on a 33 Mhz Motorola 68030, making it faster than any existing Macintosh- or Intel-based PC on the market. It boasted a clean, elegant GUI that straddled a Unix core. This system was targeted at the education market and was the first PC system to include a networking feature, and leverage the power of network communications. The system was priced at $6000 base, about twice the cost of existing Macintosh or PC computers at the time. The cost was a major factor in the lack of market penetration for the beautiful black hardware.

The public beta of Mac OS X was released in 2000, and version 10.0 was released in 2001. From the early days of Rhapsody (the code name for the public beta), it was clear to many that Apple had a strong contender on their hands. The operating system retained the visual elegance commonly attributed to the NeXTStep system, while keeping its Macintosh look and feel. There were several apparent differences between this Mac OS and previous versions, such as a dock on the desktop and the absence of the familiar trash can on the desktop (it had been moved to the dock). However, for the most part, excepting the addition of eye candy in the form of the all new Aqua interface, the system was visually similar to prior versions of the Macintosh operating system. Of course, the visual similarity was about the only thing this version of the Mac OS had in common with the prior versions. Included with version 10.0 was software called Classic. Classic is an application that, when launched, executes a software-based Macintosh emulator. The user could have both MacOS 9 and Mac OS X installed on a hard drive, and using Classic could launch the previous version of the operating system and run applications designed for that system. Early users relied on this functionality to run older versions of their software while they waited for the software to be released in Mac OS X native versions.

Today, Mac OS X leads the charge of Unix-based desktop systems, shipping more Unix-based desktop systems than all other Unix vendors combined. For the majority of users of these systems, the Unix underpinnings are all but invisible, providing increased stability and performance improvements, without any penalty in complexity or in any way changing the perception that Macintosh systems are "easy to use" and "just work." Hardware and software integrate with the same plug-and-play simplicity that Macintosh users have come to admire and expect.

Differences between Mac OS 9 and Mac OS X

There are many differences between the previous versions of the Macintosh operating system and Mac OS X; most of these differences are under the hood, so to speak, and are invisible to users who restrict their usage of the system to the GUI. However, several of the fundamental changes to the underlying system manifest themselves in ways that distinctly change the experience of working with a Macintosh system, besides simply reducing the frequency of system crashes or the need to restart the computer.

The most important distinction between the two systems is that Mac OS X is a multiuser operating system, whereas Mac OS 9 was truly a single-user OS. Like all other Unix systems, the concept of multiple users pervades all areas of working with Mac OS X. Even in a situation where you are the sole user of the computer, and it is not connected to any network, there are still multiple accounts present on the system. The accounts are added at installation time for various system daemons, which provide for privilege separation and accounting. An example of such a user is eppc, the remote AppleEvents service; and at install time a user named eppc is created. This user has neither a shell nor home directory (home directories are discussed later in this chapter). However, eppc exists for logging and other purposes. Additional pseudo-users exist for postfix, cyrus, lp, mailman, MySQL, qtss, smmsp, sshd, and the catchall daemon and unknown accounts.

Additionally, differences exist in the organization of folders on the hard drive. Whereas previous versions of the Macintosh operating system were quite flexible and forgiving regarding the names and locations of folders on the hard drive, Mac OS X has stricter requirements on folder placement, especially at the root level of the boot hard drive, where the operating system is installed.

The other major difference between Mac OS X and previous versions of Mac OS involves administrative activities and privileges. Because Mac OS 9 and below were single-user systems, there was no restriction placed on accessing files and folders or on making changes to the system configuration. As long as you had access to the computer, you could make whichever changes you desired. Mac OS X has a stricter security model, where privileges are granted to an administrative user who can delegate or grant access to files and folders as well as change system settings. Additionally, as a result of the presence of multiple users on the system (or the possibility that there might be more than one physical user), system-wide settings and preferences are becoming less common. Whereas Mac OS 9 and earlier had a single preferences folder where application settings would be stored, you will see that Mac OS X has preference settings for each user on the system.

Folders Are Directories Too

Historically, the Macintosh OS has presented groups of files nested in a directory to the user as folders. This has been part of the visual metaphor of the Macintosh OS since the origination of the operating system. The Finder in Mac OS X also uses folders and refers to them as such. However, in Unix operating systems, folders are usually referred to as directories. This stems from the command-line origination of Unix, where there was no need for the iconic reference. While working with Mac OS X, you will see references to both folders and directories. Both are correct, and neither is any more or less accurate than the other. You can use whichever terminology you are comfortable with. Generally you will use folder when referring to Finder-based views of your files, along with other GUI-based operations, and will use the term directory when referring to terminal and other command-line operations.

The major difference between Mac OS X (and Unix in general) and Mac OS 9 with regard to folder and directory navigation is in the command-line interface. Many users of previous versions of Mac OS have used AppleScript or other scripting languages to navigate the file system. For those users, folders were separated by a colon (:), as in `Macintosh HD:System Folder:Preferences`. Unix and Mac OS X use the forward slash (/) character as a delimiter, as in `/Users/craigz/Desktop`. Additionally, when using classic versions of the Mac OS, file path names would begin with the volume label, as in the following example: `Macintosh HD:Users:craigz:Desktop`. However, Unix has its own way of referring to the boot volume, and that is the forward slash (/) character. Hence, the same example in Mac OS X would be `/Users/craigz/Desktop`. These differences are of no issue when using Finder to navigate the file system, although they become quite important when using the terminal to navigate the file system, or when working on other Unix systems, as the colon-based navigation generates error messages. Keep in mind that, while on Unix, everything falls under the common root directory (which is termed `/`), and which is the leading character in all path names. On Mac OS X, different hard drives can have different labels, such as Macintosh HD and HardDisk. Finder displays additional volumes on the desktop, however, in Terminal, additional volumes are located in a hidden directory: `/Volumes`.

Required Folders

In classic versions of the Macintosh operating system, only one folder is required for the system to boot properly: the System folder. In fact, you could remove most of the contents of a System folder, leaving only the files Mac OS ROM, Finder, and System, and a classic Mac OS machine would boot normally, albeit in a depreciated state. Mac OS 9 has traditionally been quite flexible regarding folder names and locations. In developing Mac OS X, Apple has imposed a bit more organization upon the structure and naming of folders, especially at the root level. This is mostly out of necessity, because a Unix-based system requires certain things to be organized in a certain way. You will find that this does not cause much practical difference in the way you work with the system; however, you will need to be aware of this difference.

In Mac OS X, there are four permanent folders created at installation time. These folders are created when you install Mac OS X, and you are unable to move, delete, or rename these folders, because they are essential to your machine's operation. These folders are Applications, Library, System, and Users, as shown in Figure 20-1.

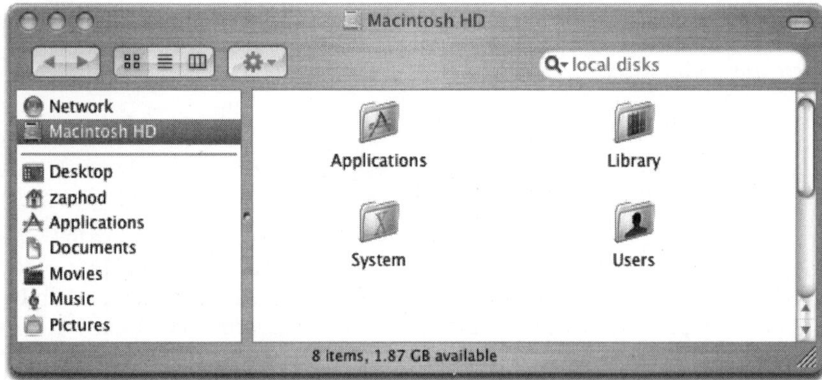

Figure 20-1

There are several other folders installed at installation time that are either Unix-specific or are related to network functionality, such as Network, Volumes, and the standard Unix folders such as etc, bin, sbin, tmp, usr, and var. These files are hidden from display by the program Finder, because they are generally not necessary for day-to-day use, and not displaying them keeps the frustration and confusion level to a minimum. For a complete list of the folders that are present on the boot drive, but are invisible to Finder, consult the file `.hidden`*, which is at the root of your boot volume. This file is also hidden from Finder, because Finder (like the Unix command* `ls`*) does not show files or folders named with a period as the first character.*

The following sections describe these folders as well as explain their purposes.

Applications

The Applications folder is designated to hold applications. All applications installed by Apple as part of the Mac OS X installation are installed in this folder. All applications in this folder are available to all users on the system. If you wish to limit the usage of a specific application to a single user, then install that application in the Applications folder within that user's home directory. The home directories are discussed later.

Within this folder is a folder called Utilities, where Apple installs applications of a utility nature at the time Mac OS X is installed. Examples of Utility software are the Disk Utility, Print Center, Installer, Console, Activity Monitor, Network Utility, NetInfo Manager, Console, and Terminal Applications, along with several other programs that can be used to configure, monitor, and maintain various aspects of your system.

Library

The Library folder is loosely equivalent to the Preferences folder contained within the classic Macintosh System folder. The Library folder is an example of the modular nature of Mac OS X. There is no formal requirement or definition for the contents of this folder. Application preferences, fonts, printer drivers, shared code libraries, and items of an informational nature (generally informational to the system) are all the types of files that are stored in the Library folder. In fact, there are three different locations where Library folders exist on a Mac OS X system. This location at the root of the boot drive contains files that are accessible to all local users on the system and that can be modified only by a user with administrative rights on the system. Additional Library folders exist in the System folder discussed later, as well as in User home directories also discussed in a later section. Files in the Library folder of a user's home directory are only available to that user.

System

This folder is roughly equivalent to the System folder on a classic Macintosh system. This folder contains a single folder called Library. This folder contains folders that are similar to those in the main Library folder, discussed previously; however, this location is reserved for Apple software and should not be modified. If there is any folder on the computer that screams "Hands Off!" it is this folder. While an administrative user can make changes to files in the System folder, it is highly advisable to avoid doing so, as it is quite likely that Apple will make changes to files in this directory over the course of software updates, so any changes to files in this directory could be overwritten at any time.

Users

The Users directory is probably the most significant change to the operating system from the point of view of a user. Previous versions of the Macintosh operating system have included various stabs at multiple users but have never come close to the Unix standard of multiuser operating system that is embodied in Mac OS X. Mac OS X is a truly multiuser system, as discussed in the beginning of this chapter.

Each file and folder on a Unix system belongs to a specific user and group. The user who creates a file is considered to be the file's owner, and, as the owner, the creator can decide whether other users can read or edit that file. Furthermore, each file or directory belongs to a group, which is similar to the owner, except that where an owner can only be a single individual, a group can contain more than one member. When Mac OS X is installed, two groups are created by default. These groups are staff and admin. All users created on the system are members of the group staff. Users granted administrative rights, either when the system is installed or at a later time, are added to the group admin. By setting files or folders to be accessible by one or the other of these groups, you can control access to those files to these classes of users. To further refine access to your files and folders, you will need to create groups and assign users to those groups. For a more detailed discussion of users and groups in Unix, please refer to Chapter 3. The Users directory is the location where all users' home directories are located on the system.

Other Folders

Also the folder Developer will be present if the Developer Utilities have been installed. Additionally, if Mac OS 9 is installed on your system, you will see several folders that relate to that operating system. These folders are:

- **Applications (Mac OS 9)** — This folder is where applications written for the classic Macintosh OS are installed. If you have upgraded your system to Mac OS X, you will find your previous applications in this folder.
- **Desktop (Mac OS 9)** — This folder contains the desktop folder from classic versions of the Macintosh OS. If you have upgraded your system to Mac OS X, you will find your previous desktop items in this folder.
- **System Folder** — This folder is the System folder from classic versions of the Macintosh OS. The application Classic will use this folder to boot the emulator.

Home Directory

Your home directory is the place on your computer where everything is personal. Everything in this folder is yours and yours alone. This is the place where you can customize everything to your heart's content and rest assured that whatever you do will not affect either the normal operation of the machine, nor other users' experience with the system. Your desktop and all the files and folders contained on your desktop reside in a folder called Desktop in your home directory. You can install your own fonts in the Library folder and they will be unseen by other users on the system. This folder is most like the top-level Macintosh HD on Mac OS 9 and older versions of the Macintosh OS. In this folder you can create folders to your heart's content, you can name files anything you like, and you will never be interrupted by an authentication dialog.

Apple has made a great effort to help you keep things organized throughout the system in Mac OS X. Your home directory comes prepopulated with several folders that have been created by default at the time your account was created. Most computer users create and use similar types of files, which could be loosely typed as multimedia. Apple has created several folders as recommendations for where to keep such common file types as music, movies, and pictures. Additionally, there is a catchall folder called Documents, which could be used for any and all files. The contents of a user's home directory are visible to only that user, with the exception of the Public and Sites directories described later. Any files in the Sites directory can be viewed with a Web browser, if the Web server is enabled on the local system. The purpose of the Public directory is to make files available to other users on the system and to network users if file sharing is enabled.

These folders that are installed by default are shown in Figure 20-2 and are described in the list that follows.

- **Desktop** — The files and folders in this directory are what you see on your desktop. This folder has always been present on Macintosh computers; however, in the past it had been rendered invisible by the Finder.
- **Documents** — This folder exists as a place for you to store documents and other things you create. It exists as a suggestion and need not be used if you do not wish.

- **Library** — This folder contains contents that are similar to those in the other Library folders you have encountered. Files in this folder are private and are available only to the user whose home directory the folder is in. This is where personal preferences, fonts, screensavers, and so on are stored. If you wish to make items accessible to all of the users on the system, they should be kept in the Library folder at the top level of the hard drive instead.
- **Movies/Music/Pictures** — These directories are used as the default locations to save media files by the various iLife applications (iMovie, iTunes, and iPhoto), and are a suggested location for you to save similar types of files. You can ignore these folders or create folders within them, whatever makes the most sense to you.
- **Public** — If you wish to share files with other users on your system or on a network, you can place those files inside the Public folder within your home directory. Additionally, there is a folder called Drop Box in this folder. Other users can put files in this folder for you but are unable to see the contents of this folder for themselves. This is referred to as a *blind drop*, because it preserves your privacy by not allowing others to see the contents within the Drop Box folder.
- **Sites** — Mac OS X includes the Apache Web Server software. If the Web server is enabled, anything in this folder is served to Web clients. Your sites folder is visible at the following URL: `http://`*`your-ip-address`*`/~`*`username`*, where *`your-ip-address`* is your computer's IP address and *`~username`* is your username (for example, `http://192.168.1.20/~craigz`).

Although these folders have been installed by default, you can do anything you like in your home directory; you can use or ignore all of these folders. You can create additional folders in this directory and name them anything you wish.

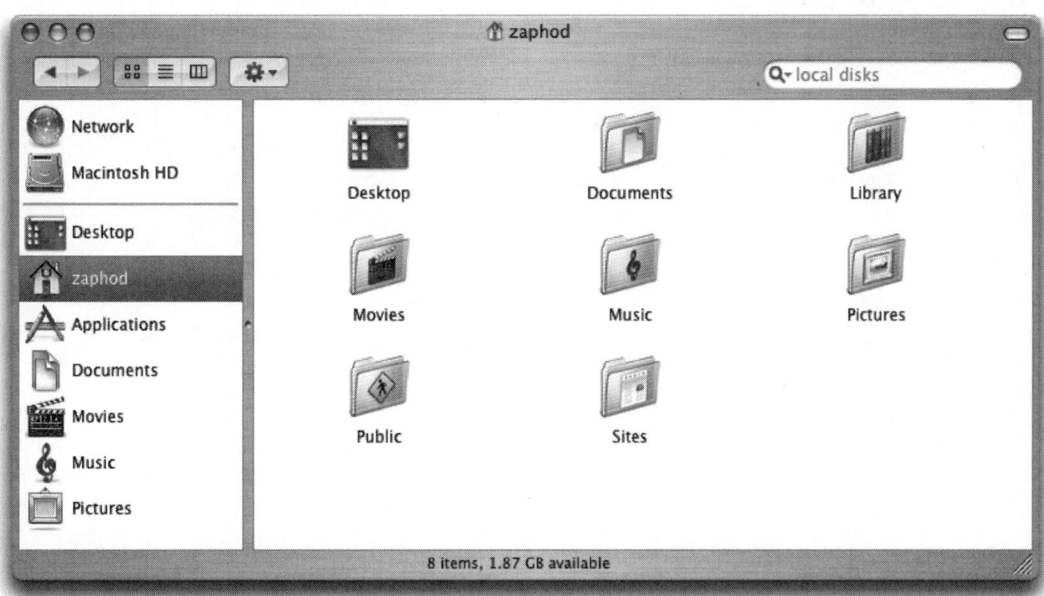

Figure 20-2

Administration

Again, the single largest change between previous versions of the Macintosh OS and Mac OS X is that classic versions of the operating system provided what was fundamentally a single-user system. That meant that by having access to the computer, you could really do just about anything. You could change settings such as network settings, configure printers, set up file sharing, and see and change all files and folders located anywhere on the computer. Due to the multiuser nature of Mac OS X, there are many more restrictions as to what system settings you can change.

Apple uses the concept of role-based administration. Rather than require a specific account to be used for administrative functions, the system allows for any authorized user to authenticate to the system to perform maintenance tasks and other privileged functions. By default the initial user created at the time of system installation is authorized to do this; however, that user can designate this authority onto any other user he or she wishes in addition to himself or herself.

When you open most of the system preferences panels, you will see a lock icon on the lower left of the window. In order to make changes to that setting, you are required to authenticate by entering the name and password of a user with administrative privileges, as is shown in Figure 20-3.

Figure 20-3

Most traditional Unix software is configured by editing configuration files, some requiring administrative access to change; Mac OS X applications are traditionally GUI-based, and each application generally provides a Preferences menu item in the Application menu. By setting preferences in the GUI, the application is thus configured. Preference files are discussed in the next section.

Preference Files

Applications typically store user-specified values that refer to settings, default behaviors, and other user-specific information in a text file on your hard drive. The application can later refer to this text file to look up the values that have been previously set when it is required, rather than to require the users to make their desired customizations with each application launch.

Classic versions of the Macintosh operating system have historically saved these files in a special location called the Preferences folder within the System folder on the hard drive. Historically, preference files have been binary data files, which were not human-readable, or even editable without the use of specialized software (ResEdit, for example). Mac OS X has changed both the format of these files and their location.

Mac OS X applications utilize plain text files that are composed of values associated with a key. These key/value pairs are stored in specially formatted files called Property Lists, which are created with the file extension .plist. Property List files organize data into named values and lists of values. These files are then formatted into XML, which allows for a uniform means of organizing, storing, and accessing data.

These .plist files serve the same function as preference files under Mac OS 9; however, by standardizing the file format, it is possible to use either a text editor to edit these files, as well as to use applications that can parse XML to provide a simpler way of editing these files. Apple provides a GUI-based tool for the editing of .plist files as part of the Developer Tools, called Property List Editor, which is located in `/Developer/Applications/Utilities` if the Developer Tools package has been installed. Contrast this with the procedure required to edit Mac OS 9 preference files, which would involve hex-editing the preference files using the ResEdit application and determining the format chosen by each individual vendor.

Unix and Mac OS X/Mac OS 9 Command and GUI Equivalents

Mac OS X provides a command-line interface to the system in the form of the Terminal application. Many actions that can be performed in the Mac OS GUI can be performed by a Unix CLI command. The following table shows how to convert from a Mac OS 9 (or earlier) GUI command to the equivalent Mac OS X GUI action, what the equivalent Unix command is, a short description of the command, and what chapter the command appears in.

On a standard Macintosh keyboard the Command key is marked with an Apple logo and a cloverleaf symbol. This key is commonly referred to as the Apple key; however, Command is more commonly used, and the Apple key is referred to as the Command key in the following table.

Mac OS 9 GUI Action	Mac OS X GUI Action	Equivalent Unix Command	Description	Chapter
Select file in Finder and select Get Info from File menu, or press **CMD + I**	Select file in Finder and select Get Info from File menu, or press **CMD + I**	`chmod`	Modify file attributes	Chapter 6
Use Finder to open folders	Use Finder to open folders	`cd`	Change directories	Chapter 4
Look at title bar of window	Look at title bar of window	`pwd`	Show current working directory	Chapter 4
Disk First Aid	Disk Utility	`fsck`	Scan hard drives for errors in files, scan for damage, and perform other administrative tasks	Chapter 4
CMD + D	**CMD + D**	`cp`	Copy a file	Chapter 6
Option + click on menu bar clock on top right of screen	Click on menu bar clock on top right of screen and select Open Date & Time	`date`	Change the date	Chapter 11
CMD + DELETE (a single file)	**CMD + DELETE** (a single file)	`rm`	Delete or remove a file	Chapter 6
CMD + DELETE (a folder)	**CMD + DELETE** (a folder)	`rm -R`	Delete the files and directories recursively	Chapter 6
Double-click a folder icon	Double-click a folder icon	`ls`	Show the contents of a directory	Chapter 4
SimpleText	TextEdit	`vi` (many others exist, vi is the one that is most likely to exist on the system)	Perform text editing on a file	Chapter 7
N/A	Select Log Out from the Apple Menu (**Shift + CMD + Q**)	`exit`	Terminate the shell	Chapter 2
Drive Setup	Disk Utility	`fdisk`	Partition hard drives	Chapter 4

Mac OS 9 GUI Action	Mac OS X GUI Action	Equivalent Unix Command	Description	Chapter
CMD + F	**CMD + F**	`grep` (the Unix command `find` only looks at filenames not inside the files)	Search files for words given as an argument	Chapter 8
Select Help Center from Help menu in Finder	Select Mac Help from Help menu in Finder	`man`	Show online help files	Chapter 2
Select TCP/IP from Control Panels menu in the Apple Menu	Select Network Pane in System Preferences Application	`ifconfig`	Display and modify network interface (shows IP address as well)	Chapter 16
N/A	Activity Monitor	`vmstat` (Solaris), top, free (Linux)	Display memory statistics	Chapter 14
CMD + N	**SHIFT + CMD + N**	`mkdir`	Create a directory	Chapter 4
Drag folder to new location	Drag folder to new location	`mv`	Move a file	Chapter 4
N/A	LoginWindow	`who`	Display information about current users logged into the system	Chapter 3
N/A	Activity Monitor	`netstat`	Display network statistics	Chapter 16
N/A	Network Utility	`nslookup`	Perform a hostname lookup	Chapter 16
N/A	Network Utility	`ping`	Transmit network packets to defined host	Chapter 16
CMD + P	**CMD + P**	`lpr`	Print named file	—
Select file then press **Enter**	Select file then press **Enter**	`mv`	Rename a file	Chapter 4
Select as List from Finder view menu, then select description bar to sort by that description	Select as List from Finder view menu, then select description bar to sort by that description	`sort`	Arrange data either alphabetically or numerically	Chapter 8

Table continued on following page

Mac OS 9 GUI Action	Mac OS X GUI Action	Equivalent Unix Command	Description	Chapter
N/A	Network Utility	`traceroute`	Display network routes to defined host	Chapter 16
Option + click on Disclosure Triangle next to folder icon in Finder's List View	Option + click on Disclosure Triangle next to folder icon in Finder's List View	`ls -R`	Recursively list directory contents	Chapters 4, 6
Open the item with the corresponding program	Open the item with the corresponding program	`cat`	Show the contents of a file or directory	Chapter 6
Select About This Computer from the Apple Menu	Select About This Mac from the Apple Menu	`uname -a`	Shows information about the current operating system version	—

Differences between Mac OS X and Other Unix Systems

As you are well aware, Mac OS X is a Unix-based system. This is of great benefit to everyone, from those who will never look at the Terminal application nor ever enter a single CLI command to the system (who will benefit from the increased system stability and software availability) to those long-time Unix users who will be able to enjoy the fruits of Apple research and development for the first time. Mac OS X is a great platform upon which to learn to use Unix, and most of what applies on a Mac OS X system will be transferable to other Unix systems, such as those that may be found at an ISP, workplace, or other location.

While the core of the Mac OS X system is a FreeBSD variant, there are many things that are quite different between Mac OS X and other Unix systems. The most important of these differences is apparent in the area of system administration, specifically with regard to account creation and maintenance and system startup.

Directory Services and NetInfo

Mac OS X inherits the concept of directory services from its predecessor NeXTStep. Because NeXTStep was designed from the beginning to be a network-centric operating system, there were hooks in each client system to consult a centrally located network resource for issues regarding authentication, access to resources, printer configurations, and so forth. Each system could act alone or as a network client, based on a local configuration, because each system had the NetInfo database and could be configured to be either a standalone database or to act as a client of a NetInfo database running on another host.

While current versions of Mac OS X still use NetInfo, Apple is moving away from this proprietary database, and toward open standards such as LDAP, using OpenLDAP.

The impact of directory services is that the traditional `/etc` files (passwd, group, protocols, etc.) are not consulted by the system during normal operations. In rare cases, such as booting to single-user mode for maintenance purposes, these files may be consulted, but this would be in a skeletal form, not the way the system would be found in a production environment.

Traditionally, a Unix administrator would look to files in the `/etc` directory to either check how the system is configured or to make changes. For example, the file `/etc/group` contains a list of groups on a standard Unix system, and if you wish to add a user to a group, this file can be directly edited, the user added to a line in the file, and the change is done. To make changes to a group on Mac OS X, the change must be made to the NetInfo database. This can be done by a GUI-based application provided by Apple called NetInfo Manager, which is shown in Figure 20-4.

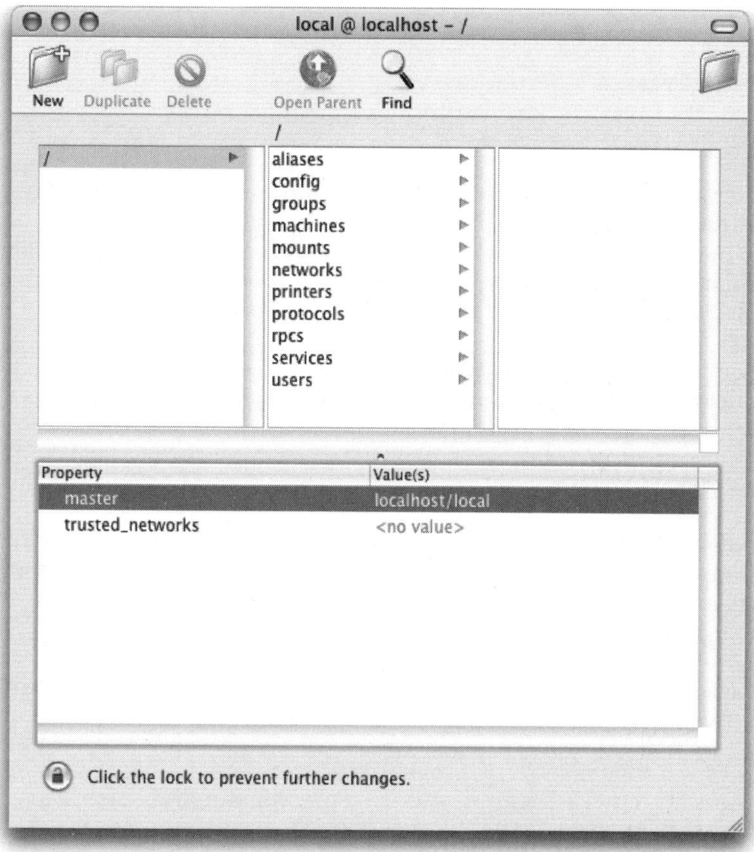

Figure 20-4

Apple also provides a command-line interface to the NetInfo database, which can be used to list, add, edit, and delete any entries in the NetInfo database.

In a standard Unix installation, configuration files are stored in the `/etc` directory. Mac OS X also has an `/etc/directory` populated with the standard files. However, unless a configuration change is made to directory services, these files will be consulted only in single-user mode and will be ignored during regular system use.

The standard Unix text files are referred to as *flat files* in the parlance of Mac OS X. If you wish to work with information stored in NetInfo via flat files, you can use the utility nidump to export the data from NetInfo to the corresponding flat file.

Using nidump and niload

For example, if you wish to create an `/etc/passwd` file using existing account information, you can type the following command sequence:

```
$ sudo nidump passwd . > /tmp/passwd
$ sudo mv /etc/passwd /etc/passwd.old
$ sudo mv /tmp/passwd /etc/passwd
```

The first step creates an appropriately formatted password file in the `/tmp` directory. To be safe, make a copy of the existing `/etc/passwd` file in the second step, then in the last step replace the old `/etc/passwd` file with the newly created file. The period (`.`) character in the first command refers to the NetInfo domain being manipulated, where the period refers to the local domain, rather than the root domain, which is referred to using the forward slash (/) character.

Conversely, you can use the utility niload to take data from flat files and import it into the NetInfo database. To import data from a standard password file located at `/tmp/passwd.txt` to the NetInfo database, you can issue the following command:

```
niload passwd . < /tmp/passwd.txt
```

Prior to importing data from a flat file to the NetInfo database, you should edit the file and ensure that there are no duplicate UID or GID entries, that the shell is pointing to an existing shell on your system, and that the home directories are in the `/Users` directory, as if you have brought this file over from another system; generally, home directories would be in the `/home` directory.

To see a complete list of the kinds of data that can be imported or exported with the niload and nidump utilities, issue the `nidump` command on its own as follows:

```
$ nidump
usage: nidump [-r] [-T timeout] {directory | format} [-t] domain
known formats:
    aliases
    bootptab
    bootparams
    ethers
    exports
    fstab
```

```
group
hosts
networks
passwd
printcap
protocols
resolv.conf
rpc
services
```

The known formats refer to the flat files typically found in the `/etc` directory on Unix systems, such as `/etc/passwd`, `/etc/group`, `/etc/hosts`, and so forth. These files are of a standard format, which Apple refers to as a *known format*. This functionality makes it extremely easy to import users and other common resources from another Unix system into a NetInfo database, and to export such information to other systems. An example of the usefulness of this is such that, on many large networks there will be a common hosts file that is distributed to all systems to aid in host name resolution. In order to get that information into a Mac OS X NetInfo database, the file can be loaded using niload, and the known host-file format can be referred to as hosts.

Backup and Restoration of the NetInfo Database

As you can gather, there is a wealth of critical information stored in the NetInfo database. For the system to function properly, it is imperative that this database is functional. For this reason, the database is backed up daily by the `cron job /etc/daily`. The file `/var/backups/local.nidump` is the backup that is created by the `cron job /etc/daily`.

For more information on NetInfo, check the man pages for niutil, nidump, and niload and download the document "Understanding and Using NetInfo" from: `http://docs.info.apple.com/article.html?artnum=106416`.

For more information on Open Directory, check the following page: `http://developer.apple.com/documentation/Networking/Conceptual/Open_Directory/Chapter1/chapter_2_section_1.html`.

System Startup

Chapter 2 discussed the boot process of a Unix system, the scripts that run when the system starts up, and how services are launched. Mac OS X follows a similar bootstrap process to that of a standard Unix system; however, it keeps things organized a bit differently. In fact, the startup process in Mac OS X is probably the greatest difference between it and other Unix systems.

When the machine is powered on, the computer is under the command of the firmware, which is like the BIOS on a standard PC. The firmware, after completing its job, hands control of the system to the BootX loader, which is responsible for bootstrapping the Mach microkernel, `mach_kernel`. Next, the device driver subsystem, I/O Kit, is initialized, and then the root file system is mounted. Following these actions, `mach_init` is loaded; `mach_init` is responsible for housekeeping within the mach microkernel. Finally, the BSD init process is fired up and given PID 1, as is standard in Unix systems.

The system at this point is fully booted, with all defined startup services launched, and is ready to accept interactive logins.

> *By default the system boots in a graphical mode, where very little information is displayed on the screen. If you want to watch the boot process in detail, for either troubleshooting or for informational purposes, boot the system into verbose mode by holding* ***CMD + V*** *while powering up the system.*

While other Unix systems use the files in the `/etc/rc.d` or `/etc/init.d` directories as startup scripts, and will use the file `/etc/inittab` to direct the init process in loading processes at boot time, the Mac OS X startup process is completely different than that of other Unix systems, as described previously. Startup items are processed from the `/System/Library/StartupItems/` and `/Library/StartupItems` directories.

Services that are installed by Apple as part of the Mac OS X installation are installed in the `/System/Library/StartupItems` directory. Like all the things in the System directory, these files are not meant to be changed, because those changes can be discarded the next time the Software Update application is run if Apple has overwritten these files. There is a Startup Items folder in the Library folder, where locally installed services can be configured to start on system boot. The `/Library/StartupItems/` folder can be used for any local services.

For more information on the I/O Kit, visit `http://developer.apple.com/hardware/iokit/`.

For more information on the Mac OS X boot process, visit `http://developer.apple.com/documentation/MacOSX/Conceptual/BPSystemStartup/Concepts/BootProcess.html`.

File Structure Differences

Historically the Macintosh has used what is referred to as a forked file structure to store files on the system. All files created on a Macintosh using the classic version of the operating system had two forks: a data fork and a resource fork. There was no requirement to use both forks, and many programs would save all their data into the data fork. The resource fork was used for data such as icons, fonts, and similar additional information.

Windows and Unix files consist of only one fork, the data fork. Mac OS X has mostly done away with resource forks, although it retains compatibility with the older file format. Applications in Mac OS X store their resources differently, and documents no longer require resource forks.

One of the challenges of working with Mac OS X files from the terminal by using the traditional Unix utilities mv and cp is that the resource forks can be unlinked from the file when using these tools to copy or move the file. Apple provides the tool ditto (`/usr/bin/ditto`) that can be used to copy files from the command line while preserving the resource fork. Additionally, if the developer tools are installed, the tools MvMac and CpMac are installed in the `/Developer/Tools` directory.

For a further explication of resource forks on the Macintosh, consult this page online at Wikipedia: `http://en.wikipedia.org/wiki/Resource_fork`.

Root User Account

The account root is disabled by default in Mac OS X. It is preferable to use the sudo utility described in Chapter 12 to perform administrative tasks. If you find yourself in a situation where a root shell is required, it can be obtained by executing the command `sudo /bin/bash`, or `sudo /bin/tsch` depending on your preference. If you wish to enable the root account for interactive use, you can do so by setting a password for the account by issuing the command `sudo passwd root`, then going to the NetInfo Manager and enabling the root account by selecting Enable Root User from the Security menu, as shown in Figure 20-5.

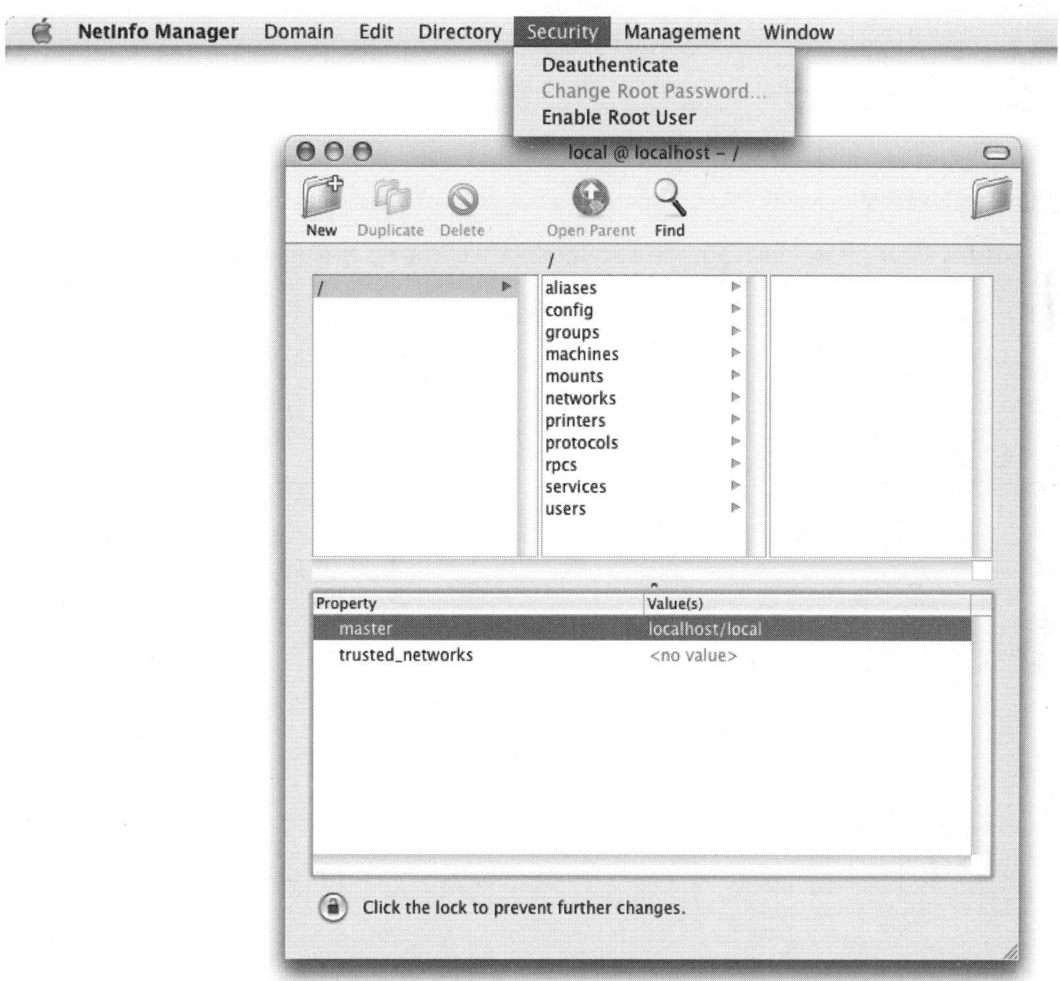

Figure 20-5

You can then log in to the root account by three different methods:

- Use the traditional `su -`.
- Enter the command `sudo su -`.
- Change the setting for "Display Login Window as:" to "Name and Password" in the Login Options section of the Accounts Panel of System Preferences. Then log out and enter root for the username with the password you set for root.

The first two options allow you to issue commands as root in a Terminal window, while the third option provides you with a fully interactive root login, complete with a desktop and a dock. Remember that when using the first command, you will have to enter the system root password; while using the command in the second example, you would enter the password for your own account.

Summary

This chapter discussed issues that are specific to Apple operating systems, including Mac OS X, the current Macintosh operating system, which is Unix-based. The chapter covered the history of Mac OS X, discussed the differences between Mac OS 9 and Mac OS X, and discussed the differences between Mac OS X and other Unix systems.

Exercises

1. You want to export your Mac OS X users to a `passwd` file for use on another Unix system. How do you do this?
2. You want to install an application that is available only to a single user on your system. Where do you install the application so that it not accessible by other users?

Conversion: Unix for Windows Users

Microsoft Windows is generally the first operating system most people encounter due to its large share of the desktop/personal computer market. Most users who learn Unix do so after they have gained an understanding of the MS-DOS/Windows environment. This chapter shows you the similarities between Unix and Windows/DOS, making the transition easier for you if you are converting to Unix from a version of DOS or Windows XP (most of these commands will work in Windows 2000 and some will work in Windows 98).

Structural Comparison

There are some fundamental differences in methodology between Windows and Unix, specifically in their file systems. In Unix, the / (slash) represents a separator and is used with commands to indicate a new directory level; in Windows, the \ (backslash) is used for the same purpose. For example, to `cd` (change directories) to the `/var/log` directory in Unix, you would type:

```
cd /var/log
```

In MS-DOS/Windows, you could navigate to the c:\windows\system directory by typing:

```
cd c:\windows\system
```

In Unix, the two directories in the preceding command are `var` and `log` (the `log` directory being subordinate to the `var` directory in this example) as noted by the / separator. The leading / (called *root*) is the top-level directory and is where all other directories start in Unix. The Windows directories are `windows` and `system` (`system` being subordinate to the `windows` directory in this example). The `c:\` indicates the starting point of this particular file system.

Windows has a different type of top-level directory (analogous to the root directory in Unix) usually called the `c:\` directory, which tends to be the top-level directory for the file system. Other devices such as second hard drives, network drives, floppy diskette drives, CD-ROM drives, and

USB key drives are often put in their own top-level directory equivalent to `c:\`. For instance, the typical Windows system uses `a:\` to represent the first floppy diskette drive and `d:\` for the CD-ROM drive, and all of these directories are equivalent to the `c:\` in that they are at the same level in the file system.

In Unix, the `/` is the uppermost directory, and there are no equivalents. Secondary devices such as CD-ROM, USB, and floppy diskette drives are subordinate to the `/` (root) directory and usually can be navigated through the `/mnt` directory. So a floppy drive in Unix might be under `/mnt/floppy`, a CD-ROM drive under `/mnt/cdrom`, and so on (the mountpoint, described in Chapter 4, differs among the various Unix implementations). A second hard drive also would be subordinate to the `/` (root) directory and would typically be attached (mounted) to the system usually in the /mnt directory.

MS-DOS/Windows is not case-sensitive when it comes to its file systems; the filename `TESTFILE.txt` is the same as `TestFile.TXT` and `testfile.txt` to the system. You could type any one of these variations or others and it would still refer to the same file. This is not true in Unix, which is case-sensitive. The file `TESTFILE.txt` would be a completely different file than `TestFile.TXT`, and `testfile.txt` would be another completely different file in the system. This applies to directories as well, so you must be cognizant of capitalization when referring to files and directories.

The Administrator account in Windows is almost equivalent to the root account in Unix. In Unix, the root (also referred to as the *superuser*) account can do anything on the system, whereas the Windows Administrator account may be prevented from performing some tasks that would damage the system.

The Windows operating system often tries to protect users and administrators from themselves by preventing them from making mistakes such as trying to remove a critical system file or deleting a file in use on the system. For instance, if the Administrator tries to delete `c:\windows\explorer.exe`, he receives an error such as the one shown in Figure 21-1.

Figure 21-1

In Unix, you can set up the `rm` command to provide a similar functionality (by setting an alias for `rm` to `rm -i` in the user's shell, as discussed in Chapter 5), but by default the system carries out the deletion or performs the function requested with no prompting.

Windows' Recycle Bin, which is used to "undelete" files, does not have an equivalent in most Unix systems, although similar functionality is implemented within many of the Graphical User Interfaces for Unix. Linux KDE, Solaris GNOME, CDE windows managers, and Mac OS X Aqua, for example, do include a Recycle Bin equivalent component, but most command-line Unix shells do not provide a way to "undelete" files.

In Unix, if you try to delete `/bin/sh` as the root user, the system deletes it without hesitation. Unix assumes that if you are logged in as the root user and you know what you are doing, even if you completely wipe out the system, while Microsoft Windows attempts to protect the system as shown in Figure 21-2.

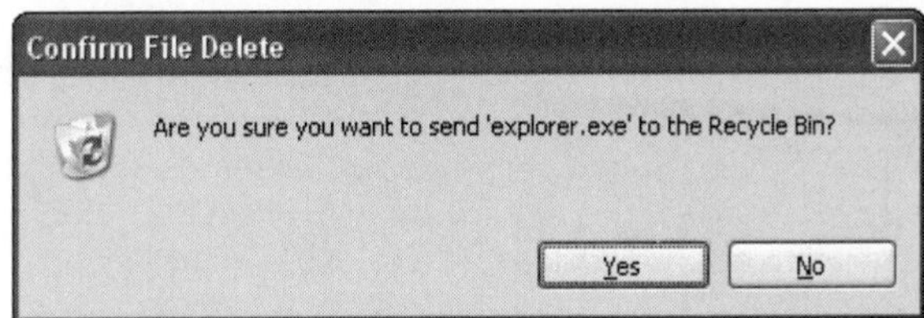

Figure 21-2

Windows provides an MS-DOS interface to the system. To access it, press **Win + R** keys to display the run dialog in which you type **cmd**. The following table shows how to convert from a Windows/DOS command line, how to perform the action in the Windows GUI, what the equivalent Unix command is, a short description of the command, and the chapter in which the command is discussed.

Windows/Dos Command	Windows GUI Sequence	Unix Command	Description	Chapter
`at`	Use Task Scheduler (found in the Control Panel)	`at` or `cron`	Run a command at a certain time	Chapter 11
`attrib`	**Alt + Enter**	`chmod`	Modify file or directory attributes	Chapter 4
`cd`	Use Windows Explorer to navigate directories in left column	`cd`	Change directories	Chapter 4
`chdir` or `cd`	Look in left section of Explorer bar or at title bar of window	`pwd`	Show current working directory	Chapter 4
`chkdsk`	chkdsk (`c:\windows\system32\cchkdsk`) or press **Win + R** and type **chkdsk** in the Run dialog's textbox	`fsck`	Scan hard drives for errors in files and damage, and performs other administrative tasks	Chapter 4
`cls`	**Win + D**	`clear`	Clear the screen	—
`copy`	**Ctrl + C** while file is selected and **CTRL + V** to put file in new location	`cp`	Copy a file	Chapter 6

Table continued on following page

Windows/Dos Command	Windows GUI Sequence	Unix Command	Description	Chapter
`date` and/or `time`	Double-left-click the time at the bottom right hand corner of the screen	`date`	Show the date	Chapter 11
`del` or `erase`	Delete	`rm`	Delete or remove a file	Chapter 6
`rmdir /S`	Delete	`rm -R`	Delete the files and directories recursively	Chapter 6
`dir`	Use Windows Explorer to show contents	`ls`	Show the contents of a directory	Chapter 4
`echo`	N/A	`echo`	Display output following echo command	Chapter 4
`edit` or `edlin`	**Win + R** then type **notepad** in the dialog's textbox	`vi` (many others exist, vi is the one that is most likely to be on the system)	Perform text editing on a file	Chapter 7
`exit`	**Alt + F4**	`exit`	Terminate the shell	Chapter 2
`fc` or `comp`	N/A	`diff`	Look for differences between two files	—
`diskpart` or `fdisk`	**Win + R** then type **diskmgmt.msc**	`fdisk`	Partition hard drives	Chapter 4
`find`	**Win + F**	`grep` (the Unix command `find` looks only at filenames, not inside the files)	Search files for words given as an argument	Chapter 8
`help` or *`command`* ?	**F1**	`man`	Show online help files	Chapter 2
`ipconfig`	Network Connections (found in Control Panel)	`ifconfig`	Display and modify network interface	Chapter 16
`mem`	**Ctrl + Shift + Esc** then select the processes tab	`vmstat` (Solaris), `top`, `free` (Linux)	Display memory statistics	Chapter 14

Windows/Dos Command	Windows GUI Sequence	Unix Command	Description	Chapter
`mkdir`	Right-click, New, Folder	`mkdir`	Create a directory	Chapter 4
`more`	N/A	`more`	Show output one page at a time (instead of scrolling)	Chapter 6
`move`	**Ctrl + X** while file is selected and **Ctrl + V** to put file in new location	`mv`	Move a file	Chapter 4
`net session`	**Win + R**, then type **fsmgmt.msc**	`who`	Display information about users currently logged into the system	Chapter 3
`netstat`	**Ctrl + Shift + Esc**, then select the Networking tab	`netstat`	Display network statistics	Chapter 16
`nslookup`	No equivalent in GUI	`nslookup`	Perform a hostname lookup	Chapter 16
`path`	**Win + Break**, select the Advanced tab, Select Environment Variables button adjust PATH variable	`echo $PATH`	Show the directory and order for executable files	Chapter 4
`ping`	No equivalent in GUI	`ping`	Transmit network packets to defined host	Chapter 16
`print`	Ctrl + P	`lpr`	Print named file	—
`prompt`	N/A	Varies depending on shell in use	Modify the prompt at the command line	Chapter 5
`rename`	Select file then press **F2**	`mv`	Rename a file	Chapter 4
`rmdir`	Delete	`rmdir`	Remove a directory	Chapter 4
`set`	**Win + Break**, select the Advanced tab, select Environment Variables, and view System Variables	`set`	Show environmental variables	Chapter 5

Table continued on following page

Windows/Dos Command	Windows GUI Sequence	Unix Command	Description	Chapter
`sort`	Select description bar in Windows Explorer to sort by that description	`sort`	Arrange data either alphabetically or numerically	Chapter 8
`tracert`	No equivalent in GUI	`traceroute`	Display network routes to defined host	Chapter 16
`tree`	Explorer will show this by selecting the icon	`tree` or `ls -R`	Recursively list directory contents	Chapter 4
`type`	Open the item with the corresponding program	`cat`	Show the contents of a file or directory	Chapter 6
`ver`	**Win + Break**	`uname -a`	Show information about the current operating system version	Chapter 2
`xcopy`	**Ctrl + C** while directory is selected and **Ctrl + V** to copy directory in new location	`cp -R`	Recursively copy all the files in named directory	Chapter 6

Major Administrative Tools Comparisons

The Unix and Windows operating systems can perform similar functions or have files that perform similar functions. This table identifies the Windows administrative tools and their equivalent in most Unix systems.

Windows File or Command	Unix File	Description
`autoexec.bat` and `config.sys`	`/etc/init.d` or `/etc/rc.`*`number`*	Related to system boot
`C:\Documents and Settings\`*`username`*	`/home/`*`username`* or `/export/home/ `*`username`*	User space on the system for personal files
`C:\Program Files`	`/opt` (by tradition but different depending on Unix)	Default location for storing file installations

Windows File or Command	Unix File	Description
C:\windows\explorer.exe or C:\windows\system32\cmd.exe	/bin/sh, /bin/ksh, /bin/csh, etc.	The shell for the system
C:\Windows\system32 and C:\Windows\system	/etc, /bin, /sbin etc.	Holds all files critical to system operation
C:\Windows\System32\Config	/etc	Configuration files for the system
C:\Windows\System32\Spool	/var/spool	Printing information
C:\Windows\Temp	/tmp	Storage area for temporary files
Event View (Control Panel - Administrative Tools)	/var/adm/messages (may differ on different Unix systems)	To view system generated messages
Network Connections (Control Panel)	/etc/hostname.*interface_name*, /etc/hosts, /etc/resolv.conf, /etc/nsswitch.conf, /etc/nodename,	Used to setup the network connections
Performance Monitor (Control Panel, Administrative Tools)	top, netstat (commands)	Monitoring the performance of the system
Scheduled Tasks (Control Panel)	/var/cron/crontab and /var/cron/at (may differ on different Unix systems)	Setting up programs to run at a specified time
Services (Control Panel, Administrative Tools)	/etc/inetd.conf and /etc/services	Setting up available services on the system.
User Accounts (Control Panel)	/etc/passwd and /etc/shadow	Setup for user accounts

Popular Programs Comparison

Many programs frequently enjoyed by Windows users have counterparts in Unix, and often these Unix programs are free. The following are some of the more popular programs in Microsoft Windows and their Unix equivalents.

Windows Program	Unix Program	Included with Unix?
Internet Explorer	Mozilla Firefox (`http://mozilla.org`), Netscape Navigator (`http://netscape.com`), Safari (included with Mac OS X), Konqueror (`http://konqueror.org`)	Sometimes
Microsoft FrontPage	Quanta Plus (`http://quanta.sourceforge.net`), NVU (`http://nvu.com`), Netscape Composer (with Netscape Navigator; `http://netscape.com`) and OpenOffice.org (`http://openoffice.org`) includes a Web editor as well	No
Microsoft IIS	Apache (`http://apache.org`)	Sometimes
Microsoft Money or Quicken	GnuCash (`http://gnucash.org`), MoneyDance (`http://moneydance.com`)	No
Microsoft Office	OpenOffice (`http://openoffice.org`), KOffice (`http://koffice.org`), GNOME Office (`http://gnome.org/gnome-office`)	Yes
Microsoft Outlook	Ximian Evolution (now under Novell, `http://novell.com/products/desktop/features/evolution.html`)	No
Notepad or WordPad	Vi	Yes
PGP	GnuPG (`http://directory.fsf.org/gnuPG.html`)	Sometimes
Photoshop	GNU Image Manipulation Program (GIMP) (`http://gimp.org`)	Not always
telnet	telnet	Yes
Winamp	XMMS (`http://xmms.org`)	No
Winzip or PKZIP	tar and gzip	Yes
WS FTP	GFTP (http://gftp.seul.org)	Sometimes

This is by no means a comprehensive list of the software available for Unix; most Microsoft Windows programs have a Unix counterpart. The following sites are large archives of Unix software that can assist you in finding the software you need:

- **Sourceforge** — `www.sourceforge.net`
- **Freshmeat** — `http://freshmeat.net` (heavily slanted toward Linux, but software for other Unix systems is available)
- **Free Software Foundation** — `www.fsf.org`

- **SunFreeware** (Sun-specific) — `www.sunfreeware.com`
- **Apple** (Mac OS X–specific) — `www.apple.com/support/downloads`

There are other locations to find software for your version of Unix, and you can use your favorite search engine to discover them.

Using Unix within Windows

You may find that you want to dabble in Unix, but you still need to maintain your Microsoft Windows environment, or you may want to see what Unix is about before totally giving up your Microsoft Windows system. There are multiple ways to do this through free software and commercial software. The following list below offers a few of the many examples:

- **VMWare** (`www.vmware.com`) — This program allows you to run multiple operating systems inside of the host operating system (which could be Windows). It emulates another system within the program to allow you to install a new operating system, which is completely segregated from the native (host) operating system. This program costs a significant amount of money.
- **Microsoft Virtual PC** (`www.microsoft.com/windows/virtualpc/default.mspx`) — This program allows you to run multiple operating systems inside of the host operating system (which could be Windows). It emulates another system within the program to allow you to install a new operating system, which is completely segregated from the native (host) operating system. This program costs a significant amount of money.
- **Bochs** (`http://bochs.sourceforge.net`) — This program allows you to run multiple operating systems inside of the host operating system (which could be Windows). It emulates another system within the program to allow you to install a new operating system, which is completely segregated from the native (host) operating system. This is open source and free software.
- **Knoppix** (`www.knopper.net/knoppix/index-en.html`) — This is a complete distribution of Linux self contained within a CD-ROM. You can boot off the CD-ROM and a Linux operating system will be fully available without overwriting or effecting the original installation of Windows or other operating system. This allows you to preview Linux on the system while making no long-term changes, as you can simply reboot your system without the CD-ROM to have your fully functional Microsoft Windows system unaffected. This is open source and free software.
- **Cygwin** (`www.cygwin.com`) — This program allows you to run a large set of Unix (Linux) commands within Windows without the need for a reboot. You can even run full Unix window environments while still logged into a normal Microsoft Windows sessions. This is open source and free software.
- **U/Win** (`www.research.att.com/sw/tools/uwin`) — This program allows you to run a large set of Unix (Linux) commands within Windows without the need for a reboot. This is open source and free software.

Cygwin is a program used by many Windows users to obtain some of the same functionality or the capability to run programs created for Linux while still within the Windows environment. The following "Try It Out" enables you use Cygwin to run the Unix commands you learn throughout this book without leaving the comfort of your Windows environment.

Try It Out — Use Cygwin

This exercise shows you how easy it is to use one of the programs that enable you to use Unix commands within Windows.

1. Download the Cygwin setup program from `http://cygwin.com/setup.exe`.
2. Double-click the file to start the Internet install, at which point you should see a pop-up box similar to that shown in Figure 21-3.

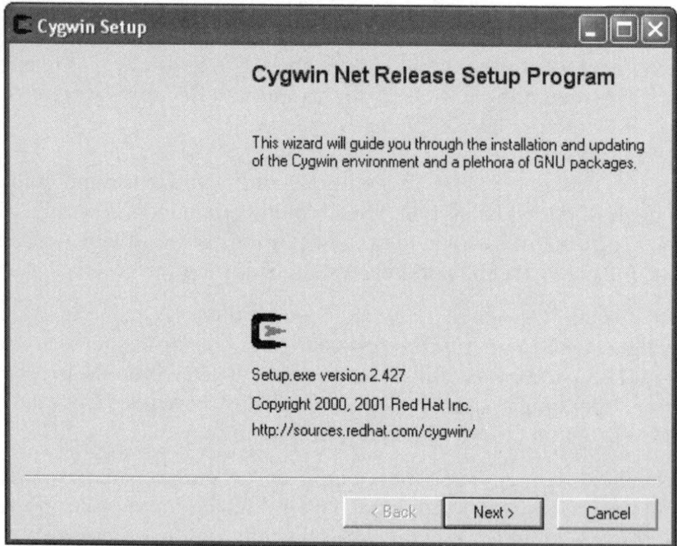

Figure 21-3

3. Click the Next button, and you will see a screen similar to Figure 21-4.

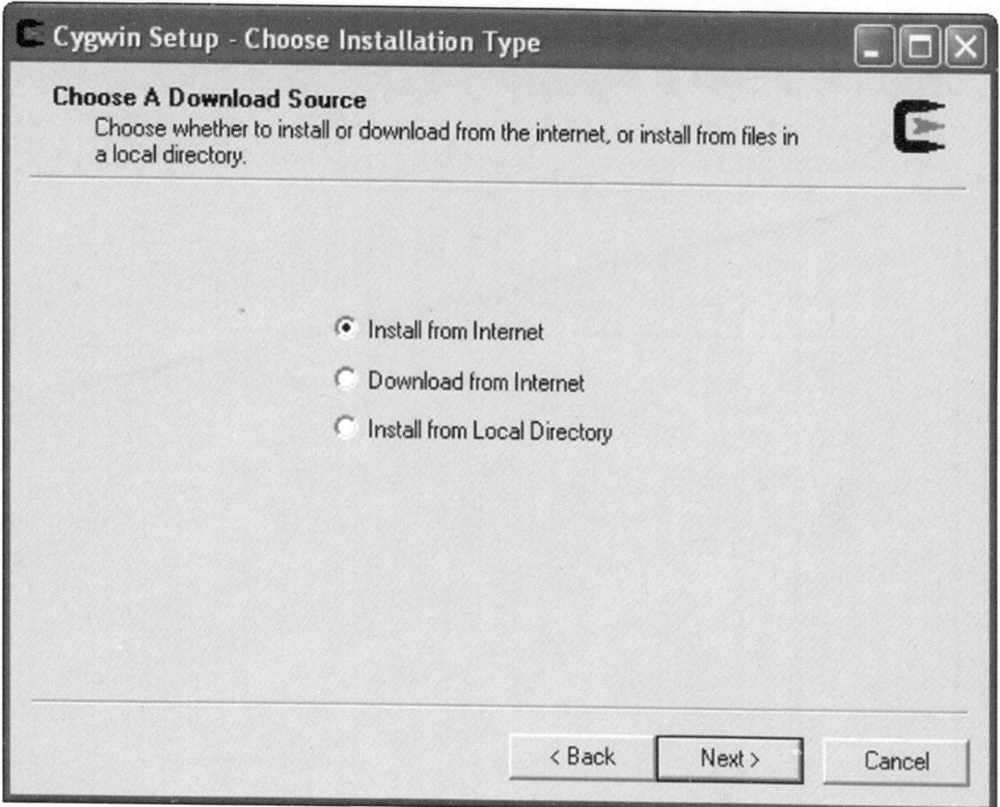

Figure 21-4

4. Select Install from Internet to download the files you need. You will now see a screen similar to Figure 21-5.

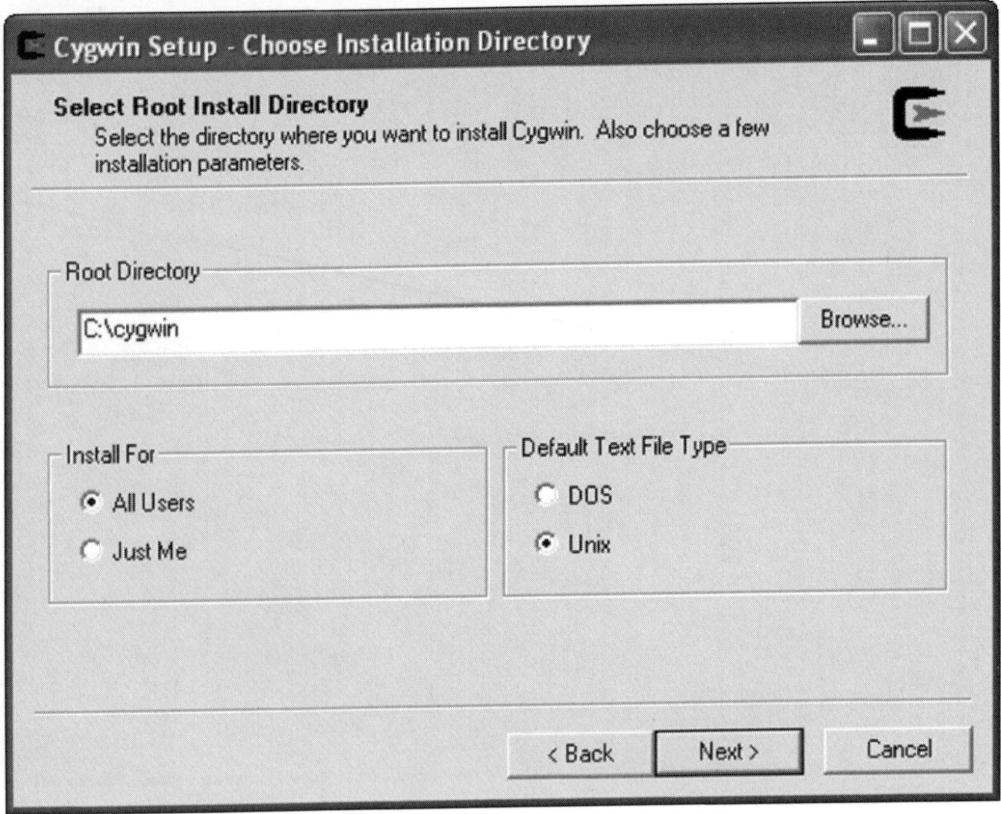

Figure 21-5

5. You should select the defaults, but if you are comfortable with choosing others selections, you may do so here. Click the Next button to move forward in the installation. That will bring you to the dialog box shown in Figure 21-6, where you can choose the Local Package Directory for storing installation files.

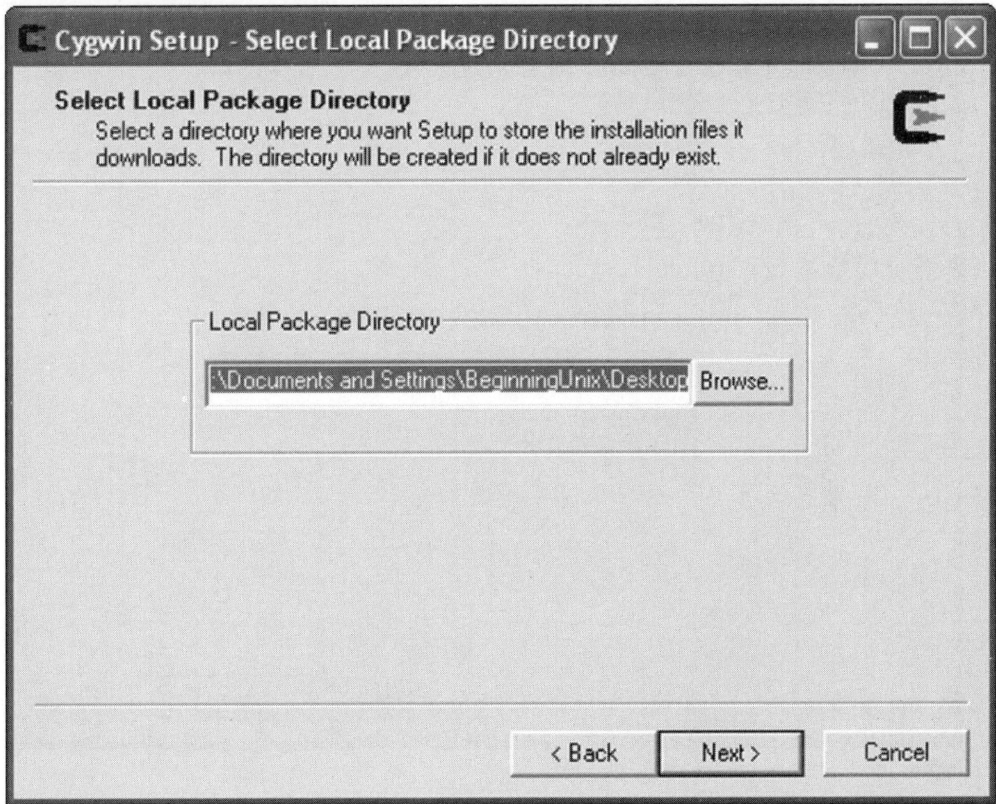

Figure 21-6

6. In the next dialog box (shown in Figure 21-7), you are prompted for the connection type you want, which you can generally leave as the default.

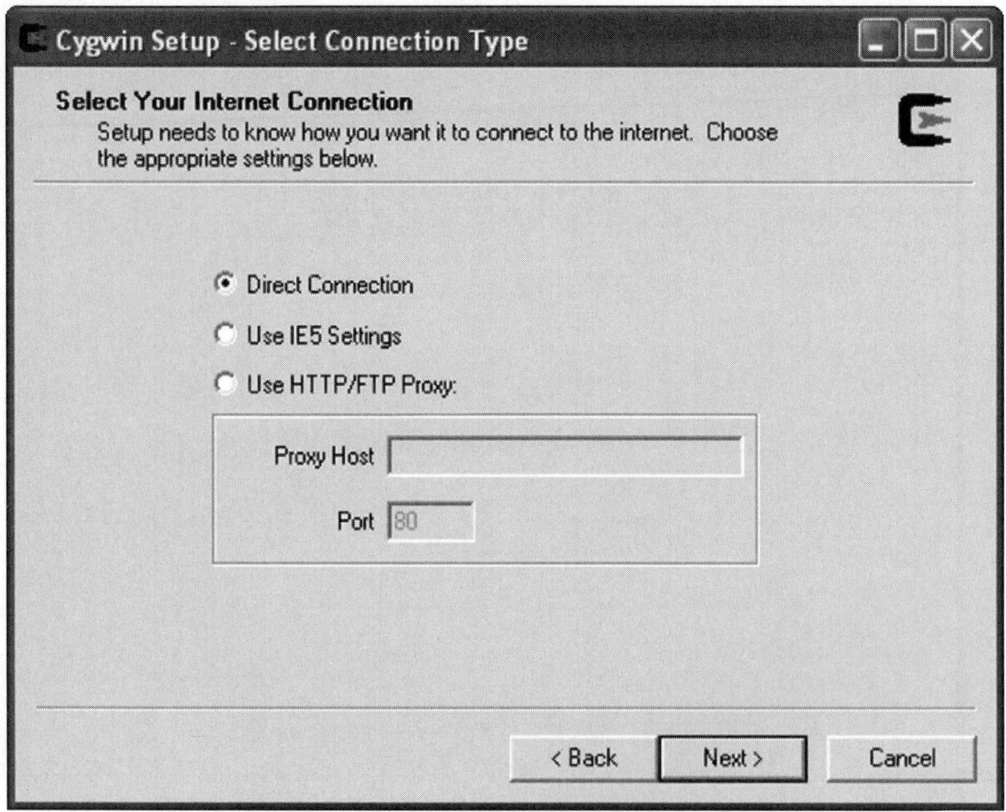

Figure 21-7

7. Cygwin then displays a list of download sites for the selections you are choosing. You can select the download site you prefer from the dialog box shown in Figure 21-8.

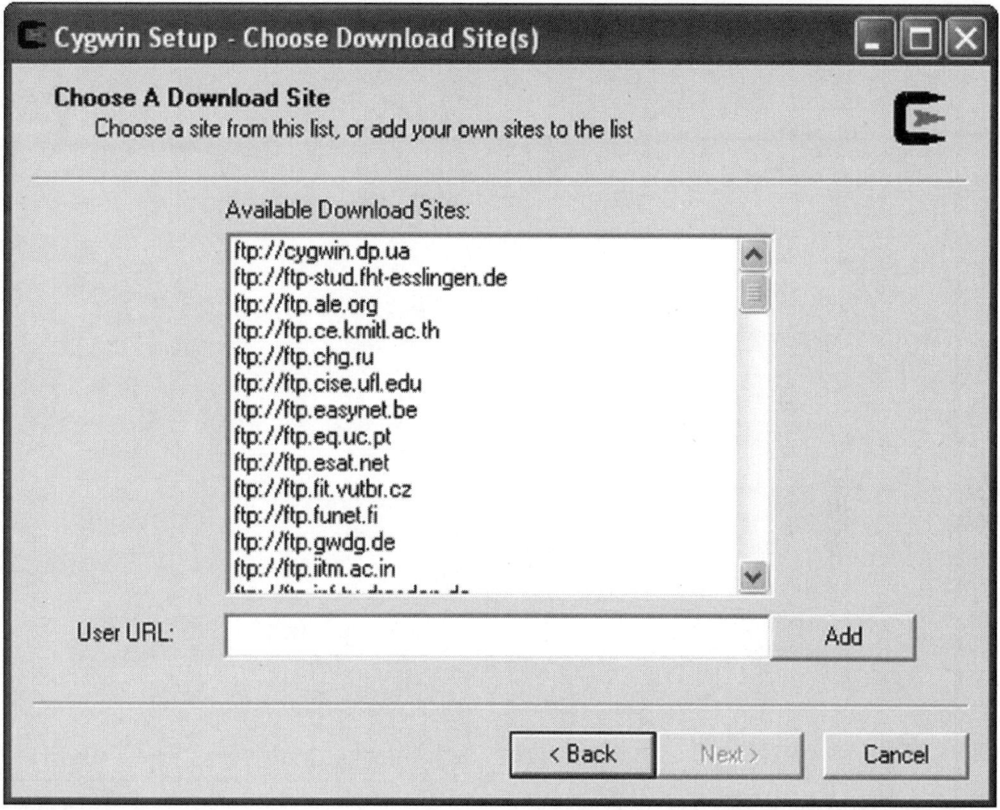

Figure 21-8

8. The download continues, as shown in Figure 12-9. A list of packages is created in the background and will display when it's completed.

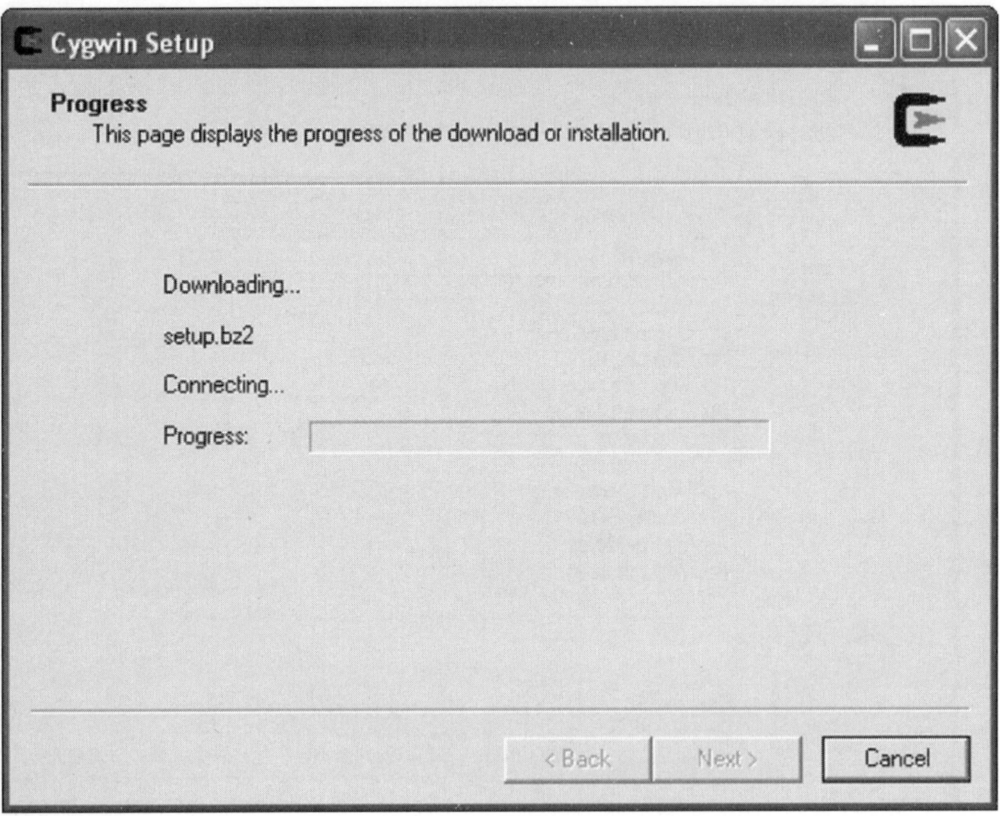

Figure 21-9

9. Figure 21-10 shows the package selection screen. For this exercise, you can choose all packages to get the most functionality if you have high-speed Internet access; otherwise, you should choose the specific packages you are interested in testing. Here is where you identify the package groups and individual packages (or programs) you want to install.

If you download "All Packages," be prepared for a very large amount of downloaded material that may take significant time to download even on a broadband connection.

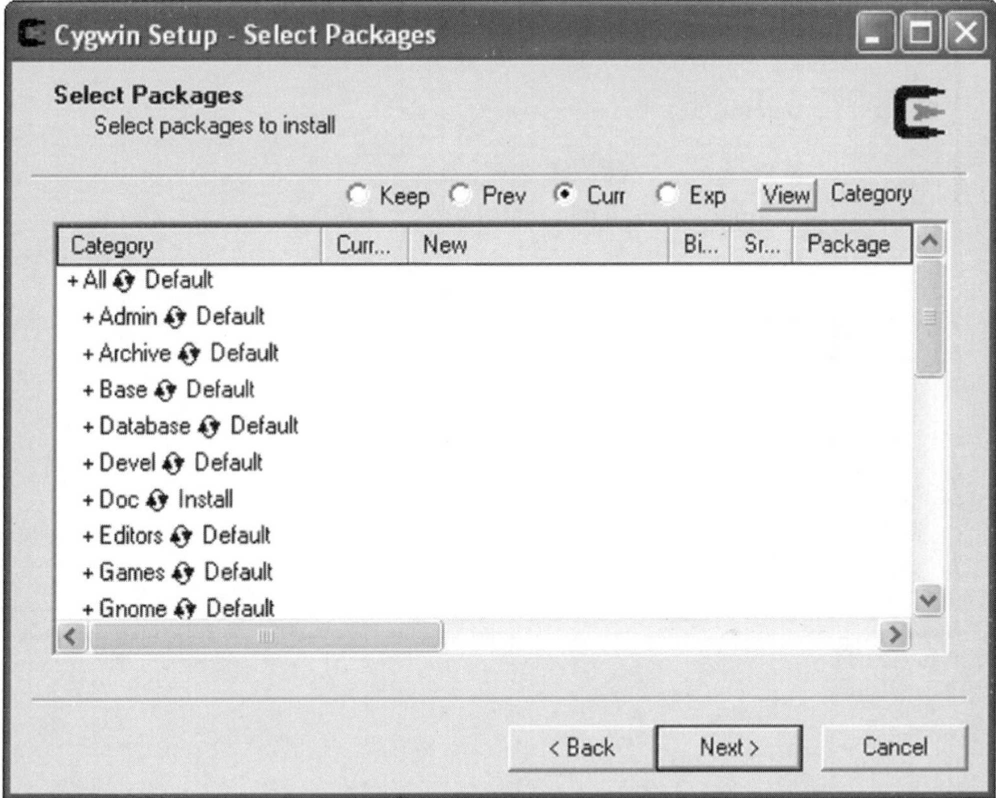

Figure 21-10

10. After you have selected the packages you want, you see the download progress dialog box shown in Figure 21-11.

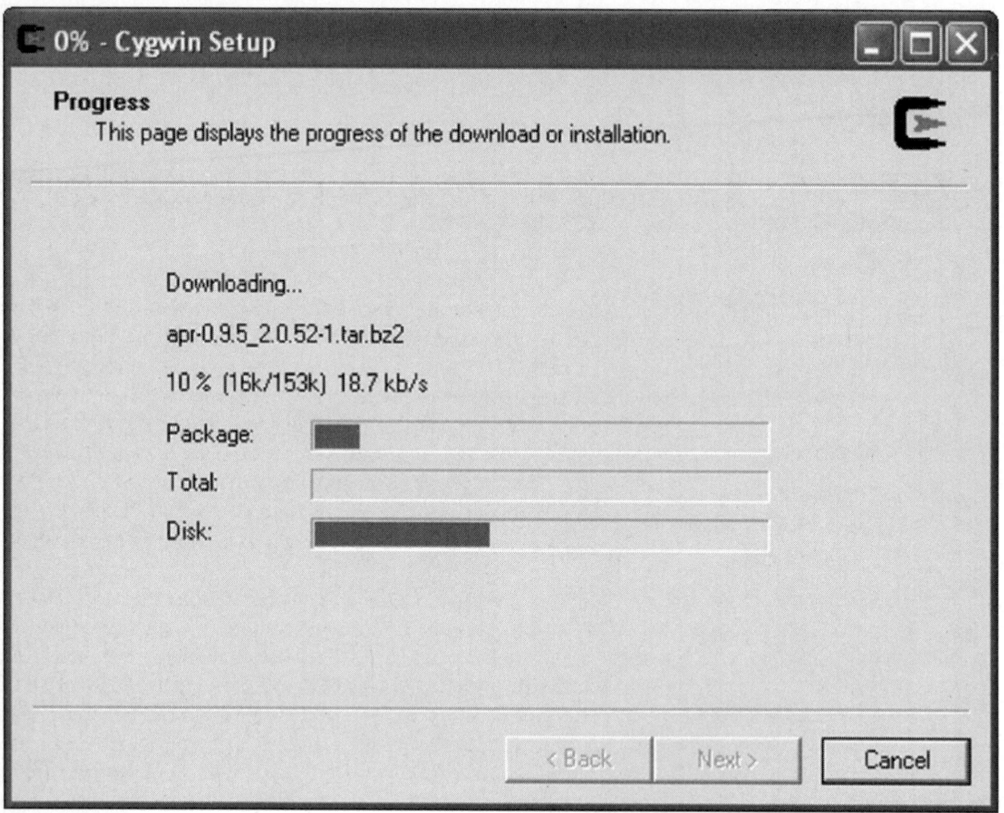

Figure 21-11

11. After the packages have downloaded, a screen displays the installation progress (see Figure 21-12).

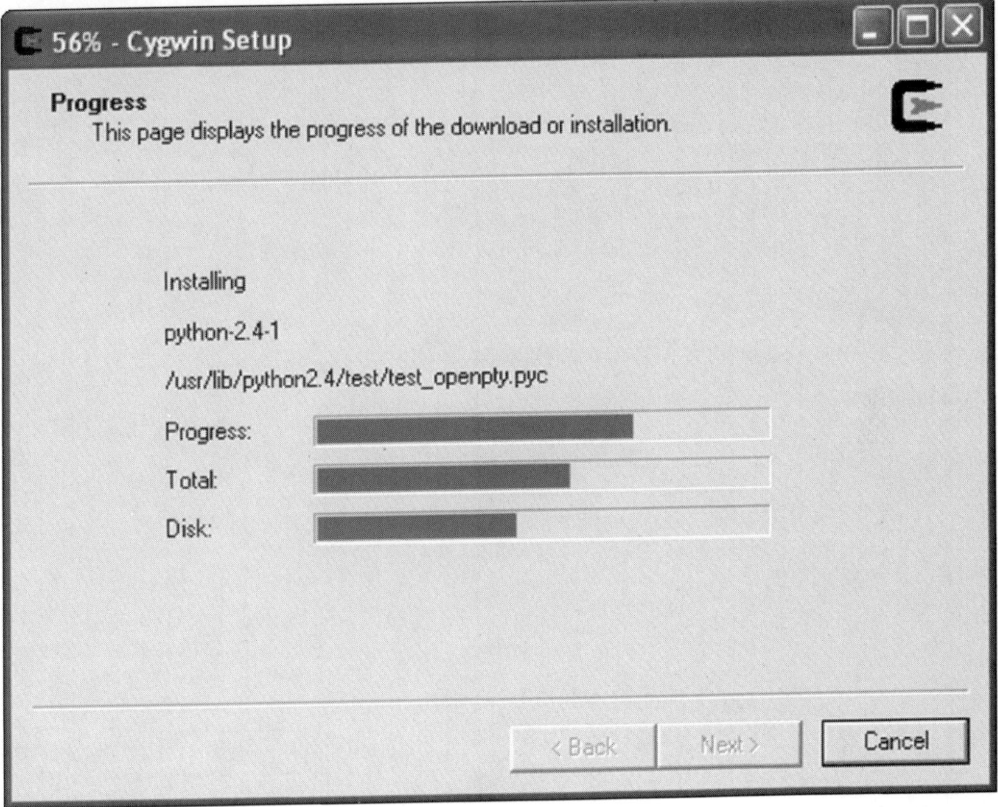

Figure 21-12

12. After installation is complete, you are asked if you want to select icons to create shortcuts to the Cygwin program, as shown in Figure 21-13.

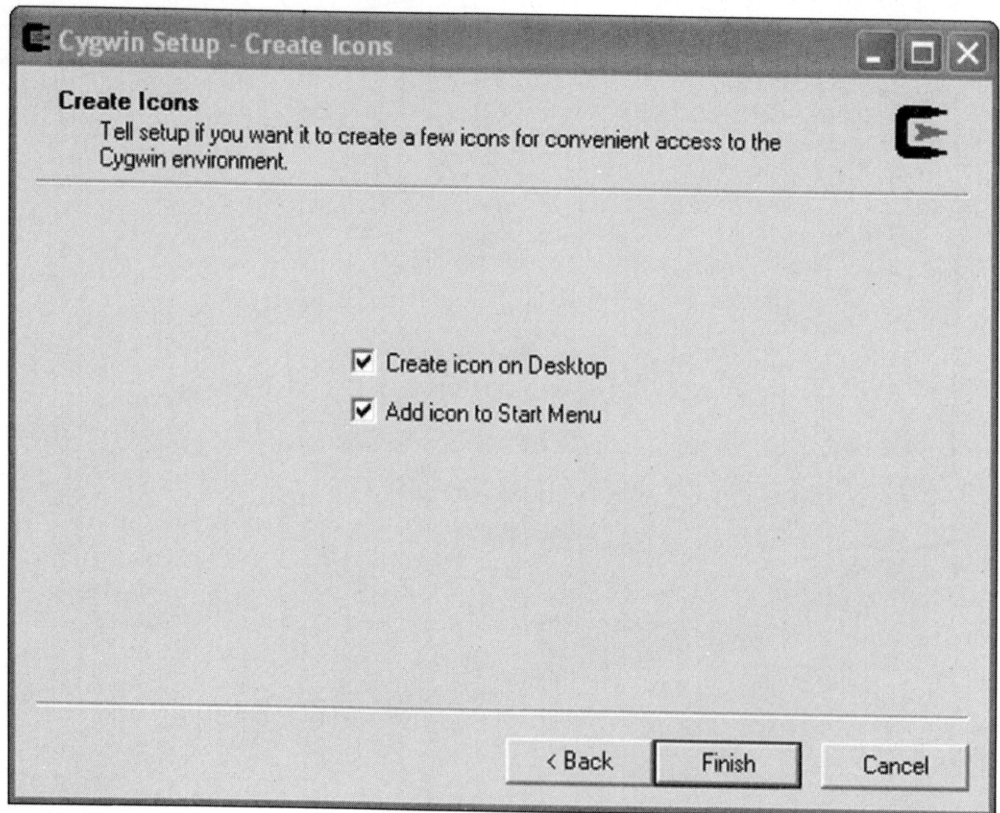

Figure 21-13

13. After installation, select the Cygwin icon on your desktop to start the program. A shell prompt (similar to the one shown in Figure 21-14) displays. From it, you can run a large number of the commands discussed in this book.

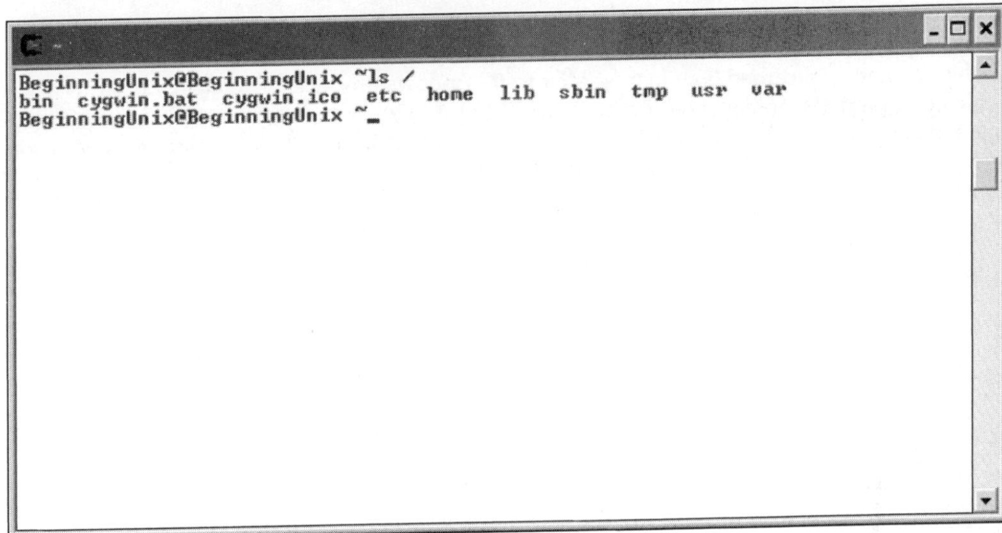

Figure 21-14

How It Works

Cygwin enables you to use Linux API emulation, providing Linux-like functionality through a Microsoft Windows DLL. You can run graphical interfaces and many programs built for Linux within your current Windows session.

More information about using Cygwin is available at `http://cygwin.com/cygwin-ug-net/cygwin-ug-net.html`.

Using Windows within Unix

If you decide you want to embark on a Unix-only environment for your system, you do not necessarily have to give up your critical Windows programs. There are tools in the Unix community that enable you to run your favorite Microsoft Windows programs within Unix. Some of the more popular are the following:

- Wine (`www.winehq.com`) enables you to run native Microsoft Windows programs from within Linux. This program is still somewhat difficult for new users to use and should be used with care.
- Crossover Office (`www.codeweavers.com/site/products`) enables you to run Microsoft Office and other programs from within Linux.
- VMWare (`www.vmware.com`) is also available for non-Windows platforms, enabling you to run Windows programs within an emulated environment.

Summary

In this chapter, you learned how to map Microsoft Windows products to Unix, including as discussion of which programs are similar, how file structures differ, and what program similarities exist. You also learned how to use Unix from within a Windows environment as well as which programs all you to use Windows within a Unix environment. With this information, you can transfer your current knowledge to a Unix system.

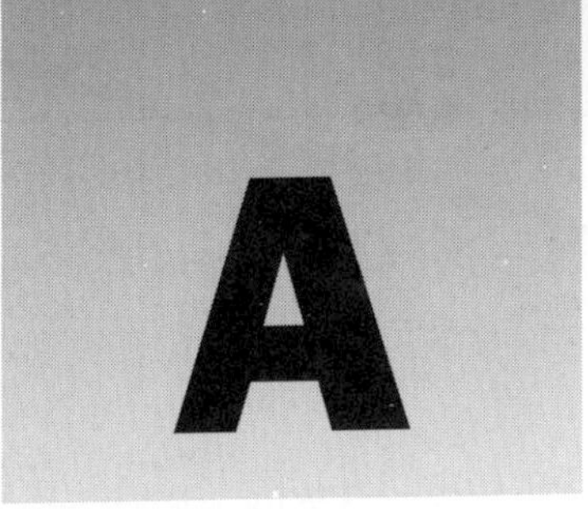

Answers

Chapter 3

Exercise 1 Solution

1. `/etc/passwd`. Holds information concerning the account name, user ID, group ID, home directory, and shell.

2. `/etc/shadow`. Holds the encrypted password for the corresponding account name in `/etc/passwd` as well as password and account-aging information.

3. `/etc/group`. Identifies the different groups available for accounts.

Exercise 2 Solution

```
# adduser -c "C Jane Doe" -d /export/home/jdoe -e 2005/05/31-f 10 -g employees
-G info_tech_1, info_tech_2, info_tech_5 -m -s /bin/ksh -u 1000 jdoe
# passwd jdoe
Changing password for user jdoe.
New UNIX password:
Retype UNIX password:
passwd: all authentication tokens updated successfully.
#
```

Chapter 4

Exercise Solution

```
chmod 755 samplefile
```

Chapter 5

Exercise 1 Solution

```
PS1="[\d \u]$"
```

Exercise 2 Solution

Find the executable file for this program. Add its directory to the value of the PATH variable, as in `PATH=$PATH:/newdirectory`.

Exercise 3 Solution

Add the command to the appropriate run control file for your preferred shell.

Chapter 6

Exercise Solution

```
ls /home/k* | wc > k-users-files
```

Chapter 7

Exercise 1 Solution

If you press the **Esc** key twice, you know you are in command mode.

Exercise 2 Solution

In command mode, type either **/ computer** or **? computer** to search for the word computer moving forward or backward respectively. (Be sure to put a space before and after the "computer" string if you want to find only instances of the complete word.) To continue the search in the opposite direction, type an uppercase **N**.

Exercise 3 Solution

In command mode, type **5yy** at the first line of the five-line sequence to be copied, and then type **10j** to move 10 lines down. Type a lowercase **p** to paste the yanked lines on the line below the current line.

Exercise 4 Solution

```
:1,$s/person/human/g
```

Chapter 8

Exercise 1 Solution

Either of the following commands is acceptable:

```
cat /etc/inetd.conf | grep telnet.d
grep telnet.d /etc/inetd.conf
```

Exercise 2 Solution

```
find /tmp -size +5000000k -atime 4
```

Chapter 9

Exercise 1 Solution

```
awk -f: '{print $4 " " $1 " " $2 " " $3}' | sort > addresses-sorted.txt
```

Exercise 2 Solution

```
s/St\./Street/g
s/Ave\./Avenue/g
s/Rd\./Road/g
s/Dr\./Drive/g
s/N\./North/g
s/S\./South/g
s/E\./East/g
s/W\./West/g
```

Exercise 3 Solution

```
sed 's/\(NY\), \(New York\)/\2, \1/' addresses.txt > addresses-new.txt
```

Chapter 11

Exercise Solution

```
crontab -e

* * /2 * * userid ls | mail -s "Directory Listing for Home Directory" userid
```

Chapter 12

Exercise Solution

Edit the sudoers file with visudo and add the following entries:

```
     # Host alias specification
Host_Alias          Backup_Host=linux_backup
     # User alias specification
User_Alias          Administrator=jdoe
     # Cmnd alias specification
Cmnd_Alias          Backup_Script=/bin/su backupuser
     # User privilege specification
Administrator       Backup_Host=Backup_Script
```

Chapter 13

Exercise 1 Solution

```
##########################################################################
# filescript.sh
#
# Dec. 9, 2004
#
# A program to find certain types of files, and report certain types
# of information, selectable by the user.
#
# CHANGELOG:
#
#   12/9/04 -- This is version 1. No changes at this point
#
##########################################################################

#!/bin/sh

# Get directory from command line. Otherwise, directory is current.

if [ $1 ]    # NOTE: This form of the 'test' command returns
             # true, as long as the value specified actually
             # exists.
then
        DIR=$1
else
        DIR=`pwd`
fi

cd $DIR
echo "Working directory is $DIR"

# Prompt for an option from the keyboard.

echo "What information would you like to know (size, permission, owner,
group, all)?"

read OPTION

# If the option is "size",  find all ".txt" files in directory and print
# their names and file sizes.
#
# If the option is "permission", print the permissions held by the file
#
# If the option is "owner", print the owner of the file
#
# If the option is "group" print the group
#
# If the option is "all", print all of the above info
```

```
if [ $OPTION = "size" ]
then
        ls -la *.txt | awk '{print $9": "$5}'

elif [ $OPTION = "permission" ]
then
        ls -la *.txt | awk '{print $9": "$1}'
elif [ $OPTION = "owner" ]
then
        ls -la *.txt | awk '{print $9": "$3}'
elif [ $OPTION = "group" ]
then
        ls -la *.txt | awk '{print $9": "$4}'
elif [ $OPTION = "all" ]
then
        ls -la *.txt | awk '{print $9": "$1", "$3", "$4", "$5}'
else
        echo "Must be size, permission, owner, group, or all."

fi
```

Exercise 2 Solution

The chain of `elif` statements in Exercise 1's solution works but seems a little cumbersome. It could be rewritten more elegantly with `case` statements, as this script shows.

```
################################################################
#  case $OPTION in
#      "size")
#      ls -la *.txt | awk '{print $9": "$5}'
#    ;;
#    "permission")
#      ls -la *.txt | awk '{print $9": "$1}'
#    ;;
#    "owner")
#      ls -la *.txt | awk '{print $9": "$3}'
#    ;;
#    "group")
#      ls -la *.txt | awk '{print $9": "$4}'
#    ;;
#    "all")
#      ls -la *.txt | awk '{print $9": "$1", "$3", "$4", "$5}'
#    ;;
#    *)
#      echo "Must be size, permission, owner, group, or all."
#    ;;
#  esac
#
########################################################################
```

Chapter 14

Exercise 1 Solution

The following function sums two values passed to it. For bonus points, write some validation to ensure that the right number of parameters is passed and that they are of the right type. To make it available to all scripts, place it in `.bashrc`:

```
#!/bin/bash

total() {
   sum=`expr $1 + $2`
}

exit 0
```

Exercise 2 Solution

Use the `tail` command with an IO redirection operator like so:

```
#!/bin/bash

tail /var/log/some_file filename

exit 0
```

Substitute `some_file` for whatever log file you want to monitor in the `/var/log` directory.

Exercise 3 Solution

```
#!/bin/bash

badsum() {
result = `expr $1 / $2`
}


function cleanup() {
   echo "You have attempted to divide by 0. You are either very brave, or very
   silly... "

exit 1

}
trap cleanup 8

badsum 3 0

exit 0
```

Exercise 4 Solution

Create and run as root user:

```
#!/bin/bash

echo "The date is: $(date +%c)"
echo
echo "The following users are logged on: $(who | more)"
echo
echo "The following files are being used: $(lsof | more)"

wall <<End
Good day! The Administrator is now in. If you have any queries please give me a
shout!
End

exit 0
```

Chapter 15

Exercise 1 Solution

Add the following line to syslog.conf:

```
kern.alert                                        /dev/console
```

Exercise 2 Solution

```
mail.debug                                        @horatio
```

Exercise 3 Solution

```
watchfor /INVALID/
echo
bell
mail addresses=root@localhost, subject="Login attempted with incorrect username"
```

Chapter 16

Exercise Solution

First, create an awk script called `top_process.awk` and enter the following:

```
/^ *[0-9]/        {
top_cpu_usage = 0
top_command = 0
top_user = 0

for (line = 0; line <= NR; ++line) {
if (top_cpu_usage > $3) {
    top_cpu_usage = $3
```

```
        top_command = $11
        top_user = $1
    }
    }

    printf "Current Top Process: " top_command ", by user: " top_user ", at:
    "top_cpu_usage "\n"
    }
```

Next, create a shell script called `top_process.sh` and enter the following:

```
#! /bin/bash
# run traceroute and parse the data with top_process.awk
ps auwx > process_results.data
awk -f top_process.awk process_results.data
```

Finally, within a local `crontab` file, enter the following automation for the shell script:

```
# run our shell script for testing the network
* */2 * * * userid cd ~/bin; ./top_process.sh | mail -s "System Performance Data"
userid
```

Chapter 17

Exercise 1 Solution

```
#!/usr/bin/perl

use warnings;


open (FILE, '/etc/passwd');
   @lines = <FILE>;
close (FILE);

foreach $line (@lines) {
   (@fields) = split /:/, $line;
   print "Username: ".$fields[0];
   print " Userid: ".$fields[2];
   print "\n\n";

}

exit (0);
```

Exercise 2 Solution

The debugger ends at different lines of code, as each invocation provides a different branch of code to take.

Exercise 3 Solution

The `else` test in the subroutine test should be changed from this:

```
} else {
   # There was a error in the input; generate an error message
   warn "Unknown input";
}
```

to this:

```
} else {
   return ('no numeric');
}
```

Chapter 18

Exercise Solution

```
tar -cvzf /tmp/etc_backup /etc
```

or

```
tar -cvf /tmp/etc_backup /etc
gzip /tmp/etc_backup
```

Chapter 19

Exercise 1 Solution

1.
   a. `http://catb.org/~esr/fetchmail/fetchmail-6.2.5.tar.gz`
   b. `tar xvfz fetchmail-6.2.5.tar.gz`
   c. `cd fetchmail-6.2.5`

      `more INSTALL`
   d. `./configure`
   e. `make`
   f. `su root -c "make install"` (provide superuser password at the prompt)
   g. `man fetchmail` (and follow the instructions shown in the manual pages)

Exercise 2 Solution

2.
   a. `www.acme.com/software/micro_httpd/micro_httpd_14dec2001.tar.gz`
   b. `tar xvfz micro_httpd_14dec2001.tar.gz`
   c. `cd micro_httpd`

      `more README`

d. `make`

e. `cp micro-httpd` *`desired-location`*

f. `man inet.d` or `man xinet.d` (and follow the directions relevant to your particular installation)

Chapter 20

Exercise 1 Solution

```
nidump passwd . passwd >> /tmp/passwd
```

Exercise 2 Solution

You should install the application in `/Users/username/Applications` and replace `username` with the short username for the user to whom you want to provide the application.

Useful Unix Web Sites

Unix Basics

- Bell Labs Unix Overview — www.bell-labs.com/history/unix/tutorial.html
- Darwin — http://developer.apple.com/darwin/projects/darwin/
- GNU — http://gnu.org
- Linux Documentation Project — http://en.tldp.org/
- Linux.com — http://linux.com
- Linux.org — www.linux.org
- Mac OS FAQ — http://osxfaq.com/Tutorials/LearningCenter/
- Mac OS X Hints — www.macosxhints.com/
- Mac OS X Basics — http://apple.com/pro/training/macosx_basics/
- SAGE — http://sageweb.sage.org/
- Unix Guru Universe — http://ugu.com
- Unix Rosetta Stone — http://bhami.com/rosetta.html

Unix History

- Dennis Ritchie's Homepage — www.cs.bell-labs.com/who/dmr/
- Ken Thompson Homepage — www.bell-labs.com/about/history/unix/thompsonbio.html
- The Unix Heritage Society — www.tuhs.org/
- Unix Timeline — http://levenez.com/unix/

Unix Security

- General Unix Security — `http://secinf.net/unix_security/`
- Linux Security — `http://linuxsecurity.com`
- SANS.org Top 20 Vulnerabilities — `http://sans.org/top20/#u1`
- Security Focus — `http://securityfocus.com/unix`
- Unix Network and Security Tools — `http://csrc.nist.gov/tools/tools.htm`
- Unix Security Checklist — `www.cert.org/tech_tips/usc20_full.html`

Vendor Sites

- Debian GNU/Linux — `http://debian.org/`
- FreeBSD — `http://freebsd.org/`
- Hewlett Packard HP-UX — `http://hp.com/products1/unix/operating/`
- IBM AIX — `www.ibm.com/servers/aix/`
- KNOPPIX — `http://knopper.net/knoppix/index-en.html`
- Mac OS X — `http://apple.com/macosx/`
- NetBSD — `http://netbsd.org/`
- OpenBSD — `http://openbsd.org/`
- OS/390 Unix — `www.ibm.com/servers/s390/os390/bkserv/r8pdf/uss.html`
- Plan 9 — `www.cs.bell-labs.com/plan9dist/`
- Red Hat Enterprise Linux — `http://redhat.com`
- Red Hat Fedora Core — `http://fedora.redhat.com/`
- SGI IRIX — `http://sgi.com/products/software/irix/`
- Sun Microsystem's Solaris Unix — `http://sun.com/software/solaris/`
- SUSE Linux — `www.novell.com/linux/suse/index.html`
- Yellow Dog Linux (for Apple systems) — `http://yellowdoglinux.com/`

Software Resources

- Apple (Mac OS X–specific) — `http://apple.com/support/downloads/`
- MacUpdate(Mac OS X–specific) — `www.macupdate.com/`
- Fink Project (Mac OS X–specific) — `http://fink.sourceforge.net/`

- Free Software Foundation — `www.fsf.org`
- Freshmeat (heavily slanted toward Linux, but software for other Unix systems available) — `www.freshmeat.net`
- RPM Find (Linux-specific) — `http://rpmfind.net/`
- Sourceforge — `http://sourceforge.net`
- SunFreeware (Sun-specific) — `http://sunfreeware.com`

Unix Magazines

- *Linux Journal* — `http://linuxjournal.com`
- *Linux Magazine* — `http://linux-mag.com/`
- *MacAddict* — `http://macaddict.com/`
- *Mac Tech* — `http://mactech.com/`
- *MacWorld* — `http://macworld.com/`
- *Sys Admin* — `http://sysadminmag.com/`

Unix News and General Information

- BSD News — `http://bsdnews.com/`
- Linux Format — `http://linuxformat.co.uk/`
- Linux Gazette — `http://linuxgazette.com/`
- Linux Insider — `http://linuxinsider.com/`
- Linux Today — `http://linuxtoday.com/`
- Linux Weekly News — `http://lwn.net/`
- Linux.org — `www.linux.org`
- Mac Minute — `http://macminute.com/`
- Mac News Network — `http://macnn.com/`
- NewsForge — `http://newsforge.com/`
- Slashdot.org — `http://slashdot.org`
- Solaris Central — `http://solariscentral.org/`
- Sun News — `http://sun.com/software/solaris/news/`
- Unix Review — `http://unixreview.com/`
- Unix World — `http://networkcomputing.com/unixworld/unixhome.html`

Fun Stuff

- KDE versus GNOME—http://freshmeat.net/articles/view/179/
- Unix Haters Handbook—http://research.microsoft.com/~daniel/unix-haters.html
- Vi Home Page—http://thomer.com/vi/vi.html
- Vi versus Emacs—http://newsforge.com/article.pl?sid=01/12/04/0326236

Index

SYMBOLS

A

B

D

E

F

G

M

N

Q

R

T

U

V

GNU General Public License

Version 2, June 1991

Preamble

The licenses for most software are designed to take away your freedom to share and change it. By contrast, the GNU General Public License is intended to guarantee your freedom to share and change free software--to make sure the software is free for all its users. This General Public License applies to most of the Free Software Foundation's software and to any other program whose authors commit to using it. (Some other Free Software Foundation software is covered by the GNU Library General Public License instead.) You can apply it to your programs, too.

When we speak of free software, we are referring to freedom, not price. Our General Public Licenses are designed to make sure that you have the freedom to distribute copies of free software (and charge for this service if you wish), that you receive source code or can get it if you want it, that you can change the software or use pieces of it in new free programs; and that you know you can do these things.

To protect your rights, we need to make restrictions that forbid anyone to deny you these rights or to ask you to surrender the rights. These restrictions translate to certain responsibilities for you if you distribute copies of the software, or if you modify it.

For example, if you distribute copies of such a program, whether gratis or for a fee, you must give the recipients all the rights that you have. You must make sure that they, too, receive or can get the source code. And you must show them these terms so they know their rights.

We protect your rights with two steps: (1) copyright the software, and (2) offer you this license which gives you legal permission to copy, distribute and/or modify the software.

Also, for each author's protection and ours, we want to make certain that everyone understands that there is no warranty for this free software. If the software is modified by someone else and passed on, we want its recipients to know that what they have is not the original, so that any problems introduced by others will not reflect on the original authors' reputations.

Finally, any free program is threatened constantly by software patents. We wish to avoid the danger that redistributors of a free program will individually obtain patent licenses, in effect making the program proprietary. To prevent this, we have made it clear that any patent must be licensed for everyone's free use or not licensed at all.

The precise terms and conditions for copying, distribution, and modification follow.

Terms and Conditions for Copying, Distribution and Modification

0. This License applies to any program or other work which contains a notice placed by the copyright holder saying it may be distributed under the terms of this General Public License. The "Program" that follows refers to any such program or work, and a "work based on the Program" means either the Program or any derivative work under copyright law: that is to say, a work containing the Program or a portion of it, either verbatim or with modifications and/or translated into another language. (Hereinafter, translation is included without limitation in the term "modification".) Each licensee is addressed as "you".

   Activities other than copying, distribution, and modification are not covered by this License; they are outside its scope. The act of running the Program is not restricted, and the output from the Program is covered only if its contents constitute a work based on the Program (independent of having been made by running the Program). Whether that is true depends on what the Program does.

1. You may copy and distribute verbatim copies of the Program's source code as you receive it, in any medium, provided that you conspicuously and appropriately publish on each copy an appropriate copyright notice and disclaimer of warranty; keep intact all the notices that refer to this License and to the absence of any warranty; and give any other recipients of the Program a copy of this License along with the Program.

   You may charge a fee for the physical act of transferring a copy, and you may at your option offer warranty protection in exchange for a fee.

2. You may modify your copy or copies of the Program or any portion of it, thus forming a work based on the Program, and copy and distribute such modifications or work under the terms of Section 1 above, provided that you also meet all of these conditions:

   a) You must cause the modified files to carry prominent notices stating that you changed the files and the date of any change.

   b) You must cause any work that you distribute or publish, that in whole or in part contains or is derived from the Program or any part thereof, to be licensed as a whole at no charge to all third parties under the terms of this License.

   c) If the modified program normally reads commands interactively when run, you must cause it, when running it for such interactive use in the most ordinary way, to print or display an announcement including an appropriate copyright notice and a notice that there is no warranty (or else, saying that you provide a warranty) and that users may redistribute the program under these conditions, and telling the user how to view a copy of this License. (Exception: If the Program itself is interactive but does not normally print such an announcement, your work based on the Program is not required to print an announcement.)

   These requirements apply to the modified work as a whole. If identifiable sections of that work are not derived from the Program, and can be reasonably considered independent and separate works in themselves, this License and its terms do not apply to those sections when you distribute them as separate works. But when you distribute the same sections as part of a whole which is a work based on the Program, the distribution of the whole must be on the terms of this License, whose permissions for other licensees extend to the entire whole, and thus to each and every part regardless of who wrote it.

Thus, it is not the intent of this section to claim rights or contest your rights to work written entirely by you; rather, the intent is to exercise the right to control the distribution of derivative or collective works based on the Program.

In addition, mere aggregation of another work not based on the Program with the Program (or with a work based on the Program) on a volume of a storage or distribution medium does not bring the other work under the scope of this License.

3. You may copy and distribute the Program (or a work based on it, under Section 2) in object code or executable form under the terms of Sections 1 and 2 above provided that you also do one of the following:

   a) Accompany it with the complete corresponding machine-readable source code, which must be distributed under the terms of Sections 1 and 2 above on a medium customarily used for software interchange.

   b) Accompany it with a written offer, valid for at least three years, to give any third party, for a charge no more than your cost of physically performing source distribution, a complete machine-readable copy of the corresponding source code, to be distributed under the terms of Sections 1 and 2 above on a medium customarily used for software interchange; or,

   c) Accompany it with the information you received as to the offer to distribute corresponding source code. (This alternative is allowed only for noncommercial distribution and only if you received the program in object code or executable form with such an offer, in accord with Subsection b above.)

   The source code for a work means the preferred form of the work for making modifications to it. For an executable work, complete source code means all the source code for all modules it contains, plus any associated interface definition files, plus the scripts used to control compilation and installation of the executable. However, as a special exception, the source code distributed need not include anything that is normally distributed (in either source or binary form) with the major components (compiler, kernel, and so on) of the operating system on which the executable runs, unless that component itself accompanies the executable.

   If distribution of executable or object code is made by offering access to copy from a designated place, then offering equivalent access to copy the source code from the same place counts as distribution of the source code, even though third parties are not compelled to copy the source along with the object code.

4. You may not copy, modify, sublicense, or distribute the Program except as expressly provided under this License. Any attempt otherwise to copy, modify, sublicense or distribute the Program is void, and will automatically terminate your rights under this License. However, parties who have received copies, or rights, from you under this License will not have their licenses terminated so long as such parties remain in full compliance.

5. You are not required to accept this License, since you have not signed it. However, nothing else grants you permission to modify or distribute the Program or its derivative works. These actions are prohibited by law if you do not accept this License. Therefore, by modifying or distributing the Program (or any work based on the Program), you indicate your acceptance of this License to do so, and all its terms and conditions for copying, distributing or modifying the Program or works based on it.

6. Each time you redistribute the Program (or any work based on the Program), the recipient automatically receives a license from the original licensor to copy, distribute or modify the Program subject to these terms and conditions. You may not impose any further restrictions on the recipients' exercise of the rights granted herein. You are not responsible for enforcing compliance by third parties to this License.

7. If, as a consequence of a court judgment or allegation of patent infringement or for any other reason (not limited to patent issues), conditions are imposed on you (whether by court order, agreement or otherwise) that contradict the conditions of this License, they do not excuse you from the conditions of this License. If you cannot distribute so as to satisfy simultaneously your obligations under this License and any other pertinent obligations, then as a consequence you may not distribute the Program at all. For example, if a patent license would not permit royalty-free redistribution of the Program by all those who receive copies directly or indirectly through you, the only way you could satisfy both it and this License would be to refrain entirely from distribution of the Program.

   If any portion of this section is held invalid or unenforceable under any particular circumstance, the balance of the section is intended to apply and the section as a whole is intended to apply in other circumstances.

   It is not the purpose of this section to induce you to infringe any patents or other property right claims or to contest validity of any such claims; this section has the sole purpose of protecting the integrity of the free software distribution system, which is implemented by public license practices. Many people have made generous contributions to the wide range of software distributed through that system in reliance on consistent application of that system; it is up to the author/donor to decide if he or she is willing to distribute software through any other system and a licensee cannot impose that choice.

   This section is intended to make thoroughly clear what is believed to be a consequence of the rest of this License.

8. If the distribution and/or use of the Program is restricted in certain countries either by patents or by copyrighted interfaces, the original copyright holder who places the Program under this License may add an explicit geographical distribution limitation excluding those countries, so that distribution is permitted only in or among countries not thus excluded. In such case, this License incorporates the limitation as if written in the body of this License.

9. The Free Software Foundation may publish revised and/or new versions of the General Public License from time to time. Such new versions will be similar in spirit to the present version, but may differ in detail to address new problems or concerns.

   Each version is given a distinguishing version number. If the Program specifies a version number of this License which applies to it and "any later version", you have the option of following the terms and conditions either of that version or of any later version published by the Free Software Foundation. If the Program does not specify a version number of this License, you may choose any version ever published by the Free Software Foundation.

10. If you wish to incorporate parts of the Program into other free programs whose distribution conditions are different, write to the author to ask for permission. For software which is copyrighted by the Free Software Foundation, write to the Free Software Foundation; we sometimes make exceptions for this. Our decision will be guided by the two goals of preserving the free status of all derivatives of our free software and of promoting the sharing and reuse of software generally.